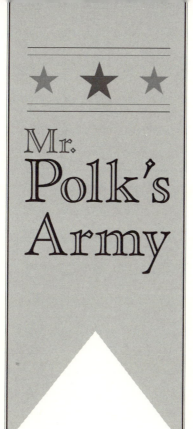

Mr. Polk's Army

TEXAS A&M UNIVERSITY
MILITARY HISTORY SERIES
51

Mr. Polk's Army

THE AMERICAN
MILITARY EXPERIENCE
IN THE
MEXICAN WAR

Richard Bruce Winders

Texas A&M University Press
College Station

The paper used in this book meets the minimum requirements
of the American National Standard for Permanence
of Paper for Printed Library Materials, Z39.48-1984.
Binding materials have been chosen for durability.

Library of Congress Cataloging-in-Publication Data

Winders, Richard Bruce, 1953–
    Mr. Polk's army : the American military experience in the
    Mexican War / Richard Bruce Winders. — 1st ed.
        p.   cm. — (Texas A&M University military history
    series ; no. 51)
    Includes bibliographical references and index.
    ISBN 0-89096-754-7 (alk. paper)
    1. United States. Army—History—Mexican War, 1846–
1848. 2. Mexican War, 1846–1848—Social aspects.
3. United States. Army—Military Life—History—19th
century. 4. Soldiers—United States—History—19th century.
5. Polk, James K. (James Knox), 1795–1849. I. Title.
II. Series: Texas A&M University military history series; 51.
E409.2.W56   1997
973.6′24—dc21   96-37753
                                                    CIP

For Margaret and Sharon

Contents

Illustrations

Tables

Preface

It has almost become standard for authors writing about the Mexican War to inform readers that the topic has been neglected. While I am starting off with the same general observation, I believe that the time soon may arrive when the claim is no longer true. New diaries and journals of participants regularly are appearing in print. The war is the topic of several coming documentaries and possibly even a feature film. Many scholars are beginning to give it closer scrutiny. Ongoing research in the field is sure to increase our understanding and acceptance of this significant episode that shaped the destinies of two North American republics, the United States and Mexico.

Mr. Polk's Army is not the book that I set out to write. More than ten years ago, I was frustrated by the dearth of unit histories dealing with the Mexican War. Most material on the war seemed to fall into two broad categories: accounts chronicling individual experiences and general histories. I began to compile a volume of unit histories of all U.S. regular and volunteer regiments that served in the conflict. That turned out to be a monumental task, but it is completed; I plan to publish these in the near future. This book presents the impressions I developed of the soldiers whom I "met" along the way—who they were, what they were like, and what they experienced.

As my research took me through scores of diaries, journals, and reminiscences, I noticed that these accounts were surprisingly similar. This led me to conclude that American participants in the Mexican War shared a common experience. It mattered little whether they served along the Rio Grande, in central Mexico, in New Mexico, or in California; they told essentially the same stories. From private to general, nearly all complained of bad food, hard marches, and long periods of incredible boredom. They complained about each other and about their superiors. Although they loved Mexico as a place, generally they disliked its people. To be sure, for all soldiers in all wars, the military experience has certain common features.

In the case of these Mexican War soldiers, however, I decided that society—the society of early-nineteenth-century America, to be specific—gave the American soldiers of the Mexican War their distinctive view of the world. I would even say that they saw events through "Jacksonian"-colored glasses. Can anyone dispute the claim that we are shaped by the times in which we live? These men carried their cultural baggage with them, along with the other implements of war.

The "common man" approach to military history is not new. Bell Irwin Wiley's groundbreaking volumes, *The Life of Johnny Reb* and *The Life of Billy Yank,* inspired others to plow the same field. One of Wiley's own students, John Porter Bloom, applied his mentor's techniques to the Mexican War. Bloom's 1956 dissertation, "With the American Army into Mexico, 1846–1848," remains an excellent study of the common soldier in the Mexican War. James M. McCaffrey's more recent study, *The Army of Manifest Destiny: The American Soldier in the Mexican War, 1846–1848,* has filled a notable void. McCaffrey's work, now available in paperback, has made its appearance in college classrooms as a supplemental text in courses dealing with the American West and with military history, giving students a rare glimpse of the lives of Mexican War soldiers.

Mr. Polk's Army builds on this tradition, examining the daily life of soldiers at war. For that reason, it might be placed in the category known as "new" military history. Like new military history, this work endeavors to link the army to the society that produced it. In addition to analyzing the expected mundane complaints of Mexican War soldiers, I discovered that many soldiers were concerned with serious political issues of the day. Contrary to the claim made by one volunteer that there were no "Democrats" or "Whigs" in the army, I found that many soldiers made great displays of their political affiliations while in uniform. Sensing the importance of politics to these men, I began to see the American military in a new light. Democrats and Whigs alike struggled for control of the army, because each group realized that military victory on the battlefield was linked to political victory at the polls. The war and the effort to raise thousands of troops gave President James K. Polk and his party an excellent opportunity to reward loyal supporters with commissions and fill the officer corps with Democrats. The army that fought the Mexican War was indeed "Mr. Polk's Army."

Modern readers may find some terms used in *Mr. Polk's Army* in ways that do not fit current attitudes; therefore a brief explanation may be helpful. I use the older term "Mexican War," the name by which the war's American participants knew it, to describe the conflict in 1846–48 between

Mexico and the United States. Other names in current use are "the Mexican-American War" and "the U.S.-Mexican War."

A second term that may draw attention is "American." While I realize that the word "American" can designate all people living from the Arctic Circle to Terra del Fuego, the term (as used in 1846–48) is needed for clarity's sake. Thus, I refer to persons from the United States as "Americans" and the combined army of regulars and volunteers as "the American army."

Several important place names have changed over the years. *Vera Cruz* has become *Veracruz*, and *Monterey* has gained an additional "r," making it *Monterrey*. Here, too, I have chosen to use the more archaic versions. *Matamoros* (which appeared as both *Matamoros* and *Matamoras* in writings and on maps of the period) is the spelling I settled on for that city. Whenever possible, I have kept the original spelling used by the war's participants. I believe that use of these words helps convey the spirit of the time in which the events described in this book occurred.

Acknowledgments

No book is the product of only one person. Having said this, I wish to acknowledge some of those who contributed in special ways to *Mr. Polk's Army*. I wish to thank Dr. Grady McWhiney for his encouragement and confidence. Thanks, too, are due Dr. Donald E. Worcester, Dr. Kenneth R. Stevens, Dr. Spencer Tucker, and Dr. Jim W. Corder. I owe Dr. Donald S. Frazier, a long-time friend and colleague, a special tip of the hat: our paths crossed many years ago, and ever since we've been going down the same trail. I also wish to acknowledge the help of several scholars who read this work and whose comments I took to heart: Sam W. Haynes, James M. McCaffrey, and Ralph W. Wooster. Thanks also go to Dr. Michael Collins and Dr. John Belohlavek for reading portions of the manuscript that appeared as professional papers. Paul R. Ackerman, armorer at the West Point Museum, was kind enough read chapter 6 on his own time. I also wish to thank William Schultz, M.D., for allowing me access to his extraordinary daguerreotype collection.

Several others read this work in various stages; they, too, have my thanks. Mary Gagné, Paul Gagné, and Nickey Winders helped find those irritating little errors that invariably crop up. For the moral support he provided, James Lee Bain forever has earned the title "friend." Thanks to C. Steven Abolt and Robert P. Wettemann, whose keen interest in the war made my research less lonely.

Others whose help made this book possible deserve to be acknowledged. My thanks go to the staffs of the various archival repositories that I visited during this project, especially the Jenkins Garrett Collection at the University of Texas at Arlington; the United States Military Research Collection at Carlisle, Pennsylvania; and the Daughters of the Republic of Texas Library in San Antonio. As we all know the immense value of Inter-Library Loan (ILL), I would be remiss if I did not salute the efficient ILL staff at Texas Christian University, Fort Worth, for tracking down a multitude of sources critical to my work. Vicki Betts, research librarian for the University of Texas at Tyler, is a credit to her profession. I can never fully repay her for all the help she has given me on this and other projects.

Several opportunities arose to travel through northern Mexico. A trip to Monterrey and Saltillo, sponsored by the staff of the Historic Brownsville Museum, still elicits pleasant memories. Dr. Joseph E. Chance and Laurier B. McDonald, Esq., provided an enlightening and entertaining tour of Camargo and Mier. My traveling companions on this jaunt, Dr. Linda Vance and Kevin R. Young, made the trip more delightful still.

Lastly, although by no means last in importance, I thank my family. Their support made *Mr. Polk's Army* possible. The old adage really is true: behind every good man is a good woman. In my case, it took two women: my mother, Margaret, and my wife, Sharon.

Mr. Polk's Army

ONE

Jacksonians at War

[Soldiers of a democratic army] do not . . . imbibe the spirit of the army, . . . they infuse the spirit of the community at large into the army and retain it there.

—Alexis de Tocqueville,
Democracy in America

Well may we be grateful that we are at war with Mexico! Were it any other power our gross follies would surely have been punished before now.

—2d Lt. George G. Meade,
U.S. Topographical Engineers

The Battle of New Orleans in 1815 added a new hero to the national pantheon—Andrew Jackson. Old Hickory, as he came to be called, towered over the political and social landscape of America for the next thirty years, until his death in 1845, less than one year before the start of the Mexican War. Supporters adored him, opponents hated him, but all feared the sting of his wrath. In the first half of the nineteenth century, Jackson became the focal point of a social and political revolution, a fact that led some historians to label the period "Jacksonian America." Early American textbooks indelibly impressed Jackson's victory upon the minds of schoolboys. The popular Peter Parley series recounted how, "on the 8th of January, 1815, 12,000 British troops came against New Orleans.

Gen. Jackson was there with 3,000 American soldiers. He knew that the British were coming; so he prepared to receive them. . . . In one hour after the battle began, it was all over. The British were defeated and marched sullenly away. . . . Thus the British had lost 2,600 men, while the Americans had only seven killed, and six wounded." What young lad growing up in the early Republic could fail to be stirred by a victory such as this? In the decades before the Civil War, Americans celebrated the anniversary of Jackson's victory at New Orleans with the same patriotic fervor they reserved for the Fourth of July.[1]

Jackson's victory had important consequences. As historian John William Ward points out in his study of Jackson, the battle reinforced the myth of the invincible frontiersman who picked off the advancing British soldiers with the same cool skill he used hunting squirrels. The victory thus enhanced the status of the American militia and the hardy men of the West. According to Noah M. Ludlow, the American theatrical pioneer, his 1822 rendition of "The Hunters of Kentucky," a song about the battle, quickly caught on; thereafter, his audiences forced him to sing the popular ballad several times during each stage appearance. As for Jackson, the battle focused national attention on him, placing him in the limelight politically. Denied the presidency in 1824 by a move that his supporters termed a "Corrupt Bargain," Jackson gathered his forces and ended by "ruling" the nation as president from 1828 to 1836.[2]

Jackson's election and his subsequent conduct as president provoked strong reactions and facilitated the formation of a new two-party system. His supporters, who claimed that they wanted to end special privilege and apply democratic principles to all white males, came to be known as Democrats. His opponents, who saw the danger of a growing "mobocracy" in the rise of the common man, viewed Jackson as a threat not only to themselves but also to the nation as a whole. Decrying his tight grasp on presidential power and his willingness to propose legislation as well as veto bills, they charged that he had assumed the power and trappings of an absolute monarch and dubbed him "King Andrew." In response to his unprecedented actions, they styled themselves "Whigs," implying that they were like the British opposition party. The election of Jackson, the first western president, signified that the two opposing forces were gathering for battle. Jackson's supporters built a formidable political machine that lasted beyond his retirement and death. One soldier in Jackson's political army, James Knox Polk, carried the party's banner high and led the Democrats in a war against both the Whigs and Mexico.[3]

President James K. Polk was one of the most successful commanders-in-chief the United States ever has produced. He led the nation in its first major war where the opponents were not Europeans or Native Americans. He formulated the strategy that sent five armies onto foreign soil. He oversaw the greatest military expansion that Americans of his day had ever witnessed. His troops won victory after victory, occupying large sections of the enemy's territory. In the end, his strong-willed negotiator, Nicholas Trist, wrested from the vanquished a land concession that in size rivaled the Louisiana Purchase. It is odd that, with all these accomplishments, Polk remains unknown to most Americans.

"Who is James K. Polk?" people asked when he ran for president. The eldest of ten children, Polk was born on November 2, 1795, in Mecklenburg County, North Carolina. His parents, Samuel and Jane, joined the stream of Americans who headed westward in the early days of the Republic. They moved to Tennessee and built a home at Columbia, on the Duck River, southwest of Nashville. The change was hard for ten-year-old James, who reportedly failed "to hold his own" in the rough outdoor games common on the frontier. Education and rhetoric proved the lad's fortes, as he found solace in learning. After studying with local scholars at Columbia and Murfreesboro, he entered the University of North Carolina in 1813 and graduated with honors in 1818. Afterwards he studied law under Felix Grundy, a lawyer and politician of national renown. As a congressman, Grundy used his considerable influence to secure the post of clerk of the state senate for his promising protégé. Polk joined the Tennessee Bar in 1820, at the age of twenty-five.[4]

A private man, James K. Polk chose to lead a public life. He embarked upon a career in politics that eventually led to the White House. An ardent follower of Andrew Jackson, Polk was elected to the Tennessee House of Representatives in 1823. Two years later, voters sent him to the U.S. House, where he served for fourteen years. Polk held the important post of Speaker of the House from 1835 until he left Washington in 1839. Polk eventually earned the sobriquet "Young Hickory," in recognition of his strong support of Jackson's policies. Polk reentered state politics in 1839, winning the post of governor of Tennessee. In 1841, however, the office slipped from his grasp; a subsequent attempt to regain the post also failed. Polk might have faded into obscurity except that Democratic delegates meeting in 1844 selected him as their presidential candidate on the ninth ballot after being unable to decide on any of the party's front-runners. The Tennessean was the first "dark horse" candidate to be elected to the White House. Sworn into office on March 4, 1845, James K. Polk became the eleventh president of the U.S. and hence the commander-in-chief of the nation's military forces.[5]

Polk assumed office during a tumultuous period when many Americans clamored for expansion. He had been elected to office by supporters who demanded the "reoccupation of Oregon" and the "reannexation of Texas." The term *manifest destiny,* signifying the young nation's right—supposedly given by God—to spread its institutions over North America, entered the American lexicon shortly after Polk moved to the White House. The president desired expansion, even at the risk of war. Although not a military man like some of his predecessors in the office, he did not shy away from using force to accomplish his goals. Polk led his country into war a little over a year after he became president.[6]

Conflict with Mexico had been long in the making. The claims of France and Spain had overlapped during the halcyon days of their North American empires, creating uncertainty about boundaries. France's humiliating loss to Great Britain in 1763, at the end of the French and Indian War, seemed to give Spain clear title to much of North America. Only twenty years later, however, the U.S. entered the picture. The newly independent nation naturally competed with Spain for control of the Mississippi River and the Gulf Coast. Although Pinckney's Treaty of 1795 permitted Americans to use the river, as well as the port facilities at New Orleans, adventurers such as Philip Nolan and Aaron Burr early gave Spanish officials notice that they intended to push into the borderlands of New Spain. France's sale of Louisiana in 1803 left many Americans with the impression that Texas had formed part of the extraordinary bargain. The 1810 loss of West Florida to a revolt staged by American frontier republicans coupled with Andrew Jackson's 1818 invasion of East Florida convinced Spanish officials that something had to be done to prevent further encroachment. The Adams-Onìs Treaty of 1819 tentatively ceded East Florida to the U.S. in return for U.S. renunciation of any claim to Texas. New Spain once more seemed secure.[7]

The map of North America changed again in 1821 when Mexicans overthrew Spanish rule and established their own republic. Concerned about the borderlands, Mexican officials continued a colonization plan begun under the Spanish that would allow settlers from the U.S. to colonize parts of Texas if they agreed to become Mexican citizens. Throughout the 1820s and 1830s, Stephen F. Austin and other *empresarios* worked to fulfill their colonization contracts with the Mexican government. Their success in establishing vibrant communities surprised Mexican officials, who realized that Anglo immigrants had become more numerous than native *Tejanos*. In a belated attempt to stem the flood of Americans by banning immigration from the U.S., the Mexican government issued the Decree of April 6,

1830. This decree, coupled with a crackdown on smuggling, heightened efforts to collect taxes, and a much stronger military presence, made the colonists fear and resent the Mexican government. In October 1835, discontented Americans and Tejanos openly revolted against the Mexican government. The brief struggle—forever linked with the names Gonzales, Alamo, Goliad, and San Jacinto—sealed the fate of Texas. In April 1836, after a brief but decisive battle at San Jacinto, Gen. Sam Houston extracted a promise of independence from the defeated Mexican president, Antonio López de Santa Anna, and Texas went its own way.[8]

Tension and resentment followed the birth of the Republic of Texas. Not only did Mexico disavow Santa Anna's coerced pledge of independence, but its leaders believed that the U.S. had encouraged the rebellion. In Mexico, it was well known that President Jackson desired to add Texas to the U.S.; he had authorized an American diplomat, Col. Anthony Butler, to negotiate its purchase several years before the revolt. Mexico could point to the great number of American volunteers who had poured into Texas to fight for independence. Large rallies had been held in cities throughout the U.S. to raise money for arms and supplies that were used against the Mexican government. More than one source claimed that U.S. troops—in the guise of deserters—even had crossed into Texas and joined the rebels at the Battle of San Jacinto. In the summer of 1836, American troops under Gen. Edmund P. Gaines briefly occupied Nacogdoches, Texas, ostensibly to prevent an Indian uprising. The Mexican government had ample proof of American involvement in the Texas Revolution.[9]

The bloody deeds of the Texas War for Independence stirred strong emotions on all sides. Mexico felt justified in executing American prisoners at the Alamo and at Goliad because it considered the men land-pirates. Americans interpreted the killings as despicable acts carried out by a savage and half-civilized people. Mexico failed to realize that the dead men had friends and relatives in the U.S. who possessed long memories. Fear and hatred dogged the short life of the Republic of Texas, with both sides eager to settle old scores whenever fighting erupted once more. Mexico made several attempts to reestablish control over its lost territory. Texas mounted an unsuccessful expedition to sever New Mexico from Mexico. These affairs added to the bitter feelings that already existed. Texans added Santa Fe, Mier, and Perote to a growing list of wrongs to be avenged.[10]

Annexation of Texas by the U.S. confirmed suspicions that many Mexicans had long held. Texas had asked for admission to the Union shortly after it achieved independence, but political matters at home, as well as diplomatic concerns abroad, had prevented early statehood. The U.S. presidential election of 1844 showed Texas annexation to be a popular issue. Democrats called for the "reannexation" of Texas, a cry reflecting the belief that the region had been taken from the U.S. in 1819 as a result of the Adams-Onìs Treaty. On March 1, 1845, outgoing President John Tyler signed a joint resolution of Congress inviting Texas to join the Union, thereby circumventing intense political opposition to the measure. Mexico informed the U.S. that it considered annexation of Texas an act of war. The new president, James K. Polk, ordered troops to concentrate at Fort Jesup, Louisiana, in order to counter any hostile move by Mexico to prevent Texas from joining the U.S. The force, commanded by Bvt. Brig. Gen. Zachary Taylor, became the nucleus of the American army that conquered Mexico.[11]

The question of Texas' boundaries complicated the matter of annexation. Mexico long had recognized the Nueces River as the southern border of the province of Texas; this river had been the boundary in the days of New Spain. Texas, and subsequently the U.S., however, wanted the border set 150 miles to the south at the Rio Grande. This claim was bolstered by the pledge made by Santa Anna at San Jacinto. Thus the boundary issue would have presented a serious problem even if Mexico had agreed to annexation. In July 1845, once Texans voted to ratify the annexation treaty, Polk ordered Taylor's small army to take up a defensive position at Corpus Christi, near the mouth of the Nueces River. Meanwhile, the war of words between Mexico and the U.S. continued.[12]

Polk searched unsuccessfully for a diplomatic solution to the problem. Mexico had refused the U.S. president's offers of money to settle the disputed boundary of Texas and had declined to sell New Mexico or California. The Mexican government, never having recognized Texas' independence, believed that negotiations could bring only further humiliation. A strong pro-war regime, headed by Gen. Mariano Paredes y Arrillaga, replaced President José Joaquín de Herrera when it appeared that Herrera might enter into negotiations with Polk's administration. As in the U.S., hawks in Mexico used the country's newspapers to build a case for war.[13]

In late February 1846, Polk ordered Taylor to advance to the southern edge of the disputed zone, a move that Mexico strongly protested. A month later, Taylor's troops were camped on the northern bank of the Rio Grande, across the river from the inland port of Matamoros. Taylor established a supply base near Point Isabel, as the U.S. Navy closed the mouth of the river to Mexican traffic, isolating Matamoros from the Gulf of Mexico. Tension increased throughout April, as U.S. and Mexican troops cautiously monitored each other's movements. Finally, on the evening of April 24, 1846, a force of Mexican cavalry crossed to the northern side of the river.

The next day, it overwhelmed a small American patrol Taylor had sent out to verify reports that the Mexican army had advanced. News of the skirmish, which killed eleven U.S. soldiers and wounded six, quickly traveled eastward.[14]

Weary of diplomatic maneuvering, Polk had decided on a military solution to the Mexican dispute even before learning of fighting on the Rio Grande. On April 25, 1846—the same day that Thornton's squadron was attacked—he and his cabinet discussed declaring war against Mexico. Informed of the skirmish on May 9, the president reworked his already partially written war message to include the latest news. Now he would explain to Congress that Mexico had "invaded our territory and shed American blood upon American soil." After hurried Congressional debate, Polk on May 13 signed into law a bill authorizing money and troops for the war. Ironically, the administration had declared war without knowing that Taylor's army had won the twin battles of Palo Alto and Resaca de la Palma. The victories mattered little to Polk, who already had told his countrymen that "the cup of forbearance has been exhausted" and the "two nations are now at war."[15]

To many observers in 1846, the U.S. Army seemed woefully unprepared for war. Congress had authorized an army of 8,613 men and officers, but illness and desertion had created nearly 3,300 vacancies. Consequently, the army, with its fourteen regiments and ten staff departments, was nearly 40 percent under strength. Those troops present for duty were dispersed at more than a hundred forts and cantonments in seven military departments charged with guarding four thousand miles of border. According to William A. Ganoe, an authority on the U.S. Army, not since 1808 had the regular army reached such a low ebb. One report in *Niles' National Register* stated that each of the five infantry regiments with Taylor's Army of Occupation required six to seven hundred additional men in order to bring it up to full strength. With war at hand, the situation had grown critical and demanded action.[16]

Several times during the war, Congress acted to raise troops against Mexico. One solution was to increase the size of the regular army. On May 13, 1846, Congress raised the number of privates in artillery and infantry companies from forty-two to one hundred. The number of privates in companies of dragoons also was increased from fifty to one hundred. Two days later, Congress authorized the creation of one company of "Sappers, Miners, and Pontoniers" (later designated Company A, U.S. Engineers), with an authorized limit of seventy-eight privates. Another bill passed on May 19 created an entirely new regiment, the U.S. Mounted Rifles. Originally intended for duty on the Oregon Trail, the regiment saw its first service in Mexico instead. These newly created troops, along with the regiments that existed before the war, made up a body of troops referred to as the Old Establishment. The above measures failed to raise the number of soldiers needed. Responding to the shortage, Congress passed an additional act on February 11, 1847, creating eight new regiments of infantry, one regiment of dragoons, and one regiment designated as Foot Riflemen and Voltigeurs. The law, known as the Ten Regiment Bill, specified that the units be disbanded at the war's end. Although officially considered part of the regular army, these ten regiments comprised the New Establishment, so called because they were not part of the prewar military and were raised only as a temporary measure. Desperate for troops, Congress called on the states to provide volunteers early in the war in order to field an army against Mexico. The Act of May 13, 1846, which increased the number of privates in regular companies, also authorized Polk to call out fifty thousand state volunteers. The Act of March 3, 1847, allowed the president to

Unidentified lieutenant, U.S. Mounted Rifles.
Courtesy Dr. William Schultz Collection

accept individual volunteers to fill vacancies. Thus, the American army that invaded and occupied Mexico was a combination of both federal (regular) and state (volunteer) troops.[17]

According to the War Department, the number of officers and enlisted men in the American military during the war exceeded one hundred thousand. That figure is, however, extremely misleading, as these were never in the field at the same time. Additionally, more than sixteen thousand of the volunteers were deemed by the War Department to have been raised illegally and were sent home from the Rio Grande shortly after they arrived. Perhaps fewer than eighty-eight thousand Americans were employed in the campaigns against Mexico. The coming and going of volunteers, coupled with the high rate of turnover in the regular service due to expiring enlistments, meant that the composition of the American army during the war constantly changed. The army of 1846 was not the same as that of 1847 or 1848.[18]

By May 13, 1846, Congress overwhelmingly had passed its response to Polk's plea for war, giving him the means needed to proceed with military action against Mexico. Opposition quickly had developed from Whigs who believed that President Polk had forced an unjust war on both Mexico and the American people. In the House of Representatives, 14 Whigs, led by John Q. Adams and Joshua Giddings, voted against the measure; but their protest seemed insignificant compared with the 174 "yes" votes. In the Senate, only 2 members opposed the measure, while 40 voted in the affirmative. When finally allowed to speak briefly during debate on the bill, Sen. Garrett Davis, a Kentucky Whig, summed up the opposition viewpoint. According to Davis, Democrats in the Senate had prevented Whigs from taking part in the discussion and steamrollered the bill through before the situation on the Rio Grande could be understood fully. He questioned whether war actually existed, musing that if indeed it did, Polk and not Mexico was at fault. Davis, concerned that Taylor faced real danger, voted money and men to aid the general but made it clear that he opposed an invasion of Mexico. Most Congressmen, inspired by patriotic motives, followed the logic of Lewis Cass, Democratic senator from Michigan, who during the debate stated, "Let's go for the [good of the] country first— let's make all the requisite preparations." Once Congress acted to save the American force on the Rio Grande, Cass concluded, the matter of fault could be determined. The issue of blame continued to be raised throughout the war and is still discussed today.[19]

Congressional opponents of the war found themselves in an awkward situation. They believed that they had to support the war measure or face serious consequences. With memories of the Federalist opposition to the War of 1812 still fresh in the nation's mind, those who opposed the war outright faced the charge of aiding the enemy. Most congressional opponents voted to support the army even while speaking out against Polk and his administration. This strategy did not sit well with many soldiers. One volunteer officer voiced his opinion about Whig opposition: "I had as soon fight some of the Damd [*sic*] Tories in the U.S. as those Yellow Devils here[.] I believe peace would have been made long ago If It had not been for some D Tories who call themselvsz [*sic*] Whigs." He was not alone in his opinion, as another volunteer proclaimed that the machinations of Henry Clay and his supporters "have been heretofore & perhaps will still prove, a barrier to the cessation of existing hostilities." These "yelpers," he said, opposed "the comsumation [*sic*] of an honorable peace" purely because it "might advance the cause of Democracy to the detriment of 'false founded Whiggery.'" The Democratic press in North Carolina went so far as to call its political opponents "Mexican Whigs" and accused them of giving "aid and comfort" to the enemy.[20]

Choosing men to command the wartime army of more than one hundred thousand regulars and volunteers intensified the political struggle between Democrats and Whigs. Each newly created regiment of regulars presented an opportunity to fill thirty-three officer positions. In addition, the problem of logistics dictated that several hundred new positions be created in the army's staff departments to clothe, feed, arm, transport, and pay the burgeoning number of American troops. The task of appointing these men fell to the president; confirming them was the duty of Congress. Filling positions offered excellent opportunities for Polk and his administration to exercise the power of patronage, as well as to extend Democratic control over the army. For the Whigs, opposing high-profile Democratic appointees became a means of drawing attention to their own emerging political favorite—Maj. Gen. Zachary Taylor.[21]

On the state level, too, raising troops had its political aspects. The Act of May 13, 1846, stated that volunteer "officers shall be appointed, in the manner prescribed by law in the several States and Territories to which such Companies, Battalions, Squadrons, and Regiments, shall belong." In some instances this meant that the officers were appointed by the governors, but more commonly volunteer officers were elected by the men of their commands. The system guaranteed that the issue of politics would enter the selection process.[22]

The practice of allowing volunteers to choose their own leaders reflected a firmly held conviction of the citizen-soldier: men free-born should be allowed to determine who would lead them in time of war. Would not neighbors know best who among themselves were the best leaders? One historian who has written on this period, Thomas W. Cutrer, terms this concept "the frontier military tradition" and posits that it dates back to America's colonial period. Throughout the war, volunteers proudly clung to their status as citizens and resented any slight, real or imagined, to the honor associated with this title. The traditions of the citizen-soldier, as embodied by the volunteer, conflicted with those of the regular army and its corps of officers trained at West Point. To many men involved in the war, this conflict exemplified the ongoing struggle against a privileged class— a struggle taken to fever pitch by the supporters of Andrew Jackson.[23]

An army reflects the beliefs and values of the society from which it is drawn. That the soldiers who fought against Mexico held the attitudes prevalent in their day is evident from their diaries and letters. Few doubted the superiority of the Anglo-Saxon and his associated institutions. Whether Democrat or Whig, all held republican notions common during Jackson's day. It seemed obvious to these men that Mexico was suffering from a severe case of tyranny and that a good "bleeding" would work wonders as a cure. These Protestant Americans had little sympathy for people of other faiths, especially Roman Catholics and Mormons. Whiskey poured though the camps, carrying many a Son of Temperance away in the flood. Volunteers charged with crimes demanded to be tried by a jury of their peers, not by a panel of regulars. The army's armaments were products of the nascent Industrial Revolution, and its medicines were those of a pre-Lister world. The soldiers who heeded Polk's call to arms carried their values and attitudes with them to war. Alexis de Tocqueville could have been speaking of these men when he wrote, "They infuse the spirit of the community at large into the army and retain it there." The product of Jacksonian America, Polk's army carried its view of democracy to the land of the Montezumas.[24]

Polk, as commander-in-chief, faced the twin problems encountered by other presidents during other wars: he had to defeat his foreign enemy as quickly as possible while at the same time fight off political threats at home. Different U.S. presidents have met the challenge differently. Abraham Lincoln used the power of patronage to build a strong coalition which bound the loyal opposition to him and thereby earned support for his policies. Other wartime presidents, however, pursued a course similar to Polk's, punishing dissent and rewarding party loyalty. During the War of 1812, critics accused James Madison of trying to revive the rank of lieutenant general in order to bestow command of the army upon his supporter, Henry Clay. Like other presidents both before and after him, Polk employed political generals, hoping to find men he could trust. Even the abolition of the volunteer system and the adoption of a professional military, which occurred at the end of the nineteenth century, failed to insure good relations between a commander-in-chief and his top generals. Generals who openly differed with their civilian bosses and were removed for their insubordination (real or imagined) have included Winfield Scott, George B. McClellan, and Douglas MacArthur. Not all the fighting that occurs in war takes place on the battlefield, and few presidents have refrained from using their powers as commanders-in-chief to support their parties. As Theodore J. Crackel notes in his study of the early American military, even the venerable West Point was created in an attempt by President Thomas Jefferson to counter Federalist control over the army. Thus, the commander-in-chief's role as party leader was well established before Polk took the oath of office on March 4, 1845.[25]

"Well may we be grateful that we are at war with Mexico! Were it any other power our gross follies would surely have been punished before now." Thirty-one-year-old Lt. George G. Meade, the future hero of Gettysburg, wrote these words to describe the political infighting that characterized the U.S. military during the Mexican War. The American military during that period was a creature of politics. Democrats and Whigs vied for control of the army in a war waged off the battlefield. The prizes included the statehouse, Congress, and even the White House. President Polk, as military commander-in-chief and as leader of his party, marshaled his forces and waged war against both Mexicans and Whigs. For many American soldiers who marched off to war, the actual experience proved very different from what they had expected.[26]

TWO

The American Military Establishment

Every regiment is a miniature army. It has all the constitu-
ents of the largest body of troops. . . . In a word, a regt., is a
unit of which larger bodies are composed, and battalions, grand
divisions, & companies the fractions.

—Fayette Robinson,
Organization of the Army

Taylor's fame is complete and his popularity will be as over-
whelming as was Genl. Jackson's.

—Colonel William B. Campbell,
1st Tennessee Infantry

The United States Army had been in existence for
nearly sixty years at the time of the Mexican War. During its history, the
officers and soldiers had been called on to quell insurrection, repel invasion, and enforce the nation's laws. Subjected to the whims of Congress,
the regular army frequently underwent change. Crises always generated a
flurry of legislation affecting the army, increasing or decreasing the number of officers and men to meet the needs of the moment. Once an emer-

gency passed, the drive for economy and the fear of a standing army prompted Congress to slash the army's budget, sometimes eliminating whole regiments at a time. In 1815, for example, Congress reduced the number of infantry regiments from forty-four to eight. If pressed for troops, the president could always call on the nation's other military force, the militia.[1]

The basic structure of the American military was established during the early years of the Republic. The Constitution reserved the office of commander-in-chief for the president, a duty that President James K. Polk embraced during the Mexican War. Although his supporters called him "Young Hickory," recalling his mentor Andrew Jackson, Polk lacked "Old Hickory's" martial background. Despite his lack of experience in military affairs, Polk played an active role in planning the strategy of the Mexican War and in the war's subsequent conduct.[2]

The nation's founders placed the defense of the United States in the hands of the War Department. Officially created in 1789 as one of the three original executive departments, the department faced the immense task of overseeing all aspects of the nation's military, both regular and militia. As secretary of war, the department's chief occupied a seat in the president's cabinet. William Learned Marcy filled the office from 1845 to 1849, consulting with Polk on departmental matters, the prosecution of the war in Mexico among them. Born in Massachusetts in 1786, Marcy had been admitted to the New York Bar in 1811. Active in state and national politics, he had held a number of governmental posts, including New York comptroller (1823–29), New York associate supreme court justice (1829–31), U.S. senator (1831–32), and governor of New York (1833–39), before joining Polk's cabinet. Marcy is best remembered for his 1832 address regarding the spoils system, in which he remarked, "To the victor belong the spoils." Such thinking would play an important role during the Mexican War.[3]

Marcy could not exercise command in the field, as the War Department did not actually constitute part of the army; but through his office he issued the orders that implemented presidential directives and federal legislation that affected the mobilization, deployment, and maintenance of the U.S. Army. The War Department periodically issued guidelines, entitled *General Regulations,* that set forth the rules of organization and the operation of the military. The last prewar edition had appeared in 1841, but a new edition was published in 1847. In the preface to the new edition, Marcy states, "The General Regulations for the Army, revised and published in 1841, being exhausted, it is found necessary to publish a new edition, . . . so as to embrace alterations and amendments promulgated in orders, or taken from former Regulations, &c." One major difference between the two editions of regulations is that the 1847 version omits many of the lengthy sections on the army's staff department. In addition to the Army Regulations, troops were governed by another set of rules known as the Articles of War. Adopted by Congress in 1806, the Articles of War laid down basic guidelines for behavior expected of officers and enlisted men. So important were these rules that the articles were supposed to be read to all enlisted men twice a year.[4]

A specialized staff, divided into ten separate departments, assisted the secretary of war in managing the standing, or regular, army. The departments included the Adjutant-General's Department, Inspector-General's Department, Commissary Department, Medical Department, Ordnance Department, Pay Department, Quartermaster's Department, Subsistence Department, Corps of Engineers, and Topographical Engineers. Each department oversaw some important aspect of army life and was commanded by a career soldier. All the department chiefs had entered the service either prior to or during the War of 1812. In theory, the general-in-chief coordinated the activities of the departments; but in reality, the department heads often bypassed this link in the chain of command and communicated directly with the secretary of war.[5]

Several categories of officers existed in the army: staff, field, and company. Staff officers planned and supervised strategic and logistical operations. Although the chief of each staff department held the rank of colonel, the ranks of other staff officers below him depended upon their level of responsibility. The second group of officers, called field officers because they were assigned to and commanded regiments in garrison and on campaign, consisted of colonels, lieutenant colonels, and majors. Company officers—captains and lieutenants—composed the third category and commanded the individual companies within each regiment. General officers, the highest ranking category of officers, exercised both staff and field duties.[6]

The issue of rank caused much discord among the officer corps prior to the war and continued to be a sore spot when the army advanced against Mexico. One internal struggle within the corps was between officers of the line (those serving with regiments) and staff officers. Line officers often believed that staff officers received preferential treatment in such important matters as promotions and duty stations. Another equally contentious issue was that of brevet rank. Congress had the authority to bestow brevet, or honorary, rank upon an officer as a reward for good service or heroism in battle. Usually an officer with a brevet, although permitted to use the higher title, did not draw any more pay. However, he could receive the additional pay, as well as fulfill the duties commensurate with the higher rank, when an officer holding the actual rank was not present for duty. Brevet rank had been employed in the army since the War of 1812, and although not entitled to automatically assume the duties and privileges associated with the honor, many older officers had begun to claim that brevet rank actually superseded actual rank. When the army was at Corpus Christi, the debate became so rancorous that President Polk used his position as commander-in-chief to declare brevet rank inferior to actual rank. The decision reversed an early one made by the commanding general of the army, Maj. Gen. Winfield Scott. Outraged by the ruling that determined that Col. David E. Twiggs actually outranked him, Bvt. Brig. Gen. William J. Worth left the army just prior to the commencement of hostilities, thereby missing the battles of Palo Alto and Resaca de la Palma. Worth quickly withdrew his resignation and returned to duty, reportedly vowing to earn either a grade or a grave.[7]

Noncommissioned officers (NCOs) formed an important level in the army's hierarchy. The army's many sergeants and corporals composed this extremely important class of enlisted men. Noncommissioned officers held their rank at the discretion of their colonels and captains and did not receive a commission from Congress. Each company had five sergeants and eight corporals who supervised the privates while the latter performed their duties. Men who were appointed sergeants or corporals had proven themselves knowledgeable both in the drill and in army regulations. Many had chosen to make the military their career. In accord with their rank, NCOs were entitled to certain privileges, such as a mess separate from that of the privates. The regulations warned officers not to reprimand a sergeant or a corporal in public, as this lessened the NCO's authority. The senior sergeant, or first sergeant, kept the company's records, conducted roll calls, and assigned men to various details. The first sergeant also was known as the "orderly sergeant."[8]

Managing the army in war and peace required the coordinated efforts of the army staff departments. These departments kept the army fed, clothed, armed, nursed, and paid, so that it could perform its duties when called upon by the commander-in-chief. Under the direction of the secretary of war and the general-in-chief, the staff departments quietly conducted their operations, engendering cohesion and standardization throughout the military. The officers and men of these departments played a crucial role, albeit one that was unglamorous and often overlooked.

The Adjutant-General's Department linked the various components of the army together by acting as a clearinghouse for all official correspondence. In addition, the members of the department kept track of the health and whereabouts of all army personnel. Official documents such as general and special orders, morning reports, and court-martial proceedings were deposited in the adjutant general's office at Washington, D.C. Army recruiting also fell under this department's jurisdiction. Col. Roger Jones, a distinguished veteran of the War of 1812, served as adjutant general.[9]

The Inspector-General's Department, the smallest of the staff departments, carried out the vital task of evaluating the army's performance. Officers in this department were attached to the office of the general-in-chief. In peacetime, two permanent members traveled throughout the country inspecting forts and camps; checking on the condition of the buildings, personnel, and material; and evaluating the army's overall state of readiness. The immensity of these tasks made it necessary for field officers from permanent regiments (regimental officers with the rank of colonel, lieutenant colonel, and major) to be detached from their units periodically and sent on inspection tours. Although this helped the overworked inspector general, Col. George Croghan, the practice had a detrimental effect on regiments by causing their senior officers to be absent, a problem the army encountered when war broke out.[10]

The Medical Department oversaw the army's health. In addition to establishing hospitals and dispensing medicine to sick and wounded soldiers, the officers of the department supervised the selection of posts and camps, to insure salubrious settings. Medical officers periodically inspected army provisions for mold, weevils, and worms. Regulations also required army doctors to examine all recruits. The surgeon general, Col. Thomas Lawson, directed the efforts of the Medical Department. The army assigned one surgeon and two assistant surgeons to each regiment. Contract surgeons—civilian doctors hired by the army—sometimes filled vacant positions. The Medical Department consisted of personnel other than surgeons. Hospital stewards (enlisted men with the rank of sergeant) acted as apothecaries and supervised hospital wards in the surgeon's absence. In times of medical crisis, such as during epidemics or following battles, soldiers were detailed from the ranks to serve as nurses. Women hospital workers, called matrons, cooked and washed for patients. U.S. Army hospitals in Mexico sometimes employed local Mexican women as matrons.[11]

The men and officers of the army eagerly looked forward to the arrival of the officers of the Pay Department. The paymaster general, Col. Nathan Townson, presided over eighteen paymasters. Although army paymasters held the rank of major, they were not entitled to field command. The department had jurisdiction over all *sutlers*, civilian shopkeepers whom the government licensed to accompany specific regiments. Although sutlers often inflated their prices, soldiers lined up to buy luxuries that the army did not supply. These government-licensed merchants, who extended credit to men without money, had the right to stand beside the paymaster on payday and collect payment from customers with tabs. Some sutlers followed their regiments to Mexico. Although payday was supposed to occur every two months, on the frontier or on campaign it was common for long interludes to pass between the paymaster's visits. In such cases soldiers did without cash or had to find other forms of currency. In one instance, volunteers and New Mexican merchants employed buttons, needles, and tobacco as currency when a paymaster failed to visit Santa Fe.[12]

Soldiers relied upon the Quartermaster Department to fulfill basic needs for food, clothing, and shelter. A permanent staff of thirty-seven officers, headed by Brig. Gen. Thomas S. Jesup, strove to meet this monumental demand. The department's duties included providing permanent and temporary shelter, as well as transporting and issuing provisions for man and beast. Civilian teamsters, hired to assist the overworked enlisted men assigned to the department, drove the caravans of wagons required to keep the army supplied. Besides American employees, the department hired hundreds of Mexican mule drivers to transport supplies into the Mexican interior. The Quartermaster Department contracted with private ship owners to carry equipment and provisions to Mexico, in addition to operating its own fleet of sailing ships and steamboats along the Rio Grande and the Gulf coast. The department also supervised the government workshops and private manufacturers that produced uniforms, tents, knapsacks, haversacks, canteens, and other items for the army. Military storekeepers were quasi-military employees who kept stocks of army supplies, inventorying all goods received and issued at government storehouses. So important were the department's duties that Quartermaster General Jesup spent several months in Mexico with the army inspecting its operations.[13]

Army procurement fell under the joint jurisdiction of the Quartermaster Department and the Subsistence Department. Quartermasters had the authority to make purchases in locations where troops were operating, in order to satisfy the army's immediate needs. Quartermasters bought meat, vegetables, fodder, and draft animals at Mexican markets. Quartermaster funds also covered the cost of transportation and lodging. Bulk rations, such as hundred-pound barrels of beef, pork, flour, and hard bread, were purchased by the eight officers of the Subsistence Department, who tried to secure high-quality provisions at the lowest possible prices. Col. George Gibson, the commissary general of the army, supervised the activities of the Subsistence Department.[14]

Arming the military was the responsibility of the Ordnance Department. In addition to issuing weapons to the army, the department also supervised the production of muskets, rifles, cannons, gunpowder, and accouterments. While the department contracted with some manufacturers to produce arms, it also operated its own arsenals turning out thousands of weapons complete with accessories. These important duties were the responsibility of Col. George Bomford.[15]

Although their duties sometimes overlapped, two separate departments of army engineers existed. Officers and men attached to the United States Engineers established and maintained the nation's permanent posts and fortifications. The corps numbered nearly forty-five officers and was commanded by the chief engineer, Col. James G. Totten. The military academy fell under the jurisdiction of the U.S. Engineers. Col. John J. Abert held the office of Chief Topographic Engineer and directed the Topographic Engineers. Officers of this department surveyed routes for new roads and recommended sites for new posts. Active on the western frontier, the Topographic Engineers conducted many mapping expeditions throughout the mid-nineteenth century. Members of both corps figured conspicuously in fighting in Mexico, reconnoitering, marking trails, and supervising the placement of guns.[16]

Infantry, artillery, and dragoons formed the combat elements of the U.S. Army. On the eve of hostilities with Mexico, the army consisted of only eight infantry regiments, four artillery regiments, and two dragoon regiments. The various companies of these fourteen regiments of infantry, artillery, and dragoons were spread out across the nation at more than one hundred military posts. The war reunited some regiments whose individual companies had not served together for ten or more years.[17]

According to one former army officer–turned-historian, Fayette Robinson, each regiment comprised "a miniature army," as it contained all the elements of command and staff that existed in the army as a whole. The senior officers of the regiment—colonel, lieutenant colonel, and major—and an appointed staff were responsible for the management of the regiment. Officers assigned to the regimental staff helped the colonel carry out his duties. Brevet second lieutenants fresh from West Point routinely were assigned to regimental staffs, a duty that familiarized them with army operations while they gained experience supervising small details. The regiment's quartermaster and commissary (officers such as the ones just described) provided for the immediate needs of the regiment. Another regimental staff officer, the adjutant, acted as the colonel's secretary, freeing his commander from mundane paperwork. Selected from among the regiment's more experienced and promising lieutenants, this important officer helped to mark the regiment's place on the line of battle and on the march. He also trained the regiment's noncommissioned officers in their duties and helped manage the regimental band. One surgeon and two assistant surgeons looked after the regiment's health.[18]

A noncommissioned staff also assisted the colonel in running his regiment. At large posts, an ordnance sergeant repaired and maintained weapons and munitions in good condition and in working order. The sergeant major, the regiment's senior enlisted man, acted as the adjutant's aide. The chief musician—a sergeant—led the twelve-man regimental band that provided entertainment as well as the music to which the army marched and fought. A quartermaster sergeant assisted the regimental quartermaster.[19]

Women played important roles in regimental life. Whenever possible, officers' wives joined their husbands at permanent posts, allowing officers to maintain regular households with their families. Army regulations permitted each company to employ four laundresses to wash and sew for the men. Like sutlers, laundresses attended payday to collect from soldiers to whom they had extended credit. Most women and children stayed behind when the troops marched off to Mexico; however, American women occasionally are mentioned in the letters and diaries of Mexican War soldiers. Writing on the first day of 1846, Col. Ethan Allen Hitchcock noted the lack of females with the army then camped at Corpus Christi, commenting dryly, "There are no ladies here, and very few women."[20]

A few women, disguised as men, made their way into the ranks of the American Army during the Mexican War. A woman in the ranks, however, was a rarity and caused a commotion whenever her disguise was penetrated. All known cases of women in the ranks involved volunteers who, unlike regulars, often did not have to undergo physical examination upon enlistment. One Alabama volunteer passed off a female companion as his frail younger brother until the ruse was discovered. Caroline Newcome took the name "Bill" and served as a private in the Missouri volunteers until pregnancy betrayed her. A similar case occurred in the Mississippi volunteers. Popular attitudes of the day prohibited women from serving as soldiers, and all known cases of females found in uniform ended in disgrace for them and their accomplices.[21]

To facilitate management and deployment, regiments were divided into smaller components called companies. Ten companies, each commanded by a captain, constituted a regiment. Besides the captain, other positions of command within each company included one first lieutenant, one second lieutenant, five sergeants, and eight corporals. Sergeants performed the functions of quartermaster and commissary on the company level. Each company was divided further into two equal parts called platoons; the platoon, in turn, was divided into two smaller parts called sections. In 1842, Congress had established the maximum strength of each infantry and artillery company at forty-two enlisted men; but sickness, desertion, and detached duty caused the enrollment in companies to fall far below the prescribed number. Wartime legislation prescribed one hundred privates per company. Soldiers considered their company "home" because they worked, played, ate, slept, and sometimes died within its familial environment. Each member of a company wore a letter denoting his company's designation: A, B, C, D, E, F, G, H, I, K. The letter *J* was omitted, as it was too easily confused with the letter *I*.[22]

Companies, battalions, regiments, brigades, and divisions provided the army with a simple framework for both logistical and combat organization. The army's basic building blocks—regiments and companies—could be arranged in various combinations. A military unit of more than one but less than ten companies was designated a *battalion* and usually was commanded by a lieutenant colonel or a major, depending upon the unit's size. A battalion usually consisted of companies from the same regiment, but under special circumstances this custom was ignored. A unit larger than a regiment, called a *brigade,* could be produced by placing two or three regiments together under the command of a brigadier general. Two or more brigades could be placed together under the command of a major general and organized into a unit called a *division*. Both brigadier and major generals were aided by officers who performed the various duties of the army's staff departments. Several divisions operating in one theater, commanded by the most senior officer present, comprised an army. The U.S. Army, however, did not retain organized brigades and divisions in peacetime and employed them only in time of war.[23]

Infantry composed the bulk of all nineteenth-century armies. Troops of this class sometimes bore the designation "foot." Armed predominantly with flintlock muskets, infantry consisted of two categories. Heavy infantry, also called infantry-of-the-line, were trained to fight shoulder to shoulder in rigid lines of battle. Light infantry, the second class of infantry, operated as skirmishers and fought in open order. In theory, a regiment's two flank companies—those on the right and left of the regimental line of battle—served as light infantry. In practice, however, all infantry companies in the U.S. Army received the same training and functioned equally well in either role. Officers instructed infantry recruits using a drill manual prepared for the army by the commanding general, Winfield Scott, and bearing the imposing title *Infantry Tactics; Or, Rules for the Exercise and Maneuvers of the United States Infantry*. For brevity's sake, officers commonly referred to the manual and its drill simply as *Scott's*.[24]

Artillery, too, was categorized as heavy and light. Heavy artillery garrisoned the nation's permanent fortifications. Artillerists of this class also manned the heavy siege guns used in wartime. Light artillery had undergone revolutionary changes prior to the war. Equipped with new, lightweight, horse-drawn guns, these mobile artillerists could maneuver and deploy rapidly, going into action quicker than ever had been possible before. Because of their speed, they were called "Flying Artillery." Although highly effective in Mexico, only five companies—or batteries, as artillery companies also commonly were called—had been equipped as light artillery at the start of the war. Although light batteries rarely exceeded six guns, instances occurred when eight guns were placed together. Capt. Robert Anderson's translation of a French manual, *Instruction for Field Artillery*, appeared in 1839 and was used to train soldiers in the methods of field artillery. In 1845, the War Department adopted Maj. Samuel Ringgold's newer manual for light artillery, *Instruction of Field Artillery, Horse and Foot*, which was based on the British system. Ironically, in the Mexican War, the majority of U.S. artillerymen were organized into a unit designated the Artillery Battalion and served as infantry throughout the war.[25]

Unlike European armies, which had several classes of cavalry, the U.S. Army used only a type of light cavalry called *dragoons*. Armed with pistols, carbines, and sabers, dragoons theoretically could fight equally well on horseback or on foot. As an economy measure, Congress in 1842 had ordered the 2nd U.S. Dragoons dismounted and converted into a rifle regiment, an act that left only one mounted regiment to cover the entire United States and its western territories. Fortunately, Congress reversed its decision and the regiment again was outfitted as dragoons in 1844, just in time to perform valuable service in Mexico. Mounted troops were referred to as "horse." Although organized as regiments, in the case of the dragoons, a slight difference in structure existed. *Squadron,* a term used only in the dragoons, referred to a unit composed of two companies; no unit of equal size existed in either the infantry or the artillery. Prior to the war, Congress had established fifty privates as the maximum number allowed for a company of horse, but on May 13, 1846, the number was raised to one hundred. A government publication, entitled simply *Cavalry Tactics,* served as the basis of instruction for the dragoons. In May, 1846, Congress authorized an additional regiment of horse, the U.S. Regiment of Mounted Rifles. Armed with the Model 1841 Rifle in addition to the usual dragoon equipment, the regiment saw action in central Mexico as both light cavalry and infantry.[26]

Two training manuals specifically written for the *militia,* or state troops, were widely used. The first, an abridged version of the manual developed by Winfield Scott for the infantry, had been in use since the early 1820s. The other, *A Concise System of Instruction and Regulations for the Militia and Volunteers of the United States,* first appeared in 1836 and was referred to as *Cooper's* after the book's compiler, Bvt. Capt. Samuel Cooper. Most regulars, however, believed that the militia generally lacked the training needed to make them useful in an actual military campaign. Many militia officers viewed the organization as a springboard to political office and used days set aside for drill for stump speaking.[27]

Disappointing the founding fathers' hopes for a citizen army, the militia in the past had proven itself unreliable. During the War of 1812, for example, the New York militiamen had refused to leave the borders of the United States to take part in the invasion of Canada. In many cases, when the militia was called to active duty, a large portion of its members' three-month term of enlistment already had elapsed; by the time they assembled and reached the front, the men clamored to go home. In many states, the militia had deteriorated into social clubs that met only a few times a year so that members could drill, eat, and drink. One other class of citizen-soldier existed within the framework of the U.S. military tradition: the volunteer. Troops of this class occupied a position between the enrolled militia and the regular army.[28]

Congress looked to Europe for models for the American military. A series of military disasters during the early years of the War for Independence convinced George Washington and others that the country needed a disciplined force for its defense, especially when the foe was a well-trained professional army like that of Great Britain. The legendary winter spent at Valley Forge under the tutelage of a self-proclaimed Prussian nobleman, Baron von Steuben, transformed Washington's collection of troops into a disciplined army that began to match the British in their own kind of warfare. Von Steuben's *Regulations for the Order and Discipline of the Troops of the United States* was adopted by the Continental Congress in 1779 and remained the standard drill for the American army until 1812. Manuals that replaced Steuben's continued to be based upon European systems of drill.[29]

More than any other, one man came to represent the European military tradition in America—Winfield Scott. Born in Petersburg, Virginia, on June 13, 1786, young Scott originally intended to practice law, but the growing tension between the U.S. and Great Britain caused him to change his plans. On May 3, 1808, following a brief period as a volunteer, he accepted a commission as captain of light artillery in the U.S. Army. Recognized for his diligence and attention to duty, Scott saw his star rise steadily. He reached the rank of lieutenant colonel in 1812, at the age of twenty-six. Assigned to the 2nd U.S. Artillery, Scott in October of that year participated in the American attack on Queenstown. There he was forced to surrender, along with the other troops, when reinforcements of New York militia refused to cross into Canada and come to their aid. Paroled the following month, Scott was both promoted to colonel of his regiment and appointed adjutant general. Like von Steuben, Colonel Scott believed in strict discipline and rigorously exercised his troops at every opportunity. Congress promoted the twenty-nine-year-old Scott to the rank of brigadier general on March 9, 1814.

Scott soon gained a reputation for commanding one of the best-trained brigades in the army. At the Battle of Chippewa on July 5, 1814, Scott's brigade—dressed in coats of militia gray instead of U.S. Army blue—met and drove British regulars from the field, causing the stunned redcoats to cry out, "Why, these are regulars!" Several weeks later, on July 25, the Americans again clashed with the British at Lundy's Lane, near the Falls of the Niagara. Although both sides claimed victory, the American army had battled it out with British regulars, at last proving itself a worthy opponent. Severely wounded in the fight, Scott recovered and won a major general's brevet for his actions at Chippewa and Lundy's Lane. After only six years in the service, the thirty-year-old Scott was the fourth highest-ranking officer in the army, inferior only to Jacob Brown, Andrew Jackson, and Alexander Macomb.[30]

In his elevated position, Scott continued to model the U.S. Army after those of Europe. Appointed in 1815 to a military board charged with formulating a new system of discipline (also called tactics), Scott went to Europe, where he observed the armies of other nations. Already familiar with the French system (which had guided the training of his regiment and brigade during the recent war), Scott borrowed heavily from it when he produced a system of tactics for the U.S. Army. An edition of the new manual appeared in print in 1817; later versions were published and republished in 1836, 1840, 1846, 1847, 1848, 1852, 1857, 1860, and 1861. An abridged edition designed for use by the militia went to press in 1830, but it was not used as widely as the version designed for the regular army. In 1818, Scott began collecting English and French books and essays pertaining to the governance of armies in garrison and on campaign. Drawing on this research, he compiled a new book, *General Regulations*. In 1825, Congress adopted this work as the official guide for governing the army. Scott's military writings greatly shaped the development of the U.S. Army in the years prior to the Mexican War.[31]

Appointed general-in-chief of the U.S. Army in 1841, Scott already had gained a reputation for skill in the fields of diplomacy and politics as well. During the Nullification Crisis of 1832, President Andrew Jackson sent Scott to Charleston, South Carolina, to calm passions and urge restraint. In 1838, President Martin Van Buren sent Scott to the Canadian border to try to calm hostilities aroused after pro-British Canadians seized and burned an American ship, the *Caroline,* killing a U.S. citizen. Returning to the Niagara frontier where he initially had made his reputation, Scott quashed attempts at retaliation while shoring up American interests in the area. Scott's high visibility in matters such as these placed him in contact with influential persons, and by 1839 leading politicians in the Whig Party were eyeing him as a possible presidential candidate. Scott, too, viewed himself a worthy candidate for the White House and stood ready to answer the call.[32]

Scott's meteoric rise caused resentment among his peers. One of them, Brig. Gen. Edmund Pendleton Gaines, developed an intense, open rivalry with Scott over the issue of seniority. Gaines, who had entered the army as an ensign in 1799, had won praise for his defense of Fort Erie in August 1814. Unfortunately for Scott and Gaines, their respective commissions as lieutenant colonel, colonel, and brigadier general had been awarded by Congress on exactly the same days: July 6, 1812; March 12, 1813; and March 9, 1814. Both men received brevets as major generals, Scott's for the action of July 25, 1814, and Gaines's for that of August 15, 1814. At the war's conclusion, the War Department declared Scott's rank higher than that of Gaines, and the feud began. Scott claimed that his brevet to major general entitled him to the top spot, while Gaines contended that his years of service prior to Scott's entrance into the army made him senior to Scott. The two generals attacked each other in the press. As late as 1845, Gaines was still pushing his case, writing that Scott had "labored for more than a quarter of a century past with far more zeal to cover me with calumny, and defeat my efforts . . . than he has ever labored to provide for the national defense and to defeat the invading foe." In the army, old grudges died hard.[33]

Some veterans of the fighting along the Niagara who had served in Scott's command survived budget cuts and made careers in the army. In 1825, Congress appointed Roger Jones, who had been assistant adjutant general in Gen. Jacob Brown's division at Lundy's Lane, to head the Adjutant-General's Department. Two regimental commanders under Scott also rose to positions of prominence within the army. Col. Hugh Brady was given command of the 2nd U.S. Infantry on May 17, 1815, and was breveted to brigadier general six weeks later. Thomas S. Jesup received both his commission as brigadier general and an appointment as quartermaster general on May 8, 1818. William Jenkins Worth, who as a young lieutenant had served as Scott's aide during the Niagara campaign, took command of the 8th U.S. Infantry as colonel on July 7, 1838. Newman S. Clarke, who acted as brigade major to one of the brigade commanders under Scott, was the lieutenant colonel of the 6th U.S. Infantry when the hostilities between the U.S. and Mexico commenced.[34]

The commander of the 6th U.S. Infantry, Col. Zachary Taylor, entered the army as lieutenant in 1808, the same year Scott received his commission as captain. Both men were Virginians, but the similarity ended there. Taylor, who grew to maturity on his father's estate outside Louisville, Kentucky, built a solid war record, although it seemed mediocre compared to Scott's successes. Assigned to duty in the Old Northwest, Captain Taylor won a brevet to major for his September 5, 1812, defense of Fort Harrison in Indiana Territory. Promotion to major came on May 15, 1814, the highest rank Taylor achieved during the War of 1812. Although many surplus officers were sent home in the reduction in force that came with peace, Taylor was told he could stay on if he accepted the lower rank of captain. He declined the offer; left the service on June 15, 1815; and briefly tried his hand at farming. Less than a year later, however, Congress reinstated Taylor as a major. Climbing slowly but steadily, Taylor was promoted to colonel in command of the 1st U.S. Infantry on April 4, 1832. During the Seminole War, Taylor and his regiment were sent to Florida, where on Christmas Day, 1837, the colonel scored a victory against the elusive hostiles at Lake Okeechobee. For this action Congress rewarded Taylor with a brevet to brigadier general. It was Bvt. Brig. Gen. Zachary Taylor—the Hero of Okeechobee and then colonel of the 6th U.S. Infantry—whom President Polk placed in command of the Army of Occupation.[35]

Other differences set Scott and Taylor apart. Scott spent much of his career in the East. Cultured and refined, he delighted in the 1815 trip across the Atlantic Ocean that allowed him to rub shoulders with the elite of Europe. But success eluded him on the frontier. Sent west at the head of a column during the Black Hawk War in 1832, Scott and his men were prevented from reaching their destination by a cholera epidemic that erupted on their transport ships while on the Great Lakes. Although Scott won praise for his humanitarian efforts to comfort his stricken troops, he missed the opportunity for new military laurels. His lackluster performance in

Florida elicited a court of inquiry to determine whether or not he had acted with vigor to subdue the Seminoles.

Taylor, in contrast, thrived on frontier duty. During the War of 1812, he fought and won several encounters against British-backed Indians. His postwar stations included Fort Winnebago, Wisconsin Territory (1816); New Orleans, Louisiana (1819); Fort Jesup, Louisiana (1822); Louisville, Kentucky (1824); Fort Crawford, Michigan Territory (1832); Florida Territory (1837); Baton Rouge, Louisiana (1840); and Fort Gibson, Indian Territory (1841). Taylor's performance during the Black Hawk War and in Florida brought him a measure of national recognition as an Indian fighter. Additionally, his purchase of Cyprus Grove plantation near Baton Rouge tied him to the land. In short, Taylor came to symbolize the rugged West and Scott the sophisticated East.[36]

The sobriquets of both men indicated the obvious differences between them. Scott, known to love fine food and fancy uniforms, early on came to be called "Young Fuss and Feathers." As he aged, the title changed to "Old Fuss and Feathers," indicating that his penchant for high living had not lessened over the years. One soldier who remembered seeing Scott's camp during the Seminole War remarked that the general "required a band of music, with a company of professed cooks and servants to attend them." These refinements, he continued, likely never had been seen before in the wilderness and included several large tents and enough furniture to fill three wagons. This "grand panoply of war," the observer contended, was "quite unsuitable for Indian bush fighting." Anyone who stumbled upon Scott's camp, he concluded, "would imagine that it was the train of some Indian nabob rather than the requisites of a republic[an] general engaged in warfare with a wild foe in a desert country."[37]

In his dress and mannerisms, Taylor was the exact opposite of the aristocratic Scott. An observer of Taylor's camp on the Rio Grande described its Spartan appearance: "There was no pomp about his tent; a couple of rough blue chests served as his table." No fancy mess gear was in sight, just a tin serving plate holding a collection of black bottles, glass tumblers, and an earthen water pitcher. Taylor spurned military finery, preferring a simple civilian coat and pantaloons. Such clothing often caused him to be mistaken for a servant, farmer, or teamster—anybody but a general officer of the U.S. Army. His troops affectionately called him "Old Rough and Ready," a name the public soon learned as well. One officer who served under Taylor in Mexico summed up the prevailing opinion regarding the general's common touch when he stated, "He is essentially democratic in his nature."[38]

As soldiers and commanders, the two leaders approached war differently. Taylor often relied on straightforward action, as when he informed his army the day before Palo Alto that the enemy held the road to Fort Texas, and he planned to "give him battle." As further evidence of his philosophy of attack, Taylor told his infantry commanders that their "main dependence must be in the bayonet." He demonstrated this style of command again during the first day's action at Monterey, when he ordered two divisions to fight their way into the fortified town. Taylor always seemed eager to find the enemy and bring him to battle. Scott, on the other hand, planned battles meticulously and avoided rushing into unknown danger. His battles in central Mexico were characterized by his ability to maneuver and turn the enemy's flanks, forcing the Mexicans to withdraw to a safer position to keep from being surrounded. Ironically, the American public, who expected heroic reports from the battlefield, failed to realize that Scott's victories were the result of military skill, while Taylor's were bought with blood.[39]

For many Americans, including the men who served under them, the war's two most illustrious generals came to represent two different military styles: Scott, the aristocrat; and Taylor, the democrat. Scott consistently praised West Point–trained officers who served in his command, remarking that the presence of these men increased the effectiveness of his army fourfold. "Old Fuss and Feathers" held lavish dinner parties for his officers, at which he lectured them on such topics as the art of wine tasting. His campaigns resembled those of European generals, incorporating movement to avoid bloodshed. Ironically, Taylor personally disliked most volunteers, but the press and the public linked him with the freer style associated with the volunteer service. Writing soon after the battle of Buena Vista, Col. William B. Campbell expressed his view of both generals: "Taylor is the people's man," contended the colonel, "and he makes an impression on the soldiery." Campbell claimed that "Gen'l Scott," on the other hand, "makes no such impression as Old Rough and Ready." Scott's main fault, thought Campbell, was that, although he was a man of "great acquirements and genius," he was "vain and light." Campbell hit upon the key to Taylor's celebrity, stating, "Taylor's fame is complete and his popularity will be as overwhelming as was Genl. Jackson's." Here was a hero cast from the mold of Old Hickory himself. Unfortunately for Polk and his party, this "democratic" general settled in the Whig camp.[40]

By the advent of the Mexican War, Winfield Scott, through his administrative ability and battlefield victories, had helped shape America's regulars into a European-style army. But the transition was not yet complete.

Although the number of professionally trained officers had grown significantly, many top officers had learned their lessons of war from experience, not textbooks. The homespun style of Taylor—the "Hero of Okeechobee"—still appealed to many Americans who had been reared on tales of the frontier. While the war would bring defeat to Mexico, it also would strike a serious blow at "democrats" in the army and so further professionalize the military.

THREE

Mr. Polk's Generals

The truth is neither Taylor nor Scott are fit for the command of the army.

—James Knox Polk,
January 14, 1847

I can assure gentlemen that all the clamor they may get up here against the old veteran [Taylor] will only attract more attention to his merits, and add new fuel to the flame already burning at the bare idea of his being superseded in his command, or being subjected to the dictation of a political general, fresh from the Halls of Congress.

—Thomas W. Newton, Arkansas congressman,
February 26, 1847

For James K. Polk, the War with Mexico became a paradox. In a conflict largely perceived as a Democratic endeavor, a Whig general was receiving credit for American victories on the battlefield. The wartime press seized upon Zachary Taylor and presented him to the public as a folksy frontier hero. Letters from Mexico described the general as unrefined and uncouth but a man sprung from the common people. The combination of military glory and mass appeal was not lost on Polk and the Democrats; America had sent successful generals to the nation's capital before. George Washington, hero of the revolution, established the precedent. Andrew Jackson, victorious over the British at the Battle of New

Orleans, followed Washington's example. The Whigs had learned to tap into this tradition and in the election of 1840 put their own war hero, William Henry Harrison of Tippecanoe fame, in the White House. Whigs began mentioning Taylor's name as a possible presidential candidate soon after the battles of Palo Alto and Resaca de la Palma. As early as July 1846, Taylor felt compelled to deny that he sought the office. Polk came to recognize the danger that Taylor presented to the Democratic Party and decided that "Old Rough and Ready" must go.[1]

Polk and Taylor had begun the war on good terms. Impressed with the old soldier's victories at Palo Alto and Resaca de la Palma, the president had bestowed upon Taylor the rank of major general. Their falling out came in the autumn of 1846, after Taylor allowed a Mexican army to retire from Monterey following the battle for the city, under terms of an unauthorized armistice. Polk believed that Taylor had missed a chance to end the war. Taylor, stung by Polk's open criticism, realized that he no longer had the support of the president and his administration. Their mutual respect for one another turned into intense hatred, as each believed that the other's actions were motivated by party politics.[2]

Obstacles to replacing Taylor existed. First, although Polk held the title of commander-in-chief, popular opinion, protocol, and even law precluded Taylor's recall without a valid reason. The public had come to adore the tough old general, and a move to oust him could backfire and create even more support for him. Second, the army traditionally promoted officers on the basis of seniority, and the list of general officers who could replace Taylor offered Polk no solution, as he found them all equally unacceptable. Finally, by law, Congress had to vote to confirm new appointments, and it was unlikely that its members would go along with a move to depose the new hero. Throughout the war, however, Polk worked to overcome these obstacles and provide the Democratic Party with a popular chieftain of its own.[3]

The obvious solution to Polk's problem was to send Taylor's immediate superior, Winfield Scott, to Mexico. But Polk disliked Major General Scott—the general-in-chief of the army—even more than he disliked Taylor. Although Polk faulted Taylor for not being resourceful, he heaped much harsher criticism on Scott. According to the president, Scott (whose Whig aspirations for the presidency were well known) not only thirsted for personal glory but also was disloyal to the administration. Polk even questioned Scott's standing as America's premier soldier, charging that the general was unwilling to "lay aside the technical rules of war found in books" and prosecute the war with vigor. The remark obviously mocked the general's military scholarship. Polk already had had several clashes with Scott over the issue of brevet rank and the appointment of officers to the U.S. Mounted Rifles. Scott, a prolific if not a prudent writer, early in the war had charged that the president was appointing only Democrats to the new regiment. In another well-publicized incident, he indicated that the president and his cabinet not only were ignorant of military affairs, but also were ready to sacrifice him for political reasons. The general claimed that he was working so hard to organize the army that he only had time for a "hasty plate of soup" and that he feared moving to the front "with a fire in his rear," directed at him from Washington. Scott genuinely was surprised when the president stripped him of the command of field operations in late May 1846 and ordered him to remain in Washington, D.C. On January 14, 1847, irritated at both generals, Polk confided to his diary, "The truth is neither Taylor nor Scott are fit for the command of the army." It was only when no other commander for the Vera Cruz expedition could be found that Polk relented and allowed Scott to take to the field. Soon after, however, the Polk-Scott feud began anew, eventually rising to a new level of bitterness.[4]

Polk was contemptuous of other high-ranking army officers, too. The president decried the fact that other top generals, such as John E. Wool and Roger Jones, were Whigs. Regular army officers, claimed Polk, jealously guarded their positions and worked to defeat the appointment of new volunteer generals. "These officers are all Whigs and violent partisans," he wrote in one passage in his diary. Polk believed that these Whig generals were "disposed to throw every obstacle in the way of [his] prosecuting the Mexican War successfully."[5]

As Polk suspected, many officers were Whigs, although just how many is not known. Various factors helped to account for the strong Whig presence in the army. Some officers had felt themselves slighted in matters of promotion by previous Democratic administrations. Many regular officers had disagreed with Jackson's policy of Indian removal. The war in Florida, carried out largely under a Democratic administration, also had been unpopular with the army. The Whigs, on the other hand, appealed to many officers with a far-reaching plan for increased public works. Projects such as harbor improvement, river dredging, and road building were a boon to the army. Thus, the Whig Party seemed to be friendly to the army, while the Democrats openly doubted its worth.[6]

Polk disliked Whiggish career officers for more than just their politics; he was convinced that years of inactivity had made them slow and unimaginative. Remarked the president, "The old army officers have become so in the habit of enjoying their ease . . . that most of them have no energy." He wanted decisive action, and he believed that these tradition-bound generals were incapable of giving him a quick victory. These men also seemed to waste public funds by their mismanagement. Taylor, for instance, continued to demand expensive wagons for his army, when pack mules seemed more suitable for Mexican roads. And could not the army purchase Mexican horses, saving the cost of transporting them from places as distant as Ohio? To Polk, who confessed his own lack of military experience to Q.M. Gen. Thomas Jesup, simple solutions such as these seemed obvious. In order to rectify the problem, the president vowed to become more active in directing army operations.[7]

One way Polk exerted control over the army was in the appointment of new generals. On June 26, 1846, Congress authorized positions for eight new generals to lead the volunteer army being raised for service in Mexico. Five of these new generals bore the title "general of volunteers" to distinguish them from generals of the permanent military establishment. On

General Taylor writing a letter to the War Department. John Frost, Pictorial History of the Mexican War, *Philadelphia: C. Desilver, 1848. Courtesy Mary Couts Burnett Library, Texas Christian University*

March 3, 1847, Congress again voted to increase the number of volunteer generals by adding two more major generals and five more brigadier generals to the volunteer corps. Although the commissions were to expire at the end of hostilities, their creation enabled Polk to appoint men whom he believed not only would push the war forward aggressively, but, even more important, were loyal to his administration and the Democratic Party.[8]

Polk followed party doctrine established by his predecessors in the appointment of volunteer generals. First, his appointment of Democrats to fill these positions underscored his belief in rewarding party loyalty. After all, Polk's secretary of war was none other than William L. Marcy, who had popularized the phrase "To the victors belong the spoils." Filling these positions with loyal Democrats therefore can be viewed as use of the spoils system. Second, Polk resented career army officers because he thought they lived privileged lives and were the antithesis of the common man. By appointing men from civilian life, Polk hoped to prove that these American Cincinnati could perform just as well as—if not better than—regular generals. His belief in the ability of the common man extended down to the men in the ranks: "Our forces are the best troops in the world, and would gain victories over superior forces of the enemy, if there were not an officer among them." Polk even favored promoting privates to vacant officer positions. Jacksonian views regarding the ability of the common man guided Polk's military appointments.[9]

Polk saw the army as a political battleground between Whig and Democratic officers and sent reinforcements, in the form of volunteer generals loyal to the Democratic Party, to aid his side. Although Polk claimed that he was "wholly uninfluenced by any reference to the political opinions of the officer[s] of the army," his actions failed to confirm this assertion. While little direct evidence exists to prove that Polk planned to fill the army's officer corps with Democrats, his wartime diary, with its numerous tirades concerning Whig officers, holds important clues. Taylor, the president claimed, had betrayed him by falling under the spell of "political partisans," despite the kindness shown in making him a major general. The general's camp, he lamented, had become a "political arena" where "injustice has been done to many officers of high merit who happen to be Democrats." In one such incident, Polk praised Col. William S. Harney—a "Democrat in politics" and "one of General Jackson's personal friends"—and sided with Harney in that officer's dispute with Scott. The president accused Scott and Taylor of arbitrary and tyrannical conduct, not only toward Harney but against other men he called "gallant Democratic officers."[10]

During the war, President Polk appointed, and Congress confirmed, thirteen volunteer generals. Although some had previous military experience, these men had one trait in common—all were loyal Democrats with years of service to the party. Nine of the thirteen had been Democratic state legislators; five had served as Democrats in Congress. One future volunteer general resigned his congressional seat to lead troops against Mexico. Nor did these men set aside their politics when they accepted their commissions. Two of Polk's volunteer generals even participated in political races while serving with the army in Mexico. An examination of the careers of the volunteer generals—"Mr. Polk's generals," one volunteer called them—prior to their appointments adds weight to the argument that these men were chosen for their political affiliation.[11]

William Orlando Butler graduated from Kentucky's Transylvania University in 1812, just in time to participate in the war with Great Britain. Enlisting in the army, he fought the British and their Indian allies on the Raisin River, surviving the massacre that followed the American surrender. Eventually exchanged, he later obtained a captain's commission

U.S. Commanders: Army, Division, and Brigade

Major Generals

	Date of Commission	Original Date of Appointment and Rank
Winfield Scott	June 25, 1841	May 3, 1808; captain, U.S. light artillery
J. P. Henderson	May 11, 1846	May 11, 1846; major general, Texas Volunteers
Zachary Taylor	June 29, 1846	May 3, 1808; 1st. lieutenant, 7th U.S. Infantry
William O. Butler	June 29, 1846	June 29, 1846; major general of volunteers
Robert Patterson	July 7, 1846	July 7, 1846; major general of volunteers
Gideon J. Pillow	April 13, 1847	July 1, 1846; brigadier general of volunteers
John A. Quitman	April 14, 1847	July 1, 1846; brigadier general of volunteers

Brigadier Generals

	Date of Commission	Original Date of Appointment and Rank
Persifor F. Smith	May 15, 1846	May 15, 1846; brigadier general of Louisiana Volunteers
John E. Wool	June 25, 1841	April 14, 1812; captain, 13th U.S. Infantry
David E. Twiggs	June 30, 1846	March 12, 1812; captain, 8th U.S. Infantry
Stephen W. Kearny	June 30, 1846	March 12, 1812; 1st lieutenant, 13th U.S. Infantry
Thomas Marshall	July 1, 1846	July 1, 1846; appointed from civil life
Gideon J. Pillow	July 1, 1846	July 1, 1846; appointed from civil life
Thomas L. Hamer	July 1, 1846	July 1, 1846; appointed from civil life
Joseph Lane	July 1, 1846	July 1, 1846; appointed from civil life

U.S. Commanders (cont.)

	Date of Commission	Original Date of Appointment and Rank

Brigadier Generals (cont.)

John A. Quitman	July 1, 1846	July 1, 1846; appointed from civil life
James Shileds	July 1, 1846	July 1, 1846, appointed from civil life
Franklin Pierce	March 3, 1847	March 3, 1847; appointed from civil life
George Cadwalader	March 3, 1847	March 3, 1847; appointed from civil life
Enos D. Hopping	March 3, 1846	March 3, 1847; appointed from civil life
Caleb Cushing	April 14, 1847	April 14, 1847; appointed from civil life
Sterling Price	July 20, 1847	July 20, 1847; appointed from volunteer service

Brevet Major Generals

William J. Worth	September 23, 1846	March 19, 1813; 1st lieutenant, 23rd U.S. Infantry

Brevet Brigadier Generals

William J. Worth	March 1, 1842	March 19, 1813; 1st lieutenant, 23rd U.S. Infantry
Persifor F. Smith	September 23, 1846	May 27, 1846; colonel, U.S. Mounted Rifle Regiment
John Garland	August 20, 1847	March 31, 1813; 1st lieutenant, 35th U.S. Infantry
William S. Harney	April 18, 1847	February 13, 1818; 2nd lieutenant, 1st U.S. Infantry

Acting Brigade Commanders

James S. McIntosh: lieutenant colonel, 5th U.S. Infantry	November 13, 1812; 2nd lieutenant
William Whistler: colonel, 4th U.S. Infantry	June 8, 1801; 2nd lieutenant
John Garland; lieutenant colonel, 4th U.S. Infantry	March 13, 1813; 1st lieutenant
Henry Wilson: lieutenant colonel, 1st U.S. Infantry	May 17, 1814; ensign
Thomas Staniford: major, 5th U.S. Infantry	October 12, 1814; ensign
Newson S. Clarke: colonel, 6th U.S. Infantry	March 12, 1812; ensign
Bennett Riley: lieutenant colonel 2nd U.S. Infantry	March 12, 1813; ensign
Samuel E. Watson: lieutenant colonel, U.S. Marine Corps	

Source: Francis B. Heitman, *Historical Register and Dictionary of the United States Army, From Its Organization, September 29, 1789, to March 2, 1903,* 2 vols. (Washington: Government Printing Office, 1903; Gaithersburg, Md.: Olde Soldiers Book, Inc., 1988).

and commanded a company of Kentucky volunteers at New Orleans under Andrew Jackson. Breveted a major for his part in the famous battle, Butler was appointed to Jackson's staff in 1816 but resigned the following year to study law. Returning to Kentucky, he became one of the state's leading Democrats, missing the governorship in 1844 by less than five thousand votes. Butler received his commission as major general of volunteers on June 29, 1846.[12]

Robert Patterson, a native of Ireland, immigrated to Pennsylvania when his father was exiled for taking part in the Rebellion of 1798. Only twenty years old in 1812, Patterson quickly rose to the rank of captain in the Pennsylvania militia, a rise followed by promotions to lieutenant colonel and colonel. He gained a commission as lieutenant in the 22nd U.S. Infantry before being transferred to the 32nd U.S. Infantry to fill a captain's vacancy. Patterson returned to Pennsylvania in 1815 after his discharge from the army and became a prosperous grocer and merchant. He entered local politics and served as a delegate to the state Democratic convention at Harrisburg that helped nominate Andrew Jackson for president in 1824. Although Patterson did not serve in either the Pennsylvania legislature or the U.S. Congress, he was a prominent figure in the state militia. In 1844, Patterson led militiamen to Philadelphia to restore order after several days of anti-Catholic rioting. He received his commission as major general of volunteers on July 7, 1846.[13]

Kentucky's Thomas Marshall had a long family tradition of leadership to uphold. Both his grandfather and father (for whom he was named) had been officers in the War for Independence and were the peers of fellow Virginians such as George Washington and Patrick Henry. His uncle, John Marshall, had been chief justice of the U.S. Supreme Court from 1801 to 1835. Like his elders, Marshall received a good education and then entered politics. From 1817 to 1844, he served several terms in the Kentucky legislature, including one term as Speaker of the House. Unlike his more famous relative, he was a Democrat. On July 1, 1846, Marshall was appointed brigadier general of volunteers. Although he had been a junior officer in the War of 1812, his only other military experience had been his involvement in the Kentucky State Militia.[14]

Gideon Johnson Pillow began a career in law after graduating from the University of Nashville in 1827. Although he never held an elected office, he often worked behind the scenes for Democratic candidates. In the 1844 presidential election, Pillow threw his influence behind James K. Polk, a fellow Tennessean who was a personal friend and a law partner of his nephew, J. Knox Walker. Thought by many who knew him to be a master of political intrigue, Pillow received a commission as major general of volunteers on July 1, 1846. True to his past reputation, Pillow was involved in several feuds with his fellow officers, including one with his commander, Winfield Scott. As Polk's friend and a man with no previous military background, Pillow was an easy target for critics, who quickly labeled him an incompetent crony of the president.[15]

Thomas Lyon Hamer, a native of Pennsylvania, had set off on his own in 1817 while not yet eighteen years old. He taught school while preparing to pass the Ohio bar exam. Involvement in local and state politics placed Hamer in the Ohio legislature in 1825 as a Democrat. In the 1830s, he served three terms in the U.S. Congress. Hamer was a figure well established in his state by the outbreak of the Mexican War but is perhaps best remembered as the congressman who sent Ulysses S. Grant to West Point. He received his commission as brigadier general of volunteers on July 1, 1846.[16]

Joseph Lane's family moved to Kentucky from North Carolina while he was still a boy. In 1816, at age fifteen, Lane left home and went to Indiana to try life on his own. Employed first as a clerk, through hard work and pluck he became a prominent Vanderburg County merchant. He won his first election to the state legislature in 1822 as a Democrat. Voters sent him to the U.S. Senate in 1844, but he was back home just in time to be swept up in Indiana's initial wave of volunteerism. Elected colonel of the 1st Indiana Volunteer Infantry, Lane resigned that position to accept the July 1, 1846, appointment as brigadier general of volunteers.[17]

John A. Quitman was born in Rhinebeck, New York, in 1799. His father, a Lutheran minister, educated his son and hoped he would follow in his footsteps. Quitman became a tutor and in 1818 he received an appointment as adjunct professor at Mount Airy College in Germantown, Pennsylvania. Restless, he moved west to Chillicothe, Ohio, where he studied law. Admitted to the bar in 1821, Quitman relocated to Natchez, Mississippi, and opened a law office. A successful trial lawyer, freemason, and militia officer, Quitman entered politics. In 1827 he was elected to the lower house of the state legislature, where he served one session. In 1832 he became chairman of the judiciary committee for the state constitutional convention. From 1827 to 1835, Quitman held the office of state chancellor. Elected to the Mississippi senate in 1835, he served as acting governor for one month. During the Texas Revolution in 1836, he led a company of Natchez volunteers to Texas, but he and his men arrived after the fighting had ended, and Quitman soon returned home. Back in Mississippi, he received an appointment as brigadier general in the state militia. Initially a Whig, he switched parties in 1838 and became a Democrat.

Quitman was appointed brigadier general of volunteers on July 1, 1846.[18]

A native of Ireland, James Shields immigrated to the United States in 1826 and settled in Illinois. He studied law and entered politics, winning his first election to the Illinois legislature in 1836. Other political positions occupied by the Illinois Democrat include state auditor (1839), state supreme court judge (1843), and federal land commissioner (1845). The transplanted Irishman perhaps is remembered best by historians as the man who supposedly fought a bloodless duel with a personal and political rival, Abraham Lincoln, using "cavalry broad-swords." On July 1, 1846, Shields received a commission as brigadier general of volunteers.[19]

New Hampshire native Franklin Pierce was born in 1804. An 1824 graduate of Bowdoin College, Pierce studied law and was admitted to the bar in 1827. He soon entered politics and was elected to the New Hampshire General Court in 1829; his father happened to be the state's governor. During the 1831–32 session, Pierce held the office of Speaker of the House in the state legislature. The following year he entered the national arena, winning a seat in the U.S. House. From 1837 to 1842, he sat in the U.S. Senate. After leaving Congress, he continued to be active in state Democratic party affairs. Pierce had declined the offer to join Polk's administration as attorney general in 1846, but he accepted a March 3, 1847, appointment as brigadier general of volunteers.[20]

Philadelphian George Cadwalader was the son of a Revolutionary War hero—Gen. Thomas Cadwalader. The younger Cadwalader practiced law and held the rank of general in the Pennsylvania State Militia. In the anti-Catholic riots of 1844, he ordered troops under his command to fire into a crowd of nativists, sparking a street battle that resulted in the deaths of ten nativists and two militia men. Approximately forty other rioters and soldiers were wounded. A Democrat, Cadwalader received his commission as brigadier general of volunteers on March 3, 1847.[21]

Enos D. Hopping, a native of New York, was appointed brigadier general of volunteers on March 3, 1847. Reported to be a "personal and political friend" of Secretary of War Marcy, Hopping had connections with the New York militia and had wanted a colonel's commission. He received a general's star instead.[22]

Massachusetts native Caleb Cushing graduated from Harvard University in 1817. A classmate of George Bancroft, he proved himself an equal of many of New England's brightest intellectuals, mastering at least four languages and contributing to periodicals such as the *North American Review*. Passing the bar, he entered politics during the 1820s as a supporter of John Q. Adams. In 1834 Cushing won a seat in the U.S. House of Representatives as a Whig but left Congress in 1843 a confirmed Democrat. The change resulted from Cushing's support of John Tyler after the Virginian assumed the presidency upon the death of William Henry Harrison. Rejected by the Senate as Tyler's choice for secretary of the treasury, Cushing accepted the post of commissioner to China. While Cushing was in the Far East, citizens of Massachusetts elected him to the state's General Court. Cushing crossed Mexico by stage upon his return from his overseas post in 1844. Cushing openly supported the administration in its war with Mexico. On April 14, 1847, he accepted a commission as brigadier general of volunteers.[23]

Sterling Price, a native of Virginia, attended Hampden-Sydney College in 1826 but left to study law after one year. In the early 1830s, he accompanied his parents to Fayette, Missouri. Soon afterward he settled on a farm in Chariton County. Entering politics as a Democrat, he was elected to two terms (1836–38 and 1840–44) in the state legislature. During his last term, he served as Speaker of the House. Voters sent him to the U.S. Congress in 1844, but he resigned his seat on August 12, 1846, in order to accept the post of colonel in the 2nd Missouri Mounted Volunteers. On July 20, 1847, after he and his regiment had helped suppress the Taos Revolt in New Mexico, Price was appointed brigadier general of volunteers.[24]

The pattern of appointing Democratic politicians as generals also can be detected in cases of men who declined commissions. One commission as major general was offered to Sen. Sam Houston, a veteran of Jackson's victory over the Creeks at Horseshoe Bend and the hero of San Jacinto in Texas. When Houston declined the appointment, the president offered it to Thomas Rusk, the other Democratic senator from Texas. Polk had hoped to fill the brigadier generalship created by Gideon J. Pillow's promotion to major general with Jefferson Davis, the Democratic congressman from Mississippi, but the hero of Buena Vista, still suffering from a painful wound, turned down the commission and returned to Congress instead.[25]

Polk's generals easily were recognized for what they were: political appointees. *Niles' National Register* reported skeptically that Thomas Marshall, Thomas L. Hamer, and James Shields had been appointed brigadier generals. Marshall, the story contended, had gone to Washington, D.C., to ask that a battalion of Kentucky Volunteers he commanded be accepted into service; instead, he left with a brigadier's commission in hand. Hamer, upon hearing that he had been considered as colonel of Ohio Volunteers, supposedly had responded that he was fit to give "speeches" but not to command a regiment, as he was "entirely destitute of military experience, even in the peace service!" As for Shields, the article continued, "He may be able to discuss a 'hasty plate of soup,' as witty editors phrase it, but as for any other portion of Gen. Scott's system of tactics, he is as completely at fault as the most ignorant militia captain of the Sucker state." Writing in August 1846, Taylor informed a friend that Pillow, Quitman, Butler, Hamer, and Shields had arrived on the Rio Grande, adding, "We have had a large accession of Militia Genls recently." More to the point, Lt. George Meade of the U.S. Topographic Engineers declared that "General Patterson and the others are good Democrats," implying that this had been their major qualification in the eyes of the president. Capt. Robert Anderson, 3rd U.S. Artillery, after supping with Shields at Scott's dinner table, referred to the general's former position as "Commissioner of the Land Office" and "a devoted friend of the President." This future hero of Fort Sumter later wrote that he could not believe that Pillow—Polk's "neighbor, friend, and partner"—actually might be slated to supersede the commanding general. Others commented on the obvious relationship between Polk and his appointees. S. Compton Smith, a surgeon with the volunteers, noted Caleb Cushing's blossoming military career, commenting that "he had become one of Mr. Polk's 'generals'." Col. Ethan Allen Hitchcock—himself an ardent Whig—contended that the president had sent "partisan parasites" to plot against General Scott. Calling the new appointees "mushroom generals," Hitchcock said these men would be indebted to the regulars on their staffs for all the fame they ever might gain.[26]

Knowing someone with close ties to the president could have its advantages. Captain Anderson, who labeled Shields a political appointee, thought that he could call on the general to support a bill creating an asylum for elderly army officers to eliminate the problem of aged and infirm officers plaguing the service. Lt. Ralph W. Kirkham, 6th U.S. Infantry, decided to ask Franklin Pierce to intercede on behalf of an acquaintance who wished to attend West Point. The lieutenant reasoned that, as "General Pierce and Mr. Polk are good friends," the president surely would grant the appointment if he could persuade the general to make the request. Thus not everyone objected to the influx of Democratic appointees.[27]

Some of Polk's generals earned poor reputations as military commanders. According to Lt. George B. McClellan, volunteer generals put their political careers at risk if they imposed strict discipline upon their men. The future commander of the Army of the Potomac wrote, "Mustang Generals were actually afraid to exert their authority upon the Volunteers. Their popularity would be endangered." Furthermore, said McClellan, "I have repeatedly seen a Second Lieutenant of the regular army exercise more authority over the Volunteers—officers and privates—than a Mustang General."[28]

Gideon J. Pillow, perhaps because of his direct ties to the president, received the most scorn. Col. William B. Campbell, 1st Tennessee Infantry, had known Pillow before the war. After serving with Pillow in Mexico, Campbell wrote that the man was "in no part a Genl. or military man." Some in the army noted Pillow's habit of blaming others for his military shortcomings. Following the Battle of Cerro Gordo, one Pennsylvania volunteer accused the general of trying to make his unit the scapegoat for Pillow's botched assault. Colonel Hitchcock thought Pillow "a brave and competent but vain commander and a pet of President Polk and Secretary Marcy." The general's constant search for praise caused Captain Anderson to remark that "Genl. Pillow's inordinate vanity has so inflated him as to disgust everybody."[29]

Caleb Cushing, who began his Mexican War career as colonel of the 1st Massachusetts Infantry, was another general who many believed lacked military skills. Both he and his former regiment arrived in Mexico late and consequently saw no combat. Cushing's unfamiliarity with commanding troops caused one volunteer in his brigade to remark, "It is evident that Genl. Cushing does not understand how to march troops. I would not fancy making a long tramp under him." Obviously the general failed to win the respect of his men. When Cushing issued "a batch of orders" calling for routine drills and roll calls, the same Pennsylvanian remarked that the new rules would be ignored "as a matter of course." Another volunteer wrote, "Brig. Gen. Caleb Cushing is the most comical looking general I have ever seen," adding that "[he] is made fun of by all the soldiers." Doubting Cushing's leadership, the writer further commented, "I hope we will never be attached to his brigade." With Cushing still in Mexico, his political friends ran him as the Democratic candidate in the governor's race. His dubious standing as a military leader undoubtedly did little to help the campaign in the Whig stronghold, and voters rejected him. Once home, Cushing's troubles were not over, as he was accused of abandoning his regiment after his promotion to general. The *Cambridge Chronicle* reported that he was heckled at a homecoming dinner.[30]

Other volunteer generals fared better in the minds of their comrades-in-arms, although few escaped the barbs of their critics. Captain Anderson found Gen. Robert Patterson "very affable and gentlemanly." Col. William B. Campbell thought the general very friendly but unsuited to the army, as he was "in military affairs decidedly ignorant." "A heavy set man without anything remarkable in his appearance" was all one volunteer had to say after seeing Patterson at a grand review. One volunteer commissary officer, Capt. Franklin Smith of Mississippi, served closely under Patterson at Camargo and had little good to say about the man, referring to him as "the

August Personage," "his Mightyness," and, in a snide reference to the general's prewar occupation, "a counting house merchant." In another slap at the general, Smith excused himself and a companion for once "mistaking a mere huckster as a grand Don," saying that the president had made a mistake in appointing Patterson a general. One Pennsylvania Volunteer thought Patterson an able administrator and a brave man but a poor commander in battle. Francis Collins, a lieutenant in the 4th U.S. Artillery, wrote that "Patterson did not belong to the regular army but was appointed for the war by President Polk, and was one of his poorest appointments." More pointedly, Collins accused the Pennsylvanian of abandoning the army while it was being withdrawn from Mexico in the summer of 1848. A politician at heart, the general, according to Lieutenant Collins, was eager to return home to receive a hero's welcome, even though he had never "shared in the dangers, or glories of the battlefield with the men" he commanded.[31]

Maj. Gen. William O. Butler's position insured him high visibility during his service in Mexico. He commanded a division of volunteers at Monterey, where, according to Lieutenant Meade, the general "behaved most handsomely." Butler, who had fought the British under Andrew Jackson, evidently expected his men to behave themselves as well. One Illinois volunteer likened Butler to General Wool, who he thought too rigid and prone to false alarms. Capt. Leander M. Cox of the 3rd Kentucky Infantry credited Butler's rise to the fact that the general was "a favorite of Mr. Polk." Another officer confirmed this perception, writing to his wife, "General Butler . . . is supposed to be more in the secrets of the President and his cabinet than even General Taylor himself." Colonel Campbell thought Butler "a very ordinary" man but one of the president's best appointments, praising him as a "gallant fellow." The general seemed never to forget that his position enhanced his political standing. In 1847, soon after the anniversary of the Battle of New Orleans, Lt. Isaac Bowen of the 1st U.S. Artillery wrote his wife from Saltillo: "Major General Wm. O. Butler of Kentucky gave a 'grand treat' in honor of the event, and General Jackson and himself who participated largely in the glory in which the event conferred. Nearly all officers in town called upon him to offer their congratulations." A civilian who spent time with Butler in northern Mexico left this assessment of the general: "The truth is, as a military man, though brave as he be, no doubt, he is rather an imbecile. His forte is most probably politics." Another officer also thought that Butler worried too much about his political career to the detriment of the army. According to this critic, once the Kentuckian received the Democratic nomination for vice president in May 1848, the general, "like the politician that he is, left the army to shift for itself."

Captain Cox, whose regiment was part of Butler's command in central Mexico, thought the general "wholly incompetent & the most vain & empty headed man" he ever knew. He charged that "Gen. B[utler] was playing Billiards in Jalapa . . . while his men were starving." Another volunteer officer credited Butler's rise to overall command of the army in Mexico to fact that "Gen. B[utler] is a favorite of Mr. Polk."[32]

Opinions about Maj. Gen. John A. Quitman varied. Captain Anderson, so hard on other volunteer generals he met, thought Quitman a "brave and honorable" man. Surgeon S. Compton Smith thought the general kind, with a "paternal regard of the men of his command," and told how Quitman personally helped move sick volunteers into a new hospital at Cerralvo. Colonel Campbell—a confirmed Whig—expressed a much different view of the man, writing, "Genl. Quitman is weak, vain, ignorant, [and] ambitious to do something to signalize himself, and has the supreme contempt of nearly every officer in the command." Furthermore, according to Campbell, the general was "not liked by his men" and in his opinion would "not do at all for a commander." Overall, though, Quitman earned a reputation as an effective officer who performed his military duties extremely well. General Scott demonstrated his confidence in Quitman by appointing him military and civil governor of Mexico City after its capture by the Americans in September 1847.[33]

Brig. Gen. James Shields seems to have made a favorable impression wherever he served. One officer of an Illinois regiment recorded that the general had "won the hearts of the men by shaking hands with several of the privates." These privates, he continued, were "quite high-headed about" such treatment from a general. A few days later, the same officer called upon the general at his headquarters and was received with brandy and small talk, causing him to remark that Shields was "very opposite of what is the mode [of other generals, who are] distant and haughty." Others echoed this sentiment about Shields. One Pennsylvania volunteer stated that the general was a favorite of the army, who thought him brave and skillful, and lacking the "stinking pride" that characterized many officers. Another volunteer testified, "I am very much pleased with General Shields. He preserves his dignity and commands respect although he is entirely sociable and communicative." He seemed to have the ability to make others feel comfortable in his presence but still retain their respect. Wounded at Cerro Gordo by a piece of grapeshot that passed through his chest, Shields astonished the army with his miraculous recovery. Although everyone expected him to die, Shields healed rapidly and soon was back leading his brigade in the battles for Mexico City. One South Carolinian wrote that both General Quitman and General Shields were "much loved by the Palmetto Regiment." According to one Pennsylvania volunteer in Puebla, Shields "was received with six cheers and a regular yell which lasted for several minutes, which made his horse rear on his hind feet, in regular Jackson style." No doubt the general did not object to the comparison to Old Hickory.[34]

Another of Polk's appointees who won high praise was Joseph Lane. The general commanded troops in actions in both northern and central Mexico, building a reputation as a hard fighter. Lane earned the sobriquet "The Francis Marion of the Mexican War" for his anti-guerrilla activity along the supply route linking Vera Cruz and Mexico City. Others called him "Rough and Ready No. 2." He disliked deference shown men of his rank. On one occasion he asked a group of soldiers for a bite to eat but was turned away until they realized who he was. Lane then refused to eat with the men because they would not share willingly with a stranger. The general expected fair treatment for the Mexican populace, once giving a farmer fifty dollars from his own pocket because he thought the man had been underpaid by a quartermaster who had taken corn from his fields.[35]

Some volunteer generals failed to win much recognition for their services in the war. One Pennsylvania volunteer most remembered Gen. George Cadwalader for his speaking ability. Lt. Col. Henry S. Lane of the 1st Indiana Volunteers found Gen. Thomas Marshall "clean and kind," but, unfortunately for the general, Marshall had little chance to build a reputation for himself due to his assignment which placed him in charge of troops along the Rio Grande when Taylor's army advanced on to Monterey and Saltillo. Fate was cruel to Franklin Pierce. Well-wishers from his home state had given the general a high-spirited war horse. The steed, however, was not used to the sound of gunfire and lurched forward when guns opened up near Churubusco and threw Pierce violently forward onto the pommel of his saddle. Struggling hard to stay mounted, Pierce severely twisted his knee. His injuries nearly caused him to pass out, making it impossible for him to lead his brigade forward into the battle. One regular officer, unaware of Pierce's condition, called out that he was a coward, a label the general had trouble living down.[36]

Death denied two of Polk's appointees opportunities for fame. Gen. Thomas Hamer survived fierce fighting at Monterey only to sicken and die two months later. The general had become a favorite among the officers of the regular army, who knew him as "a conspicuous member of the Democratic party." Elected by his constituents back home to a seat in Congress, Hamer died at Monterey before he could fill the office. Lt. Isaac Bowen observed, "His death has cast a gloom . . . over the whole Army . . . His character was such to command universal respect and esteem, and among the officers of the Army he ranked as a man of sense, judgment and discretion, immeasurably above any other officer of the Volunteers." The death of Gen. Enos D. Hopping at Mier, coming at nearly the same time as the climactic battle for Mexico City, passed virtually unnoticed by an army and a public that, after nearly a year and a half of war, had grown accustomed to such news.[37]

These volunteer generals did not give Polk what he needed. No Democratic general gained enough national acclaim to topple Taylor from his pedestal. All of Polk's volunteer generals held temporary commissions, which made them inferior in rank to both Taylor and Scott. What Polk needed was a way to advance a trusted confidante over the heads of both these Whig major generals, thereby gaining control of all armies in the field. To do this, he would have to resurrect the rank of lieutenant general.

Sen. Thomas Hart Benton, a colonel in the War of 1812 and a member of the U.S. Senate since 1821, was the trusted confidante Polk needed. On several occasions, the president discussed the problem of Whig generals with the Missouri senator, who expressed both sympathy and concern. In the fall of 1846, Benton approached the president with a solution: appoint him lieutenant general. The rank (last held by George Washington) would make the Democratic congressman the highest ranking officer in the army. Polk showed interest but acknowledged that the plan would meet stiff opposition in Congress. Consulting key Democrats on the matter, Polk learned that the move likely would fail. In December, nevertheless, the president presented Benton's proposal to Congress. The measure passed the House but died in the Senate. Whigs balked at the idea of sending a "political general" to replace the beloved Taylor. The senator, during his long tenure in Washington, apparently had made enemies in his own party, who feared the power the rank would give Benton. Offered the lesser position of major general of volunteers, Senator Benton, his pride hurt, declined. Although the plan to resurrect the rank of lieutenant general failed, it demonstrates that Polk sought Congressional aid in placing a reliable Democrat at the head of the army.[38]

The opportunity to gain control finally came early in 1848, four months after the fall of the Mexican capital. With fighting seemingly at an end, Taylor had returned to the United States in November on a leave of absence. Soon after, a controversy erupted in Mexico City over missing war trophies and slanderous letters. The principals in the dispute were Polk's nemesis, Winfield Scott, and Gideon J. Pillow, a man who had been instrumental in nominating Polk for president. Scott contended that Major General Pillow had taken two cannons captured at Churubusco and planned to carry them home to Tennessee. Although the missing guns were found in Pillow's baggage train, the general disavowed any larcenous intention and turned them over to the Ordnance Department. Around the same time, a letter signed "Leonidas" appeared in newspapers in the United States, praising Pillow in glowing language as the true genius behind the capture of Mexico City. Citing regulations prohibiting officers from publishing private accounts of military operations, Scott placed Pillow and other Democrats implicated in the scandal under arrest. The army divided into two camps: supporters of Scott and supporters of Pillow. His disdain for Scott well established, Polk naturally sided against the general-in-chief and judged the time right to oust him. In choosing his replacement, Polk ignored suggestions from some of his own cabinet members that Taylor be ordered back into the field. He dispatched orders removing Scott and appointing Maj. Gen. William Orlando Butler as his replacement. At last both Taylor and Scott were gone and a Democratic general commanded the army in Mexico. Unfortunately for Polk and the Democratic Party, the war was nearly over.[39]

Victory rang hollow as the war neared its conclusion. Polk, who had exerted tremendous effort to find a Democratic general, seemed to withdraw from party concerns as his term neared its end. Without a strong candidate of their own, fellow Democrats asked him to renounce his pledge to serve only one term and to run again. The president refused. He even failed to suggest a successor, merely saying that he would support whomever the party selected. In need of a champion of their own, the Democrats passed over Polk's generals and picked an older war horse, Lewis Cass. A general in the War of 1812, Cass had served as secretary of war in Jackson's administration. Scott's replacement in Mexico, William Orlando Butler, joined the ticket as the vice-presidential candidate. The combined appeal of these two generals, however, was not enough to overcome the popularity of Zachary Taylor, who carried the election by 140,000 votes.[40]

For Polk and the Democrats, the war had assumed a significance beyond mere victory over Mexico; the future of the Democratic Party was at stake. The Mexican War had become a battle between rival parties for national supremacy. As Polk recorded in his diary after one visit from Benton, "He alluded to what was apparent to everyone, that the Whigs were endeavoring to turn this war to party and political advantage." The president and his party counted on Democratic generals to counter the threat. And although the tactic failed in 1848, it bore fruit four years later, when voters elected former Brig. Gen. Franklin Pierce president, at last carrying one of Polk's generals into the White House.[41]

FOUR

The Regulars

Not only will the officers no longer be the 'idle vagabonds' draining the public treasury, but the soldiers will be free from being styled the 'scum of society,' 'hirelings' and other epithets too numerous to mention.

—Lt. Isaac Bowen,
1st U.S. Artillery

Tut, tut, good enough to toss, food for powder; they'll fill a pit as well as better; tush, man, mortal men, mortal men.

—Shakespeare, *Henry IV,*
as quoted by Pvt. George Ballentine,
1st U.S. Artillery

"We have been marching, fighting, &c. and furnishing subjects of conversation and excitement to those, who at the next session of Congress, may perhaps style us epauletted loafers . . . as they have done heretofore." With these words, Lt. Isaac Bowen, 1st U.S. Artillery, expressed the view, held by many regular officers during the Mexican War, that their government—and the public in general—failed to appreciate their hard work and dedication. Underpaid and ill-accepted, the United States Army formed a unique class living beyond the bounds of a society that valued industry and achievement. Americans asked themselves why, in a land filled with an abundance of opportunities, any man willingly would enter an undemocratic system where little chance of advancement existed.

In the minds of some critics, men became soldiers only when they lacked the enterprise to do anything else. Those with influence, the logic continued, became officers. Young Lt. Ulysses S. Grant, returning to his hometown as a recent West Point graduate, found out first hand what the public thought of his profession, when he encountered a young boy in the street who saw his uniform and cried out, "Soldier! will you work? No, sir-ee; I'll sell my shirt first!" The incident illustrates the image of soldiers, common in the 1840s, as slackers on the public dole.[1]

The Mexican War offered the officers and men of the U.S. Army the opportunity to exchange that image for a new one, as they put down the pick and shovel (tools of the peacetime army) and took up arms in the defense of their nation. According to Bowen, "Victories on the battlefield certainly would enhance the army's reputation. Not only will the officers no longer be the 'idle vagabonds' draining the public treasury, but the soldiers will be free from being styled the 'scum of society,' 'hirelings' and other epithets too numerous to mention." As war approached, one officer stationed in North Carolina mused to a friend, "We sigh, and I suppose you sigh, to be let slip as dogs of war."[2]

Unidentified sergeant, U.S. Army. Courtesy Dr. William Schultz Collection

The army already stood positioned for the coming war. In October 1845, President Polk had ordered Bvt. Brig. Gen. Zachary Taylor to Corpus Christi, Texas, with the Army of Occupation. Camped along the Texas shore of the Gulf of Mexico, Taylor collected a force numbering about 3,900 troops. Five regiments of infantry, four regiments of artillery, and one regiment of dragoons were represented at this gathering, the largest since the last war against Britain. These troops, the president informed Congress, represented more than one-half the regular army. Taylor remained at this spot until March 1846, when he obeyed new orders directing him to advance to the Rio Grande. The army used the five months at Corpus Christi to prepare for the approaching war.[3]

Prepare as it might, the army faced serious personnel problems. Many of its companies were below their authorized limits of privates. One source states that the infantry companies on the Rio Grande with Taylor averaged only twenty-six privates. Administration officials had been aware of the problem for some time but had been slow to correct the situation, even though they had known of a potential crisis on both the northern and southern U.S. borders. Maj. Gen. Winfield Scott, in his 1845 report to the secretary of war, had recommended increasing the number of privates in existing regiments, but Congress failed to act on the plan until after war was declared. Secretary of War William L. Marcy then admitted that it would be "difficult to fill the regular regiments," because the "volunteer service is regarded, generally, by our citizens, as preferable to that in the regular army." Thus, not only did the army begin the war under strength, but it soon had to compete with volunteer units for recruits.[4]

The army also faced a critical shortage of field officers. Marcy informed Polk, "The efficiency of the regular troops in the field has much been impaired for the want of officers, especially regimental field officers." The problem had developed over the years because Congress had failed to pass legislation providing pensions to aged or infirm officers. Unable to retire without an income, elderly officers refused to leave the army, often filling their positions in name only. To make matters worse, a number of field officers were detached from their regiments and served in such positions as departmental commander. Thus, as the war began, many field officers were absent from their regiments.[5]

The situation demanded action, but action was slow in coming. Adj. Gen. Roger Jones described the plight in a report to the secretary of war dated July 31, 1846, in which he detailed the status of the colonels of the artillery and infantry. Col. Ichabod B. Crane, 1st U.S. Artillery, was ill and unfit for field service; Col. James Bankhead, 2nd U.S. Artillery, commanded army operations in New York City; Col. William Gates, 3rd U.S. Artillery, was commanding at Charleston, South Carolina; Col. John B. Walbach, 4th U.S. Artillery, was listed as commanding at Fort Monroe and not fit for field service; Col. William Davenport, 1st U.S. Infantry, was on duty west of the Mississippi River; Col. Hugh Brady, 2nd U.S. Infantry, was a brevet brigadier general in command of the 4th Military Department and too old for field service; Col. James B. Many, 3rd U.S. Infantry, had been on leave for many years and was disqualified from field service due to his advanced age and constant infirmity; Col. William Whistler, 4th U.S. Infantry, had been placed under arrest and was awaiting trial for drunkenness on duty; Col. George M. Brooke, 5th U.S. Infantry, was a brevet brigadier general, commanding the army's Western Division from his post at St. Louis, Missouri; Col. Zachary Taylor's recent promotion to major general had left his regiment without a commander; Col. Matthew Arbuckle, 7th U.S. Infantry, was a brevet brigadier general, stationed at Fort Gibson, Indian Territory; and Col. William J. Worth, 8th U.S. Infantry, was a brevet brigadier general, commanding a division in Mexico. Lieutenant colonels exhibited the same pattern of absenteeism: three disqualified from field duty due to illness; three recovering from wounds or illness suffered in Mexico; two serving on detached duty in the United States; one commanding a brigade in Mexico; one commanding a battalion in Mexico; and one en route to Mexico to join his regiment. Only six out of twelve majors assigned to the infantry and artillery were available for duty in Mexico; the remainder either were too ill or were detached from their regiments. Adjutant General Jones remarked that two majors reportedly were unable even to walk or ride and had not served with the army for the last seven years! Lieutenant Grant related the demise of the 4th U.S. Infantry's commander in New Orleans while the unit awaited passage to Texas. A veteran of thirty-three years, Col. Josiah H. Vose, collapsed and died one evening after a short drill session at Jackson Barracks. Grant postulated that the stress of conducting troops through maneuvers, something that most field officers had not done in years, had brought on a heart attack. A court martial found Vose's replacement, Col. William Whistler, guilty of disobeying orders, drunkenness on duty, and misconduct; but the need for field grade officers was so great that the president ordered him back to duty.

Jones complained to Marcy that there never had been an army so "inadequately provided with field officers as that under General Taylor." The commander of the 3rd U.S. Infantry, Lt. Col. Ethan Allen Hitchcock, claimed that most of the field officers with the army were ignorant of their duties. "Egotism or no egotism," he boasted, "I am the only field officer on the ground who could change a single position of the troops according to any but a militia mode."[6]

The lack of field officers meant that the army had to make adjustments. Command of many regiments and battalions fell to senior captains, while lieutenants commonly led companies. Lt. William S. Henry, who published an account of his experiences during the war, summed up for his readers the situation at Palo Alto and Resaca de la Palma: captains had commanded three regiments and one battalion engaged in the battles. Elderly and broken-down officers who clogged the promotion pipeline irritated officers like Henry, who asked, "Is it fair, is it just, the juniors should be performing their duty and reap none of the advantages?" The shortage of field officers continued throughout the war, although Congress attempted to alleviate the problem by authorizing an additional, or second, major for each regiment, as part of the Act of February 11, 1847, that enlarged the regular army.[7]

The situation may have proven dire except that many of the army's company, or line, officers were alumni of the U.S. Military Academy. The institution had been established in 1802, and its graduates slowly had been filling the lower echelons of the officer corps, so that, by the time of the Mexican War, the majority of lieutenants and captains were West Pointers. In contrast, only five of the army's field officers and none of its generals were products of the Military Academy. These middle- and lower-level officers—trained in drawing, mathematics, and French, as well as in the art of war—brought real skills as well as new professional spirit to the army. The absence of so many field officers actually may have been a blessing in disguise, for it allowed better trained officers a more active leadership role. The top performers from each West Point graduating class had been assigned to the engineers and those just below them to the topographical engineers. A posting to the artillery (still an honorable placement) had awaited graduates unable to enter the engineers. Cadets who failed to demonstrate the high standards needed for the scientific branches entered the infantry and dragoons, with the lowest achievers going to the latter corps. These officers were eager to prove their worth to the nation.[8]

Graduates of the U.S. Military Academy worked closely with their friends and old classmates during most of their careers, an experience which created a strong esprit de corps. Proud of their profession, many graduates credited the army's early successes to the training they had received at West Point. "You Say truly this Mexican affair is a glorious thing for West Point," wrote one captain of U.S. Engineers, Robert E. Lee. "Every one must See the difference between the commencement of the present war & the last,

& every one must acknowledge that this difference is caused by the difference in the officers. See how well every officer of every grade & arm has behaved."[9]

Many supporters of West Point believed that laurels garnered in Mexico by its graduates would blunt criticism of the academy's existence. In a society which celebrated the common man, West Point graduates seemed to comprise an undemocratic elite, trained and maintained at the public expense. An "eleemosynary [charitable] school for the education of the aristocracy of political favorites" is how one critic characterized the institution. Indeed, many of these officers believed themselves superior, having learned by their senior year to act dignified and condescending toward their "inferiors." Lt. George G. Meade recognized that army officers formed a clique. Himself a West Point graduate, he had spent several years in civilian pursuits before reentering the service. Having lived outside the army, Meade declared that he was not "filled with all the prejudices of an exclusive class," as were some of his military comrades. Soldiers who knew nothing but military life, he contended, often displayed contempt for those outside the profession.[10]

From its founding in 1802, the U.S. Military Academy had faced periodic attempts to close its doors by opponents who saw it as a threat to the existence of the citizen-soldier. Several years before the war, one critic charged that the Military Academy claimed the "exclusive privilege of making officers for our army." This pernicious practice, he explained, denied positions to deserving young men and placed an obstacle in the path of those who tried to gain entrance to this favored group. In Congress, disparaging West Point had become a popular pastime prior to the war. One West Point graduate wrote to his wife about a former Ohio congressman serving in Mexico, who had been commissioned a lieutenant colonel in a volunteer regiment. The man was well known for "the most violent attacks against the Army, speaking against officers on all occasions." Asked why he opposed the Military Academy and the officers it produced, the man "acknowledged that he spoke without a knowledge of the subject, merely because it was popular so to speak." After meeting many of its graduates, however, the man vowed to speak out in favor of the institution upon his return to the U.S.[11]

Graduates, however, were concerned with more than vindicating West Point; they longed for personal advancement as well. Although fresh out of West Point, Lt. George B. McClellan accurately summed up the feeling of most career officers: "I came down here with high hopes, with pleasing anticipation of distinctions, of being in hard fought battles and acquiring a name and reputation as a stepping stone to a still greater eminence in some future and greater war." The system of brevet, or honorary, rank presented the fastest means of advancement. Awarded by Congress, a brevet conferred a higher rank on the officer for "gallant actions or meritorious services." Thus each battle became an opportunity for officers to demonstrate their courage and ability, in the hope of attracting their superiors' attention. Capt. Robert Anderson believed that the actions of line officers often escaped official recognition. The injustice, he explained, stemmed from the practice of awarding credit to commanders of battalions and regiments, not to the officers who led individual companies. "It is only by a captain's being detached with his Compy. on some service that he has a chance to distinguish himself," lamented Anderson, who predicted that he would return home still a captain. Lieutenant Meade privately accused Taylor of mentioning the names of commanding officers merely because they were in charge of a regiment or battalion. "At Resaca de la Palma," he explained, "the action was fought entirely by the platoon officers . . . [but] all the rewards [went] to the old men of rank, some of whom were not [even] in the action." A captain in the 5th U.S. Infantry, Ephraim Kirby Smith, compared winning a brevet to winning a lottery, saying it had little to do with one's merit. According to this disenchanted officer, "It is too frequently the sycophant who flatters the foibles of his commanding officer, he who has political family influence, or who some accident makes conspicuous, who reaps all the benefits of the exposure and labors of others." All knew that their brevets came from catching the eye of a superior and were happy when their names appeared in official reports. After the Battle of Monterey, Lieutenant Bowen wrote, "I feel no little pride in being mentioned by my commanding General favorably, and this my first battle," adding in jest, "at least since I was a schoolboy."[12]

As Captain Smith observed, politics often played an important part in an officer's advancement. Edward M. Coffman determined in his study of the army that regulars he could find who left some indication of their views were split almost equally into Democrats and Whigs. Custom and public opinion dictated that officers should refrain from openly engaging in political activity. Officers found it difficult to comply with this restriction, however, because Congress controlled pay, promotion, and all other important aspects of their lives. Coffman noted that many officers routinely visited the nation's capital when on leave, offering this explanation: they hoped to find a benefactor who might take interest in their careers. Capt. John Charles Frémont, who married the daughter of Sen. Thomas H. Benton, is perhaps the best-known example of an officer with influential political connections. Officers knew the importance of political friends. Asst. Surgeon John S. Griffin, who observed the feud developing between Frémont and Brig. Gen. Stephen W. Kearny in California, quipped, "I only wish I could marry a Senator's daughter; I might then set at defiance the orders of my superiors and do as I pleased." Griffin continued, "Genl Kearny has been most outrageously used by both Frémont and [Commodore Robert F.] Stockton, they are both men of political influence, and of course they will go scot free." Lieutenant Grant gave the following advice to his fiancee, Julia Dent, to pass on to her brother, who wanted an officer's commission: "Tell him to apply to Mr. Benton to use his influence right off." Even the relatives of deceased politicians gained favor. Andrew Porter, the son of George B. Porter, received a commission as captain in the U.S. Mounted Rifles; his father previously had been appointed governor of Michigan Territory by Andrew Jackson.[13]

Officers without political influence found themselves at a disadvantage. Lt. John J. Peck confided to his diary after he failed to receive a well-deserved brevet that he had "no friends at court to urge [his] merits." Scorning a system which appeared to pit merit against influence, Peck deplored "the petty wire-workings and intrigues at Washington by which politicians hope to perpetuate power." Lieutenant Meade mulled over his lack of a brevet and concluded, "I was always aware that the nomination of the commanding general was one thing, and the nomination by the 'President' another." The first required hard service, but the latter required "political influence." He wrote, "If I had strong Locofoco friends at Washington . . . I might have hoped to have been rewarded; but in its absence, my claims will meet with no attention."[14]

Regular officers generally believed that President Polk treated the army poorly, with blatant disregard for its achievements. Having won battles, they wanted recognition for their years of sacrifice. The creation of the U.S. Mounted Rifles in May 1846 seemed a colossal snub to the army, since almost all officers appointed to the new regiment came directly from civilian life. The appointments caused dissatisfaction among officers who had wanted to transfer to the unit, hoping to gain a promotion in the process. Writing in July 1846, Capt. Robert E. Lee remarked, "We however cannot much hope that merit will be Sought . . . after the manner in which the appointments to the Mounted Rifles have been filled." He further contended, "No Army ever deserved more from an administration than that on the Rio Grande." While the new regiment gave Polk ample opportunity to reward deserving officers, "every man was passed over, many of whom, Graham, May, [and] Duncan had made direct application for this very

Corps." The creation of additional regiments authorized by the Ten Regiment Bill of February 11, 1847, brought more disappointment for the army. The nature of the new regiments—raised only for the war—meant that officers who sought transfers risked dismissal from the service once these additional troops were no longer needed. Thus, although the size of the army increased during the war, it did not benefit the officer corps because the vast majority of officers for these new units were commissioned directly from civilian life. Writing of the injustice of the situation from his perspective, Lieutenant Peck asserted, "More than four hundred officers have been commissioned and only five have been taken from the army." Peck lamented, "What is the use of graduating from West Point if we are to be rated thus by the executive?" His sentiments were shared by others who felt overlooked.[15]

In the case of the U.S. Mounted Rifles, Polk had plans that did not take the wishes of the army into consideration. He intended for the new regiment to reflect an increasingly important faction of American society—the West. Polk admitted that "upwards of 100 officers of the army have applied for promotion," but he had "determined to select officers from civil life." The move, he reasoned, would prevent jealousy from developing between current officers whose service and merit made it impossible to select who deserved appointment to the new regiment. The president made one major exception to this rule, however, in granting Capt. John Charles Frémont (who happened to be the son-in-law of Sen. Thomas H. Benton, chairman of the important Senate Committee on Military Affairs) the post of lieutenant colonel. Frémont, he contended, was "peculiarly fitted" for the regiment because of his explorations of California and Oregon. As "it is a peculiarly Western regiment," he vowed to "give a larger proportion of officers to that part of the Union than to any other." Some junior officers joined the regiment, however, through the intervention of Adj. Gen. Roger Jones. The high percentage of officers appointed from civilian life prompted him to assign to each company a brevet second lieutenant "to instruct it in drill and discipline." All these instructors were recent graduates of West Point.[16]

Captain Anderson, himself a Whig, thought he knew the real reason behind Polk's appointments to the Mounted Rifles. According to him, "The decided hostility evidenced by President Polk to the Army" was the result of "his eager desire to secure political influence in his appointees." The army could expect no rewards from a president whose actions "spoke as plainly to the Army as actions could speak." Anderson cited the case of

Capt. Charles Ferguson Smith, a man universally admired and respected by his fellow officers for his courage and military skill. "Over this man's head," said Anderson, "are placed a score of men whose sole recommendation is that they or their friends have proved faithful in their worship of the President's party." "Enough, enough," Anderson cried.[17]

Some officers became so disgruntled that privately they threatened to leave the army. Anderson, disgusted at the favoritism he witnessed, was uncertain about his own career. He predicted that "some [officers] will undoubtedly resign as soon as peace is declared." Lt. Napoleon Jackson Tecumseh Dana echoed this sentiment. "The army is done for . . . dead as a doornail, and at the end of the war every young officer who possibly can will leave it in disgust and contempt." The reason behind the discontent, said Dana, was that "new corps have been raised and new military offices created, but the benefits of them are all given to the sovereign people whose friends have votes to give pro or con [to] J. K. Polk." Lieutenant McClellan, irked at volunteer officers who outranked him, contemplated leaving the army unless he received a promotion, saying, "I cannot stand the idea of being a Second Lieutenant all my life."[18]

Army regulations prohibited Peck, Meade, Anderson, and Dana from censuring their superiors, but they and many others routinely took Polk and his administration to task in their letters and diaries. Private letters when made public could spell trouble for the authors. Lieutenant Bowen, like many married officers, wrote home regularly. Disgusted at rancorous scandals spawned by certain officers, he remarked, "Really, 'letter writers' are a scourge to the Army." Applauding his wife, Bowen thanked her for not allowing his letters to be printed, as they were intended "only for thee and a few intimate friends." Some of his letters to her had been extremely venomous toward the administration, blaming Polk for plunging "the country into an expensive, unjust, and cruel war." Knowing that these ideas might sound slanderous to others, Bowen warned, "You need not read my abuse of the President and his party to Father, Shepard, or Holman. They are such good democrats that they may not take it kindly." Passages similar to Bowen's that excoriate "Polk, Marcy, and Co." frequently appear among the writings of regular officers.[19]

Politics affected the army's enlisted men only indirectly. Their lowly status indicated that they lacked the political influence sought by the officers who ruled over them. Although pay, enlistment terms, rations, and other important issues were determined by Congress, enlisted men were powerless to lobby on their own behalf. Promotion to the rank of noncommissioned officer depended upon one's captain and colonel, not the grace of Congress. Thus, the bulk of soldiers ignored the squabbles of politicians and their supporters and concentrated on their own daily existence.

Men enlisted in the army for various reasons. Some, like the 3rd U.S. Infantry's Pvt. Barna Upton, reportedly joined out of a desire for excitement. Others enlisted to escape problems at home or with the law. Most, however, turned to the army out of economic necessity. Seven dollars a month, room, and board lured many needy men into the service. In his memorandum book, Pvt. John F. Meginness, a native-born American in the 5th U.S. Infantry, explained his decision to sign up with "Uncle Sam": "Having nothing to do, and being foiled in every attempt to get employment, I finally thought of Enlisting in the Army." George Ballentine, a Scotsman recently arrived in New York City, could find no work by which to support himself. He at first considered shipping on a whaler, but a sailor turned him from the sea with tales of horror and danger. Ballentine, a veteran of the British Army, determined to offer his skills to the 1st U.S. Artillery as the best means of supplying his immediate wants. Frederick Zeh, a German immigrant, claimed that hunger drove him to enlist. Whatever their individual reasons, the majority of men entered the army as privates only when their civilian lives had taken a wrong turn and they needed time and a place to recover from life's storms and recoup their losses.[20]

Foreigners like Ballentine comprised a significant proportion of the ranks. One former enlisted man estimated that, during the 1830s, two-thirds of the soldiers were born outside the U.S. Men from Germany, Ireland, and Great Britain found ready homes in the army. Some of their own officers expressed contempt for these men who were forced into the army by economic circumstance, a fact that reflected growing nativism. Capt. George A. McCall, assigned to recruiting duty in Philadelphia in 1836, disliked dealing with the "unsophisticated, untutored, and intractable sons of Erin" who made up the majority of the applicants who came before him. According to the captain, Congress recently had repealed a ban restricting service to natives of the United States because "it had become plain that the ranks of our army could not be filled with men whose intelligence and industry enabled them to fill the higher places in the walks of life." According to one German recruit, Americans called him and his countrymen names such as "sauerkraut" and "G— D— Dutch." During the war, the status of immigrants in the army was not improved by the scores of foreign-born soldiers who deserted to the Mexican Army and served in the San Patricio Battalion, a unit thought to have been composed at one time mainly of Irish deserters from the U.S. Army. Pamphlets encouraging desertion distributed among U.S. soldiers in Puebla by Mexican agents were printed in German, French, and English, so that men of all nationalities serving with the Americans could read the message.[21]

Hostility toward foreign "ne'er-do-wells" explains why many Americans believed that soldiers were the "scum of society." The public may have been surprised to learn that not all soldiers were uneducated misfits only one step ahead of the law. Once, when traveling to a new post, Ballentine overheard a cynical passenger describing him and his fellow soldiers as "a fine set of candidates for the States prison." The Scotsman responded to the slight by quoting lines from *Henry IV:* "Tut, tut, good enough to toss, food for powder; they'll fill a pit as well as better; tush, man, mortal men, mortal men." His mastery of Shakespeare astounded the crowd, earning him free drinks and a private cabin aboard the vessel. Private Upton also knew learned men in the ranks. He told friends at home, "Almost every kind of men you will find in the Army and a good many are well educated." He listed professionals he had met, including preachers, schoolteachers, clerks, and tradesmen such as shoemakers, carpenters, tailors, blacksmiths, and more. The army of the 1840s—as crude as it could be in some ways—also was replete with debating societies, lending libraries, and theatrical troupes organized and managed by enlisted men. Certainly it was a creature of marked contrasts.[22]

The differences between officers and enlisted men in matters of power and privilege created a sharp division that could not be overlooked. Some officers, aware of the control they had over men's lives, tried to rule benevolently. Lieutenant Peck was so popular that every man of his company volunteered to accompany him on a hazardous assignment. Other officers, however, ruled with an iron fist and earned the hatred of those they commanded. One volunteer remarked, "Some of the Regular officers are contemptible, insolent scoundrels." He further observed, "The lower their grade[,] the more insulting they generally are." These "whelps fresh from West Point," the volunteer contended, enjoyed exercising the prerogatives that came with their new rank. Private Meginness voiced the same opinion of officers who, he claimed, abused poor, defenseless soldiers. Enlisted men, he warned, should be prepared to endure physical pain, "so that when a young Lieutenant chooses to amuse himself by Knocking them down with his sabre, it will make no more impression on them than on a block of marble." Meginness reported seeing a lieutenant slash one soldier on the shoulder for making a mistake during drill. "The poor fellow was of course disabled at once and had to be assisted to the hospital by a couple of soldiers. He presented a pitiful spectacle as he was brought back, the blood flowing profusely from a gaping wound." In another incident, Meginness described how a lieutenant ordered a soldier to be given 180 lashes with a rawhide whip for missing a roll call. Such harsh treatment was not confined to junior officers. One volunteer witnessed Capt. John H. Winder (later associated with the infamous Andersonville prison during the Civil War) strike several guards with his sword when they refused the order to kneel as a Catholic procession passed them in the streets of Puebla. Even Brig. Gen. David E. Twiggs reportedly "grabbed [one soldier] by the head, and tore out a handful of hair" for buying a glass of whiskey. Such abuse, although officially frowned upon, evidently was not uncommon.[23]

Punishment, which sometimes exceeded the legal limits, created considerable friction between officers and enlisted men. In theory, no punishment could be administered unless ordered by a court martial. Authorized punishments included "death; stripes [marks left by a whip] for desertion only; confinement; hard labor; ball and chain; forfeiture of pay and allowances; and dishonorable discharge from service, with or without marking [tattooing or branding]." Mild forms of punishment included extra guard duty, or carrying a log or cannonball back and forth over a given route. Other punishments not spelled out by the Articles of War made their way into common use. Several regulars described "bucking and gagging," in which a prisoner was forced to sit on the ground, hands to the front, with his wrists and ankles tied. A musket or stick was passed under the knees and over the elbows to lock the victim's arms and legs together. As a final measure, a tent peg or bayonet was forced between the prisoner's teeth and tied in place. Unable to move, the bound soldier might be forced to endure hours of pain and humiliation before being released. In another painful practice, the prisoner "rode" a tall wooden "punishment horse." The structure was designed so the feet would not touch the ground, causing pain to any unfortunate soldier forced to straddle the top rail. These punishments excited sympathy for the prisoners and resulted in hard feelings toward the officers responsible. Ballentine and others mused that resentment over severe punishment might have motivated many a soldier's desertion.[24]

Some soldiers believed that the harsh discipline reflected the poor opinion their officers had of them. One enlisted man who served during the Seminole War thought he had discovered an unwritten military truth: "My opinion of the other soldiers is that they were a congregation of the most thoughtless [beings], and I suppose such are considered by the officers to make the best soldiers. Men as machines are highly prized by officers. Many a time I heard them tell their men that they were paid to think for them."

According to Private Meginness, "An individual who enters the U.S. Army as a private Soldier . . . must expect to be treated more like a vicious dog, than a civilized, intelligent, human being." A private, he contended, needed only enough brains to keep himself and his equipment "scrupulously clean" and master the use of his arms. Furthermore, "he is also supposed to have just language enough to Answer when he is haughtily spoken to by his very excellent humane and dignified superior officers." Soldiers who showed more intelligence than this, he wryly reported, were punished. Meginness wondered why officers did not try to win their men's respect "by pursuing a different course, and attempting to govern [soldiers] as moral agents instead of [as] brutes." Writing after the fall of Mexico City, he coldly stated that the high casualty rate among the officers at Molino del Rey was not the work of the Mexican army, but was the result of American soldiers settling old scores under the cover of battle.[25]

Men responded differently to soldiering. Old hands like Ballentine, who had served in a foreign army, recognized the division between officers and enlisted men and stoically served out their time. Barna Upton, a young man fresh from the farm, grew to like the army because it provided him the excitement he had lacked in rural Massachusetts. For hungry immigrants like Zeh, the army became a shelter in a strange land. Most enlisted men were unable or unwilling to speak out against those who were providing them with the necessities of life. Thinking back on his experience, John F. Meginness, however, seethed with rage. An urbane product of a democratic society, he could not accept such a rigid system and used his pen to protest. "Aristocracy, that bane of society, reigns supreme in this department, and of course soldiers are not to be considered as human beings by their officers." In addition to poor treatment at the hands of officers, Meginness resented the lack of opportunity for advancement he found in the army. Privates never could "expect to be promoted above the rank of Sergeant, for the graduates of West Point step in above them as brevet Second Lieutenants, and fill all vacancies." According to him, merit did not matter, and good men were doomed to be oppressed by what one volunteer called the "shoulder-strapped gentry." Old Hickory himself could not have issued a stronger plea against special privilege.[26]

To a nation based on republican principles, the existence of a standing army presented a dilemma. This simple fact lay at the root of criticism leveled against the officers and men of the U.S. Army. President Polk summed up the argument in his first annual message, clearly stating that standing armies "are contrary to the genius of our free institutions." The nation's true defense must rest, he continued, "on our citizen soldiers." In this speech, while discussing the tariff, Polk revealed a basic ideal that governed his actions as commander-in-chief: "The Government in theory knows no distinction of persons or classes, and should not bestow upon some favors and privileges which all others may not enjoy." Regular officers—especially West Point graduates—constituted a class of aristocrats, a fact that contravened Jacksonian doctrine. Enlisted men also failed to live up to the model, because they had removed themselves from the democratic process and the opportunities it was thought to offer, a sure indication to the public that these men were molded from inferior clay and deserved to be called the "scum of society." Although Americans recognized the need for an army, as a rule they still loathed its existence—a peculiar trait for a people imbued with martial spirit.[27]

Polk's image of the army as a marriage of aristocrats and hirelings shaped his actions throughout the war. The creation of new regiments allowed him to bypass the established hierarchy by appointing men directly from civilian life. Thus he attempted to break the monopoly of the officer corps that West Point graduates had begun to develop. Polk's reliance upon men from the West underscored his great faith in that region. After all, the West was fresh and free of the vices of the eastern seaboard, especially places like "Federalist" New England. He planned for the new rifle regiment to be officered by westerners. In addition, Polk extended the initial call for volunteers largely in the western states. He explained his admiration for the region by stating, "Experience has proven that no portion of our population are more patriotic than the hardy and brave men of the frontier." Polk felt that no other Americans were "more ready to obey the call of their country and to defend her rights and her honor whenever and by whatever enemy assailed." Opening up the army to these "hardy pioneers of the West" would purify the establishment.[28]

Something else occurred that Polk failed to mention: his appointment of officers infused the army with Democrats. The exact number of Democrats commissioned by Polk is impossible to ascertain, but a brief examination of field officers appointed to the new regiments reveals a pattern similar to that seen in the appointment of volunteer generals. William Trousdale, colonel of the 14th U.S. Infantry, had served as a Democrat in the Tennessee State Legislature. The lieutenant colonel of this regiment, Paul Octave Hébert, was a graduate of West Point who had left the army to pursue a career as a civil engineer. While living in Louisiana, however, Hébert had become involved with the Democratic party. Henry Livingston Webb, a former Democratic state legislator from Illinois, received a commission as lieutenant colonel of the 16th U.S. Infantry. George A. Caldwell, a major in the Regiment of Voltiguers and Foot Riflemen, was a Democrat from Kentucky who had served in the state legislature and in Congress. The colonel of the 16th U.S. Infantry, John W. Tibbats, was another Kentucky Democrat. Both Caldwell and Tibbats had been delegates to the Democratic Convention of 1844, which had nominated Polk for president. Polk's own brother, William H. Polk, received a major's commission in the 3rd U.S. Dragoons. Polk also appointed Lewis Cass, Jr. (the son of Democratic hopeful Lewis Cass, Sr.), to the 3rd U.S. Dragoons with the rank of major. The overwhelmingly Democratic affiliations of the president's appointees did not go unnoticed by his contemporaries, as some of these facts were brought to light toward the end of the war in a speech by William M. Cooke to the U.S. House of Representatives. In his speech, Cooke charged that Polk had abused his patronage power. In retrospect, however, we might ask whether a Whig president in Polk's situation would have acted any differently.[29]

The Mexican War reshaped the image of the regular army, which emerged from the conflict with newfound confidence, born on the battlefield. Through Polk's appointment of Democrats to the army, the officer corps had changed. The aged and infirm officers who had burdened the army were on their way out, although it would take Congress twelve years to pass the retirement act sought by the army. Some of the army's brightest stars lay dead, but new ones appeared to take their places. Hundreds of officers commissioned from civilian life entered the army. Most left at the war's end, but they had gained valuable experience and a taste for battle. The attempt to diminish West Point's influence failed, as the professionalism displayed by its alumni brought acclaim to the institution. The war offered regulars the opportunity to prove that they were not merely "epauletted loafers" and "idle vagabonds."

FIVE

The
Volunteers

*Our reliance for protection and defense of the land must be
mainly on our citizen soldier, who will be ready, as they ever
have been ready in the times past, to rush with alacrity, at the
call of their country, to her defense.*

—James K. Polk, U.S. President

*The American volunteer is a thinking, feeling, and often a
capricious being. He is not and never intends to become a
mere moving and musket-holding machine.*

—Maj. Luther Giddings,
2nd Ohio Infantry

The popular image of the American fighting man
had been well established by the time of the Mexican War. He was the
minuteman chasing Gage's redcoats back to Boston, the frontiersman defending his home against Tecumseh's braves, and the Kentuckian teaching
Pakenham's veterans a bloody lesson at New Orleans. The American fighting man was not a soldier by trade. He spent his days in the fields and
workshops of his country until called to battle; only then did he take up
arms and become a warrior. With Cincinnatus as their model, Americans
exalted the citizen-soldier and relied upon him to form a major part of the
nation's armed forces in time of need.

The citizen-soldier existed officially within the militia system. Congress in 1792 enacted a law requiring military service from "every free able-

bodied white male citizen" between the ages of eighteen and forty-five. Exemptions existed for those engaged in running the nation's government and commerce. The rest formed a body of men designed to supplement the small regular army during emergencies spelled out by the Constitution. The militia could be used only in certain circumstances: to execute the laws of the Union, to suppress insurrections, and to repel invasions. Writers of the 1792 bill patterned the militia after the U.S. Army, so as to provide a recognized standard for the militia's peacetime training and its employment during war. Three years later, in 1795, Congress passed a law declaring that militiamen called into service by the president would be subject "to the same rules and articles of war as the troops of the United States." An additional stipulation established three months as the amount of time that militiamen legally could be retained on active duty. Americans feared that commerce and agriculture would suffer if civilians were kept from their livelihoods too long. The short time period, deemed

Unidentified militia soldier. Courtesy Dr. William Schultz Collection

adequate in most foreseen emergencies, doomed the system to failure in time of war.[1]

Each state maintained control of its own militia, making the militias essentially state armies. Each governor served as commander-in-chief of his state's militia. Some states actually authorized the governor to command troops in the field, but most intended for him merely to act as an administrator. Aided by a state adjutant general, each governor organized the militia into companies, battalions, regiments, brigades, and divisions. State constitutions, like the federal Constitution, placed their military forces under strict civilian control. One rule adopted by the states seriously hampered the effectiveness of the militia in assisting the regular army: service outside a state's boundary was prohibited unless the governor, the legislature, and in some instances the militiamen themselves consented. This restriction precluded combined operations between militia units and the regular army, as the cases of Queenstown and Plattsburg demonstrated during the War of 1812 when militia commanders refused to commit their troops to battle in Canada.[2]

Another body of troops emerged on the early American military scene. This hybrid of militia and regulars was called "volunteers." The militia act of 1792 authorized one company each of artillery and dragoons to serve with each militia division. The men of these elite units, composed of volunteers from the enrolled militia, were required to be "uniformly clothed in regimentals, to be furnished at their own expense." Officials recognized a difference between militia and volunteers, with the latter assigned a higher status. Congress expanded the role of volunteers during the War of 1812 by authorizing the president to accept an entire corps of these troops to augment the regular army. Another body of volunteers was raised in 1836, at the beginning of the Seminole War. The federal government came to rely upon volunteers during national emergencies because their use evaded the two great problems associated with militia: volunteers would serve for extended periods and could leave their state's boundaries.[3]

The militia performed an important, although largely administrative, role during the Mexican War. A few militia units did serve actively with Taylor on the Rio Grande. Authorized by the War Department to call upon Texas for additional troops, General Taylor relied on five companies of Texas Rangers to help protect the newly acquired region from both Mexicans and "Camanches" [sic]. In addition, Maj. Gen. Edmund P. Gaines sent Taylor two companies of the famed Washington Artillery from New Orleans to supplement his force at Corpus Christi. Although the militia failed to win laurels on the battlefields of Mexico, these troops had a significant impact on the war. The work of raising volunteers was much easier with the organizational framework of the militia already in place.[4]

Polk planned that volunteers would play a major role in the war against Mexico. The president already had made his views clear in his first annual message, when he informed Congress: "Our reliance for protection and defense of the land must be mainly on our citizen soldiers, who will be ready, as they ever have been ready in the times past, to rush with alacrity, at the call of their country, to her defense." The war bill passed by Congress on May 13, 1846, authorized the president to call fifty thousand volunteers into service. In a meeting with his cabinet a few days later, Polk stated that he intended to draw troops from "each State and Territory in the Union, so as to make each feel an interest in the war." The volunteers, however, were not all to enter the service at once. He issued an immediate call for twenty thousand volunteers from the "Western and Southern States," with the remaining thirty thousand volunteers to be held in reserve until they were needed. Addressing Congress in December 1846, Polk declared, "The events of the last few months afford a gratifying proof that our country can under any emergency confidently rely for the maintenance of her honor and the defense of her rights on an effective force, ready at all times voluntarily to relinquish the comforts of home for the perils and privations of the camp." He added that the temporary expense of this force, although seemingly great, far outweighed keeping a large peacetime standing army.[5]

Maj. Gen. Edmund P. Gaines temporarily disrupted Polk's plans for mobilization by issuing his own call for volunteers. Headquartered at New Orleans, the sixty-eight-year-old general believed himself to be the most senior officer in the army and therefore entitled to exercise the prerogatives of rank and experience. As early as September 2, 1845, Gaines informed the government that Taylor (whom he considered to be acting within his department) should be augmented by "fifty battalions of mounted gunmen." He stood ready to send these "sober citizen soldiers of the Union to the city of Mexico," but the War Department ignored his plan. When news arrived at the Crescent City in April 1846 that Taylor likely faced attack by the Mexicans, Gaines acted immediately, without consulting Polk, Marcy, or Jones. The general, who had acted similarly during the Seminole War, issued his own call for volunteers. Louisiana responded by raising three artillery companies and six regiments of infantry. Alabama, Missouri, and Texas together raised another ten regiments. Neither Taylor, Polk, nor the War Department had anticipated Gaines's action, and the uncontrolled rush of Gaines's volunteers became an impediment to the war effort. These troops, who arrived on the Rio Grande unexpected, taxed Taylor's quartermaster and commissary departments beyond their limits. Another question arose regarding the status of Gaines's volunteers: were they militia or volunteers? No one seemed to know. The war bill that was passed on May 13, 1846, granted Polk the authority to extend the traditional three-month term to six months, but the men who answered Gaines's illegal call for troops found themselves in a difficult situation. The army and their country seemed ungrateful for their sacrifice, making them feel like unwanted stepchildren. Informed that they must enlist for six months instead of three, most units voted to return home, thereby depriving Polk of the service of nearly twelve thousand volunteers camped along the banks of the Rio Grande. In dismissing the short-term volunteers, Taylor applauded their zeal, writing in General Orders No. 90, "The commanding general would do violence to his feelings were he to omit the expression of regret that these brave men have been disappointed in their wish to meet the enemy, and now must, under an inevitable necessity, be discharged from the service." Polk relieved Gaines of his command of the Western Division and ordered him to Washington, D.C., to appear before a court of inquiry. Although praised by the court, Gaines nevertheless was rebuked, reassigned to New York City, and prevented from taking an active part in the war. Wrote one biographer about the affair, "No one . . . [not] even his most inveterate enemies and calumniators, has dared to hint a doubt of the lofty and patriotic motives that actuated him." Even as these events unfolded, the War Department went about the business of raising Polk's volunteers.[6]

The volunteers called up by the War Department formed two distinct groups. Men who enlisted in the spring of 1846 took advantage of ambiguous wording in the war bill that allowed them to serve for "twelve months after they have arrived at the place of rendezvous, or to the end of the war, unless sooner discharged." The clear implication—that the war would be over before a year passed—seemed to present no problem to the administration during the summer of 1846. The situation changed, however, when, after a year in Mexico and with no end in sight, the twelve-month volunteers chose to return home almost *en masse*, as the government had no way legally to keep them in the service. The second call came in the fall of 1846, after the war had ground to a halt. Polk and the War Department, now much less optimistic that the war would be short, closed the loophole by requiring men answering the second call to enlist "for the war." Volunteers of the first wave saw duty mainly in northern Mexico; a few twelve-month regiments had the distinction of serving under both Taylor and Scott. Others who responded to this call seized New Mexico and California. A major portion of volunteers enlisted "for the war" were doomed to guard territory already won by their predecessors, a duty made more odious by the fact that they had signed up for an indefinite period of time.[7]

Spurred on by patriotic fervor, thousands of men initially joined the rush to the colors. One song of the period told Americans to "Strike for Our Rights, Avenge Your Wrongs," wrongs which the author said included the mistreatment of the Santa Fe prisoners and the murder of American officers on the Rio Grande. Another patriotic tune that attempted to capitalize on the nation's Revolutionary past said that Americans should not "mind fatigue or pain, for they were borne by Washington." In some communities, veterans of the Texas War for Independence addressed crowds of recruits eager to march to the Rio Grande. An estimated thirty thousand Tennesseans answered the governor's call for volunteers—twenty-seven thousand more than were needed to fill the state's quota. Across the country, men scrambled to join up, hoping to be lucky enough to make it to the "Halls of the Montezumas." Throughout the South and West, rallies were held and recruiting offices were opened. Women sewed flags and uniforms for friends and relatives lucky enough to find a place in the ranks of the volunteers. In Indiana, Lew Wallace (future Union general and author of Ben Hur) did not wait for official sanction, but instead took it upon himself to recruit a company of volunteers. Employing a drummer and fifer and displaying a flag and a four-sided transparency that beckoned, "FOR MEXICO. FALL IN," he filled his quota in less than three days. Scenes like this were repeated as others like Wallace endeavored to transform their friends, neighbors, and relatives into soldiers.[8]

Motives other than patriotism prompted some volunteers to enlist. Many men were drawn to the war by the promise of excitement. Volunteer service also offered men down on their luck an opportunity to escape problems at home. Leander M. Cox, a captain in the 3rd Kentucky Infantry, almost regretted entering the service but wrote, "I could not see what I would have done better at home as the business of my profession was very trifling [sic], and I had involved myself greatly beyond my ability." Great opportunities existed in Mexico for volunteers who could free themselves from their military commitment. Noted one volunteer, "I cold [sic] make three Dollars a day working at the carpenter trade or I cold [sic] get 35$ pur [sic] Month for to drive a wagon." Other volunteers, lured by the promises of "new bright dollars" and "farms as big as Texas," joined the rush to Mexico. The bounties, land warrants, and pensions offered to entice recruits into the regular army also were offered to volunteers. The government promised volunteers who completed twelve months of service 160 acres or $100 in land script; those who volunteered for a lesser period could choose either 60 acres or $25 in land script.[9]

The total number of volunteers who enlisted during the Mexican War is of little significance unless it is analyzed. At the end of the war, the War Department reported 73,260 volunteer enlistments. The figure included 1,390 three-month volunteers, 11,211 six-month volunteers, 18,210 twelve-month volunteers, and 33,596 volunteers for the war. Only a small percentage of these volunteers ever served with Taylor or Scott; an even smaller number ever saw combat. Some went to California, some to New Mexico, and some nowhere at all. The men of Gaines's illegal call, for example, were mustered out before Taylor advanced on Monterey. Most of Florida's volunteers stayed home to man posts vacated by regulars ordered to Mexico. Several battalions of Texas volunteers patrolled the state's borders, keeping Indians in check. One battalion of Missouri volunteers guarded travelers on the Oregon Trail, while another watched Indians on the plains of Colorado and Kansas. Iowa volunteers manned forts and escorted Indians to a new reservation. Several thousand volunteers, including Ohio's twelve companies who were called the "Camp Washington Volunteers," never saw service of any type at all, being mustered out almost as quickly as they were mustered in because the state had exceeded its quota. Volunteer service in the Mexican War entailed a wide variety of duties as well as a wide range of geographical postings. It is a mistake to assume that all volunteers served south of the Rio Grande.[10]

Raising volunteers involved several steps. The War Department first informed a governor that Congress requested his state to provide a specific number of volunteers, denoting the type of troops to be raised—foot, horse, or artillery. The governor, after receiving official word of the requisition, announced the call in newspapers throughout the state, naming the time and place of the rendezvous. Most governors worked through their state's militia system to help spread the word and utilized militia officers to organize the volunteers into companies, battalions, regiments, and, in a few instances, into brigades. Once accepted by the governor, volunteers were inspected by an officer of the U.S. Army who mustered them into federal service. Although "federalized," volunteers retained the characteristics of state troops, being raised by the state and commanded by officers commissioned by the governor instead of Congress.[11]

Governors usually accepted companies in the order in which they reported for duty, but charges of favoritism and incompetence were leveled by disappointed companies unable to find places within their states' quotas. In Illinois, the citizens of Clark County drew up a resolution condemning Gov. Thomas Ford for refusing the service of a company commanded by Capt. William B. Archer—a veteran of both the War of 1812 and the Black Hawk War—after first indicating that it would be accepted. Recruits from Natchez, Mississippi, fumed at Gov. Albert G. Brown's decision to designate Vicksburg as the site of the rendezvous, thereby ensuring that two companies from that city were selected for the 1st Mississippi Rifles. Twenty companies in Indiana—enough to form two full regiments—had to be turned away once the state's quota had been filled. In Ohio, enough extra men answered the call for volunteers to form another regiment; but they, too, were told to go home. Disappointed Memphis men watched from the city's bluffs as volunteers from Indiana, Ohio, Illinois, Kentucky, and even eastern Tennessee sailed down the Mississippi River on their way to join Taylor. Polk and the War Department could have saved considerable time, effort, and money, had they been able to utilize the masses of potential volunteers, numbering in the thousands.[12]

An important part of raising a volunteer unit came with choosing officers. The selection usually followed common militia practices codified by state law. Some states, such as New Hampshire, Delaware, and Maryland, empowered the governor to appoint all militia officers. North Carolina left this duty in the hands of the general assembly. Vermont left the selection of field officers up to the governor but allowed companies to elect their own company officers. Massachusetts, New York, and Virginia allowed the men of each company to elect their company officers, with the company officers in turn electing the regimental field officers. Tennessee, Indiana, Mississippi, Illinois, Alabama, and Arkansas left the election of field officers up to the men of the regiment and allowed every man of the command to cast a ballot in this important election. Much was at stake, as a state's reputation rested upon the selection of its volunteer officers.[13]

Inexperienced officers, many of whom had commanded troops only on militia days, struggled to learn their new craft. Winfield Scott, aware that many volunteer officers lacked the technical skill needed to command their troops, issued an order shortly after the war began for the War Department to make his tactics manual available "for the use & instruction of the volunteers called into service." He directed that fifty copies each of volumes 1 and 2 be placed on deposit at Cincinnati, Nashville, and Louisville; five copies each of volume 3 were to be sent to these same cities. New Orleans, the gateway to the war, was to receive one hundred copies each of the first two volumes and ten copies of the third. The manuals were intended to provide volunteer officers with the rudiments of company, battalion, and brigade drill. Evidence shows that some volunteer officers made use of these books. Capt. Leander M. Cox studied tactics on the voyage to Mexico. Col. William B. Campbell equipped himself with a copy each of *Cooper's* and *Scott's* (training manuals), as well as the *General Regulations*. Shortly after his regiment arrived on the Rio Grande, he boasted that he already had taught his men several battalion maneuvers, including forming column by company and by division, changing front on any company or division, closing column at both company and division distance, deploying into line of battle, passing defiles, and forming a square. He wrote of his men, "The manual of arms they perform very well, and [they] are getting to march pretty well with the step." Lt. Lew Wallace recalled that the colo-nel of the 1st Indiana Infantry, James P. Drake, had an "uncommon apti-tude for tactics" and mastered the School of the Battalion in only three months. Luther Giddings, major of the 1st Ohio Infantry, contended that officers of his regiment followed the army regulations and that most, hav-ing been elected for their ability, regularly drilled their men. He ridiculed some field officers who rarely practiced battalion maneuvers but instead conducted stationary exercises from in front of their tents. One commander, he claimed, spent a great deal of time teaching his regiment to "fire by battalion" but neglected almost all other aspects described in the tactics manual. How well a company, battalion, or regiment of volunteers mas-tered drill depended on the ability and dedication of its commander.[14]

A number of West Pointers who had left the army took up their swords again to lead volunteers. Writing as the twelve-month volunteers arrived on the Rio Grande, Lt. William S. Henry proudly declared that the states showed "sound appreciation and respect for the advantages which must arise to their troops by being commanded by officers expressly educated for that purpose." The fact that these men had left their civilian pursuits to put their training to use proved to Henry that graduates of the Military Academy took their obligation to the nation seriously. A number of U.S. newspapers even carried a story entitled "West Point Vindicated" that re-ported a number of professionally trained officers at the head of volunteer units. The list of former regular officers who led volunteers in the Mexican War was indeed long: eleven (almost all West Pointers) commanded regi-ments with the rank of colonel; four served as lieutenant colonels; six served as majors; six more served as captains. Included in this group of West Point alumni were Henry Clay, Jr.; Humphrey Marshall; Meriwether Lewis Clark; Albert Sidney Johnston; Samuel Ryan Curtis; Jubal Early; and Jefferson Davis.[15]

Other current and former officers of the regular army found positions in the volunteer corps. Lt. Isaac Bowen informed his wife that one second

Generals of Volunteers, 1846–48

Name and Rank	State	Party	Political Experience
William Orlando Butler Major General of Volunteers June 29, 1846–Aug. 15, 1848	Kentucky	Democrat	Democratic candidate for governor in 1844 (lost the election)
Robert Patterson Major General of Volunteers July 7, 1846–July 20, 1848	Pennsylvania	Democrat	delegate to the 1824 Democratic convention at Harrisburg that nominated Andrew Jackson
Gideon Johnson Pillow Major General of Volunteers April 14, 1847–July 20, 1848 Brigadier General of Volunteers July 1, 1846–April 13, 1847	Tennessee	Democrat	lawyer and acquaintance of Polk; never held an elected office but had gained a reputation as a powerful man behind the political scene
John Anthony Quitman Major General of Volunteers April 14, 1847–July 20, 1848 Brigadier General of Volunteers July 1,1846–April 14, 1847	Mississippi	Democrat	chancellor of Mississippi Superior Court from 1828 to 1831, and again from 1832 to 1835
Thomas Marshall Brigadier General of Volunteers July 1, 1846–July 20, 1848	Kentucky	Democrat	nephew of Chief Justice John Marshall; served in Kentucky Legislature; rose to the post of speaker of the house
Thomas Lyon Hamer Brigadier General of Volunteers July 1, 1846–December 2, 1846 (died, Dec. 2, 1846, at Monterey, Mexico)	Ohio	Democrat	Ohio Legislature in 1825; three terms in the U.S. Congress; elected to Congress while serving in Mexico
Joseph Lane Brigadier General of Volunteers July 1, 1846–July 20, 1848	Indiana	Democrat	Indiana Legislature; U.S. Senator
James Shields Brigadier General of Volunteers July 1, 1846–July 20, 1848	Illinois	Democrat	Illinois Legislature; state auditor; state supreme court; land commissioner

Generals of Volunteers (cont.)

Name and Rank	State	Party	Political Experience
Franklin Pierce Brigadier General of Volunteers March 3, 1847–July 20, 1848	New Hampshire	Democrat	New Hampshire Legislature; U.S. Congress; offered post of U.S. Attorney General by Polk, but declined
George Cadwalader Brigadier General of Volunteers March 3, 1847–July 20, 1848	Pennsylvania	Democrat	lawyer; militia general
Enos D. Hopping Brigadier General of Volunteers March 3, 1847–Sept. 1, 1847 (died, Sept. 1, 1847, at Mier, Mexico)	New York	Democrat	Marcy's personal and political friend
Caleb Cushing Brigadier General of Volunteers April 14, 1847–July 20, 1848	Massachusetts	Democrat	U.S. Congress; rejected by the Senate as President John Tyler's choice for secretary of the treasury; commissioner to China; Massachusetts General Court; involved in governor's race while in Mexico
Sterling Price Brigadier General of Volunteers July 20, 1847–Nov. 25, 1848	Missouri	Democrat	Missouri Legislature, speaker of the house; U.S. Congress, resigned seat to command a regiment of Missouri Volunteers

lieutenant he knew had gained a commission in the volunteers: "Mr. [James Allen] Hardie, our old friend, is really Major of the California Regiment." Some officers of the U.S. Navy received commissions in volunteer units in California, where John C. Frémont (a captain of Topographic Engineers, but a lieutenant colonel of volunteers) appointed them as company commanders in the force raised to wrest the region from Mexico. Volunteers from the District of Columbia also were placed under the command of regular officers. Some officers, such as Col. William B. Campbell, who had commanded a company of Tennesseans in the Seminole War, brought experience gained in other conflicts. Texas was an extremely rich source of battle-tested officers. The infusion of West Point alumni, officers on active duty, and veteran volunteers benefited the volunteer units in which they served.[16]

West Pointers resented the return of former comrades who had been forced from the army prior to the war. More than sixty men who had attended West Point but failed to graduate received state commissions. Lt. George G. Meade made his feelings clear on the matter when he wrote his wife that "dismissal and rejection from the Military Academy have proved very fortunate events for several young men, who are placed far above the heads of their more fortunate classmates, 'who were fools enough to graduate.'" Most of these men returned as lieutenants or captains, but a few gained much higher rank: George W. Morgan commanded the 2nd Ohio Infantry; Gaston Mearse was elected lieutenant colonel of the 1st Arkansas Cavalry; and William Gilpin served as a major under Alexander Doniphan before commanding his own battalion of Missouri Volunteers as a lieutenant colonel. Writing generally of volunteer officers who flocked to Mexico, Lt. George B. McClellan remarked in disgust, "I found that every confounded Voluntario in the Continental Army [out]ranked me."[17]

One returnee especially irked regular officers, who were shocked to see him back in uniform. William E. Aisquith, an 1823 graduate of West Point and a native of Maryland, had been dismissed from the army in 1832 for being absent without leave. Reinstated five years later, Aisquith once more found himself in trouble and was cashiered from the army in 1845 for "drunkenness on duty and un-officerlike conduct." At the commencement of the war, Aisquith was appointed the orderly sergeant of Company E, 1st Battalion of Maryland and District of Columbia Volunteers. The men of the company later elevated him to the rank of second lieutenant, and soon after he became the battalion's adjutant. His comeback failed to impress Lieutenant Bowen, who, after seeing Aisquith on the march to Monterey, wrote, "Mr. Aisquith, formerly of our regiment, is in the Regiment of Baltimore volunteers as a sergeant. I have not recognized him as an acquaintance." Reputation was hard to regain among comrades who believed in honor.[18]

Some volunteers wanted experienced officers to lead them. Capt. John R. Kenly explained why members of his company overlooked Aisquith's shady past and elected him lieutenant. The men had learned "that playing soldier at home and practicing it [in Mexico] were two very different things, and that their lives and comforts would mainly depend on the skill and discretion of their officers." Of those men answering the second major call for volunteers, thirty-three captains, ten majors, nine lieutenant colonels, and six colonels already had served in Mexico with older units. Units raised late in the war often sought officers "who had seen the elephant." Nearly one hundred veteran officers returned to Mexico at the head of fresh troops.[19]

Officers were not the only volunteers who chose to return to Mexico. Almost all twelve-month volunteers left the service at the end of their term, but enough stayed on to form seven new companies: Capt. Gaston Mearse's Company of Remustered Arkansas Cavalry; Capt. C. Roberdeau Wheat's Company of Remustered Tennessee Mounted Volunteers; Capt. James Boyd's Company of Remustered Maryland Mounted Volunteers; and Maj. Robert Walker's Santa Fe Battalion of Remustered Missouri Mounted Volunteers. Other volunteers returned home long enough to visit their families before reenlisting in new regiments raised for the war. The remustered volunteers numbered 631 officers and men, but it is impossible to determine how many enlisted men later joined other units.[20]

Politics affected the selection of volunteer officers. Lt. Lew Wallace contended that the election of Indiana's top-ranking officers had been prearranged by presenting the candidates as a "slate." Only one of the four colonels chosen by Hoosier volunteers in 1846 was a Whig. Wrote Wallace in retrospect, "Certainly the able Democratic governor knew how to provide for himself and his party." Colonel Campbell of the 1st Tennessee Infantry expressed surprise at having won his post. Writing to a relative, he explained, "The old political companies were those called for by the Govr. and it so hap[p]ened that ¾ of those in my Regt are democratic officers, [and although] there is a majority of 200 Democrats of the rank and file, . . . I beat a Major Genl., and a Democrat [by] 169 votes." Campbell believed that he had achieved more than a Whig could have expected under the circumstances. A few other Whigs gained high rank in the volunteers, including Col. Edward D. Baker (Illinois), Col. Baile Peyton (Louisiana), and Col. William T. Haskell (Tennessee), as well as Lt. Col. Henry S. Lane (Indiana) and Lt. Col. James L. D. Morrison (Illinois). North Carolina's Whig governor appointed two Whigs, Robert T. Paine and John A. Fagg, colonel and lieutenant colonel, respectively, of his state's only regiment of volunteers. The lion's share of these positions, nevertheless, overwhelmingly went to Democrats. An attempt to determine the political affiliation of forty field officers revealed that seventeen had strong links to the Democratic Party; fewer than ten were found to be Whigs (the party loyalty of the remainder could not be discovered). Campbell believed partisan activity harmed the service, and he blamed "Democratic Gen's, Col's, and Major's, and officer's" [sic] for trying to bring down General Taylor. "I feel myself not safe amongst men who seem to have no other objective here but to advance the political party to which they owe their elevation." Campbell, who claimed that Democratic generals were bent on advancing themselves and their party, feared for "any poor Whig who fell under" the power of men like Gen. Gideon J. Pillow.[21]

Politicking was an integral part of being a volunteer officer. Although a few states appointed men to command volunteers, most field and company officers had to win election. A large number of volunteer officers were lawyers, a profession closely associated with nineteenth-century politics. In one company of Pennsylvania volunteers, the first lieutenant, both second lieutenants, two sergeants, and three corporals listed their prewar occupations as lawyers, while two more sergeants claimed to be law students. While this case may be extreme, lawyers frequently held leadership positions in the volunteer camps. The same study of field officers to determine political affiliations revealed that nearly 60 percent of the group examined were lawyers in civilian life. Newspaper editing, another profession closely associated with Jacksonian politics, was significantly represented in the volunteer officer corps. The editors of the *American Star* noted, "There is quite a number of the editorial profession attached to the army, and we rejoice that it is so." They continued, insightfully remarking, "Those who fight the political battles in their States, ought not to be backward when their country calls for the services of its citizens on the tented field." By the *American Star*'s count, at least ten editors had left their desks and were commanding troops in Mexico.[22]

Democrats dominated many early-war volunteer regiments, a fact perhaps due as much to the party's enthusiasm for the war as to any special treatment. A few examples illustrate the extent of Democratic involvement throughout the command structure of the volunteers. Col. Archibald Yell, a personal friend of Andrew Jackson, was a former Democratic congressman and ex-governor of Arkansas; his second-in-command, Lt. Col. John S. Roane, was a Democrat who had served as speaker of the Arkansas General Assembly; and Maj. Solon Borland edited the *Arkansas Banner*, a Democratic newspaper. Georgia's Col. Henry Jackson Roote was a Democrat and U.S. district attorney. Col. William H. Bissell was a Democrat and the prosecuting attorney for Saint Clair County, Illinois. Col. William A. Bowles of Indiana edited the *Panoli Times*, another Democratic newspaper. Indiana's Col. James P. Drake, a Democrat, held the posts of county clerk, auditor, and probate judge, and was an agent in the U.S. Land Office. Col. William A. Gorman was a Democrat who had been secretary of the Indiana senate. Lt. Col. Christian C. Nave never had won election, but he had been a Democratic candidate in several state races in Indiana. Col. Sterling Price, a Democrat, left his seat in the U.S. Congress to accept command of a regiment of Missouri volunteers. Another Democrat, Jefferson Davis, also was serving in the U.S. Congress when elected colonel of a regiment of Mississippi volunteers. Maj. Alexander Bradford, third in command of Davis's regiment, had been a major general in the Mississippi militia and had been a leading Democrat in state politics; Col. Reuben Davis, commander of another regiment of Mississippi volunteers, abandoned a bid for governor as the Democratic candidate to lead his troops to Mexico.[23]

Some volunteer officers proved to be better politicians than soldiers. Capt. Robert Anderson, unimpressed by Edward D. Baker, wrote that the colonel "looked like a regular electioneering hero." One civilian observer voiced similar opinions about other volunteer officers. Josiah Gregg, famed chronicler of the prairies, traveled with the 1st Arkansas Cavalry to northern Mexico. Of the regiment's commander, he wrote, "Col. Yell is a very clever[,] pleasant, sociable fellow, but decidedly out of his element—in a sphere so different from his forte of political demagogary [sic] and duties using tact, that he succeeds, as yet not very well; and I fear he may not improve very rapidly." The unit's lieutenant colonel, John S. Roane, fared no better, causing Gregg to remark, "Col. Roane is . . . a clever jovial companion, but too dull and indolent to succeed, . . . He is also rather stiff and aristocratic in his manners to be very popular; yet a necessity for electioneering would doubtless greatly change his deportment." Maj. Solon Borland also failed to pass muster with Gregg; even though he was "a gentleman of decidedly literary talent and acquirements, and good education," he was "'out of his element' in a military career." In addition, Gregg found him "rather [too] petulant to be an agreeable commander." The Arkansas volunteers, under the loose leadership of these politicians, gained a reputation for rowdy behavior. In one incident, troops of this command massacred unarmed Mexicans in a cave near Patos in retaliation for the murder of one of their comrades. On another occasion, Mexicans captured a detachment commanded by Borland at Encarnación when he and his men failed to place guards around their camp before retiring for the night. Colonel Yell's heroic death at Buena Vista focused attention away from his inability or unwillingness to discipline his regiment. Gregg, who saw the colonel's body on the battlefield, remarked, "Col. Yell, I had for some time been convinced (whatever doubt I may have previously had) was brave . . .

but lacked a sufficient degree of prudence. The truth is, he mistook his talent, when he entered the army—he was much better suited to politics."[24]

For many volunteers, reality failed to measure up to their image of war; army life turned out to be much more difficult than many had expected. Deriding gentlemen volunteers from Louisiana, Lt. George G. Meade cautioned, "Soldiering is no play, and those who undertake it must make up their minds to hard times and hard knocks." Capt. John R. Kenly of the 1st Battalion of Baltimore and Maryland Volunteers recorded that his battalion spent five hours at drill, in addition to their usual camp duties. Writing from Monterey several weeks after the fall of the city, Kenly remarked, "Our volunteers are pretty generally disgusted with volunteering, for it is no child's play, the daily labor now being done in earnest." Lt. Chesley Sheldon Coffey of the 2nd Mississippi Rifles, serving near Saltillo, warned in a letter home, "I Do not want any of my Brothers to volenteer [sic] as they ar [sic] So much Exposed here that one in 10 will not Stand it."[25]

Volunteer officers soon learned they could not expect citizen-soldiers to behave like regulars. Volunteers expected to retain the privileges of citizenship and to be treated according to their status as free men. Lamented one volunteer, "It is hard for a free American to accustom himself to the discipline and aristocracy of the army." Colonel Campbell explained that regular soldiers "are but machines and will obey implicitly without murmur. Hence it is an impossible task to drill and discipline an army of volunteers like the Regular Army." One volunteer officer who tried reasoning with his men told fellow officers that "freemen must not be insulted." Luther Giddings, major of the 2nd Ohio Infantry, stated, "The American volunteer is a thinking, feeling, and often a capricious being. He is not and never intends to become a mere moving and musket-holding machine." Many volunteers, clinging to their status as citizen-soldiers, believed that they should not be subjected to the same degree of discipline as regulars. Sgt. Thomas Barclay, a member of one Pennsylvania regiment, set down his philosophy on volunteers in his journal: "The policy of frequent roll calling and drill is good when applied to regulars but the volunteers should be exempt from all duties except such as are absolutely necessary. They are composed of a different material from the regulars and should be differently managed."[26]

Most volunteer officers recognized that their men could not be ruled with tight reins. Maj. Luther Giddings listed the qualities he thought an officer of volunteers should possess: he should not assert his authority to enforce small issues; he should be as ready to offer encouragement as to find fault; he should be mindful of the comforts of his men; he should be friendly and try to govern through affection rather than fear; and, above all, he must set an example for them through his own behavior. Lieutenant Wallace pointed to one officer who evidently had developed a similar creed. Although "careless as a soldier," Maj. Henry S. Lane was esteemed by the regiment, because "no one knew better than he that with volunteers, at least, respect for an officer is more important than fear." Volunteers preferred their own officers to regulars, who they thought were "too strict." Sergeant Barclay admitted that, in contests of will, "we are generally more successful with our own officers." Volunteer officers who demanded too much discipline from their men often encountered trouble. Josiah Gregg, who had noted the lack of military ability of the field officers of Yell's Arkansas volunteers, found one captain of the regiment, the poet Albert Pike, to have been "the most conspicuous, in fact, . . . the best disciplinarian and drill officer of the corps." But, continued Gregg, "Pike is too stiff and aristocratic in his manner to be popular so I doubt if he could be elected by a general vote to any office in the regiment." His main complaint against Pike was that "he is in truth in his deportment what unfortunately too many officers of the regular army are."[27]

Commanding volunteers could be vexing. Captain Kenly noted this about his men who behaved like children constantly seeking his attention:

> One wanted a pen, another a sheet of paper; one wanted me to read a letter he had just received; another wanted me to write one for him; another wanted me to send his money home; another wanted me to keep it for him; one wanted a wafer, another ink; one complained that his uniform was too large, another that his was too small; one said that he was sick and wanted me to give him medicine, another that he couldn't find the surgeon.

Capt. William P. Rogers lamented, "One who has never commanded a company of voluntiers [*sic*] can form no idea of the unpleasantness of the life." Mulling over his situation as commander of a regiment of volunteers, Colonel Campbell reflected that "it is too much trouble and responsibility for the honor. He that undertakes to command a volunteer Regt. will have his hands full." The commander of the 2nd Mississippi Rifles, Reuben Davis, recalled his first day on duty after his election to the rank of colonel. "Never shall I forget the exasperation of seeing the officers of the regiment sitting around much at their ease, and evidently taking malicious pleasure in answering every application with a careless, 'Go to the colonel.'"[28]

Internal politics caused discord in volunteer regiments. Candidates who sought high rank had to gain support from a majority of the companies in order to be elected to office. After the elections, it was hoped, the losers would put their defeats behind them and work for the good of the regiment. In some cases, however, grudges developed that divided a regiment into opposing camps. One member of a company from Jackson, Mississippi, claimed that Jefferson Davis showed great partiality to his neighbors from around Vicksburg, stating, "The regimental staff has been taken entirely from the two Vicksburg companies, and when any post of honor or profit is to be filled temporarily, a Vicksburgian is appointed to fill it." So obvious was the favoritism, claimed the writer, that the name of the regiment should have been "The Vicksburg Regiment." A member of the 1st South Carolina Infantry described a similar situation in his regiment. Pvt. William S. Johnson claimed that many were dissatisfied because "the only road to preferrement [*sic*] in this Regt. Seems to be a man's position at home, not his merits as a Soldier here—all who are connected in the remotest degree with the aristocracy of South Carolina have more than an equal chance of advancement." Col. Reuben Davis, the commander of the 2nd Mississippi Rifles, also noted considerable dissent in his unit. According to him, his victory over a rival for the office of colonel gave the loser, Capt. Benjamin C. Buckly, "great offense which he cherished to the day of his death." At Matamoros, when Buckly refused to form his company for parade, Colonel Davis ordered the other companies to load their muskets and fire on the mutineers if they persisted in disobeying. Bloodshed was averted when Buckly belatedly brought his men onto the parade ground. More trouble lay in store for the Mississippians. All three of the regiment's field officers became sick and had to leave Mexico, causing new elections to be held in the field.[29]

Supporters campaigned for their candidates with the zeal characteristic of Jacksonian political races. Opponents accused Col. John Geary, the commander of the 2nd Pennsylvania Volunteers, of sending certain popular officers from Mexico City to Vera Cruz so that his favorites would have a better chance in regimental elections. "Electioneering is going on in great style," said one Pennsylvanian who claimed that Col. Geary promised to use his patronage power to make some enlisted men lieutenants if they would support his man in the election. "Liquor was gotten up for the occasion" when Geary's faction carried the election. Candidates for the colonel of the 2nd Mississippi Rifles did not wait for the election results to come in before bringing out the whiskey. Gen. John E. Wool stopped the election, saying, "Officers who could, by means of intoxicating liqurors [*sic*] . . . obtain votes for the high and dignified office of colonel, are unworthy to hold that or any other office in the United States Army." One member of the 2nd Mississippi Rifles, unhappy with the results of the new election when it finally was held a month later, informed his brother that "the officers in our Regiment acted verry [*sic*] bad with Capt. [Adam] McWillie [when] they Brought out McWillie to run for Lieut. Col.—and when [John A.] Wilcox was beatin [*sic*] for Col. it made his friends mad and they Brought him out for Lieut. Col. and he beat McWillie." He added, "We had a grate [*sic*] excitement about the election."[30]

The independent attitude of volunteers stemmed from the democratic ideas they held. Volunteer officers, placed in their positions by the ballots of the men they commanded, found themselves in the awkward position of giving orders to their peers. Maj. Luther Giddings summed up the situation, stating, "The position of an officer of volunteers, elected from the ranks, as the majority of us were, is one of peculiar delicacy. While he should not allow himself to forget that he owes his rank and power to the kindness of those he commands, he must yet know how to maintain discipline and exact obedience." Volunteers felt they had a right to voice their opinions regarding those whom they had placed in office. Members of Capt. Leander M. Cox's company proposed to him and his lieutenant that "whenever a majority of the men in the com. petitioned either of them to resign [they] would do so." Comparing service in the regular and volunteer armies, Colonel Campbell declared, "In the volunteer service the officers are constantly subjected to a public opinion even in camp, which has an influence on him in spite of all the regulation of the army." He explained further, "The soldiers are writing home constantly and can annoy an officer very much and then when the short term of service is over he goes back to a society composed in part of his soldiers." The fact that volunteer officers were accountable to their men, he concluded, explained why volunteers could never reach the degree of discipline found in the regular army.[31]

Crimes committed against Mexicans and fellow Americans marred the record of the volunteers in the Mexican War. Rowdy behavior appeared even before the troops left home. One story in *Niles' National Register* discussed criminal acts committed by volunteers, exclaiming, "The public journals from the vicinity of routes taken by volunteers, bring to us, we are sorry to say, innumerable proofs of the lack of discipline and the prevalence not only of insubordination, but also of disgraceful rowdyism amongst the volunteers." The writer blamed the "rowdyism" on "lawless spirits" who entered the ranks. Company D, 1st Pennsylvania Infantry, took the moniker "The Killers," a name that aptly described their behavior as they made their way to Mexico. Local militia units were called out in New Orleans when a rumor spread that angry Mississippi volunteers had mutinied and were planning to sack the city. The adjutant of one regiment of Ohio volunteers, who evidently had considered the problem, attempted to explain to Capt. Franklin Smith that, although many volunteers were "honorable men at home," the war imbued them with "a strange sort of morality." Others, too, noticed this new morality. Col. Reuben Davis concluded that once a recruit had taken the oath of allegiance to the U.S. and was mustered into the service of his country, a drastic change occurred. The volunteer, the colonel contended, felt absolved of any obligation to God or man and, as a consequence, considered himself free to disregard every law of honesty, with the exception of fidelity to the flag and his own personal courage. Another Mississippian, Capt. William P. Rogers, considered the effect of this aspect of volunteer service and concluded that "voluntiers [*sic*] I am satisfied will never do for an invading army—They will do well enough to defend their own firesides, but they can not endure the fatigues incident to an invading army." Rogers also believed volunteers unfit for foreign duty, because it was too difficult "to keep them under proper discipline." Anxious to return to Tennessee and escape the burdens of a volunteer command, Colonel Campbell vowed that he would "never enter the service again as a volunteer unless it be to defend [his] native land, and [his] own hearth stone."[32]

Volunteers jealously guarded their rights and reacted indignantly when they believed themselves wronged. According to one witness at Camargo, twenty-nine Indiana volunteers preferred laboring in irons to serving under an officer from another state. Volunteers with Scott's army at Puebla balked when ordered to remove their caps and kneel whenever a Catholic procession passed. One volunteer called the order an insult to American soldiers and stated, "Many swear that they will undergo every punishment before they obey such orders." Authorities averted trouble only by abolishing the requirement to kneel. Unpopular officers sometimes caused near-riots when volunteers thought they overstepped their authority. Capt. Preston S. Brooks sparked a small revolt in Mexico City with his overbearing attitude. Volunteers frequently refused to submit to officers' conduct which they perceived as tyrannical.[33]

Punishment proved a sore spot with the rank-and-file volunteers, who thought military justice too severe for citizen-soldiers. By the advent of the Mexican War, many states had outlawed corporal punishment except for persons serving in the army, navy, or militia. Volunteers viewed such punishment as inappropriate for men born free, and they worked to subvert their officers. Friends of one man whom Captain Brooks ordered "bucked and gagged" set the prisoner free as soon as the unpopular officer turned his back. Sergeant Barclay, who witnessed three regulars whipped at Jalapa, reported that the sight disgusted the crowd of volunteers assembled to watch and created sympathy for the culprits. "The men were no doubt scoundrels who deserved punishment," but he thought it incredible that "in the nineteenth century an American citizen is subjected to the dishonor of being publicly whipped." Said Private Tennery after seeing another five soldiers punished, "It chills one's blood to see free born Americans tied up and whipped like dogs, in a market yard in a foreign land." Volunteers disliked other forms of punishment as well. When Gen. Caleb Cushing ordered a pair of stocks and a wooden punishment horse placed in his camp at Mexico City, volunteers carried the devices away under the cover of darkness and destroyed them. Always ready to poke fun at an unpopular officer, volunteers posted advertisements around the camp offering a reward for a "runaway horse."[34]

Volunteers railed against the military justice system. Many of those accused of crimes, as well as their friends, thought that regular officers were prejudiced against them and that volunteers could not get a fair trial. One Pennsylvanian in Mexico City angrily denounced the sentences of two Baltimore men found guilty of sleeping on guard duty: "They were not allowed the privilege of defending themselves, to show their innocence of the crime, and nothing convicted these poor soldiers except that they were privates belonging to a volunteer regiment." A popular officer of the 2nd Mississippi, Lt. John Amyx, ran into trouble and was sentenced by a military court to a three-month reduction in rank, without pay. Said one Mississippian of the trial: "He was tried by regular officers and they hate Volunteers as they do the devil and there is no love lost for the Volunteers hate them." Members of Amyx's company expressed their contempt for the system when they promptly elected him captain at the end of his court-imposed sentence.[35]

Many discipline problems resulted from the fact that volunteers came to Mexico ready for a fight and were in no mood to tolerate offense from anyone, Mexican or American. These men longed for battle, but the majority of volunteers who arrived after the initial rush to the front were destined to serve out their entire enlistments without participating in a single engagement. Lt. Andrew Jackson Trussell turned down the opportunity to return to Mississippi on recruiting duty, upon hearing a rumor that a battle might not be far off. As he informed a relative back home, "If my Regt. & Company gets into a fight I want to be there for them." Without Mexicans to battle, some volunteers took to fighting one another. On the night of

September 7, 1846, a riot occurred near Camargo aboard the steamboat *Corvette,* as two companies of the 1st Georgia Infantry battled each other over a choice spot on the ship's upper deck. Col. Edward Baker arrived with a detail from his own regiment, the 4th Illinois Infantry, to quell the disturbance. Baker and several Georgians were injured, and one volunteer died before the disturbance ended. In another incident, a catfish became the focus of a dispute between Maryland and Ohio volunteers. Capt. John R. Kenly reported that angry volunteers from both regiments ran for their muskets before cooler heads prevailed. One Mississippi lieutenant survived the battles of Monterey and Buena Vista, only to lose a leg in a drunken escapade; he was shot by a guard while trying to break his friends out of jail. While other incidents occurred where groups of volunteers battled each other *en masse,* usually they maimed and killed their fellow citizens in individual disputes.[36]

Volunteers certainly were made differently from the regulars of the Old Establishment. Reared in Jacksonian America, the former clung tightly to the privileges they had known in civilian life. The melding of democratic institutions and the army never was completed, as the "citizen" never really became transformed into the "soldier." Although volunteers were hard fighters when called to battle, their staunch defense of their "rights" made them difficult to control in camp and on the march. In the minds of most Americans, however, the citizen-soldier remained the ideal fighting man.

SIX

Tools of the Trade

Company I to which I belonged, though nominally artillery, had precisely the same duties to perform as infantry; being armed with muskets, and in every respect equipped and drilled in the same manner, with the exception of an occasional drill at the battery guns at the Fort.

—George Ballentine,
1st U.S. Artillery

I would throw Uncle Sam's blue uniform frock-coat, and my handsome forage cap, in the corner of my tent, and enjoyed the luxury of a very course pair of tow pantaloons, a red calico shirt, and a very high-crowned Mexican hat.

—Lt. Albert G. Brackett,
4th Indiana Infantry

Soldiers, like all craftsmen, are distinguished by the distinctive tools and clothing associated with their trade. The soldier's tools included the cannon, musket, and the sword; his clothing, of course, was the uniform. All armies have unique characteristics that reflect their own place and time. Although the weapons and uniforms of the United States military in the Mexican War were similar to those employed in the country's previous wars, a change had occurred that became more obvious as time passed. With the advent of the Industrial Revolution, flintlock gave way to percussion cap and the single-shot pistol to the revolver. The Mexican War stood midway between the battlefields of Napoleon and those of the Civil War.

Prior to the Mexican War, American field artillery had undergone a period of renewal that left it with new arms to support a new tactical philosophy. Light artillery truly had become mobile, "flying" across the battlefield to deliver its fire wherever it was needed most. The primary field guns were the Model 1841 bronze 6-pounder and the Model 1841 bronze 12-pounder. Both guns were mounted on two-wheeled gun carriages, which were pulled by a horse-drawn limber. The 6-pounder, using a 1.25-pound charge, could throw a 6-pound solid shot 1,700 yards. The 12-pounder, with a 4-pound charge, could throw a 12-pound solid shot 1,800 yards. One point worth noting is that the long reach of these guns allowed their crews to operate well beyond the range of musket fire. Thus artillerymen could work their pieces in the safety that distance provided. The success of the American field artillery in northern Mexico gave the corps an aura of invincibility and covered its commanders with glory.[1]

Siege artillery, although less spectacular than the field variety, saw important service in the war as well. The sheer weight of these guns, however, posed problems in transporting them over rough Mexican roads. The Model 1841 iron 12-pounder weighed 3,500 pounds—more than four times as much as its bronze counterpart. The weight of the M1839 iron 18-pounder and the M1839 iron 24-pounder increased proportionally with their sizes. The 18-pounder, with a 4.5-pound charge, threw a solid shot 1,592 yards. The massive 24-pounder, using an 8-pound charge, threw a solid shot 1,900 yards. Oxen and wagons were required to transport the siege artillery guns and their ammunition, making up what was called the siege train.[2]

In the reforms of 1841 and 1844, the army also adopted a series of howitzers. Howitzers had trajectories higher than those of field and siege pieces. Guns of this class included the M1841 bronze 12-pound Howitzer, the M1844 bronze 24-pound Howitzer, the M1844 bronze 32-pound Howitzer, the M1841 iron 24-pound Siege Howitzer, and the M1841 iron 8-inch Siege Howitzer. The bronze 12-pound Howitzer used a 1-pound charge to throw a 12-pound solid shot 1,100 yards. The bronze 32-pound Howitzer, with a 3.5-pound charge, could hurl a 32-pound solid shot 1,500 yards.[3]

The army possessed yet another class of artillery: the mortar. The mortar had an even higher trajectory than the howitzers. These short, stubby guns, when emplaced in well-protected positions, could lob heavy projectiles into their targets with near impunity. Like the other classifications of artillery, mortars came in different weights and materials. They included the M1841 iron 8-inch Siege Mortar, the M1841 iron 10-inch Siege Mortar, the M1844 iron 10-inch Sea Coast Mortar, M1841 iron 13-inch Sea Coast Mortar, and the M1844 bronze 24-pound Coehorn Mortar. Mortars were used during the siege of Fort Brown and at the battles of Monterey and Vera Cruz. But, as with siege artillery, the weight of the mortars limited their use in the war.[4]

Two other items in the American arsenal deserve mention: the M1841 bronze 12-pound Mountain Howitzer and the Hale Rocket. The Mountain Howitzer had been designed as a highly mobile, lightweight gun ideal for places where roads were poor or nonexistent. With a half-pound charge, the Mountain Howitzer could throw a 12-pound solid shot 1,000 yards. The Hale Rocket was another mobile type of artillery. The rockets came in two sizes—2-inch and 3-inch—and were fired from a ten-foot-long por-

Ordnance Commonly Used by the U.S. Army in Mexico

Field Guns

			(Maximum Range)
Model 1841	6-pounder	bronze	1520 yards
Model 1841	12-pounder	bronze	1663 yards

Mountain Service

Model 1841	12 mountain howitzer	bronze	1005 yards

Siege and Garrison Service

Model 1839	18-pounder	iron	1592 yards
Model 1839	24-pounder	iron	1901 yards

Howitzers

Model 1841	12-pounder howitzer	bronze	1680 yards
Model 1841	24-pounder howitzer	bronze	1322 yards

Mortars

Model 1841	10 inch	iron	2100 yards

Source: War Department, *Ordnance Manual of the Use of the Officers of the United States Army* (Washington, D.C.: J. and G. S. Gideon, Printers, 1841), 1, 4; War Department, *Ordnance Manual of the Use of the Officers of the United States Army* (Washington D.C.: J. B. Lippincott and Company, 1861), 13–14, 384–90.

table trough. The range of the rockets at maximum elevation was 2,200 yards. Beginning at Vera Cruz, the Mountain Howitzer and the Hale Rocket saw service throughout central Mexico.[5]

The battlefield situation determined the type of ammunition to be used. Solid shot had the greatest range and was used against massed troops as well as to batter down structures. Shells, hollow-cast iron balls filled with a powder charge, were used against structures and against troops protected by cover. Spherical case was similar to shell, except that it contained lead musket balls in addition to the powder charge and was effective against bodies of troops. Both shell and spherical case employed a fuze cut to cause the projectile to explode at the appropriate time and distance. Grape shot consisted of several tiers of irons balls held together by a series of circular plates and rings connected by an iron bolt. Both it and canister, a metal can filled with musket balls, were used against enemy troops. Ammunition usually was loaded into the gun in two steps; a bag containing the powder was loaded first and then the actual projectile. Artillery implements included the *rammer* to ram the powder and projectile down the barrel, the *sponge* to dampen sparks and embers, the gunner's haversack to carry the charge and projectile to the piece, the leather *finger stall* to seal the vent and prevent air from fanning sparks while the powder bag was being rammed, the *priming wire* that pricked the cartridge bag, the *tube pouch* to hold the priming tubes and quick match, the *trail spike* used to point the piece, the *hausse* with which to measure the gun's elevation, the *portfire case* in which to keep the portfires, and the *portfire-stock* which the gunner used to fire the gun. *Friction primers* had not yet come into vogue, although some guns were fitted with percussion locks, creating a much surer ignition system.[6]

Loading any piece of artillery involved the same basic steps. Under normal circumstances, eight men were required to carry out the procedure of preparing the rounds and loading the piece. One man handled the rammer used to drive the charge and projectile down the tube, as well as the sponge to put out any embers left after firing. A second man assisted the first in ramming and sponging; he also received the round and inserted it into the muzzle of the piece. A third man covered the vent with a leather finger stall to prevent embers from flaring up while the charge was being rammed. He also helped point the piece, pricked the cartridge bag with a priming wire, and inserted the quick match into the vent. A fourth man held the portfire-stock used to light the quick match that fired the piece. The other four men assisted in pointing the piece, setting its elevation, preparing the ammunition at the limber, and carrying it to the gun. Crews were encouraged

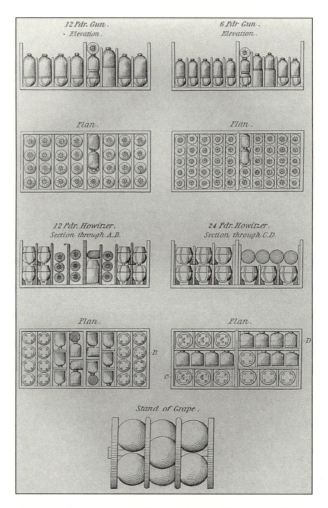

Artillery Ammunition. Ordnance Manual for the Use of the Officers of the United States Army, 1841, *Washington, D.C.: J. and G.S. Gideon, 1841. Courtesy New York State Library*

to practice with reduced numbers to simulate battlefield conditions, where members might be killed or wounded and so be unable to perform their duties. The loading and firing sequence included the following commands: (1) To your post, (2) To action, (3) Load, (4) Sponge, (5) Ram, (6) Fire, and (7) Cease firing.[7]

The American infantryman was armed primarily with the flintlock musket, a weapon not too different from that used by these soldiers' forefathers in the American Revolution. Based on a French pattern, the musket was 57.64 inches long, weighed ten pounds, and fired a lead ball slightly less than .69 caliber. A 16- to 18-inch-long socket bayonet could be affixed to the end of the barrel, effectively turning the weapon into a pike. According to Dennis Hart Mahan, a noted instructor of military science at West Point, the musket was "sighted" for a range of 120 to 130 yards; for closer targets, the piece had to be aimed lower, while for targets further away, the piece had to be aimed higher. He further states, "Beyond 220 yards the effect of the fire is very uncertain. Beyond 450 yards the ball seldom gives a dangerous wound." Besides the ball cartridge, the musket could fire a cartridge containing twelve buckshot, as well as a cartridge called "buck & ball," containing one ball and three buckshot. Although today viewed as a quaint curiosity, on the battlefields of the past, the flintlock musket was a deadly weapon.[8]

Soldiers learned to load the flintlock musket during a phase in their instruction called School of the Soldier. The procedure, although not complicated, required twelve separate steps. The commands to load included: (1) LOAD, (2) Open-PAN, (3) Handle-CARTRIDGE, (4) Tear-CARTRIDGE, (5) PRIME, (6) Shut-PAN, (7) Cast-ABOUT, (8) Charge-CARTRIDGE, (9) Draw-RAMMER, (10) Ram-CARTRIDGE, (11) Return-RAMMER, and (12) Shoulder-ARMS. At the beginning of the exercise, the soldier stood at the position of Shoulder-ARMS, with the butt of the weapon held in the left hand with the stock resting against the left shoulder. At the command LOAD, the piece was brought to the right side, balanced in the left hand with the barrel sloped forward. The right thumb was placed on the *frizzen* that covered the pan designed to hold the priming powder. When ordered to Open-PAN, the soldier flipped the frizzen open to expose the priming pan and then reached with his right hand into the cartridge box that rested on his right hip. At the command Handle-CARTRIDGE, the soldier removed a paper cartridge from the box and brought it to his mouth. Commanded to Tear-CARTRIDGE, he tore the tail of the cartridge with his teeth and placed the open cartridge near the priming pan. At the command PRIME, he poured a small portion of the powder from the open cartridge into the pan, saving the bulk of the charge for the barrel. Shut-PAN was the command to flip the frizzen back over the pan. At Cast-ABOUT, the soldier placed the butt of the musket to the left of his left foot, causing the barrel to slant to the right. At Charge-CARTRIDGE, the soldier tipped the cartridge and poured the remaining powder down the barrel; he then inserted the ball and paper wrapper into the barrel. Draw-RAMMER, Ram-CARTRIDGE, and Return-RAMMER were the steps for seating the ball. The last command, Shoulder-ARMS, readied the

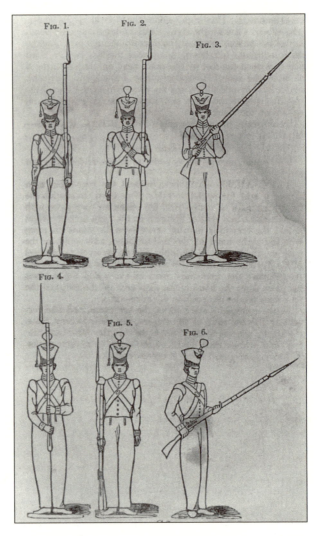

Manual of Arms. School of the Squad. Brevet Capt. S. Cooper, Concise System of Instruction and Regulation for the Militia and Volunteers, *Philadelphia: Robert P. Desilver, 1836. Courtesy Richard Bruce Winders*

soldier for marching or firing. Repetition of the drill was essential for learning its clocklike movements. With proper training, each infantryman was expected "to fire at least three rounds in a minute with ease and regularity."[9]

Troops habitually were formed into two ranks, from which several modes of firing could be employed. Preparatory to firing, the officers first cautioned the line about how the firing was to be conducted, as in FIRE BY SQUAD, FIRE BY PLATOON, FIRE BY COMPANY, FIRE BY BATTALION, FIRE BY RANK, or FIRE BY FILE. This caution was followed by three more orders given in quick secession: READY, AIM, FIRE. In all the firings—except FIRE BY FILE, when the men automatically would load and fire on their own after the first command—the commander gave the order LOAD for the troops to reload unless they had been told to FIRE AT WILL. Flintlocks were temperamental weapons and often failed to discharge. In some instances, the vent (located in the side of the barrel next to the pan) became clogged and prevented the flame from reaching the charge, creating a "flash in the pan." Massed shoulder to shoulder, soldiers sometimes were unaware when their pieces failed to discharge. Smoke issuing from the touch hole indicated that the weapon had fired. A soldier who failed to notice that his weapon had misfired and loaded his piece with a second round merited a stern warning from his sergeant or captain; a soldier who loaded a third round on top of two unfired rounds was punished.[10]

The War Department encouraged target practice before the war. Captains were advised to divide the men and corporals of their companies into three categories according to skill and accuracy: the best, the average, and the worst marksmen. The ammunition intended for each season's practice was divided unequally among these groups of men, with the worst receiving the greatest number of cartridges. Post commanders provided incentives to motivate soldiers to improve. The scheme devised by the commander at Fort Pickens, Florida, incorporated target practice with a duty the soldier already had to perform. The men stood guard with loaded muskets that had to be unloaded when they were relieved. Rather than simply have the ball removed with a ball puller and waste the cartridge, the sergeant of the guard marched the detail to a firing range and recorded where each man's shot struck the target. The incentive to aim true was that the man closest to the mark was excused from his next tour of guard duty. According to one soldier who liked the system with its reward, the men at Fort Pickens "soon became excellent shots." During the war, however, commanders placed a premium on ammunition and curtailed most target practice. In fact, replacing lost weapons and ammunition became such a problem in central Mexico that captains were instructed to charge their men the following amounts for missing items: three dollars per bayonet, six cents each per cartridge, and three cents each per percussion cap. The order explained the reason for the steep prices: "Their value being greater here than at home."[11]

The development of the percussion cap was destined to make the

Drilling recruits. John Frost, Pictorial History of the Mexican War, *Philadelphia: C. Desilver, 1848. Courtesy Mary Couts Burnett Library, Texas Christian University*

flintlock musket obsolete. In fact, just prior to the war, the War Department had authorized the production of a new-model long arm. The Model 1842 Percussion Musket, although similar to the older muskets, used the new percussion system instead of the flint and steel that had served armies on countless battlefields. In 1844, the War Department issued General Order No. 44, prescribing the loading sequence for the improved model, explaining, "The introduction . . . of arms with percussion locks and bayonets with clasps, render necessary some INSTRUCTION, in the way of a supplement to the Manual of Arms, INFANTRY TACTICS." The twelve steps were reduced to ten, eliminating Open-PAN and Shut-PAN as they did not apply to the percussion musket. The commands were (1) LOAD, (2) Handle-CARTRIDGE, (3) Tear-CARTRIDGE, (4) Charge-CARTRIDGE, (5) Draw-RAMMER, (6) Ram-CARTRIDGE, (7) Return-RAMMER, (8) Cast-ABOUT, (9) PRIME, and (10) Shoulder-ARMS. The major differences came at the command LOAD, when the soldier placed the butt of the musket on the ground, and Cast-ABOUT, when the soldier brought the piece to his right side with the barrel pointing to the front, balanced it with his left, and placed a percussion cap on the cone with his right hand. The firings remained the same. The great advantage of the percussion system over the flintlock was that the cap, filled with the explosive compound of fulminate of mercury that exploded when struck by the hammer, worked in damp and windy conditions. The small copper caps first were carried in a pocket on the front of the fatigue jacket, but this proved impractical, and a new accouterment called the cap box was introduced. Worn on the waist belt, the leather pouch protected the caps from the weather and prevented them from being scattered in the soldier's exertions.[12]

Some percussion muskets saw service in the war, but the actual number or type issued is unknown. Evidence indicates that some regiments of artillery serving as light infantry received the arms. At least one regiment of volunteers, the 1st Pennsylvania Infantry, received percussion muskets in the last months of the war. Enough percussion muskets found their way to Mexico to cause a problem for the military authorities there when some troops mixed flint and percussion weapons within the same companies. On February 3, 1848, Scott issued General Order No. 42 that said in part, "The percussion muskets issued to certain regiments will not be tolerated in flint musket companies." The predominant weapon throughout the war remained the flintlock musket.[13]

Military rifles also saw use during the Mexican War. Rifles had been produced by U.S. arsenals as early as 1803 but had remained largely a specialty weapon. The range of a rifle in the hands of a trained soldier was twice that of the musket. An obstacle limiting use of early model rifles in military situations was that it took a soldier a minute or more to load each shot, because the ball had be forced down the barrel to insure a tight fit. Although the tactics of the day specified rifles for the right and left flank companies of an infantry regiment, officers such as Winfield Scott opposed their issue to an entire regiment. The War Department had authorized the manufacture of several patterns of military rifles prior to the Mexican War. The Model 1803 Rifle, sometimes referred to by civilian observers as a Yager Rifle, reportedly went west with Lewis and Clark. The .54-caliber flintlock weapon served through the War of 1812 but was replaced by the Model 1817 Rifle. Called a Common Rifle, the M1817 was a .54-caliber flintlock rifle. Neither the M1803 nor the M1817 was fitted for a bayonet, as they were long-range weapons. An interesting innovation appeared in 1819—the Hall's breech-loading rifle. Although still a single-shot flintlock, the weapon had a novel hinged loading mechanism located at the back of the barrel that swung up to allow the user to insert powder and ball directly into the breech. Although this loading system was an improvement, some critics complained that hot gases escaped from the firing mechanism when the weapon was discharged, burning the user's hands and face. Unlike the M1803 and M1817, the Hall's had a bayonet, making it more suitable for infantry in mass formations. One other model appeared before the war, the Model 1841. This new rifle returned to the muzzle-loading method but replaced the flintlock mechanism with a percussion lock. Like the M1803 and the M1817, the M1841 had no bayonet.[14]

All models of military rifles saw service in Mexico. The loading sequence for rifles differed from that for the musket. The major difference was that a leather bullet pouch and a powder flask were used instead of paper cartridges. In August 1846, the War Department published General Order No. 38, outlining the eight-step loading procedure for percussion-lock rifles: (1) LOAD, (2) Charge-WITH POWDER, (3) PATCH AND BALL, (4) Draw-RAMMER, (5) RAM, (6) Return-RAMMER, (7) PRIME, and (8) Shoulder-ARMS. But cartridge boxes with pre-rolled ammunition had begun to replace the rifleman's pouch and flask, a change that led to a variation on the loading procedure: (1) LOAD, (2) Handle-CARTRIDGE (3) Tear-CARTRIDGE, (4) Charge-CARTRIDGE , (5) Draw-RAMMER, (6) RAM, (7) Return-RAMMER, and (8) Shoulder-ARMS. In the second method, the percussion cap was placed on the cone at the command READY. The Model 1841 is the best-known military rifle used in the Mexican War, as several regiments were armed entirely with the weapon. Although carried by the Regiment of U.S. Mounted Rifles and by the Regiment of Voltigeurs and Foot Riflemen, it was at the Battle of Buena Vista that the rifle gained fame in the hands of the 1st Mississippi Rifles and became known forever after as the "Mississippi Rifle."[15]

Muskets and rifles, with their long barrels, were difficult for mounted troops to use. In response to this problem, the War Department, through its arsenals, had developed the Model 1833 Hall Carbine. Shorter than the rifle that bore the same name, it employed a percussion rather than a flintlock firing mechanism. Other models followed in 1840, 1842, and 1843, utilizing several different calibers, from .52 to .69. All originally were smoothbore, although some barrels were cut with rifling at a later date. The Hall carbine had several unusual features worth noting. The first was a triangular spike, fitted beneath the barrel, that slid forward to form a bayonet. The second was a removable receiver, or firing mechanism, that some dragoons, when off duty, carried as a single-shot pocket pistol. Late in the war, the army added a new weapon for use by mounted troops, the Model 1847 Cavalry Musketoon. The .69-caliber percussion weapon was essentially a shortened percussion musket. One adaptation made for mounted service was a swivel that permanently attached the ramrod to the barrel, preventing the trooper from losing it. The cavalry musketoon had no bayonet.[16]

Two other patterns of musketoon were introduced in 1847, in time for use in the war. These were the Model 1847 Artillery Musketoon and the Model 1847 Miner and Sapper Musketoon. The new Cavalry, Artillery, and Miner and Sapper models were improved versions of the Model 1839 Musketoon. The Artillery model was fitted with a socket bayonet. The Miner and Sapper model had a heavy Roman-style sword-bayonet. Like the Cavalry model, both the Artillery and the Miner and Sapper models were .69-caliber percussion weapons.[17]

Mounted troops also carried pistols. The first in a series of military pistols was the Model 1806, a .54-caliber flintlock pistol. One year later, a newer model appeared, with a bore increased to .69 caliber. Arsenals produced two more models of .69-caliber flintlock pistols, the M1811 and the M1813, before returning to the smaller .54-caliber in 1819. Two additional .54-caliber flintlock pistols were issued, the M1826 and the M1836,

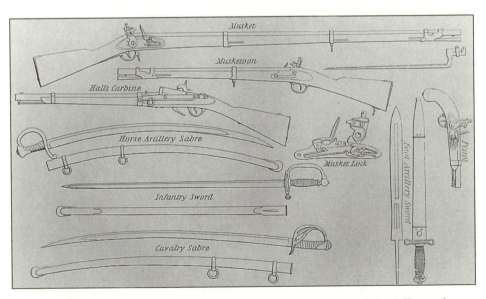

Small Arms. War Department, Ordnance Manual for the Use of the Officers of the United States Army, 1841, *Washington, D.C.: J. and G.S. Gideon, 1841.Courtesy New York State Library*

before the army finally abandoned the flintlock mechanism. The Model 1842 and Model 1843 pistols kept the .54-caliber bore but utilized the percussion lock mechanism. These pistols, sometimes referred to as horse pistols, were carried in leather holsters that mounted on either side of the pommel of the saddle. It was not until after the Mexican War that troopers officially began to carry their pistols in a holster on their sword belts.[18]

Multi-shot revolving arms made their first major appearance in the hands of soldiers during the Mexican War. Samuel Colt had found a ready market for his revolvers, rifles, and carbines in Texas, and the weapons had gained fame in the hands of Texas Rangers such as John C. Hays. Colt's first pistols were .36-caliber five-shot percussion revolvers. The 1836 model had no attached loading lever, which made it difficult to reload. Colt's company later issued an improved version with an attached loading lever, a feature that became standard on almost all subsequent models. In 1838, during the Seminole War, Colt convinced the War Department to issue one hundred .52-caliber six-shot revolving rifles to the 2nd U.S. Dragoons for trial. Although the weapon received favorable reviews, the army remained wedded to the single-shot carbine long after the Mexican War. Shortly after the war began, Samuel H. Walker, a former Texas Ranger who was newly commissioned captain of the U.S. Mounted Rifles, helped Colt obtain a contract with the government for several thousand of the newly designed revolver. Called the Walker Colt after the Texan, the pistol was a .44-caliber six-shot revolver intended for use by mounted troops. Colt's agents followed the army into Mexico and offered his wares for sale to individual soldiers and civilians, claiming that the arms had been proven by "Texians" in fifty battles. In an early form of gun control, however, soldiers were required first to obtain the permission of their commanders, and civilians the permission of the military governor, before purchasing the arms in Mexico. The observation of one historian that these weapons "were a surprise and a terror to Mexicans and to Mexican dogs" undoubtedly was true.[19]

Military swords fell into two categories: weapons and symbols of rank and distinction. The dragoons originally had been equipped with an American version of a British light-cavalry saber called the Model 1833 Dragoon Saber. Critics complained that the piece, nearly 36 inches in overall length with a slightly curved blade, was too lightweight. Responding to the complaints, the army adopted a different sword, the Model 1840. Based on a French cavalry sword, the M1840 was longer than its predecessor by nearly five inches. All the cavalry swords were "edged weapons" in the true sense of those words and were designed to wound or kill. The artillery had two patterns of swords: one for the foot artillery and another for mounted artillery. The Model 1833 Foot Artillery Sword was a straight-bladed sword, 26 inches in overall length in the scabbard. Although patterned after a French model, it resembled a Roman short sword, with a short, straight, wide, double-edged blade. The Model 1840 Light Artillery Saber, designed for use by mounted artillerymen, was 38.6 inches in overall length including the scabbard and had a blade with a pronounced curve. Private companies produced the dragoon and light artillery sabers in officer-grade models.[20]

Other military swords were used primarily as symbols of rank or distinction. Officers usually purchased their own swords, selecting one based upon a pattern prescribed by the War Department. For years the most popular style of sword for officers had been the "eagle-head" sword, named after the decorative eagle head that adorned its pommel. These were lightweight swords, with straight blades for infantry and curved blades for artillery and dragoons. In 1840, the War Department authorized a new line of swords denoting rank and distinction. These included the M1840 Foot Officer's Sword, the M1840 Noncommissioned Officer's Sword, and the M1840 Musician's Sword. These were similar in design, all having a straight blade. Several other swords appeared as part of the 1840 specifications: the Model 1840 U.S. Engineer's Sword, the Model 1840 Medical Staff Sword, and the Model 1840 Pay Department Sword. Lightweight rapier-style swords, these last three models were not intended as combat weapons. The U.S. Topographic Engineers had received their sword, patterned after the 1833 Dragoon Saber, a year earlier. General and staff officers were authorized to wear the Model 1832 General and Staff Officer's Sword. The delicate eagle-head sword was still a favorite with the militia. Volunteers were guided by their own tastes in the matter of swords, relying on both private purchase and government issue. At least one volunteer officer thought that buying a sword an unnecessary expense but did so anyway, under pressure from his colonel. "Bought a sword from Capt. Robinson and am inclined to think myself a fool for doing it," wrote Capt. James L. Kemper. "A private's sword out of the Ordnance Depart. would answer, but [Col. John F.] Hamtramck advised me to get this and away my money went." Evidence suggests that infantry officers—both regular and volunteer—sometimes carried dragoon sabers instead of the lighter foot officer's sword because they preferred the sturdier weapon.[21]

Accouterments were the soldiers' accessories. They included all the leather belts, boxes, and slings worn by soldiers, as well as saddles, bridles, and harnesses. The standard set of accouterments issued each infantryman consisted of a black leather cartridge box designed to hold thirty-two .69-

caliber cartridges, suspended on a 2.25-inch-wide white shoulder belt; and a 1.5-inch-wide white buff waist belt held together with a small oval-shaped brass belt plate stamped with the letters *US*. Another *US* plate was fastened onto the cover of the cartridge box. Regulations also called for a 2.3-inch-wide white buff shoulder belt, on which hung a black leather bayonet scabbard. Troops armed with flintlock muskets also received a small brass chain on which were attached a needlelike iron pick for clearing the touch hole of obstructions and a horsehair whisk for brushing the powder residue from the lock. Troops armed with percussion muskets wore a cap box on the waist belt as a receptacle for percussion caps. The cartridge box belt was slung over the left shoulder, and the bayonet belt was slung over the right shoulder. These two belts were referred to as "cross belts" because they crossed one another. By the time of the Mexican War, however, the bayonet belt had been abolished in most regular regiments and the bayonet scabbard moved to the waist belt. A circular brass plate embossed with an eagle fastened the bayonet belt together. After the abolition of the bayonet belt, a similar plate was placed on the cartridge box belt as an ornament. A bayonet belt made with a double rather than a single frog carried the Model 1840 Noncommissioned Officer's and Musician's swords.[22]

The main dragoon accouterment was a 2-inch-wide white leather saber belt, fastened by a oval brass buckle stamped with the letters *US*. Attached to the belt were two straps that hooked to the iron scabbard and another longer strap that passed over the right shoulder to help support the weight of the saber. A brass wire hook on the left side of the belt allowed a dismounted trooper to wear the saber in a raised position. A black leather carbine cartridge box, pistol cartridge box, and cap box were worn on the belt. The first two boxes had small oval brass plates stamped *US* affixed to their covers. Two safety devices prevented the trooper from losing his weapons while mounted. The first was a white leather sword knot connected to the hilt of the saber that could be wrapped around the trooper's wrist. The second was the carbine sling, a 2.5-inch-wide white buff leather strap, slung over the trooper's left shoulder and snapped to a ring on his carbine. Pistols were stored in saddle holsters located on either side of the pommel.[23]

Each branch of artillery had its own accouterments. Artillerymen serving as infantry received standard infantry accouterments. Mounted artillerymen were issued a 1.7-inch-wide white buff leather saber belt for use with the Model 1840 Light Artillery Saber. This one lacked the shoulder strap of the dragoon saber belt and closed with a circular, two-piece brass buckle bearing the letters *US*. The white leather saber knot was also issued to mounted artillerymen. Foot artillerymen wore the heavy Model 1833 Foot Artillery Sword. The weight of the piece required a more sturdy belt. Made in three sections, the 1.7-inch-wide belt had a frog suspended from the left side, from which the sword hung. The foot artillery belt used the same buckle as the belt for light artillery.[24]

Riflemen received accouterments that differed from those issued to infantrymen. A single 1.4-inch-wide white buff leather shoulder belt held the rifleman's two main accessories: a black leather ball pouch and a brass powder flask. Soldiers using the Hall's rifle also wore a 1.7-inch-wide white buff leather shoulder belt which carried the bayonet. Evidence indicates that troops issued the Model 1841 Rifle received the carbine cartridge box instead of the pouch and flask. The riflemen used the same waist belt as the infantry before the addition of the cartridge box, but the added weight of this heavy accouterment necessitated the issue of a wider, sturdier belt.[25]

The U.S. Congress specified the uniform worn by the regular army. The dress uniform for both officers and enlisted men was a dark blue wool tailcoat worn with sky-blue wool trousers. A woolen fatigue jacket (sky blue for infantry and artillery but dark blue for dragoons) also was worn with the wool trousers. The fatigue uniform was the soldier's basic service clothing, although lithographers of the period commonly depicted American soldiers charging lines of Mexicans attired as if dressed for parade. The summer uniform, which consisted of a white cotton fatigue jacket and white cotton trousers, was worn from May 1 until September 30. The white cotton trousers and the dress coat were worn together during the summer. Insp. Gen. George Croghan, on his tour of western forts made just prior to the war, observed that some commanders deviated from the prescribed dress and allowed their men to wear the woolen fatigue jacket with the white cotton trousers. Croghan thought white trousers should not be issued to mounted troops because, in addition to wearing out quickly, the "rubbing of the horses against each other, so stained [them] as to become offensive to the sight."[26]

A soldier who served out an entire enlistment was entitled to the following items, issued at specific intervals throughout his five years:

> 1 greatcoat
> 3 dress coats
> 2 fatigue frocks (a style of coat, for dragoons only)
> 4 wool fatigue jackets
> 4 cotton jackets
> 10 pairs of wool trousers

12 pairs of cotton overalls
10 cotton shirts
10 flannel shirts
20 pairs of boots
20 pairs of stockings
8 pairs of drawers
2 dress hats, or schakos
1 forage cap and letter
3 pairs of epaulettes
3 pairs shoulder straps
1 aiguillette
2 leather stocks
3 blankets

The government encouraged soldiers to care for their uniforms, telling them that, at the end of a man's enlistment, they could receive in cash the value of any item not drawn. Conversely, the government fined soldiers who needlessly lost or destroyed items through their own fault and had to be issued extra shirts, pants, caps, etc., withholding the money from their pay. Knapsacks, canteens, haversacks, and sergeant's sashes were provided by the government and were expected to last a soldier the full enlistment. Colonel Croghan, however, observed that, while the regulation issue might do for troops stationed in eastern garrisons, it was insufficient for troops in the West, who wore out clothing and equipment at a much faster rate. In one instance, General Taylor recognized the unfair burden placed upon soldiers and ordered extra trousers, shoes, and socks issued to troops who had theirs ruined by constant exposure to salt water while unloading transports at Point Isabel.[27]

Color and style signified branch of service in the army and helped to signal rank. Infantry uniforms were trimmed in white wool lace and fastened with pewter buttons. Dragoon uniforms were trimmed in yellow wool lace; artillery uniforms were trimmed in red wool lace. Both dragoons and artillery wore brass buttons on their coats and jackets. The trim on officers' uniforms varied with their branch: silver metal lace and bullion for infantry officers; gold for all others. Sashes were color-coded as well. First sergeants of all branches wore red wool sashes around their waists. Company, field, and staff officers wore sashes of red silk; general officers wore buff-colored silk sashes. Musicians were authorized to wear red dress coats instead of the dark blue dress coats worn by the rest of the army. The design of buttons also aided in unit identification, with each branch and department having its own. Infantry buttons, for example, bore an eagle clutching a shield with the letter I stamped in the center of the shield. The letter A on the shield signified artillery, and the letter D dragoons. Officers and sergeants also had 1-½-inch-wide stripes, each bearing the color of his respective branch or department, sewn down the outside seam of his trousers. At one time it was intended that officers and men would wear colored bands around their forage caps, but this plan never was fully implemented. The distinctive colors and designs helped foster esprit de corps within the various branches.[28]

Several regular units had their own distinctive uniforms. Maj. Samuel Ringgold's company of light artillery at one time was authorized to wear dark blue jackets trimmed in red wool lace, with sky blue trousers and knee-high boots. The Regiment of U.S. Mounted Rifles wore dragoon-style jackets with eagle buttons marked *R* in the center of the shield, and dark blue wool trousers. Company A, U.S. Engineers, wore dark blue jackets with collars trimmed in Prussian yellow lace, along with sky blue trousers with a black welt down the outer seam. Congress authorized a unique uniform for the Regiment U.S. Voltigeurs and Foot Riflemen: dark gray jackets and trousers with eagle buttons marked with the letter *V* in the center of the shield. It is unclear, however, if the regiment ever received this uniform while in Mexico.[29]

Officers traditionally bore the cost of their own uniforms, without aid from the government. All large cities had tailors who specialized in making military garments. An officer, therefore, visited his tailor, who took his measurements and made the required items. The tailor kept the measurements on record, in case the officer needed his services again but was unable to visit the shop in person. We get a glimpse of such a transaction in a letter from Lt. Simon B. Buckner to his tailor, written shortly after the war. Young Buckner, returning from Mexico, placed an order for an infantry dress coat, a pair of epaulettes, and a chapeau trimmed for an infantry officer on detached duty. He asked the tailor to make the coat from the best material he had and to forward the items to his new post as soon as they were ready. An officer such as Buckner often required several trunks just to hold his kit, which was comprised of a cloak, dress coat with epaulettes, dress trousers, schako with feathered plume, silk neck stock, gloves, frock coat with shoulder straps, vests, shirts, drawers, sword, sword belt, sash, and shoes. The regulations advised officers how and when to wear their uniforms. For fatigue duty, officers were permitted to wear jackets in place of the frock coat. Officers sometimes had trouble paying the bills they accrued in outfitting themselves. Napoleon Jackson Tecumseh Dana, a lieutenant in the 7th U.S. Infantry, unexpectedly encountered his tailor, who had come to the army camp at Corpus Christi. Upon learning of the man's arrival, the chagrined officer sought him out to confess his poverty, promising to pay his debt of a hundred dollars as soon as possible. "He appeared satisfied, was very polite, and said that he had not come out here to press me, and dropped the subject." Pleased that matter was over, the relieved officer told his wife, "I had no idea a tailor had so much delicacy."[30]

Many soldiers used campaigning as an excuse to escape the confines of the prescribed uniform. This seemed especially true of those serving under General Taylor, who was notoriously lax in enforcing the dress regulations. According to Lieutenant Dana, it would have been easy to mistake the officers and men of the Army of Occupation as "militia ragamuffins" because of the odd assortment of clothing they wore. Wrote Dana to his wife: "We wear all kinds of uniforms here, each one to his taste, some shirtsleeves, some white, some purple, some fancy jackets and all colors of cottonelle pants, some straw and some Quaker hats, and that is just the way, too, that our fellows went into battle." Dana's own wardrobe at the time included a checked coat, a dark purple woolen shirt, an old hickory shirt, a blue shirt, blue checked pants, and a straw hat. He particularly liked the purple shirt because it could be worn for two or three weeks at a time before it began to show dirt. Dana told his wife that, decked out as he was on the march to Camargo in his straw hat, blue checked pants, and checked coat (now turned white through many washings), he was in little danger of being shot by a Mexican for being an American officer, because, as he told her, his "trimmings don't show much." Knowing Old Rough and Ready's penchant for undress uniforms, it is easy to accept Dana's description of the army along the Rio Grande as true. Corroborating evidence of lax enforcement of dress regulations comes from another regular with Old Rough and Ready. "The older men dropped their coats soon," recalled an enlisted man of the 7th U.S. Infantry; as the temperature increased, "they abandoned their coats altogether and wore flannel or hickory shirts." Regular officers who had seen service in Florida thought the regulation uniform impractical. One claimed that the profession was ill-served by "dressing up men within an inch of their lives, until they looked more like a flock of eastern flamingos, or Florida wood-peckers, than the descendants of the race of men who fought and bled to establish civil liberty and republican simplicity in our country."[31]

Not all commanders allowed flagrant deviation from the uniform regulations. Winfield Scott's reputation as "Old Fuss and Feathers" convinced Lieutenant Dana to forsake his bohemian look. Dana commented, "As we

are going to join General Scott we will expect to have to pay more attention to the regulations of dress, hair, whiskers, and so forth." Some volunteers had a particularly difficult time conforming to the edicts concerning
proper dress. General Wool caused a "big holler" among the volunteers of
his command bound for Chihuahua, when he ordered all officers to keep
their coats buttoned and their ties on, especially when on guard duty. Lt.
Adolphus Engelman, an officer in the 2nd Illinois Infantry, who recorded
the incident, actually agreed with the general, although he still displayed
the attitude of a volunteer in saying that Wool issued too many orders. Lt.
Albert G. Brackett, 4th Indiana Infantry, said that he wore the prescribed
uniform while on duty near Mier, but when in camp he threw "Uncle
Sam's blue uniform frock-coat, and my handsome forage cap, in the corner
of my tent, and enjoyed the luxury of a very course pair of tow pantaloons,
a red calico shirt, and a very high-crowned Mexican hat."[32]

Deviation from the uniform standards in central Mexico evidently became enough of a problem to cause Scott's inspector general, Ethan Allen
Hitchcock, to issue an order calling it to the army's attention. He wrote, "I
have the honor to report that the Army dress appears to be continually
diverging from the prescribed pattern." One source of the problem, he
acknowledged, was the breakdown in supply caused by the long distance
from suppliers in the United States. Even so, he said, "this affords no excuse for officers, not entitled to them, wearing gold or silver lace on their
pantaloons, and there is no reason why the prescribed shoulder insignia of
rank should be departed from." According to Hitchcock, the "evil" practice had been adopted by noncommissioned officers, hospital stewards,
wagonmasters, and even teamsters, making it nearly impossible in some
cases to tell the real officers from the offenders. General Order 367 admonished the army to adhere to the regulations. It thus appears that altering or
embellishing the uniform was a practice common throughout Mexico.[33]

Long hair and beards, although a natural product of campaigning,
were frowned upon by commanders. The regulations were specific on these
matters: "The hair is to be short, or what is generally termed cropped; the
whiskers not to extend below the lower tip of the ear, and in a line thence
with the curve of the mouth; moustaches will not be worn, (except by
cavalry regiments,) by officers or men on any pretense whatever." Evidence
indicates, however, the soldiers skirted these rules whenever possible. Shortly
after the battles of Palo Alto and Resaca del Palma, Pvt. Barna Upton of
the 3rd U.S. Infantry informed his sister that he had "fine, black, savages
mustaches." Dana reported at one time that he had not shaved in seven
weeks and that another officer he knew had grown a red beard. When he

finally rid himself of the growth, he told his wife that his "clean, smooth face feels mighty funny." The celebrated and flamboyant hero of the 2nd U.S. Dragoons, Capt. Charles May, sported shoulder-length locks, mustache, and goatee; his fame appears to have rendered him scissors-proof. If the depiction of dragoons by Samuel Chamberlain was accurate, other dragoon officers, as well as enlisted men, skirted the regulations concerning facial hair. Capt. John William Lowe, an Ohio volunteer, reported that in Mexico City he saw his childhood friend, Ulysses S. Grant, with "a beard reaching half way down his waist." If true, this may indicate that beards were more prevalent in Scott's column than thought. Volunteers, who resented most orders anyway, came close to revolting when Lt. Col. Thomas Childs, the military governor of Puebla, demanded that they cut their hair according to regulations. Childs had stated in his order, "The troops are in garrison and have ample time to attend to their personal cleanliness." J. Jacob Oswandel, a Pennsylvania volunteer who heard the order read, said that volunteers "will not suffer or allow their hair to be cut short, and look like a jail bird." He further complained, "It is true we are soldiers, [but] we don't care about being treated like slaves or prisoners." As it developed, the haircut order came to naught because Childs and his small garrison were about to be besieged by a superior Mexican force, making hair length seem a trivial matter. One Missouri volunteer who made the journey to Chihuahua and back claimed that he neither shaved nor cut his hair until he was mustered out at New Orleans. The War Department republished the rules governing grooming when the army returned to the United States, saying that "the non-observance of the above regulations (tolerated during the war with Mexico) is no longer permitted. It is enjoined upon all officers to observe and enforce the regulations."[34]

The Quartermaster Department did not have enough uniforms to clothe the volunteers at the start of the war, as its warehouses held only the scant supplies needed to supply the small peacetime army. To meet the emergency, Congress authorized a clothing allowance for volunteers in lieu of uniforms at a rate of $3.50 per month. Upon being mustered into the service of the United States, the army advanced volunteers $21 (sometimes the full $42) to ensure they had money to purchase clothing before their regiments left for Mexico. Merchants, who for months had been anticipating war, had stocked coats, trousers, hats, boots, shoes, bridles, and saddles, hoping for brisk sales to soldiers bound for the "Halls of the Montezumas."[35]

Uniform styles often reflected the individual tastes of the volunteers themselves. Some regiments wore clothing resembling a military uniform, patterned after their state's militia or the federal army. The 1st Battalion of

Baltimore and District of Columbia Volunteers adopted the uniform worn by regulars. The uniform provided by the state to the 1st Virginia Infantry consisted of a navy blue cloth cap, navy blue cloth jacket and pantaloons, bootees, flannel shirt, light blue overcoat, and a leather stock. The 1st Massachusetts Infantry wore gray jackets and trousers. The men of the 1st and 2nd Pennsylvania Infantry Regiments wore dark blue jackets and trousers. The colonel of the 1st North Carolina Infantry contracted for a uniform that consisted in part of a dark blue jacket trimmed in white, sky blue trousers, a red flannel shirt, and a blue forage cap with an oilcloth cover. Some companies had their own distinctive uniforms. According to Samuel Chamberlain, each member of Company A of the 2nd Illinois Infantry had "jackets and pants of blue mixed Kentucky jeans with yellow stripes across the breast like a Dragoon Bugler." For himself, however, he commissioned the tailor to make a uniform of dark blue cloth with yellow sergeant chevrons. Chamberlain's action demonstrates how individual variation crept in, even when a design had been decided upon. One critic of this policy offered a suggestion to units looking to obtain their uniforms: "This should be entrusted to a few, all the uniforms and equipments should be purchased at one and the same time, and then they may be alike; but when each member supplies himself, much diversity exists, in the quality and appearance . . . and some it is to be feared will not be uniformed at all." A dress parade held by volunteer regiments must have presented a varied and colorful spectacle.[36]

Lt. George B. McClellan compared one group of volunteers he encountered on the march to Tampico to "Falstaff's company." According to this future Union commander, "Most of them were without coats; some without any pants [other] than the parts of pants they wore; all had torn and dirty shirts—uncombed heads—unwashed faces—they were dirt and filth from top to toe." The assessment, however, was rather harsh on his part and shows a young West Pointer's disdain for volunteers. The men he saw had been in constant service for six months, with little chance to replace the clothing they had worn to Mexico. The wear and tear on shoes, trousers, and jackets from hard campaigning left men looking more like ragamuffins than the polished soldiers people at home were used to seeing march down their streets on patriotic holidays. Some soldiers, at least, kept a sense of humor about the deteriorating condition of their clothing. One South Carolina volunteer wrote that his shoes were "like unto Sin[n]ers, [because] their Soles are in sad condition." Several days later, when the shoes finally gave up the ghost, he mixed pragmatism with his humor: "Poor old shoes! I lay you off with many regrets—not that you have untruly failed, but that I may get another pair broke for Service." A more serious plight faced Capt. William P. Rogers, 1st Mississippi Rifles, when he lost his shoes during the fighting at Monterey, exposing his feet to painful cactus thorns. When the shoes of the 1st Baltimore and District of Columbia Volunteers gave out in the weeks following the fighting at Monterey, the battalion donned Mexican sandals. Said one of their officers, "There are a good many without jackets, yet they look soldier-like and trim with their cross- and waist-belts." A member of the 1st Pennsylvania Infantry described his regiment's appearance at a dress parade after only a few months of service: "Some with straw hats, some with caps, and others with Mexican hats; some with one boot or shoe on, and others with no hats, boots or shoes; some had on Mexican coats, and some had hardly anything on except shirt and pants."[37]

Replacing old uniforms was a difficult task for volunteers serving in Mexico. A letter from Mexico written by George T. M. Davis, an officer in the 1st Illinois Infantry, warned potential volunteers of certain indispensable items they needed to bring with them, as clothing in Mexico could be obtained only at exorbitant rates, if at all. He suggested men new to the service should provide themselves with "two red flannel shirts, three hickory, or checked linen shirts, one pair of boots [of the] best quality, and two or three pairs of woolen socks." Davis also recommended a "good substantial forage cap" as headgear. To prove his point concerning inflated prices, he listed examples of what dry goods were selling for in Mexico: coarse flannel shirts, $3 each; coarse satinet pantaloons, $6 to $8 a pair; coarse boots, $5 to $6 a pair; and hickory shirts, $1 to $1.50 each. On a private's pay of $7 a month, these prices were high indeed. A Mississippi volunteer provided much the same information, confirming Davis's contention that prices were high and quality goods hard to find. "I was compelled to pay $7 for pants that would have cost $2 at home—$3 for ticking shirts—$3.50 for the commonest shoes." The writer admitted that not all shortages were caused by wear but that some were the fault of men who threw articles away while marching to lighten their loads as well as theft by other soldiers.[38]

One article of clothing, the red overshirt, seemed to be ubiquitous. Lieutenant Davis recommended them to volunteers, but these garments already were standard frontier wear. George W. Kendall, the New Orleans newspaperman, had worn one on the ill-fated Santa Fe Expedition of 1841. Francis Parkman, the historian, had worn such a shirt while on the journey described in his famous work, *The Oregon Trail*. Red overshirts appeared throughout Mexico. One volunteer officer, Capt. Franklin Smith, observed Capt. Seth Thornton's company of the 2nd U.S. Dragoons attired in "red flannel shirts" near Camargo and thought they presented "a very warlike appearance." Smith's cousin, a member of Capt. William R. Shivor's Company of Independent Volunteers, had visited him earlier, dressed in a similar red flannel shirt. One veteran recalled seeing "Texans with broad hats and red shirts" driving wagons along the Rio Grande. Red shirts also appear in the paintings of both Robert Walker and Samuel Chamberlain. The most famous red shirts of all were those worn by Col. Jefferson Davis's 1st Mississippi Rifles, whom Taylor and the American press credited with saving the day at the Battle of Buena Vista.[39]

The Quartermaster Department tried several strategies to provide the army with adequate clothing. Capt. James R. Irwin, Scott's chief quartermaster, took the unusual step of contracting with Mexicans to supply uniforms. The patterns were similar, the material coarser, and the cost about 50 percent higher than similar items produced in the United States. But troops isolated in Mexico City needed clothing, and this was Irwin's solution. The practice was discontinued, however, once supply lines were firmly established. By 1848, the warehouse at Vera Cruz reported quite a large stock of uniforms and equipment on hand, receiving in a single shipment 4,800 infantry private wool jackets and overalls, 200 infantry sergeant wool jackets and overalls, 1,000 dragoon private wool jackets and overalls, 50 dragoon sergeant wool jackets and overalls, 960 artillery private wool jackets, 2,000 greatcoats, 6,800 flannel shirts, 6,800 drawers, 2,000 blankets, 13,500 pairs of stockings, 504 infantry forage caps, 1,760 artillery forage caps, 25 infantry sashes, 20 dragoon sashes, 6,800 rubber haversacks, 4,000 knapsacks, 3,304 canteens, and many assorted drums, fifes, guidons (small flags carried by the cavalry and artillery to mark their lines of battle), cooking gear, tools, and tents. A notice in the March 7, 1848, edition of the *North American* informed the army that a large supply of clothing had arrived and asked all regimental quartermasters to present their requisitions to the Clothing Bureau. Thus, clothing shortages seem to have been less severe later in the war.[40]

Resupplying volunteers presented the army with a serious problem throughout the war. So acute was the problem that, shortly after the Battle of Cerro Gordo, the Quartermaster Department handed out a quantity of captured Mexican uniforms for volunteers to wear. Upset with the clothing situation in Mexico City, Private Oswandel stated that, "if it had not been for the clothing we captured from the Mexicans[,] one-half of our army would have to go naked." Hearing complaints about soldiers' suffering from a lack of proper clothing, Congress explored a plan to eliminate the clothing allowance and issue uniforms from quartermaster stocks. But the law which finally authorized this did not go into effect until the war was nearly over and the troops were on their way home. Some volunteer commanders earlier had taken action on their own, taking uniforms stockpiled at clothing depots intended for regulars. As expected, the regulars were outraged that supplies intended for them had been given to volunteers. Some volunteers themselves were incensed at the change in clothing. The idea of giving up their individuality and putting on the uniform of a regular was an affront greater than some citizen-soldiers could bear. According to Lieutenant Brackett, volunteers in northern Mexico strongly objected to exchanging their tattered clothing for regular uniforms. In another incident concerning regular uniforms, several members of the 1st Massachusetts Infantry chose imprisonment at Vera Cruz rather than don the offensive garments. Thus, even something ostensibly as simple as clothing proved a bone of contention between regulars and volunteers. One volunteer, who had worn the same clothing for nearly a year, said in disgust, "Every member of the head of our Government, from the President down, ought to be made a present of a *leather medal* for their faithful performance in providing for the comfort and the welfare of her sons."[41]

The weapons and clothing of the American military in the Mexican War represented the state of industry in antebellum America. The sewing machine had not yet come into wide use, so the government contracted with thousands of seamstresses to hand-sew enough coats, pants, and shirts literally to outfit an army. The clothing shortages that occurred during the war can be blamed largely on a government that historically had failed to plan on supplying its troops during times of war. Left largely on their own in regard to clothing, volunteers fended for themselves until Congress finally recognized their plight. While sometimes poorly clad, American soldiers carried some of the most modern and innovative weapons available into battle. In the future, American industry would come to play an increasingly important role in warfare.

SEVEN

Life in Mr. Polk's Army

There is no place like an army, to develop the peculiar traits of each individual. Selfishness, generosity, and all the best and worst features of the human heart reveal themselves.

—S. Compton Smith, surgeon

If any one had told me only a few months ago, that I could with impunity, sleep upon the ground in the open air, and rise at reveille in the morning, and drill two hours before breakfast, I should certainly have been at a loss to know what kind of materials he thought I was made of.

—Benjamin Franklin Scribner,
2nd Indiana Infantry

Soldiers in Mr. Polk's Army shared many of the same experiences, regardless of their political affinity or military designation. For most regulars and volunteers, the war was a series of grueling marches and inhospitable camps. More than a few soldiers included descriptions of sore feet, bad water, dusty roads, and leaky tents in their diaries and letters home. Americans struggled to occupy their hours off duty and make the time pass faster. Despite the occasional excitement of battle, mundane details of daily living were the stuff of army life.

Transporting men and material to the front was the government's first task in prosecuting the war. Recent technological changes in the nation's transportation system sped troops to war in ways never envisioned before. Steamboats and railroads carried thousands of Americans to war, giving mobilization and deployment a modern look. The War Department, in order to ensure a steady supply of ships for its use, hired private vessels to carry army personnel and supplies. Not content with this arrangement, the Quartermaster Department purchased its own oceangoing ships and riverboats, as well as embarking on a construction project of its own to meet its burgeoning transportation needs. By the end of the war, Thomas Jesup's department had amassed its own fleet of both deep-water and shallow-draft vessels.[1]

New Orleans was the gateway to Mexico for troops from the Ohio and Mississippi valleys. One of the most cosmopolitan centers of the United States, the city awed most visitors. By 1840, its population exceeded one hundred thousand, a size surpassed only by New York, Philadelphia, and Baltimore. The city's days under the rule of the French and the Spanish had given it a strange and exotic flavor. Many street names sounded foreign, and the buildings bore an antique look, unusual in such a young country. Called the Crescent City because it lay sprawled around a great bend in the Mississippi River, New Orleans, even in peacetime, was a busy port.[2]

Regiments came to New Orleans by steamboat to await passage to Mexico. The journey presented new sights for the soldiers, most of whom never had ventured far from home. Some soldiers experienced the thrill of a riverboat race, as captains and pilots vied with their competitors to be first to dock at cities and towns along the route. Some soldiers used the frequent refueling stops to explore the land along the shore. One volunteer, Pvt. J. Jacob Oswandel of the 1st Pennsylvania Infantry, had quite a time on these short side trips. At Allegheny City, Pennsylvania, he and his companions visited several small factories and met working girls who, he claimed, fell in love with them. He warned one such lass that "it was a bad time to fall in love with soldiers now." Local girls evidently were a major interest, as Oswandel reported that, further downriver in Kentucky, several of his friends tried to "make love to some of the 'yellow gals'" who lived on a nearby plantation. The owner, he said, did not mind as long as the men did not take the girls with them when they left. The inhabitants of the banks of the rivers where volunteers passed often lavished hospitality on soldiers destined for war, laying out huge feasts, complete with plenty to drink. The trip downstream was not without its hazards, though. Many diarists recorded the demise of unfortunate souls who perished when they fell overboard into the dark waters below. In most cases, these incidents were thought to be accidents, but more than one homesick young man was suspected of ending his life with a quick plunge, rather than face the unknown hardships that lay ahead or the disgrace of returning home a deserter.[3]

The thrills began to fade away and the realities of military life dawned, once the boats reached New Orleans. The city was home to Jackson Barracks, an army post located east of the city. Regulars passing through New Orleans were lodged in the wood-and-brick buildings there. Lt. Ulysses S. Grant's regiment, the 4th U.S. Infantry, spent several weeks there in the summer of 1845, while on its way to Corpus Christi as part of Taylor's Army of Observation. Volunteers, however, were denied access to these quarters and instead camped on the site of General Jackson's 1815 victory over the British. "Our condition is rendered more insupportable from the fact that the 'Barracks' are so short a distance from us, presenting so much comfort," wrote Pvt. Benjamin Franklin Scribner, a volunteer from Indiana, who added, "We truly envy the regulars." According to one Illinois volunteer who stayed at the campground, the remains of the breastworks still existed to remind everyone of Old Hickory's glorious deeds. A stone's throw from the Mississippi River, the battlefield was on low ground and flooded whenever it rained. In some volunteer regiments who stayed there, the unhealthy location caused more deaths than Mexican bullets. The 2nd Mississippi Rifles, who camped on the boggy site in January 1847, suffered the most. Sent to war in summer clothing, the men were unprepared for a cold snap that hit the Deep South. Rain sent torrents of water into their camp and inundated the site. Scores of sick and dying volunteers had to be taken into the city and placed in private homes and hospitals. Although most regiments that stayed on the battlefield fared better, they resented the fact that regulars had comfortable quarters, while they had only thin tents along the river bank to ward off the heat, cold, rain, sun, and mosquitoes.[4]

Sailing on the open seas proved to be a daunting experience for many of these landsmen. The small size of vessels prevented regiments from traveling together as whole units. The common arrangement was to break the command into detachments of several companies and place each detachment on a separate ship. A field officer accompanied each vessel to supervise the conduct of the companies' officers and enlisted men. Housed between the decks, the troops often slept on hastily constructed bunks. These wooden ships presented a real danger of fire, a danger compounded by the difficulty of feeding such a large number of men. Although an effort sometimes was made to feed everyone at once, usually the commands were divided into messes, with each mess allotted a specific time to use the galley. Capt. John R. Kenly reported that his ship nearly caught fire twice when several Maryland volunteers tried to cook in unauthorized areas. In bad weather, when no fire could be started or kept going, soldiers made do with cold rations of water, pickled pork, and hard crackers. Stormy weather also meant that the soldiers were confined below deck, virtually prisoners in a damp, rolling hell-hole. Seasickness frequently plagued officers and men alike, providing a source of entertainment for those fortunate enough not to be stricken with the malady. One volunteer unaffected by the continuous motion claimed that he could not help laughing at the seasick men aboard his ship, explaining that "such heaving and sitting and hooping and hollowing [*sic*] and groaning and growling you never did hear." Another volunteer, Capt. James L. Kemper, described a similar scene, writing, "A man in no other sickness receives so little sympathy from others. Today one man was vomiting at the elbow of another eating, while a group sat near drinking and playing whist." He observed that "peals of merriment and the hard retching of the sick ran through the cabin at the same moment." Kemper recorded his own bout with the illness, saying, "I was the sickest of suffering mortals . . . for more than three days and nights I ate nothing, and I could not drink water . . . I could only lay with a dry, parched and husky mouth and nauseated stomach." In good weather, the seasick men lined the ships' rails, while in bad they lay trapped in their bunks. In either case, they most certainly wished their ordeal to end quickly. Ships could be dangerous places, as one Mississippi volunteer found out when he fell into a ship's hold and sustained a crippling injury. In another incident, a block fell from a masthead and struck four men of the 5th U.S. Infantry, injuring three and killing one.[5]

Rules designed to promote safety and discipline regulated life aboard ship. Most rules were similar to those issued by General Scott in General Order No. 21, prior to the landing at Vera Cruz:

1. Men will be assigned quarters and not allowed to loiter elsewhere.
2. Arms will be secured, with bayonets in their scabbards.
3. Ammunition will be stored away from fires.
4. A detail, armed with bayonets as sidearms, will stand guard.
5. The men will be divided into details to help stand ship's watch.
6. An officer of the day will be assigned.
7. Sailors serving in the ranks may, if needed, serve as part of the ship's company for an extra ration.

8. Men will stay at their assigned quarters in bad weather.
9. Guards will be placed over fires, and no smoking will be permitted between the decks.
10. Messes will not be allowed to cook out of turn.
11. Water will be issued twice daily at the rate of one gallon per man and two per horse.
12. Officers will enforce upon their men personal cleanliness as much as possible.
13. Privies will be rigged over the sides of the ship's bows.
14. The ship will be fumigated frequently with brimstone.
15. Stalls and horses will be inspected.
16. Care must be taken in loading stores that those needed first can be gotten to easily.

Even aboard ship, soldiers could not escape the edicts of the army.[6]

The experience of sailing could be enjoyable at times. Men raised in the nation's interior marveled at the variety of birds and fish that followed the ships in search of food. An officer of the 2nd Indiana Infantry caught a shark and served it up in a chowder to his men. A group of Tennessee volunteers also sampled a shark they caught, pronouncing it a "first rate" meal. The scenery of the open sea was breathtaking. Capt. Ephraim Kirby Smith—the only officer, he claimed, who was "sailor" enough to take the risk—climbed aloft to escape the confusion and crowding below and had an unobstructed view of the ocean from his perch nearly one hundred feet above the deck. Some ship's officers endeavored to make the journey as pleasant as possible under the circumstances. Pvt. George C. Furber recalled that the captain of his vessel opened his personal library to him and his fellow Tennesseans, distributing "histories, novels, and romances, with a liberal hand." Captain Smith also took advantage of the well-stocked library of his ship's captain.[7]

Men found other diversions, too. Officers of the 3rd Kentucky Infantry used the time aboard ship to play cards and study tactics. Men of the 2nd Indiana Infantry read Shakespeare and listened to a discourse on Napoleon and his marshals, presented by one of their members. Impromptu debating societies sprang up on several ships, an indication of how popular the art of rhetoric was with these men. Furber and his companions were entertained by one of their own, who launched into a mock political speech. The orator jokingly claimed at one point that he had enlisted primarily to gain a military record that would vault him into the state legislature when he returned home. The man must have possessed great skill, as he held a crowd of listeners for an hour and a half while he lampooned current topics of the day. These incidents show that the soldiers could find ways to entertain themselves, under even the most difficult circumstances.[8]

Landfall may have marked the end of one ordeal, but it heralded the beginning of soldiering in earnest. Sandbars and shallow water all along the Gulf Coast prevented deep-draft vessels from coming close to shore to unload their cargoes. Sailors manning lighters ferried men and supplies from ship to dry land. But thousands of troops, as well as tons of material needed to fight a war, were successfully landed using manpower alone. The Quartermaster and Commissary departments established huge depots to house mountains of pork, beef, hard crackers, coats, hats, belts, knapsacks, blankets, and other stores vital to the upkeep of an army in the field.[9]

Feeding thousands of troops presented a great challenge to the government. For each enlisted man, army regulations prescribed a liberal daily ration, consisting of "three-fourths of a pound of pork or bacon, or one and one-fourth pounds of fresh or salt beef; eighteen ounces of bread or flour, or twelve ounces of hard bread, or one-fourth pounds cornmeal." Additionally, every hundred men were to share "four pounds of soap; one and one half pounds of candles; two quarts of salt; and four quarts of vinegar; eight quarts of peas or beans, (or in lieu thereof) ten pounds of rice; six pounds of coffee, and twelve pounds of sugar." Regulations further stipulated that "on campaign, or on board of transport at sea and on the lakes, the ration is one pound of bread." But, as with many things in life, theory and practice failed to come together, as the Quartermaster and Commissary departments could issue only whatever rations were available to them.[10]

Soldiers complained about the poor quality and occasional shortages of their rations. Illinoisan Adolphus Engelman, a volunteer officer with Gen. John E. Wool's column bound for Chihuahua, thought the Commissary Department especially incompetent for not bringing enough coffee to last the march. He also complained that the men were placed on short rations, for a time receiving only meat and flour. Issuing flour to men on the march was a colossal mistake, claimed Engelman, because there was no way to bake it into bread when the column halted for the night. The quality of rations also raised the soldiers' ire. Private Scribner, revolted by the amount of fat on the pork issued by the commissary, quipped that he truly was living off the "fat of the land." He also complained of once finding black bugs in his hard crackers. Col. William B. Campbell actually professed a fondness for hard crackers but expressed his concern that government agents were perpetrating a great fraud upon the people in some of their transactions. He contended that Secretary of War William L. Marcy should have paid more attention to the operation of the Subsistence and Quartermaster departments. Some soldiers seemed to thrive on army rations, as illustrated by 1st Sgt. John B. Duncan, 1st Illinois Infantry, who reported that his weight had increased from 149 pounds at the time of his enlistment to 170 pounds at Saltillo. Although shortages sometimes occurred, in army rations the lack of variety was more a problem for soldiers than supply or quality.[11]

Preferences in diet reveal interesting sectional differences among the Americans. Mississippians at Cerralvo, "tired of hard bread and musty flour," delighted in the issue of corn, as they could make the "'corn-dodgers' they had left at home." Yet Illinois volunteers with Wool's column objected when the quartermaster issued them corn instead of wheat flour. According to one disappointed lieutenant, his men said that they "didn't care about wearing out their feet by marching any more" if the government could not properly supply them. Blaming General Wool for their plight, the Illinois troops brayed like mules when he rode through the camp, indicating that they thought they were being made to eat food usually reserved for livestock. The men raised such a fuss that the quartermaster collected the offending article and issued flour in its place. Hence, whenever possible, volunteers retained the eating habits of their own regions.[12]

Many opportunities existed for soldiers to augment the prescribed army diet with local foodstuffs. Soldiers who were camped along the Gulf took advantage of a bountiful harvest of fish, crabs, and oysters. Members of the 3rd U.S. Infantry at Corpus Christi had their own seine, in which they caught as many as fifty to sixty bushels in one haul. Missouri volunteers used their brief halt at Bent's Fort to "catch bass, perch, catfish, and chubs" from the Arkansas River. Hunting game also proved to be an enjoyable means of supplementing their diets. Inhabitants of towns, villages, and *ranchos* welcomed soldiers who paid cash for their products. "We distribute more money than they ever dreamed of and it goes to the poorer classes for labor, vegetables, chickens, eggs, and so on," exclaimed Lieutenant Peck. Surgeon S. Compton Smith wrote that *rancheros* brought "carne seco [dried meat], and carne fresco [fresh meat], leche de cabra [goat's milk], chile con carne, tamales, frijoles, tortillas, pan de maiz [cornbread]," and other items to his camp near Monterey. According to Sergeant Duncan, the market near Saltillo offered gingerbread, onions, carrots, radishes, and milk. The market at Matamoros, said Captain Kenly, offered similar fare: eggs, red peppers, peaches, melons, and many varieties of vegetables unknown to citizens of the United States. Capt. Robert Anderson, 3rd U.S.

Artillery, listed items available at the Tampico market: cakes, chocolate, pots, hats, blankets, peppers and beans of many varieties, eggs, a vegetable that looked like eggplant but wasn't, poultry, sugar cane, fish, turtles, rice, dried corn, salt, soap, raisins, garlic, cabbage, mint, parsley, cigaritos [small cigarettes], lard, both sweet and Irish potatoes, tomatoes, radishes, green peas, and jerked beef. The inhabitants of New Mexico found willing customers in hungry volunteers. Mexican markets became so much a part of military life that American-run newspapers such as the *American Star* and *North American* regularly published prices of commodities.[13]

Sutlers who followed their regiments to Mexico also provided soldiers with a change of fare. These military merchants charged high prices, and soldiers sometimes ran up high bills without realizing it until it was too late. At Corpus Christi, Lt. Napoleon Tecumseh Jackson Dana wrote to his wife, "I ordered some potatoes and onions [from the sutler of the 7th

A camp kitchen. John Frost, Pictorial History of the Mexican War, *Philadelphia: C. Desilver, 1848. Courtesy Mary Couts Burnett Library, Texas Christian University*

U.S. Infantry] for our mess, but when I heard that the potatoes were five dollars a barrel and the onions were six dollar a barrel I very soon countermanded the order." Lieutenant McClellan preferred to buy rations straight from the Commissary Department, saying, "You can get things from them at one-half the price you pay sutlers." One Missouri volunteer at Santa Fe recalled that his company had to settle their tabs before leaving town. "We had a peep at our accounts and I found mine to be $30.75." Some men found that, after settling up with their sutler, they had no money left at all.[14]

Prepared meals were available to soldiers who did not want to cook. Matamoros boasted of several eating establishments, including the Tremont House, the Washington House, and the American Hotel. Near the market in Matamoros, Kenly purchased a meal of rabbit, eggs, kidney, and coffee. In a café in Tampico, Anderson breakfasted on fried fish, venison, steak, eggs, buckwheat cakes, fried bananas, and coffee, enjoying his meal so much that he returned to the same establishment for a dinner of soup, baked fish, broiled and roasted duck, lettuce salad, and potatoes (Irish and sweet)—all washed down with champagne. During the Battle of Monterey, the members of Jefferson Davis's 1st Mississippi Rifles found a Mexican landlady willing to provide them with a warm meal of beef and tortillas, even as the fighting raged. After traveling over the prairies for nearly four months, a group of Missouri volunteers feasted at the tables of the American Hotel in Santa Fe. "All were hungry, and it was amusing to see how we tried to eat our landlord out of house and home." Not all were satisfied by their experiences in Mexican eating establishments. One German private who entered Vera Cruz shortly after its fall and found a restaurant open for business wrote, "The portions were small and expensive, and I can hardly say I found them tasty." His later encounter with a bowl of spicy chile did little to change his opinion of Mexico's fare.[15]

Mexico City abounded with eating establishments. Frederic Guilleminot's Progeso Hotel featured "Breakfast, Dinners, and Suppers in the American and Parisian fashion, at moderate rates." The Eagle Coffee House, a "Hotel on the American style," had two billiards tables in addition to serving fine food. Another restaurant, Henry Panoli's Garden, catered to both the "public and the military gentlemen of the U.S. Army" and served "Beefsteaks, Mutton Chops, good Liquor, Coffee, Tea, &c." Mrs. Sarah Foyle, a woman who, the *American Star* claimed, had followed the army throughout Mexico, opened the Theatre Coffee House and Restaurant, where "her rosy, smiling face may be seen every night, looking more like home than anything else since we left it." These soon were joined by the

Selected Pay Scale for the Army

Rank	Pay per month	Rations per day	Servants allowed
General Officers			
Major General	$200.00	15	7
Brigadier General	104.00	12	3
Dragoons, Topographic Engineers, Engineers, and Ordnance			
Colonel	90.00	6	2
Lieutenant Colonel	75.00	5	2
Major	60.00	4	2
Captains	50.00	4	1
1st and 2nd Lieutenant	33.33 1/3	4	1
Addition pay for Adjutant	10.00	-	-
Sergeant Major	17.00	-	-
1st Sergeant	16.00	-	-
Sergeant	13.00	-	-
Corporal	10.00	-	-
Bugler	9.00	-	-
Private	8.00	-	-
Artillery and Infantry			
Colonel	75.00	6	2
Lieutenant Colonel	60.00	5	2
Major	50.00	4	2
Captain	40.00	4	1
1st Lieutenant	30.00	4	1
2nd Lieutenant	25.00	4	1
Addition pay for Adjutant	10.00	-	-
Sergeant Major	17.00	-	-
1st Sergeant	16.00	-	-
Sergeant	13.00	-	-
Corporal	9.00	-	-
Private	7.00	-	-
Principal Musician	17.00	-	-
Musician	8.00	-	-
Medical Staff			
Surgeon (after ten years)	60.00	8	2
Assistant Surgeon (after ten years)	50.00	8	1
Hospital Steward	16.00	-	-
Hospital Matron	6.00	-	-

Source: War Department, *General Regulations for the Army of the United States, 1841* (Washington, D.C.: J. and G. E. Gideon, Printers, 1841), 346–47.

Lone Star House, the United States Hotel, the Orleans House, the Mansion House, the Olive Branch Coffee House, the Anglo-Saxon House, the Soldier's Home, the Alhambra, the Lafayette House, the St. Louis House, the Washington Hotel, the Bella Union Hotel, and the Albion House.[16]

Mexican vendors frequently came to camp to seek out customers. Most of them provided soldiers with palatable food. One Alabama volunteer, however, later recalled two incidents near Vera Cruz that seemed to reinforce the warning, "Let the buyer beware." Men with a sweet tooth lost their craving for honey after it was learned that the container from which they had been served was an old cowhide bag with hair still on the inside. The demand for "turkey eggs" plummeted when volunteers discovered that the source of these popular items were buzzards' nests at the city's animal graveyard. There is little evidence, though, that Mexican vendors intentionally tried to harm Americans by selling them poisoned or tainted products.[17]

Although they thought it strange at first, most Americans developed a taste for Mexican food. One officer observed, "In all the dishes, meats and

> ## BELLA UNION HOTEL, BALL AND CONCERT.
>
> THE BELLA UNION HOTEL, having been newly fitted up, and undergone a thorough change, in order to make it one of the finest resorts in this city, is now open under the direction of MATTHEW DANIELS, whose long experience in this line of business, warrants him in saying, that regularity and good order will always be maintained.
>
> The Director has spared neither pains nor expense in rendering this establishment worthy of support, and he flatters himself that his exertions to please the public, will meet with commensurate patronage.
>
> Gentlemen will pay for admission to the Ball ONE DOLLAR each; but in every instance, Respectable Ladies will be received gratis—in fact, none others will be admitted.
>
> At 10 o'clock, an excellent COLD SUPPER will be served up in a splendid Saloon, the tickets to which will be ONE DOLLAR each person.
>
> None but the most respectable persons of either sex will be admitted.
>
> A splendid band of music will always be in attendance.
>
> The Saloon will also be open during the day.
> TICKETS for sale at the Bar of the Hotel.

Bella Union Hotel. The North American, *Mexico City, Mar. 22, 1848.*
Courtesy Daughters of the Republic of Texas Library

Mrs. Sarah Foyle. American Star, *Mexico City, Oct. 16, 1847.*
Courtesy Daughters of the Republic of Texas Library

vegetables, a great deal of chili pepper is used, and little or no salt." In central Mexico, at least, he also noted that the Mexicans ate sliced bananas in their soups. Tortillas, the traditional bread of Mexico, became a staple. One Mexican item, hot chocolate, met with universal approval. William P. Rogers, a captain in the 1st Mississippi Rifles, said that Mexicans, unlike cooks in the United States, knew how to make it. Lieutenant Engelman drank hot chocolate in a cantina in Saltillo. Captain Anderson described a visit to a café in Tampico where chocolate was prepared by a Mexican woman who made the concoction in a large tin urn heated over charcoal and served it with a piece of sponge cake on the side—all for sixpence. The drink also was popular in central Mexico. Some food had little appeal to the faint of heart: Surgeon S. Compton Smith dined on a meal of armadillo and found it tasty; but other, more discriminating Americans in his party could not bring themselves to partake of the dish.[18]

It is difficult to believe some of the items that turned up in Mexico. Enterprising New England merchants routinely delivered ice to the Texas and Mexico coasts. In central Mexico, the snow-capped volcanoes provided ice to nearby towns and villages. Thus, soldiers had ice to make refreshing beverages such as lemonade, limeade, and juleps. While detained at Brazos Santiago, Capt. Luther Giddings wrote, "Much to my surprise and satisfaction, I was enabled to procure some ice, sold from a Boston vessel at one dollar a pound." The supply of ice, however, was not unlimited, and shortages led to disputes. Private Scribner related how an officer and an enlisted man of the 2nd Indiana volunteers came to blows after a ship's steward reportedly sold them both the same piece of ice. The piece ultimately went to the officer—which was no surprise to the enlisted men of the regiment. According to South Carolinian William S. Johnson, there was no reason to fight over ice at Vera Cruz while he was there in April 1847: "Plenty of Ice and watermelons landed to day [sic]." Americans reported finding ice cream for sale throughout central Mexico and even in Chihuahua.[19]

Officers had to fend for themselves when it came to food, as they were not entitled to government rations. Each officer received a daily stipend instead of rations, a sum based upon his rank. The practice worked when pay was regular and supplies were plentiful, but there were times when officers went hungry, while their men ate. According to Lieutenant Engelman, this was the situation with General Wool's column. Even though he received 20 cents a day to purchase rations at prices fixed by the commissary (bacon, 15 cents per pound; beef, 17 cents per pound; coffee, 13 cents per pound; sugar, 10 cents per pound; and rice, 10 cents per pound), some of the items could not be had. Capt. Robert Anderson, camped near Vera Cruz, wrote that Irish potatoes were selling for $6 a barrel, sheep for $5 apiece, and pigs for $2.50 each. With prices at such levels, he said, "You may readily suppose that we cannot indulge frequently in such expensive luxuries." For officers, dining sometimes assumed the character of feast or famine.[20]

Communal cooking was common for both officers and enlisted men. According to army regulations, the privates of each squad comprised a mess. One camp kettle and two mess pans were allotted to every six noncommissioned officers, musicians, privates, and authorized washerwomen and servants. Cooking had to be done jointly, in order to make use of the available cookware. Enlisted men, however, were not left on their own, as several regulations governed the preparation of meals. "Bread must not be served warm," and "soup must be boiled for at least 5 hours until vegetables are soft." Officers were supposed to inspect cook fires when meals were being prepared, to ensure that these admonishments were followed and that the cook gear was clean. In the field, though, officers probably did little to oversee what their men ate, a fact that may have contributed to the high number of men suffering from dysentery and diarrhea. Volunteers at Puebla, who had become accustomed to cooking in small groups, resented an order to break up their messes and instead appoint two cooks per company. Wrote one disgruntled Pennsylvanian, "The most of the men swear they won't stand it." As with many other unpopular orders, the volunteers ignored the decree and did as they pleased.[21]

Officers formed their own messes separate from the ranks and, when possible, attempted to maintain an air of gentility, setting their tables with crystal, china, and silver. Although they sometimes cooked for themselves while on campaign, officers tried to take advantage of money allotted to them by the government for servants. As in the case of the ration stipend, the number of servants allowed depended upon one's rank. Officers seeking cooks and waiters usually had to look outside the army; by law, no private soldier could be made to act as a servant unless he and his captain consented. New Orleans proved a fertile hiring ground for officers bound for Mexico. For example, Capt. Julius Raith, 2nd Illinois Infantry, recruited an educated German immigrant as a cook and personal servant when the regiment passed through the Crescent City. Southern officers brought their slaves with them to take care of camp chores. Capt. James L. Kemper spent several weeks scouring Washington, D.C., for a servant before finally finding one who agreed to work for eleven dollars a month. Once in Mexico, officers turned to the local populace for cooks, maids, laundresses, grooms, and servants of all types. At Tampico, however, one officers' mess was fortunate enough to hire "a couple of French cooks." If lucky, an officer might have a servant as attentive to duty as that of Capt. Leander Cox, whose "boy" continued cooking, unfazed by the report of an enemy attack on the camp. Servants were not immune to the hazards of war. Lightning killed one of Lt. Braxton Bragg's Negro servants near Corpus Christi; and David, the black servant of Capt. Samuel H. Walker, died by his master's side at the Battle of Huamantla.[22]

Messes had an importance far beyond providing food; they provided the setting for social interaction. "Our messmates are well chosen," claimed one volunteer. Messmates' names frequently appear in the diaries and letters of Mexican War soldiers. George C. Furber, author of *The Twelve Month Volunteer*, explained this phenomenon by comparing a camp of several regiments to a city where most of the inhabitants would be unknown to one another. "A person will get acquainted with all his own company in two or three weeks," wrote Furber, "but not his own regiment in as many months" and only rarely then. If lucky, a soldier might meet a few men from other regiments, but, as Furber observed and as most Mexican War diaries and letters bear out, "Soldiers get into the habit of staying in their own companies;—not only so, but they have a peculiar attachment to their own tents." While officers sometimes attended dinners hosted by the officers of other units, enlisted men tended to socialize on their own company streets.[23]

Friendship made the rigors of army life bearable. As one Indiana volunteer stated, "To find one here and there, who can sympathize with us in misfortune, and feel interested in our welfare, when we least expect it, is calculated to give us better views of humanity." Enduring hardships to-gether created a tight bond between companions that was difficult to achieve in civilian life. Lt. Andrew Jackson Trussell informed his brother of the relationships he had forged in Mexico, saying what many others like him probably felt: "These is [*sic*] my friends for they have been tried in places where a man can tell whether men is [*sic*] his friends or not." Acquain-tances from home sometimes were encountered unexpectedly in other regiments. Private Scribner noted one such instance when his regiment, the 2nd Indiana Infantry, met the Louisville Legion upon its return from Monterey. "We had many a welcome recognition of friends in the Legion," he wrote, and "allusions [were] made to brighter days." Their respective units, as prewar militia, had attended military encampments together, "little dreaming that such a meeting as this was in store." Parting with friends after months of shared hardships was difficult. "This parting with com-rades in arms is no easy matter, I can assure you," wrote one officer after learning he was being sent back to the United States on recruiting duty. The death of a close friend evoked pain, even in battle-tested veterans. Lamented Lieutenant Peck upon learning of the death of a fellow officer, "He was ever a warm friend of mine and I feel his death keenly." Another officer, returning to his quarters after the death of a friend, sadly wrote, "I feel very lonely tonight, I assure you, with my roommate and companion dead, and I sit here alone."[24]

Soldiers passed judgment on the character of their companions. Samuel E. Chamberlain, a colorful "rogue" in the 2nd U.S. Dragoons, penned this description of the varieties of men in the regular army:

> Soldiers of the army may be divided into three classes: FIRST, the DEAD BEATS, men who never can be trusted; they are dirty or on the sick report most of the time. This class is hated by their comrades, and despised by the officers. SECOND, the OLD SOLDIERS, men who do their duty in a quiet mechanical sort of way, always in hand in camp, never in the guard house, never known to get drunk or spend their money, often made corporals but rarely sergeants. They are disliked by the men, who suspect them of being tale bearers to the officers. THIRD, the "DARE DEVILS." These men are the first in a fight, frolic or to volunteer for duty, with uniforms fitting like a glove and faultlessly clean, arms, horses and accoutrements always in inspection condition, faithful in the discharge of every duty, but when off [duty] no camp can hold them. They often turn up in the guard house, but never in the hospital; they are the "orderlies" of the regiment, the pride of the officers and the admiration of their companions.

Chamberlain's great praise for the third class probably stemmed from the fact that he considered himself a fine representative of this category. Lt. Albert G. Brackett, an Indiana volunteer, left a similar sketch of the men with whom he served in central Mexico. "Toodles" had neither character nor stamina; "Slashers" were gay, rollicking devils; "Ladies Men" were handsome and dressed well; "Polar Bears" were slovenly in appearance. Surgeon Smith summed up the issue of character when he wrote, "There is no place like an army, to develop the peculiar traits of each individual." According to him, "A few months' companionship in camp, makes men better acquainted with each other, than a lifetime spent together under any circumstance." In an army camp, "selfishness, generosity, and all the best and worst features of the human heart reveal themselves."[25]

Soldiers esteemed personal honor and bravery above other traits. Illinois volunteer John B. Duncan expressed a sentiment felt by many soldiers when he wrote, "If we ever get into a fight I will return home with honor or not at all for I would rather die than be a coward." Deserters were particularly odious to soldiers who endured the hardships of army life. Another Illinois volunteer, Thomas D. Tennery, expressed pity for two men who left the regiment before it departed for Mexico and who then were caught. Knowing that the men had ruined their reputations, he lamented, "How bad they must feel after disgracing themselves." At the siege of Puebla, Pennsylvania volunteer J. Jacob Oswandel noticed that his name was called for guard duty much more frequently than it should have been. "I think I am imposed upon by men who are as brave at the table and as in good health as I am, but when duty calls them, they all at once become ill." Shirkers like these were dubbed "Hospital Rangers" and "Diarrhea Blues" by those who had to take up the slack for them. Oswandel promised to keep a record of those who went on guard and those who did not, perhaps intending to settle the score later. A brave act could wash away past sins, as in the case of Col. John J. Hardin, a volunteer officer killed at the Battle of Buena Vista. Wrote one man from Hardin's regiment, the 1st Illinois Infantry, "There has been many curses and imprecations heaped upon him but all seems to be forgotten and everyone deeply laments his loss. . . . his actions on that fatal day will keep him alive in the memory of his countrymen for ages yet to come."[26]

Most days, however, were spent in the dull routine that constitutes most of a soldier's existence. The daily tasks required patience and endurance—bravery of a sort different from that needed on the battlefield. Even on foreign soil, the regimen differed little from that described by Pvt. Barna Upton back on Governor's Island: reveille at daybreak; roll call; fatigue duty; drill; roll call; breakfast; sick call; guard-mount; drill; roll call; dinner; more drill; supper; roll call; retreat; and finally tattoo, followed by one last roll call. Drums and bugles called soldiers to their tasks. Despite clever names given to them, such as "Peas-upon-a-trencher" and "Roast-beef," the endless calls and chores wore on some men's nerves. As one Missouri volunteer at Santa Fe tired of soldiering put it, "The town is dull and time drags along heavily." James K. Holland, a Texas volunteer, compared civilian and military life while encamped along the Rio Grande: "I have been thinking of home to day [sic] and feel disposed to wish [myself] there enjoying the luxuries that are offered in the way of fruits—melons—camp meeting—clean clothes—good Razor—corn bread—and pretty women—[rather] than here knee deep in dust in the boiling sun—beef and crackers to eat and nasty water to drink."[27]

A musician or two in one's mess was guaranteed to lighten spirits. Benjamin Franklin Scribner's mess had several; according to him, others frequently sought out their quarters "to listen to our music, and look upon our merry dances." When his mess later united with another, he thought the merger a boon: "We now think we are the greatest mess alive. Every one possesses some peculiarity of taste and disposition, that affords fun for the rest. Every meal is attended with the life and jollity of a public dinner." Lieutenant Brackett, whose regiment attend a camp of instruction near Mier, heard music wafting through the air every night. Some sentimental pieces brought tears to the eyes of men so far away from home. Private Furber recalled a night in Texas when he listened to a clarinetist play such tunes as "The Girl I Left Behind Me," "[Home] Sweet Home," and "Oh! No, I'll Never Mention Him." While at Camargo, Captain Giddings reported that some of his regiment were fond of the "Ethiopian style of minstrelsy, long popular in the United States, and [we] awoke to the echoes of the grove with the untutored, but not unpleasing, music of the banjo and the bones." One group of officers' servants even formed a minstrel group in Mexico City, providing nightly entertainment at various coffee houses around the town. Regimental bands provided an official source of music for soldiers. In their writings, almost all diarists mention hearing "Yankee Doodle" and "Hail Columbia" played at one time or another. One enterprising soul, who claimed to be an American officer, collected songs popular with the army and published them as *The Rough and Ready Songster.* Music accompanied Mexican War soldiers wherever they traveled.[28]

Private Furber vividly illustrated the ways his comrades spent their off-duty hours by taking his readers on an imaginary tour of his regiment's camp near Tampico. The occupants of the first tent he described were busy writing letters home, using the heads of old barrels as desks. In the second tent, a man interrupted his work on a bridle to sell whiskey surreptitiously from a bottle hidden under his blanket. At the third stop, men were lazily cooking a communal pot of soup. One man read a well-worn novel, while others played a game of "Old Sledge" in the fourth tent. In the fifth tent, a soldier grumbled about having to do more than his fair share of chores, while his tentmates slept and mended their tattered clothing. In the next, men munched on hard crackers and fried pork. The seventh tent was a site of merry making and singing, fueled in part by several bottles of brandied cherries. The occupants of the eighth tent were again writing, sewing, and playing a game of euchre. In the next tent, men looked over clean clothes just returned by Mexican laundresses, while outside a few men groomed their horses. The last tent was the scene of an animated game of poker, where a green blanket served as a table. Vignettes of camp life similar to those observed by Furber are described time and time again in the diaries and letters of other Mexican War soldiers.[29]

Receiving a letter from home was more than a needed diversion; it was the next best thing to being there. The arrival of a letter brought joy; failure to receive a letter brought despair or anger. Sgt. Lewis H. Wunder informed a friend back home that two letters had finally caught up with his regiment: "I tell you it made rather an excitement when it was announced that some of the men had received letters from home." Lt. Chesley S. Coffey, a Mississippi volunteer, wrote to his family upon finally receiving a much-looked-for message: "I have frequently thought [*sic*] that my Friends Could not apreciate [*sic*] the plasure [*sic*] it would afford me in writing to me oftener." He pleaded, "if the Rest of my Friends Neglect writing you must not." Private Scribner took his sister to task for not writing: "I felt assured you would not forget me. How much I have been disappointed you can judge for yourself." He told her that any news, no matter how insignificant to her, "would be hailed . . . as a God-send in this dreary place." The Indiana volunteer claimed that he once walked sixteen miles from his camp on the Rio Grande to Brazos Santiago, merely on the chance that a letter might be waiting for him there. One Tennessee volunteer begged his father for more letters, saying, "You must write me oftener than you do for I plainly see you are the only one that will pay me that favour." Soldiers continued to send letters home in hope of receiving a reply. Even illiterate men sent letters home, dictating their words to better-educated friends. One group of officers with Scott's column in central Mexico, desperate for their letters to reach home, paid two hundred dollars to a Mexican courier who was willing to slip a mailbag through to Vera Cruz. Soldiers frequently included their army addresses for the folks back home: 1st Sergt. [*sic*] Lewis H. Wunder, Company A, 2nd Regiment Pennsylvania Volunteers, in care of Colonel Roberts; Captain Leander Cox, in care of Fra Don digo Ramiaes Samdote Macillo en Seologia Rector del cologio de Sn Louis, Puebla; Colonel William B. Campbell, Matamoros, Mexico, 1st Regiment Tennessee Volunteers, Army of Invasion; Lieutenant Adolphus Engelman, 2nd Regiment Illinois Volunteers, San Antonio, Texas; Lieutenant Andrew Jackson Trussell, Company F, 2nd Regiment Mississippi Volunteers, in care of Colonel Reuben Davis; and Lieutenant Ralph W. Kirkham, 6th U.S. Infantry, General Scott's Army, Mexico. Bandits sometimes intercepted the mail and prevented letters from reaching their destinations. Colonel Campbell admonished persons mailing letters to soldiers to pay the postage or the letters would not be delivered. In spite of all the obstacles to delivery, Captain Rogers voiced the feelings of many others when he entreated his wife: "You must all write me as often as there is some chance that I may get your letters." In his diary he wondered plaintively, "Why do they not write[?]"[30]

Newspapers also linked soldiers to home. Papers from the United States usually contained the latest war news, a fact that prompted Sergeant Wunder to comment, "I presume you almost know more at Reading [Pennsylvania] than what we know here." The men at the front did not always agree with the accounts they read. According to Lieutenant Engelman, an article in the *Missouri Republican,* written by his colonel, William H. Bissell, slighted his company by claiming that others kept a neater camp. Captain Rogers noted that several newspapers had arrived from home, one with an article about him. Commenting on the story, he observed, "A fool of an editor recants a lie he told on me some time ago and another one thinks I have been treated badly." While acknowledging that he had been wronged, Rogers stated, "I have no desire to have newspapers quarreling over me." Hungry for news from home, Lieutenant Trussell asked his brother in Mississippi to send a paper, saying, "I wish you to Send me a niews [*sic*] paper for I wold [*sic*] be verry [*sic*] glad to See a paper from the States." Another officer, Lieutenant Kirkham, asked his wife to send him newspapers and even old news clippings. "Hope on; hope ever," he sighed during one long period without mail. Finally he reported home, "I received today a number of the *Hampton Post* and the *Christian Witness*. Do not stop sending them." Another soldier in Santa Fe wrote after a disappointing mail call, "There was nothing for me, not even a newspaper."[31]

Newspapers published by and for soldiers were a source of news and entertainment for Americans in Mexico. The army seemed to have an inexhaustible supply of printers and editors who joined up to fight. Taking over

Mexican printshops in occupied towns, they went to work exercising their First Amendment right. American printers ingeniously overcame the absence of the letter *W* from the Spanish type they found by substituting two *Vs* in its place or by using an inverted *M*. In Matamoros, soldiers helped publish the *American Flag*. In Saltillo, Illinois volunteers christened their paper the *Picket Guard*. In central Mexico, the publishers of the *American Star* followed Scott all the way to the Halls of Montezuma, stopping to print editions at Vera Cruz, Jalapa, and Puebla before finally setting up shop for good in Mexico City. There the publishers had to compete with a rival, the *North American*. In order to gain a local readership, both papers printed news in both English and Spanish. The *American Star's* editors even published an edition for the reading public back home, called the *Weekly Star* for the United States. Newspaper names often revealed the republican zeal of the Americans who published them: from Monterey, the *American Pioneer;* from Vera Cruz, the *Genius of Liberty* and the *Free American;* from Puebla, the *Flag of Freedom;* from Jalapa, the *Watch Tower;* from Mexico City, *Yankee Doodle;* from Toluca, the *Outpost Guard;* and from Chihuahua, the *Anglo-Saxon*. Although one Tennessee volunteer complained that the American paper printed in Matamoros had no real news, most soldiers probably appreciated the mix of camp gossip, official reports, patriotic editorials, markets prices, and advertisements that filled the familiar sheets. Lieutenant Trussell evidently thought the American newspaper published at Matamoros interesting enough to send several editions to his brother back in Mississippi.[32]

Theatrical productions drew soldiers to the footlights to escape the boredom of camp. Professional acting troupes and musical acts took advantage of the relatively short distance between New Orleans and Mexico to play before grateful audiences of soldiers. One such troupe visited Taylor's camp at Corpus Christi in January 1846 and played to packed crowds at a hall called the Army Theatre. Theatergoers were entertained by plays such as *The Idiot Witness; Or, A Tale of Blood* and *Ambrose Gwinett; Or, The Sea-Side Murder!* But not all was drama; farces such as *The Irish Tutor; Or New Lights* and *The Spectre Bridegroom* promised to make the audience laugh. Musicians played while stage hands changed sets. The Texan Chaparral Serenaders performed an "Ethiopian Concert," aided by Mr. Austin D. Look, who danced the "celebrated GRAPEVINE TWIST, and other popular Extravaganzas." A New Orleans troupe followed Taylor's army to the Rio Grande, setting up shop in Matamoros. Passing an evening at the theater became a popular diversion in central Mexico, where American troupes had to compete with local Mexican acting companies. One South Carolina volunteer who attended several productions at Puebla pronounced "Spanish" performances superior to those put on by his own countrymen. Elaborate productions of *Rob Roy* and *Soldier's Return from the War* impressed J. Jacob Oswandel, who said they were a hit with the audience. Theater thrived in Mexico City, although the performances sometimes received mixed reviews. Barclay claimed that, although he could not understand the Spanish dialogue of *Don Juan Tenorio* at the National Theatre, the performance and the scenery were the "most magnificent" that he had ever witnessed. American officers presented Señora Cañete, a member of the Spanish Dramatic Company, a purse of more than two thousand dollars for a single night's performance. When W. G. Wells, one of the owners of the American Theater in Mexico City, died, fans escorted his body to the grave. Soldiers in Santa Fe who attended the theater there seemed to be more pleased with the "Ethiopian" acts than with the actual play. While a writer for the *American Star* extolled the virtues of circus rider Madame Armond, Sgt. Thomas Barclay of the 2nd Pennsylvania Infantry found that the only thing remarkable about the great female equestrienne was "the unusually heavy proportions of her features and limbs." The *Star* editors were chagrined by Madame Turin's performance on horseback, saying that, if she were going to ride like a man, decency dictated that she should dress like one as well. The *Star* found that national pride made it necessary to chide American theatergoers in Mexico City. The paper published a list of rules that should be observed by all who attended the theater:

1. No gentlemen should mount the stage, lest they be mistaken for actors.
2. Gentlemen should refrain from yelling.
3. Gentlemen should not hang their boots over the edge of their boxes.
4. Distinguished officers, no matter how popular, should not be cheered.
5. Mexican women, who were becoming "Yankee-fied" in their dress, should remove their bonnets in the theater.[33]

Soldiers sometimes staged plays themselves. Corpus Christi's Army Theatre had been the brainchild of regular officers, who built the structure speculating that they would recover their investment at the box office. According to James Longstreet, a lieutenant in the 8th U.S. Infantry, officers intended to stage plays themselves, playing all parts, regardless of gender. The practice ended, however, when objections developed to casting Lt. Ulysses S. Grant as Desdemona in *Othello;* a real actress named Mrs. Hart was recruited from New Orleans to play the female roles. Eventually, the productions proved so profitable that entire professional acting troupes were booked. In Puebla, the theater manager hired a file of Pennsylvania

Theatre Del Progreso. American Star No. 2, *Puebla, June 12, 1847.*
Courtesy Daughters of the Republic of Texas Library

volunteers to appear as extras in *Romeo and Juliet.* One of the men later employed as an extra commented in his diary, "Whoever would have thought, that I . . . would ever become a theater actor!" In Mexico City, Sergeant Barclay judged the production of a troupe of army followers, *The Lady of Lyons,* poor, even though the actors spoke a language he could understand.[34]

Americans also found diversion in fraternal organizations. Texas volunteers on their way to the Rio Grande held a "Court of Inquiry" to look into charges that one of their members had divulged "the secret of masonry." Officers of the same regiment later buried one of their members with "masonic honors." Masons held meetings throughout Mexico and even formed lodges whenever enough brothers were stationed together. Saltillo seemed to be a particularly fertile site for Masonic activity; according to Lieutenant Coffey, members of the 2nd Mississippi Rifles had their own lodge there. One man who died at Santa Fe was followed to his grave by a procession of nearly sixty fellow Masons. A Mason with the army in Mexico City hinted to the editors of the *American Star* that some "Brother"

PUEBLA, July 14, 1847.

NOTICE.—The Officers of the Army occupying private quarters, are requested to send to Captain J. McKINSTRY, Depot Quartermaster at this place, certificates of the time and of the number of rooms they have occupied, as well as the price, if agreed on.   J. R. IRWIN, Acting Q. M. General.

DAGUERREOTYPE NOTICE.

Messrs. BETTS & GARDINER respectfully inform the citizens of Puebla, and the public generally, that their rooms are a few doors from the principal plaza, one square above Gen. Scott's quarters, at the sign of the "*White Flag,*" where they are prepared to táke MINIATURES in every style and to the entire satisfaction of the setter.   july 15

DENTAL SURGEON.

The subscriber takes leave to offer his services to the public at his rooms in Santisima street, No. 4, a few doors from the principal plaza, one square above Gen. Scott's quarters, at the sign of the "*White Flag.*"

Persons wishing ARTIFICIAL TEETH inserted, or any operation performed on the Teeth, can have it done at his office without incurring the least delay or disappointment. All operations warranted. july 15   J. C. GARDINER.

Daguerreotype Notice and Dental Surgeon. American Star No. 2, *Puebla, July 15, 1847. Courtesy Daughters of the Republic of Texas Library*

should undertake the task of forming a lodge where members could meet under the banner of "Friendship, Love, and Truth." Officers who accompanied Scott to Mexico City formed their own social organization, called the Aztec Club. Members met at the home of Señor Boca Negra, a former minister to the United States. The club became so important to its members that they voted to make it permanent and continue their association after the war.[35]

Most entertainment, however, was not as elevated in tone as plays and fraternal meetings. Soldiers in the Mexican War had many vices, and chief among them was drinking. American commanders issued orders forbidding the sale of liquor in camp, but regulars and volunteers had no trouble locating whiskey, brandy, and wine to slake their thirst. When a Mexican was spotted selling his wares near a group of soldiers at drill, one officer "called to a drummer [and] ordered him to take the bottle and pour the contents on the Mexican's head, which he done [*sic*], hitting him two or three times with the empty bottle." Soldiers sometimes banded together to protect the illicit trade. According to Lieutenant Engelman, members of his regiment convened a court near Saltillo to try a man for informing on a local liquor vendor who had been arrested and whipped for his crime. Found guilty by an impromptu jury of his peers, the Illinois volunteer was sentenced to be ridden around the camp on a pole in order to teach him a lesson, as well as to serve as a warning to others. Private Furber and his companions found several barrels of liquor on the beach at Vera Cruz that had washed up from a wrecked brig. The volunteers caved in the head of a barrel of wine and filled their canteens, while a group of regular officers came over and confiscated a barrel of porter for their own use. No stranger to drink, the men of Furber's company previously had drained a barrel of whiskey they found in an army wagon near Matamoros. Once the entire regiment had drunk itself into a stupor as a way of passing a stormy Texas night. In Santa Fe, Lieutenant Gibson noted, "Grogshops do a thriving business" due to the many Indians and soldiers in town. Even generals were known to tip the glass. While traveling to Mexico, Winfield Scott provided "light wine" from his own stock to the officers in his mess, along with instructions on how properly to enjoy it. Old Fuss and Feathers certainly would have been appalled had he known that some of his officers were so desirous of drink that they once downed the liquor from jars containing the bodies of preserved animals. Drinking became such a problem in Mexico City that the governor of the city, Gen. John A. Quitman, ordered all coffee houses and grog shops closed at 6 P.M.[36]

Soldiers who could not obtain American and European whiskey, brandy, or wine turned to the plentiful supply of Mexican liquor. Tequila in its modern form did not exist, but several other strong drinks made from the maguey plant—*pulque, mescal,* and *aguardiente*—were omnipresent. Pulque had two interesting characteristics. The first was a color said to be pleasing to the eye. The second was an odor similar to rotting meat, which made it unpopular with some Americans. Observed one volunteer, pulque "is the favorite drink amongst all the Mexican people, and I see some of our Yankees are becoming used to it." Pulque could be distilled further into a stronger drink called *aguardiente*. From the accounts left by soldiers, they overcame any repugnance they felt toward these drinks and downed them quite regularly.[37]

Some soldiers tried to keep the bottle at bay. The Temperance Movement had not left the army unaffected. In fact, Lieutenant Colonel Hitchcock had noted back in 1843 that "nearly 400 [of the 3rd U.S. Infantry] have signed the pledge, including several officers." The temperance spirit followed some to Mexico. Robert Bruce Wynne, a Tennessee volunteer, informed his mother that he was "still a Son of Temperance though some scoundrelly slander reported in Sumner [Tennessee] that I had been drinking before I left Nashville." With the coming of 1847, Captain Rogers resolved, "I will drink no more ardent spirits." A month later he confided to his diary, "My resolutions have not been cared for again and again have I abandoned them." Sgt. Thomas Barclay at Jalapa reported that "the Temperance pledges are in many instances forgotten. Aguardiente, Mexican brandy, and egg nogs are all the go." Unfortunately for one Kentucky volunteer, it took the accidental shooting of his cousin while the two were on a spree to make him swear off the bottle. Another volunteer familiar with the sad incident exclaimed, "One young man dead, the other wretched for life. There are the triumphs of the demon of intoxications!"[38]

Gambling vied with drinking as the top vice. In fact, the two usually went together, making it easier for the players to be separated from their money. Professional gamblers followed the army wherever it went, setting up shop on the outskirts of camp or taking over buildings in town. Popular games included faro, poker, seven up, whist, euchre, vingt-et-un, and chuck-a-luck, but soldiers would bet on almost anything. Samuel Chamberlain described one game played with a machete, in which the prize was a hard sugar cone called a *pelloncillo*. Although it was possible to win at these games, losing much more commonly was the outcome. Lieutenant Engelman visited a San Antonio gambling hall, where he saw Capt. Albert Pike, the famed poet, step up to a faro table and lose fifty dollars in five minutes. Surgeon S. Compton Smith of the volunteers claimed that gamblers often sought employment with the Quartermaster Department, masquerading as teamsters by day and fleecing soldiers by night. The disguises worked well; who would suspect that the "unkempt, coarsely dressed, and dirt-and-tar-begrimed teamster" was the same "over-dressed and Frenchified swell" who had dealt him cards the night before? Gamblers he saw enticed soldiers with the promise of a free drink for all who risked a quarter on their games. Men who found themselves losing often would bet all their money away, hoping that their luck would change before they went broke. Gambling often led to violence, as in the case a South Carolina volunteer who killed another member of his regiment in Mexico City after a dispute at a roulette table.[39]

Another activity often associated with drinking and gambling was dancing. *Fandangos,* as these dances were called, drew large numbers of American soldiers, who danced for hours with dark-eyed señoritas to the music of violins, guitars, and mandolins. According to Captain Giddings, the dances were held frequently, as they afforded the common people of the country "their chief Amusement." Mexicans usually overcame their fear of the soldiers and welcomed them, selling the Yankees food and drink in the process. Although the hosts of a fandango held at Wheeler's public house in Matamoros charged a two-dollar admission fee, most seemed to be much less formal and more spontaneous. Mexican women, much more sensual than the women Americans were used to seeing at home, had quite an effect on American men. Wrote Lieutenant Trussell to his brother, "We had a fine fandango, Ball, at Saltillo and they [*sic*] was some fine Looking Girles [*sic*] at It as I Ever saw in the Stats [*sic*]." In another letter Trussell wrote that he and his friends had "some fine frolicks [*sic*] here with the Mexican sinoreturs [*sic*]." According to soldiers' accounts, Mexican women returned their affection. "Many of our young officers frequent [fandangos] and cut all kinds of capers among the girls," wrote Lieutenant Dana. Curious, he attended one himself to see what it was like and reported to his wife that the ratio of the dancers was uneven, with two Americans to every Mexican girl. Unimpressed, he said that he left after a few minutes. One wonders if this was his true opinion, as the wife to whom he sent this account tended to be very jealous. She need not have worried, however, for, in proper Mexican style, chaperones usually accompanied unmarried señoritas to these social affairs. The army had little to say about these dances, but U.S. officials in Santa Fe placed a $1.50 tax on fandangos as a way to limit their frequency.[40]

Army life was a new experience for most American soldiers in the Mexican War. "What emotions thrill the heart at the sight of a military camp," penned one Illinois volunteer shortly after joining up. "All the vain-glory of war will rush onto the mind." The realities of army life, however, disappointed men who had expected a picture-book war. Without the thrills of battle, army life was dull and monotonous. Lieutenant Trussell summed up the situation faced by most American soldiers: "If we could be in activ[e] survice [*sic*] I would not care for staing [sic] here one or two years longer but to be here in garison [*sic*] [with] nothing to do but Drill and about evory [*sic*] Eight or ten days guard duty to do, this I am tiard [*sic*] of." Many probably came to feel as did Private Oswandel, who wrote to a friend, "I would sooner be home eating cakes and sausages than out here fighting Santa Anna."[41]

EIGHT

Dog Cheap to the Living

Such are the chances and fate and a soldier should always be prepared for death or life without a moment's notice.
—Thomas D. Tennery,
4th Illinois Infantry

Only about twenty of the Americans [were killed] while engaged in the Bombardment—Dog cheap to the living.
—William S. Johnson,
Palmetto Regiment

"The Mexican War was the deadliest war the United States ever fought," Thomas R. Irey writes in an essay on the human cost of the war. The number of deaths was staggering: 110 out of every thousand participants died of disease, accident, or wounds. The only other war that approaches this high rate of mortality is the Civil War, with its rate of 65 per thousand. To put this in perspective, out of a typical Mexican War regiment, more than one-tenth of its men did not survive their term of service. Much has been made of the ease with which Americans marched across Mexico, scoring victory after victory on their way to the Halls of Montezuma. A trail of bodies, however, marked their path.

The 1st South Carolina Infantry suffered more losses than any other unit in the war. Out of 1,007 officers and men on its rolls, 56 died as a result of battle, and 349 died of disease and other causes. It is little wonder why one South Carolinian wryly commented that victories like Vera Cruz were "Dog Cheap to the living." The dead and disabled paid the butcher's bill.[1]

Disease killed and prostrated far more men than battle. While only 1,548 officers and men died of wounds sustained in action with the enemy, 10,970 reportedly fell to illness contracted during their service. Thus, it was seven times more likely during the war that a soldier would die from disease than in battle. In addition, nearly 10,000 more soldiers received surgeon certificates that declared them unfit and allowed them to return home. The diaries and letters of participants are filled with tales of men struggling against illness, far from the comforts of home.[2]

The army experienced health problems even before war broke out. Surgeon John B. Porter, assigned to Taylor's Army of Occupation, observed a high rate of illness at Corpus Christi. After studying the situation, he determined several causes: bad water, poor tents, impure air, unsanitary privies, variable temperatures, and a scarcity of fuel. Had they seen his list, soldiers might have added poor diets and hard marching. Armed with knowledge of modern medicine, historians see how these factors—themselves not the real causes of infection—left the army weak and vulnerable to bacteria and viruses. One study of antebellum medicine determined that, although knowledge of anatomy had increased greatly, medical science had not advanced very far beyond that practiced in the Middle Ages, as atmospheric conditions and imbalance of the body's humors still were thought to cause disease.[3]

The Quartermaster Department faced the heroic task of sheltering the army against the elements. Efforts to supply enough tents eventually yielded results; by the end of the war, contractors each month were producing more than seven hundred tents of various designs. Throughout the war, however, constant exposure to the weather helped to break down some men's resistance to disease. The problems with shelter encountered at Corpus Christi were legion, as the tents could keep out neither rain nor windblown dust, making them practically useless. In the rush to forward tents for the army, the Quartermaster Department had allowed some contractors to use muslin instead of canvas. Surgeon Porter found it odd that, in the army of the United States, "men are better paid, better clothed, and better fed than those of any other army in the world; while they are worse lodged in peace and war, than any other troops." Some volunteers arrived on the Rio Grande without tents at all. One Texas volunteer wrote near

Matamoros, "Slept in water and mud . . . the whole regiment got wet . . . your humble svt. never was as sick in his life—never thot [*sic*] of dying before—scared to death." Barracks, when they could be procured, sometimes presented their own risks. As one Pennsylvania volunteer at Jalapa remarked, "After lying so long and cruelly exposed at Camp Patterson we were glad to get into any quarters." But he continued: "Nothing, however, can well be conceived more filthy than the barracks where the men now lay." Although an effort had been made to clean it up, he astutely predicted that disease inevitably would follow. One officer at Santa Fe attributed illness in his men to the fact that they had been sleeping on dirt floors. He hoped that the addition of bunks would restore their health.[4]

Inadequate supplies of clean drinking water resulted in widespread illness. The drinking water at Corpus Christi and Brazos Santiago contained sea salts, which made it unhealthy as well as brackish tasting. Some soldiers tried to mask the salty taste with liquor. Benjamin F. Scribner, a private of the 2nd Indiana Infantry, described how volunteers who camped near the mouth of the Rio Grande had to carry kettles more than a half-mile from camp, slogging through a slough on the way, to obtain fresh water. One Illinois volunteer blamed his poor health and weight loss on his trip through Texas, saying, "The water in Texas did not agree with me." Lt. Andrew Jackson Trussell, a Mississippi volunteer, wrote to his brother from Camargo, "I have not had [a] good drink of water sence [*sic*] I left Mississippi this is the worst watter [*sic*] I nearly Ever Drank it is river water and thare [*sic*] is ded [*sic*] cows and horsis [*sic*] in the river." He added, "I haven't saw a Spring or a well Sence [*sic*] I have been in this country." Soldiers sometimes had to dig wells to obtain drinking water. Volunteers on Lobos Island had to dig from four to eight feet before striking water, and even then it was "disgustingly brackish." Soldiers during the siege of Vera Cruz had to dig four or five feet before a "muddy looking fluid" could be scooped up in their tin cups. A fourteen-foot well had to be dug by Illinois volunteers crossing the Texas prairie on their way to San Antonio, when no surface water could be located. Missouri volunteers on their way to Santa Fe also resorted to digging wells. Inexperienced soldiers—especially volunteers—gulped down the water in their canteens, not knowing how to make it last on a long march. Wracked with thirst, they hoped to reach water, "if only in some foul mud-hole." The same Illinoisans later stopped at a "swamp, [with] green scum around the edges but clear in the middle." Wrote one who partook of its contents, "I would not have believed that swamp water could taste so good." Thirsty men were ready to drink nearly anything, as Missouri volunteers demonstrated on their way to New Mexico.

One of their officers wrote, "All the low places were dry, except a few buffalo wallows and ruts in the road, muddy, filthy, and covered with scum, which the horses of the mounted men refused to drink. Yet the men drank it with avidity." Members of the Mormon Battalion following the same route to Santa Fe also drank from these mud holes, finding that "it was very welcome to the most of us." Soldiers near Vera Cruz drank with relish from a marsh, being too thirsty to complain that the water was "not exactly transparent." Water was so scarce during one march in central Mexico that it reportedly was sold for five dollars a drink. With watering holes such as these, it is little wonder that dysentery and diarrhea ran rampant in the army. One officer, Lt. Ralph W. Kirkham of the 6th U.S. Infantry recognized the connection between bad water and illness and declared, "I accustomed myself on the march to drink as little as possible." So great was one soldier's thirst after the Battle of Cerro Gordo that he "slurped down huge gulps" of muddy water from a pond filled with bodies of dead horses and Mexicans soldiers.[5]

Hard marches created their own medical emergencies. Each infantryman had to carry his musket, bayonet, cartridge box and belts, canteen, haversack full of rations, and knapsack, a load estimated to weigh at least forty pounds. Baggage wagons often were reduced to the bare minimum. When the 4th Indiana Infantry marched inland from Vera Cruz, the quartermaster allotted only one wagon per every two companies. The heat and humidity soon had men discarding uniform jackets, knapsacks, empty canteens, haversacks, and cartridge boxes—anything that would relieve them of some of their burden. After the 2nd Illinois Infantry's "swamp water" march across the Texas prairie, many men were too ill to continue and had to be left behind. Missouri infantrymen had a hard go of it marching across the Kansas plains on the way to Santa Fe. After a day of marching in the July heat, one wrote, "Many were sick, lame, and exhausted—completely overcome by the heat, thirst, and long march." Soldiers along the Rio Grande had to march through "Shoe mouth deep" dust, drawing it into their lungs with every breath. Rations of salt pork only intensified thirst. Shoes and feet were natural casualties of a march. One notable march made by General Wool's column covered 116 miles in four days. One of the marchers reported, "It is no wonder the men had sore feet and tired legs, . . . and that when the day drew to a close the Inft. Regts. were without men."[6]

Most accounts of marches by Mexican War soldiers contain the same elements: heat or cold, sun or rain, sore feet. Private Scribner's description of his regiment's march to Mier in northern Mexico conveys a sense of the experience. He wrote, "My feet were very blistered, and every sudden movement of my arms, was like the piercing of sharp instruments. These acute pains were occasioned by the straps and weight of my knapsack, which contained all I possessed." He asked his reader to imagine his discomfort: "Fancy to yourself the burden I was bound to support. The cartridge box with forty rounds of ounce ball cartridges, bayonet scabbard and belts, the haversack of provisions, canteen with water, musket and knapsack." "Let the stoutest carry such a load twenty miles through the dust and hot sunshine," surmised Scribner, "and I assure you they will gladly stop for the night." The straps of his knapsack cut across his chest and made it difficult for him to breathe, while the heat, thirst, and exertion caused him almost to give up. Others did give in to the fatigue and fell by the wayside or flung gear aside to lighten their burdens. But Scribner, like so many other soldiers, grimly placed one foot in front of the other and made it to that night's camp. He explained, "Pride forbade me complaint and I jogged on." Capt. Leander M. Cox, 3rd Kentucky Infantry, saw his men exhibit the same type of determination while marching in central Mexico. Although many were suffering from the effects of diarrhea, "They trudge along, curse the war, obey my orders, but look like they have harder times than expected."[7]

Danger existed for those who did not "jog on" but stopped to rest or simply found it impossible to keep up. American bones littered the roads of Mexico. Victims of sunstroke sometimes crawled off to find shade and never were seen again. One officer of the 4th U.S. Artillery noted that several men fell down "dead from the effects of the sun" on the march from Vera Cruz to Mexico City. After one thirty-mile march in central Mexico, empty wagons were sent back over the route to pick up stragglers. The help arrived too late for several who already had died. Stragglers also were easy prey for the guerrillas and bandits who shadowed the lines of march. According to Lt. George B. McClellan, lancers harried marchers near Plan del Río in central Mexico. A pool of blood in the road drew this comment from him: "Some poor devil of a straggler from Worth's Division probably murdered." Everyone knew the dangers, but still men lagged behind. As Lieutenant Kirkham observed, "The men seem to have little judgment about leaving the main body, but go just where their inclination leads them," even if it led them to their deaths.[8]

Poor diet also took its toll on the soldiers. One volunteer officer, Capt. John R. Kenly, contended that badly prepared food "laid the foundation for the discharge of many soldiers from the army." A surgeon of volunteers, S. Compton Smith, listed poorly cooked rations as a cause of dysentery and diarrhea. Dr. George Johnson, surgeon with the Saint Louis Legion, claimed that many volunteers lacked the skill to prepare their rations properly and ate their beans undercooked until they learned better. Scurvy was reported in the 7th U.S. Infantry's camp at Matamoros, as well as in troops stationed in New Mexico. Mexico abounded with fresh fruit and vegetables, and there was no reason for the appearance of the disease except the Commissary Department's ineptitude. Writing of the fruits of central Mexico, one officer said, "They are the finest I have ever seen, and soldiers, particularly the Volunteers, seem to use no discretion, and many are sick." Americans, unused to the wide variety of tropical fruits available to them, often gorged on these delicacies. Lieutenant Gibson noted that New Mexico's "melons, plums, and other things have been offered in abundance." He added, "Many of the men were sick last night, which we attributed to the dissipation and change of diet." An army surgeon in California blamed unripe fruit for diarrhea and dysentery in his patients. Men who spent time in the country learned to moderate their eating habits. When Capt. Leander Cox encountered several fellow Kentuckians at Vera Cruz on their way home, they all admonished him to "avoid the fruits of the country and to drink but little spiritous [sic] liquor." He tried to follow their instructions but became seriously ill anyway. Pvt. Frederick Zeh and his companions "feasted on cactus fruits" during their march inland from Vera Cruz. The only warning he offered to others was that they should to pick off the thorns "or they will pierce one's mouth."[9]

Crowded camps promoted the spread of disease, causing outbreaks to reach epidemic proportion in some regiments. Influenza, smallpox, and measles wreaked havoc among the army's ranks. Disease attacked the 2nd Mississippi Rifles even before the regiment left their home state. Camped for two weeks under the Vicksburg bluffs without tents, the unit endured a January storm that weakened the spirits and bodies of its men. Hundreds sickened, and scores had to be hospitalized when they reached New Orleans. The regimental surgeon diagnosed the illness as "cold plague." The travail of the Mississippians continued as smallpox broke out on the passage to Lobos Island. Eventually the regiment's three original field officers all resigned and returned home ill. Of the 1,037 men of the regiment, 186 died from disease, and another 178 were discharged due to illness. One officer of the 2nd Mississippi remarked on the regiment's plight, noting that they had endured "as many plagues as was inflicted on the Pharo [sic]." Other regiments were stricken, too. Said one Indiana volunteer of another regiment, "The soldiers of the 13th Infantry died in swarms." The 1st North Carolina Infantry suffered from a disease called "black tongue." Wrote Private Johnson of the 1st South Carolina Infantry during the halt at Puebla,

Regimental Losses in the Regular Forces

	Battle Deaths	Disease and Accident	Total
Old Establishment			
General Staff	2	15	17
U.S. Engineers	2	16	18
Topographic Engineers	1	1	2
Ordnance Department	10	20	30
1st U.S. Dragoons	31	90	121
2nd U.S. Dragoons	43	146	189
U.S. Mounted Rifles	54	178	232
1st U.S. Artillery	42	211	253
2nd U.S. Artillery	54	180	234
3rd U.S. Artillery	41	183	224
4th U.S. Artillery	32	210	242
1st U.S. Infantry	20	162	182
2nd U.S. Infantry	29	133	162
3rd U.S. Infantry	56	251	307
4th U.S. Infantry	74	178	252
5th U.S. Infantry	90	208	298
6th U.S. Infantry	62	206	268
7th U.S. Infantry	46	226	272
8th U.S. Infantry	102	178	280
New Establishment			
9th U.S. Infantry	16	211	227
10th U.S. Infantry	1	100	101
11th U.S. Infantry	24	254	278
12th U.S. Infantry	26	289	315
13th U.S. Infantry	—	150	150
14th U.S. Infantry	14	257	271
15th U.S. Infantry	37	373	410
16th U.S. Infantry	—	106	106
U.S. Voltigeurs	20	226	246
U.S. Marines with Scott			
U.S. Marines	9	36	45

"Our men are dying off very fast." According to him, some companies in his regiment were reduced to ten to fifteen men fit for duty. A regular officer substantiated the claim of rampant illness in the army, saying, "Have been sick since the 1st of June. A great deal of sickness prevails and much mortality."[10]

Volunteers suffered a much higher rate of infectious disease than regulars. One regular officer remarked on the disproportionate amount of illness in volunteer regiments, "They cannot take care of themselves; the hospitals are crowded with them, they die like sheep." Mississippi surgeon Thomas N. Love made an interesting observation about his regiment's ill: most of those stricken were young farmers of temperate habits. The explanation, although he failed to realize it, was that farm boys lacked the well-developed immune systems of city dwellers whose constant exposure to disease had made them more resistant. Surgeon John Porter further explained the reason why a disease such as smallpox ran wilder among the volunteers than the regulars. By regulation, all recruits entering the army were vaccinated for the disease when they joined their regiments. Porter praised the practice, saying, "In the whole course of my service in the regular regiments of the army . . . I have never seen a case of variloa, or varioloid, in man, woman, or child; and the only cases I have ever seen were among irregular troops, and persons over whom we have no control." Surgeon Nathan S. Jarvis informed his superiors in Washington that the Mexican heat had spoiled his stock of vaccine, making it impossible to prevent the disease. Untold suffering and death could have been prevented, had the practice of vaccination been extended to all army personnel, regular and volunteer.[11]

Surgeon Love identified another reason why a high number of volunteers broke down under the stress of campaigning: poor screening of recruits. According to him, medical examinations that would have helped to screen out the weak were inadequate or nonexistent. As Love saw it, many who should not have been accepted were allowed to enlist. Unfortunately, in many cases this charge was true, even though army regulations required that each recruit undergo a medical examination to determine his fitness, prior to being accepted into service. The requisite examination for volunteers seems to have been ignored in the rush to raise troops. Love also claimed that many knew they were not fit to soldier but wanted to go anyway, in hopes that a hearty outdoors life would restore their health. These men found out too late that they were mistaken, and many paid with their lives.[12]

Some medical practices hurt more than they helped. One student of

Regimental Losses in the Volunteer Forces

Volunteer Unit	Enlistment	Battle Deaths	Disease and Accidents	Total
1st South Carolina	for the war	56	349	405
6th Illinois Infantry	for the war	1	296	297
2nd Pennsylvania Infantry	for the war	4	225	229
3rd Tennessee Infantry	for the war	—	219	219
2nd Mississippi Rifles	for the war	—	187	187
2nd New York Infantry	for the war	41	141	182
1st North Carolina Infantry	for the war	—	181	181
3rd Kentucky Infantry	for the war	—	178	178
1st Louisiana Infantry	for the war	3	172	175
1st Michigan Infantry	for the war	—	164	164
Calhoun's Georgia Mounted Battalion	for the war	6	142	148
5th Indiana Infantry	for the war	—	146	146
1st Pennsylvania Infantry	for the war	28	118	146
4th Kentucky Infantry	for the war	—	144	144
4th Tennessee Infantry	for the war	—	140	140
4th Indiana Infantry	for the war	—	128	128
1st Mississippi Rifles	12 months	59	63	122
1st Arkansas Cavalry	12 months	21	96	117
2nd Illinois Infantry	12 months	51	64	115
5th Illinois Infantry	for the war	—	113	113
1st Tennessee Infantry	12 months	29	78	107
Hay's Texas Mounted Battalion	12 months	8	98	106
3rd Illinois Infantry	12 months	1	101	102
4th Illinois Infantry	12 months	13	89	102
Price's Missouri Mounted Regiment	12 months	—	102	102
1st Georgia Infantry	12 months	—	100	100
Rall's Missouri Mounted Regiment	for the war	—	97	97
1st Virginia Infantry	for the war	—	94	94
2nd Kentucky Infantry	12 months	46	48	94
Fiesca's Louisiana Infantry Battalion	for the war	—	88	88
1st Kentucky Cavalry	12 months	30	54	84
4th Ohio Infantry	for the war	—	83	83
5th Ohio Infantry	for the war	—	83	83
1st Alabama Infantry	12 months	—	82	82
1st Indiana Infantry	12 months	2	80	82
2nd Indiana Infantry	12 months	36	46	82
1st Massachusetts Infantry	for the war	—	82	82

Volunteer Unit	Enlistment	Battle Deaths	Disease and Accidents	Total
Biscoe's Louisiana Mounted Battalion	12 months	9	72	81
2nd D.C. & Baltimore Battalion	for the war	—	77	77
Doniphan's Missouri Regiment	12 months	9	67	76
3rd Indiana Infantry	12 months	9	63	72
5th Tennessee Infantry	for the war	—	70	70
1st Kentucky Infantry	12 months	6	63	69
2nd Tennessee Infantry	12 months	20	48	68
Dunlap's Illinois Mounted Battalion	for the war	2	64	66
1st Ohio Infantry	12 months	17	47	64
2nd Ohio Infantry	12 months	1	61	62
3rd Ohio Infantry	12 months	—	61	61
1st Illinois Infantry	12 months	30	26	56
*Gray's Arkansas Mixed Battalion	12 months	—	54	54
Texas Infantry Battalion	12 months	15	34	49
Easton's Missouri Infantry Battalion	for the war	6	39	45
1st New York Infantry	12 months	2	40	42
1st Tennessee Mounted Volunteers	12 months	—	42	42
Battalion of Mississippi Rifles	for the war	—	38	38
Pennsylvania Infantry (indp. cos.)	for the war	3	31	34
Livingston's Florida Rifle Company	for the war	—	34	34
Bell's Texas Mounted Battalion	12 months	3	30	33
Chevallie's Texas Mounted Battalion	for the war	—	29	29
+Boyd's Mounted Company	for the war	5	22	27
1st New Jersey Infantry Battalion	for the war	—	26	26
1st D.C. & Baltimore Battalion	12 months	11	15	26
+Wheats Mounted Company	for the war	—	24	24
*Gilpin's Missouri Mixed Battalion	for the war	—	23	23

Regimental Losses in the Volunteer Forces (cont.)

Volunteer Unit	Enlistment	Battle Deaths	Disease and Accidents	Total
*Clarke's Missouri Mixed Battalion	12 months	1	22	23
+Walker's Battalion	for the war	—	21	21
Powell's Missouri Mounted Battalion	for the war		21	21
Willock's Missouri Mounted Battalion	12 months		21	21
Wood's Texas Mounted Regiment	6 months	2	17	19
Kenneally's & Riddles Companies	for the war	—	19	19
Texas Mounted Battalion	12 months	3	12	15
Texas Mounted Battalion	for the war	1	13	14
1st Louisiana Infantry	6 months	—	13	13
4th Louisiana Infantry	6 months	—	13	13
McCullough's & Gray's Texas Spy Co.	12 months		13	13
MaGee's Alabama Mounted Company	for the war		12	12
Blanchard's Louisiana Infantry Co.	12 months	3	8	11
+Meares's Mounted Company	for the war	—	11	11
Knowlton's Wisconsin Infantry Co.	for the war	—	11	11
6th Louisiana Infantry	6 months	—	10	10
Hay's Texas Mounted Regiment	6 months	2	8	10
Cooper's Texas Mounted Regiment	6 months	2	8	10
Engart's Mounted Ark. Company	for the war	—	9	9
1st Missouri Infantry	6 months	—	9	9
5th Louisiana Infantry	6 months	—	8	8
Johnston's Texas Rifle Regiment	6 months	—	8	8
Raiford's Alabama Infantry Battalion	6 months	—	7	7
Knowlton's Wisconsin Infantry Co.	12 months	—	7	7
Mormon Infantry Battalion	12 months	—	7	7
Gally's Artillery Battalion	3 months	—	5	5
2nd Lousiana Infantry	6 months	—	5	5

Regimental Losses in the Volunteer Forces (cont.)

Volunteer Unit	Enlistment	Battle Deaths	Disease and Accidents	Total
3rd Louisiana Infantry	6 months	—	5	5
Duncan's Ohio Mounted Company	for the war	—	4	4
Platt's Alabama Infantry Battalion	6 months	—	3	3
Henderson's Texas Volunteers	3 months	—	3	3
Hay's Texas Mounted Regiment	6 months	—	3	3
Holt's Missouri Battalion	12 months	—	3	3
Smith's Texas Mounted Battalion	6 months	—	2	2
Davis's Mormon Infantry Company	12 months	—	2	2
Morgan's Iowa Company	12 months	—	2	2
Seibel's Alabama Battalion	for the war	—	1	1
Morgan's Iowa Infantry Company	for the war	—	1	1
Gally's Artillery Battalion	6 months	—	1	1
Johnson's Florida Infantry Company	12 months	—	1	1
Kelley's Florida Infantry Company	12 months	—	1	1
1st Alabama Infantry	6 months	—	—	—
Fremont's California Battalion	war in California	—	—	—
Maddox's California Company	war in California	—	—	—
Burton's California Detachment	12 months	—	—	—
Fisher's Florida Infantry Company	for the war	—	—	—
Seymour's Georgia Infantry Battalion	for the war	—	—	—
Parker's Iowa Mounted Company	12 months	—	—	—
Gage's Michigan Infantry Company	for the war	—	—	—
Blackbeaver's Mounted Company	6 months	—	—	—
Camp Washington Ohio Volunteers	12 months	—	—	—

Regimental Losses in the Volunteer Forces (cont.)

Unofficial Volunteer Units

Battalion of Santa Fe Traders	Chihiuahua expedition	Losses not recorded
Company of Santa Fe Traders	Taos Revolt	Losses not recorded
McKinstry's Quartermaster Company	Mexico City Campaign	Losses not recorded

+ Indicates units formed from reenlisted volunteers are officially designated "remustered volunteers."

*Mixed battalions contained various combinations of infantry, cavalry, and artillery companies.

Source: U.S. Congress, House, *Military Forces Employed in the Mexican War: Letter from the Secretary of War Transmitting, Information in answer to a resolution of the House, of July 31, 1848, relative to the military forces employed in the late war with Mexico*, 31st Cong., 1st sess., Executive Document No. 24.

antebellum medicine labeled the period "the heroic age of medicine," quoting one contemporary source whose rule of thumb was: "Desperate diseases require desperate remedies." Surgeons Love and Porter both detailed treatments for various illness they encountered in their service in Mexico. In the case of the "cold plague," the prescription was bleeding, cupping, tincture of opium, pediluvia with mustard, and brandy. Some men responded to the treatment, but others did not. The common cure for dysentery and diarrhea was a combination of sulfates of copper and opium, and acetate of lead and opium. Fevers of various descriptions called for quinine, sulfate of zinc and myrrh, and arsenic. Ice also was employed to help bring fevers down. For the dreaded *vomito,* or yellow fever, the course of action called for cupping, doses of calomel and quinine, and frequent enemas. Leeches applied to the temples, forehead, and epigastrium also seemed to help in some cases. Only patients with strong constitutions survived these conventional cures. Mundane ailments—hemorrhoids, ulcers, and inflammations, for example—received a relatively safe application of tincture of iodine.[13]

The dangers presented by yellow fever may have been exaggerated in the minds of the American military, but the perception of these dangers undoubtedly affected the conduct of the war. Once begun, Scott pressed the siege of Vera Cruz forward quickly, wishing to capture the city and the fort so his troops could move inland before the onset of the yellow fever season. Once out of the coastal plains, he halted at Jalapa and allowed the twelve-month volunteers in his column to return to the United States early, so they would not have to pass through the port at the height of the fever season. His actions undoubtedly prevented much illness, as the disease did strike the American garrison, as well as other troops who passed though the area. From April 1, 1847, through March 31, 1848, doctors treated 421 cases of yellow fever at Vera Cruz. This figure seems less important, however, when compared to the 2,026 diarrhea and dysentery cases reported during the same period. Surgeon Porter observed that, although yellow fever was greatly feared, the real killers were diarrhea and dysentery. As he explained, cases of yellow fever were diagnosed quickly and the victims taken to the hospital, where they received timely treatment. Men with diarrhea and dysentery, on the other hand, often stayed in camp untreated and were taken to the hospital only after their condition had deteriorated too far for them to recover. The fear of yellow fever was a real factor, as it prompted American planners to act as quickly as they could in central Mexico to bring the war to an end, but the disease itself failed to reach the epidemic proportions anticipated.[14]

Wherever American soldiers went in Mexico, the army hospital became a common feature. While ordinarily each regiment would establish a place to care for its own sick, the sheer number of cases to be treated led to the establishment of brigade and divisional hospitals, under the command of the most senior medical officer present. A staff was assembled to aid the surgeons and assistant surgeons in tending the patients. Regulations determined the ratio of hospital staff to patients: one steward and one wardmaster (both noncommissioned officers) per regimental hospital, one nurse to every ten patients, one matron to every twenty patients, and one cook to every thirty patients. Patients' weapons supposedly remained with their respective companies, but all other equipment and valuables brought with them were inventoried and stored in the ward property room. By regulations, each soldier admitted to the hospital had to have a certified copy of his descriptive roll—a record that included information on his pay and clothing issue—so that it could be kept current. Any soldiers determined unfit for further service received a "certificate of disability" and was discharged from the army.[15]

The Medical Department grew quite large by prewar standards. The Act of February 11, 1847, raised the number of medical officers within the regular army to 115. More than half of these positions went unfilled, though, meaning that a shortage still existed in some units. Records for the regular army indicate that 18 surgeons with the rank of major, 22 assistant surgeons with the rank of captain, and 19 assistant surgeons with the rank of 1st lieutenant served in the Mexican campaigns. The number of surgeons and assistant surgeons authorized for the volunteers was 135, but not all these positions were filled. The stewards, wardmasters, nurses, matrons, and cooks who worked for the department numbered in the hundreds.[16]

Almost any building or shed could serve as an impromptu hospital for the army. At Cerralvo, General Quitman ordered Surgeon Smith "to take possession of such buildings, belonging to the citizens [of the town], as [he] deemed most convenient for the purpose." Smith selected a vacant convent. Hospitals sprang up wherever the army went: New Orleans, Point Isabel, Matamoros, Reynosa, Camargo, Cerralvo, Monterey, Saltillo, Tampico, Vera Cruz, Jalapa, Puebla, Mexico City, San Antonio, Santa Fe, Los Angeles, San Diego, San Francisco, and Pascagula. Surgeon Porter, in charge of a general hospital at Vera Cruz, described the conditions of most of these facilities at their outset: "When this hospital was established I had not a single steward . . . no ward master . . . not a kitchen, or sink, or bunk, table, bench, spit box, close stool—in a word, there was nothing but the miserable sick." General Scott ordered the establishment of a general hospital in Mexico City under the charge of Surgeon Charles Stuart Tripler, with wards located at the Bishop's Palace, the Governor's Palace, Iturbide's Palace, the Inquisition [building], and the convents of Santa Isabel and Minerva. Obviously, some of the places used by the army during the war were hospitals in name only.[17]

Full recovery often depended on the quality of care provided in the hospital. Surgeon Porter emphasized the importance of a proper hospital diet but claimed that no steward or cook he met ever "knew how to prepare the most common article of diet for an invalid." Items thought best for hospitalized men included broth (chicken or beef), beef soup, coffee, fresh meat, and "in certain cases, an allowance of wine or even brandy." Unsanitary conditions and the dearth of antiseptics undoubtedly resulted in numerous infections, which slowed recovery and even killed some patients. Incredibly, Porter reported, "not a single case of hospital gangrene, tetnus [sic], or secondary hemorrhage was seen by the writer during the war with Mexico." Private Tennery nevertheless reported that a man from his regiment had contracted lockjaw from an untreated foot wound and was expected to die. Capt. Robert Anderson contended that the 2nd New York Infantry's colonel, Ward B. Burnett, contracted tetanus from a leg wound he received at Churubusco. No medical report, however, backs up his claim.[18]

Surgeon Porter found fault with some of the staff he encountered in the hospitals at Vera Cruz, blaming their incompetence for the poor care and even the deaths of some patients. As stipulated by regulations, the cooks and nurses for hospitals were drawn from the ranks of army privates; one common practice was to assign these duties to convalescing patients. One claimed that his main qualification was that he spoke both German and English, enabling him to translate for some of the patients. A problem even more serious than untrained nurses was the "employed physicians," who often were unskilled in their profession. The problem at Vera Cruz, according to Porter, arose from the fact that Scott took almost all the military surgeons and assistant surgeons, as well as all able-bodied stewards and other attendants, inland with him. The result was that the incompetent and infirm were left to take care of the sick and dying. One Mississippi colonel refused to let his surgeon appoint attendants, claiming that the regulations applied only to regulars.[19]

Unable to care for themselves, patients were at the mercy of the medical staff. Overworked doctors and an uncaring staff sometimes committed acts of cruelty and neglect. In one instance, a surgeon in Vera Cruz ordered attendants to gag a dying man whose screams disturbed the ward. A visit to a hospital at Puebla upset Sgt. Thomas Barclay, 2nd Pennsylvania Infantry, who called the surgeons he saw there "insolent ruffians." He angrily said, "A man in the States would be ashamed to speak to his dog in the way these men address the sick." Barclay blamed his regimental surgeon for the death of a friend, claiming, "The surgeon at first refused [to grant him a discharge] because he was not low enough and when he was far gone he again refused because if discharged he would not get home." Members of the Mormon Battalion complained bitterly over the rough treatment and rude manner of the regular army surgeon attached to their column. The men came close to mutiny when one of their comrades died shortly after the surgeon forced him to take medicine the man had refused, claiming it was against his religion. Wrote one Mormon of the incident, "The general feeling was that the Doctor had killed him." An ailing Pvt. William H. Richardson said an army doctor turned him out of the hospital at El Paso with "tender and endearing epithets." A Pennsylvania volunteer, Pvt. Chauncey Forward Sargent, told of one uncaring doctor who reportedly told a man to "go to hell" when he asked for some medicine to give a dying friend. In another case, a wounded soldier passed away only hours after a doctor pronounced him fit and returned him to the ranks. Detailed to attend a member of his own company, Private Sargent said the doctor "damned me upside down" when he asked for a cloth in which to wrap a poultice that this same doctor had just ordered applied. Hospital staffs came in for their share of criticism. Sergeant Barclay lamented, "It is sad to see men who left home full of high hopes, young, gallant and patriotic, pinning away in a hospital, exposed to the carelessness of nurses and attendants and daily insulted by ruffians." Another Pennsylvania volunteer remarked upon learning of an acquaintance's appointment to the position, "Elliot is [a] hospital steward at Vera Cruz with eighteen dollars a month besides the stealing from dead men and winning at Monti." Another volunteer seconded the notion that hospital stewards were thieves, saying, "The breath is scarcely out of the body of the deceased before the 'stewards' are rifling his pockets." With the sick seen by the staff mainly as a source of revenue, he lamented, "many died from the want of proper attention." At Camargo, Surgeon Love with the 2nd Mississippi Rifles dismissed his hospital steward for drunkenness and another attendant for failing to feed the patients their supper.[20]

The plight of the ill stirred pity in the hearts of their comrades. Sgt. Lewis H. Wunder sadly described the sick at Lobos Island, saying that it was difficult to stand "the idea of seeing a man lying sick on the point of Death on the ground with nothing but his blanket around him and then for his diet not anything more than hard crackers and coffee." Private Scribner painted a similar picture of sick soldiers along the Rio Grande, adding that many, in their fevered sleep, dreamed of loved ones at home. Even allowing for the fact that the army was on campaign, charged one soldier, there was no excuse for the deplorable state of the hospital at Jalapa. There patients lay on the bricks in the same vermin-infested clothes they had worn for weeks. Sergeant Barclay wrote of one hospital at Puebla: "It presents a bad sight. Crowded with sick whose wants are not as well provided for as they should be." Surgeon Love said hospital scenes depressed even the physician, who often heard his prostrate patients "muttering the sweet words of 'Mother,' 'Sister.'"[21]

Overcrowding led to poor conditions that hampered treatment and resulted in criticism of the Medical Department. Surgeon Porter claimed that the very size of the hospital at Vera Cruz led to some needless deaths; too many patients were massed together to be properly cared for at one place. Pvt. Thomas D. Tennery, an Illinois volunteer who visited a hospital at Matamoros, wrote, "It presents quite a sorrowful aspect; there are some five or six different places [around the city] where they are kept; these though large and spacious are crowded with sick from all parts of the Union." He further observed that many men had no beds but simply were lying on the brick floor with only a blanket beneath them. He ended by saying, "The care taken of them is according to the nurse's disposition." Pvt. William S. Johnson, a South Carolina volunteer, was more generous in his assessment during his visit to an army hospital at Puebla. Admitted for "inflammation of the bowels," he was pleased with the treatment he received, remarking, "The Hospital (owing to the exertions of Dr. Clarke) is as well organized as could be expected—for the Doctor is unremitting in his attention to the sick." A much more typical response to a stay in an army hospital was Private Sargent's exclamation: "Hope I shall never get into the hospital again." Wounded twice in the assault on Chapultepec, Sargent asked to leave the hospital after only a week's time. When the doctor denied his request, the resolute young man escaped from the hospital by climbing through a hole in the roof and returned to his own company, rather than remain in the hands of the Medical Department.[22]

Soldiers sometimes tried to cure themselves rather than be admitted to the hospital. A lieutenant of Texas volunteers restored his own health after breakfasting on "a drink of burnt brandy with sugar, and about twenty drops of laudanum" and a "burnt biscuit." When Captain Cox developed diarrhea at Vera Cruz, his self-medication included "peppermint & Brandy" and a self-imposed diet of a little "rice and parched corn." Later suffering from chills and fever on the march to Mexico City, the captain downed "a pint of Cayenne pepper tea" as a remedy; his fever broke, but his diarrhea returned. Lt. Adolphus Engelman and a companion spent an entire day on a twenty-mile ride around New Braunfels, Texas, hunting for a root said to cure diarrhea. On the march into Mexico, he reported that their regimental surgeon's haughty attitude prevented men from seeking medical attention. Engelman claimed that Dr. Price "expects the sick men who come to him to take off their caps when they come, with the result that many will go without medicine before they do it." George Ballentine, an Englishman in the 1st U.S. Artillery, "suffered a good deal with the prevalent complaint" but resolved to stay out of the hospital as long as possible. His remedy: a few grains of opium each night before going to sleep. Observed Lt. Francis Collins, an officer of the 4th U.S. Artillery left behind at Jalapa ill when Scott's main column moved on to Mexico city, "If one is sick on a campaign he must take care of himself the best way he can, for others have but little time to look after him." Sgt. Daniel Tyler, a member of the Mormon Battalion destined for California, claimed that his religion promoted prayer instead of medication as a cure for illness. Brigham Young even sent his followers a message, saying, "If you are ill, live by faith, and let the surgeon's medicines alone." Some men circumvented the army surgeon and found their own doctors. Two brothers in the Tennessee volunteers sought out medical treatment on their own in Mexico City. Although they hired a physician, they were not certain that he actually was responsible for their recovery. One of the brothers wrote home, "In the house where we stopped, there was an old Mexican woman who nursed us in the most motherly manner & two beautiful young girls who daily visited us so we are rather in doubt to attribute our recovery to skill, attention, or beauty." A patient of Dr. Claudon's Hospital in Mexico City felt compelled to write to the editors of the *North American* to recommend its facilities to all who wished a speedy recovery. The setting and the staff, he said, "combine to make it one of the most agreeable places an invalid can desire." This certainly stands in stark contrast to the descriptions of army hospitals. The editors of the *American Star*, however, warned soldiers against visiting Mexican doctors, saying of one local dentist, "He had formidable looking instruments, but knew no more about handling them than a cat knows how to play a violin."[23]

Venereal disease constituted a serious health problem in some areas of Mexico. According to Surgeon Porter, although Saltillo and Mexico City were hard struck, other cities, such as Matamoros, Camargo, Monterey, and Vera Cruz, were almost free of sexually transmitted diseases. He wrote, "Syphillis [*sic*] at Saltillo was very common and very malignant" and recalled a warning from a local inhabitant that the town was "mucha mala" and had many "putas y ladrones y matadores." Infected prostitutes evidently conducted a brisk business with American soldiers, as evidenced by one regiment of regular infantry that required "several wagons for those who were hors de combat" when recalled from that city. Gonorrhea also was diagnosed at Saltillo, as well as at Mexico City. The treatment for venereal disease called for doses of mercury and cauterization of chancres with an acid solution. He noted the extraordinary case of one young artillery officer, who was threatened with the loss of his "organ" to a sloughing chancre. The desperate situation caused Porter to cauterize the sore with pure acid, and the unfortunate man recovered from the ordeal with his "organ" intact. But venereal disease was not confined only to Mexico. The surgeon of the 1st Regiment of Mounted Tennessee Volunteers reported treating cases of syphilis and gonorrhea while his men were camped near Memphis, Tennessee, waiting to be mustered into service. As syphilis and gonorrhea take time to run their course, it is impossible to tell how many soldiers eventually died years after the war from the effects of these diseases.[24]

In addition to disease, accidents accounted for a number of deaths and injuries in the army. Two of the army's most promising officers died not on the battlefield but from accidents. Lt. Jacob E. Blake, U.S. Topographic Engineers, distinguished himself at Palo Alto, but on the morning following the battle, he was struck by a ball from his own pistol when the gun slipped from his belt and accidentally discharged. The ball, although of small caliber, passed through his bladder, intestines, stomach, liver, and diaphragm, and lodged in his right lung. Capt. Randolph Ridgely also had distinguished himself at Palo Alto, assuming command of Maj. Samuel Ringgold's famed battery upon that officer's death. Recognized as one of the best horsemen in the army, Ridgely died after his mount slipped and dashed him head first onto a Monterey street while he was on his way to a dinner engagement. Another officer, Lt. George Stephens, 2nd U.S. Dragoons, drowned while crossing the Rio Grande the day that Taylor's forces occupied Matamoros. An explosion killed Lt. William Armstrong, an officer of the 2nd U.S. Artillery who had been detailed to inventory the contents of a Mexican magazine following the battle of Molino del Rey. Enlisted men were not immune to accidents, as one man reported in central Mexico: "A dragoon fell from his horse and his pistol went off and wounded him badly in the leg." One sergeant of artillery was killed when members of another company fired at a Mexican courier but struck him instead. Assistant Surgeon John S. Griffin treated a number of accidents in California while on duty with General Kearny. In one case, a dragoon had shot himself in the hand, blowing off two fingers. Two other Americans were accidentally injured during a skirmish with Californios: one gored by an ox and another shot by a sailor. Later that same day, reported Griffin, a marine accidentally shot and killed a sailor from the USS *Cyanes*. Capt. Robert E. Lee and Lt. P. T. G. Beauregard narrowly missed injury when a frightened sentinel fired at them as they returned to the American lines after a scouting expedition. The ball passed between Lee's left arm and his body, with the flame from the discharge singeing his coat.[25]

Accidents plagued volunteers, too. Private Tennery witnessed several incidents in the camp of the 3rd Illinois Infantry. On one occasion, a lieutenant shot his captain in the leg with a pistol. On another, two volunteers were trying to free a rammer stuck in the barrel of a musket when the weapon suddenly went off. The iron rod passed through the breast of the man pulling on it, killing him instantly, and lodged in the neck of a passerby. Not all accidents involved firearms. A boiler burst on a ship during a Gulf passage, killing an Indiana volunteer. Another Hoosier fell to his death from a scenic overlook during a march though central Mexico. A wagon crushed an Illinois volunteer while he was loading it. A Tennessee man burned both his hands severely while playing with gunpowder. A heavy artillery wagon rolled over the feet of a Pennsylvania volunteer, mangling them and crippling him for life. Missouri volunteers lost one man at a river crossing; another was injured when a wagon rolled over his chest; and

Death of Samuel Ringgold. Henry B. Dawson, Battles of the United States By Land and Sea, *New York: Johnson, Fry, and Co., ca. 1860. Courtesy Richard Bruce Winders*

another was injured from the accidental discharge of a "revolving pistol." One member of the Mormon Battalion shot himself in the arm and had to be left along the route at an Indian village, where he died a few days later. One young Kentuckian accidentally shot his cousin to death while the two were on a drinking spree. Few men ever imagined that fate would play such cruel tricks on soldiers, killing and maiming them without a chance for winning glory on the battlefield.[26]

Dueling accounted for a number of deaths and injuries in the army. The practice was strictly forbidden by Sections 25 and 26 of the Articles of War, but the threat of punishment—cashiering for officers and corporal punishment for enlisted men—failed to prevent some from settling their disputes on the field of honor. Dr. Price of the 2nd Illinois Infantry (the surgeon who, according to Lieutenant Engelman, made patients remove their caps before he would see them) shot it out with another surgeon at ten paces when his regiment was at San Antonio. Price fired first but missed; his opponent's aim was true, and he sent a ball into Price's abdomen. As serious as the wound appeared to some of the witnesses, he recovered. Not so fortunate were two officers from the 1st Virginia Infantry. Lt. Carlton R. Mumford accused Lt. Washington L. Mahan of making a false report and publicly branded him a "damn liar." Mahan, whose reputation was at stake, asked for a retraction but instead received more insults. The two men, each carrying a musket, met outside their regiment's camp at China. When sixty yards apart, both fired but missed. They reloaded, moved closer, fired, and missed again. Reloading a third time, they moved forward until separated by only thirty-five paces and fired—both men fell. Mumford died the next day; Mahan lingered for a week before he, too, passed away. Surgeon Porter was called upon to treat a Louisiana captain shot through both thighs by a pistol ball sustained in a duel with another officer. Firearms were not the only weapons used in these affairs. In central Mexico, two officers fought each other using dragoon sabers. The swordplay ended when one had his hand "cleft to the bone." Several duels were narrowly averted, such as one at Camargo involving Col. Baile Peyton and Brig. Gen. Thomas Marshall. Gen. Joseph Lane arrested several officers in his command in order to prevent a duel slated to be carried out with fencing foils. In California, Gen. Stephen W. Kearny prevented a duel between John Charles Frémont and Col. Richard B. Mason, which was to have been fought with double-barrel shotguns at twenty paces. In almost all these cases, the participants were volunteers or recent appointees to the regular army.[27]

Military medicine had not changed much since the days of Napoleon. Surgeon Porter described the treatment of gunshot wounds in several articles published after the war. In wounds where a musket ball passed through the flesh without striking bone, he recommended a simple dressing of lint and adhesive plaster, followed by an application of lead lotion. A poultice of linseed, corn meal, or slippery-elm bark was found to be very helpful in speeding recovery. Poultices were applied cold unless the wound was stiff and painful, in which cases they were applied hot. If a bone was involved, the doctor removed all visible chips or bone fragments before applying the dressing. Men with simple gunshot wounds stood a good chance of recovery, but the more extensive the damage, the less chance there was of surviving. Surgeons automatically considered any wound to the head, chest, or pelvic region "dangerous." Abdominal wounds almost always proved fatal. Suppuration, or the formation of pus, was expected in most cases and was thought by some doctors to be a sign of healing.[28]

The prognosis for injured extremities depended on the severity and location of the wound. Wounds to legs and feet took longer to heal than those to arms and hands. Amputation was viewed as a lifesaving practice and was not resorted to unless bones and joints were shattered and beyond the surgeon's ability to repair them. Wounds to the face and neck, although disfiguring, had a good chance of healing as long as no major nerves or blood vessels were damaged. Some surgeons had access to sulphuric ether, but they generally believed that its use harmed their patients. Hence, most surgeries during the Mexican War almost always took place without anesthetics. Surgeon Porter exclaimed, ". . . we do not need the chloroform bottle on the battlefield." One noted military surgeon claimed that a skilled physician needed less than eighty seconds to remove an injured limb successfully, cautioning, however, that too much haste in the procedure might cause the patient months of suffering. Unfortunately for the wounded, not all surgeons possessed the talent to perform the procedure effortlessly. As barbaric as the practice sounds today, medical historian John Duffy observed of the era, "Pain and healing were traditionally associated."[29]

Projectiles striking a body forced bits of clothing, leather, and other debris into the wound; if this was not removed, conditions were established that promoted infection. As careful as they were, surgeons could not always clean all foreign matter from gunshot wounds. One surgeon described the problem, saying, "The presence of foreign substance in the simplest wound frequently caused protracted suppuration, and the formation of abscess, and thus retarded their cure, in many instances for a long times." That was what happened to Lieutenant Engelman when he was wounded in the shoulder at Buena Vista. The ball carried pieces of his jacket and shirt into the wound, causing the shoulder to swell and Engelman to suffer. He rejoiced when the fragments worked their way to the surface nearly a month later, exclaiming, "I may now look forward to a speedy recovery. Oh! This is a lucky day." A musket ball pierced the foot of Isaac J. Stevens, a lieutenant in the U.S. Engineers, during the fighting at San Cosmé gate in Mexico City; the wound healed only after an application of poultices finally caused shoe leather driven deep into the wound to surface. Foreign matter of a different kind interfered with Lt. Col. Alexander Keith McClung's recovery. He was stuck in the left hand while holding his scabbard, and the musket ball carried bones from his fingers with it as it tore into his hip. Surgeons opened his wound and removed five finger bones—one an inch and a half in length—before the officer began to recover.[30]

Artillery rounds produced catastrophic trauma to the human body, often leaving the victim beyond the skill of the surgeon. The butchery caused in this manner had quite an unsettling effect on soldiers who witnessed it at first hand. At the Battle of Palo Alto, a Mexican cannonball mortally wounded Maj. Samuel Ringgold, passing through both his thighs as well as the body of horse on which he was mounted. A captain of the 4th

U.S. Infantry, John Page, had his entire lower jaw carried away; horrified by the extent of his wound, the army watched as he lingered for more than a month before finally dying. Another shot at Palo Alto took off the head of a soldier, splattering those around him with brains and blood. Artillery fire claimed the life of Maj. Jacob Brown, the American commander of the fort across from Matamoros that was to bear his name; although the shot took off his leg below the knee, he did not die until several days later. Capt. Henry McKavett died instantly when a ball passed through his chest at the Battle of Monterey. At the siege of Vera Cruz, the concussion from a ball that passed inches from Capt. John R. Vinton's head killed the officer without leaving a mark on his body. At the same battle, another ball decapitated Capt. William Albertis as he sat on a log reading a letter from home. As for Capt. Seth Thornton, the officer whose skirmish on the Rio Grande ignited the war, an 18-pound shot "tore him to pieces" outside Mexico City. Projectiles rolling across the ground presented a threat, striking men at ankle level and tearing off their feet. Injuries caused by artillery—if the victim survived being struck by shot, shell, or grape—received the same treatment as that described for regular gunshot wounds.[31]

Surgeon Porter devoted many words to discussing gunshot wounds, explaining, "Bayonet and lance wounds were not common." He stated that Mexican lancers, although thought to be among the best troops Mexico had to offer, actually performed poorly in battle. American soldiers run down by lancers on the plains of Monterey probably would have had a different opinion, as would the dragoons of Kearny's command at the Battle of San Pascual. The surgeon who treated the Americans wounded at San Pascual reported that, of the seventeen men killed and eleven men wounded, only one suffered from a gunshot wound. Assistant Surgeon Griffin noted that some of the wounded he treated had "as many as eight wounds on a side"; he deduced that the attackers "seem to aim with their lances so as to strike a man near the kidneys." Lieutenant Kirkham noted that an American officer near Mexico City "was lanced in his back whilst in the act of cutting down a Mexican in front of him." Bayonets, not lances, were the weapons Pvt. Barna Upton saw used at Cerro Gordo. As he told his brother, "Here for just a short minute ensued a kind of fighting which I hope never to see again. It seemed like murder to see men running bayonets into each other's breasts." At Resaca de la Palma, Mexican soldiers attacked the colonel of the 5th U.S. Infantry after his horse was shot from under him, inflicting several severe wounds and pinning him to the ground. One possible reason why surgeons treated few bayonet and lance wounds was that men wounded by these murderous instruments rarely made it to the operating table.[32]

Many men were unprepared for the carnage of battle. Witnessing war at first hand provoked reactions of horror. Barna Upton, a private in the 3rd U.S. Infantry, wrote to his brother shortly after the action at Resaca de la Palma: "The wounded, both friend and foe, were collected on the bank of the pond. Their groans were heart-rending as the dreadful and rapid progress of amputation was going on. The dead lay in a heap beside." According to Lt. John Peck, an officer of the 4th U.S. Artillery present at the battle, "While fighting, onward was the word, and we paid little attention to the dead Mexicans, but after the excitement of the battle had passed away our sympathies were aroused and I keenly felt the horrors of war." Although a veteran of Taylor's northern battles, Peck was shaken by his experiences at Churubusco, where a classmate was struck down by his side: "My heart sickened at the thought of the battlefield. I did not expect to live for a moment, so fierce was the contest." Following Cerro Gordo, Capt. Robert Anderson said, "The field was strewn with the dying and dead," He added, "Our Surgeons amputated the arms and legs of some of the wounded," and swore, "I never want to see such again." Pvt. Frederick Zeh described the "melancholy spectacle" of several infantrymen wounded at Vera Cruz, who were carried off to the hospital "in their woolen blankets, leaving behind a continuous trail of blood." After seeing the fighting for Mexico City, Lieutenant Kirkham told his wife, "I had no idea until within a few days past what horrible sights a battlefield presented." He described the carnage in gruesome detail: "The road and its vicinity on both sides, for the most of three miles, were covered with the dead and dying, bodies without heads, arms, legs, and disfigured in every horrible way!" Kirkham closed his letter exclaiming: "Oh! it was awful and I can never forget this day!" Later, upon reflection, he told her, "A person can get accustomed to anything so as to be indifferent to the most revolting sights." Lieutenant Gibson, an officer present at the Battle of Sacramento outside Chihuahua, said that there would be few such scenes if politicians had to view the results of their actions. Even so, he continued, "The little care the wounded must from necessity receive blunts and hardens men's feelings until they become perfectly indifferent." Most soldiers probably agreed with Pvt. J. Jacob Oswandel, who wished for a quick death rather than a crippling wound: "I would rather be dead than have my body mangled and shattered like I have seen some poor soldiers . . . with both arms shot off, others with both legs off, and others badly wounded." "Rather kill me outright, at once," he reasoned, "than have the suffering hereafter." Private Scribner remarked after visiting the hospital at Point Isabel, where the wounded from Palo Alto and Resaca de la Palma were housed, "It is an affecting sight for an American to behold his countrymen wounded in carrying out the demands of his government, to see them with their arms and legs blown off, rendering them ever afterwards incapable of enjoying active life." At Buena Vista, he saw one of his friends struck down and "quivering in death." "I was loading when he fell, and compressing my lips, and smothering my emotions, I stepped over him and fired."[33]

As shocking as death could be, soldiers like Scribner learned to step over the bodies of the slain and continue carrying out their duties. They actually became quite used to death, a transition one can follow in their diaries and letters. Pvt. Thomas D. Tennery's early entries contain lines such as these lamenting his unit's dead: "Though universally beloved by all who knew him . . . we have consigned him to the grave to be forgotten by all his friends but those dear to him by the nature of law." Again: "Alas, what tears of contrition will flow for those who die in the army without a mother, wife or sister to smooth the pillow or close their eyes in death and weep over their briar." Barely two months later, he recorded the scene following a volunteer's funeral: "We smoothed the mound and returned to quarters, but the countenance of everyone changed, the stern soldiers who a moment before stood before the open grave of their companion, with sad countenance and heavy faces, had acquired cheerful appearances and jokes went around as lively as if death had never been with us." A bit of a philosopher, Tennery remarked, "Such is the effect of war. A soldier becomes the football of passion; from grief to mirth or ambition, his life regarded as public property, as nothing, he is prepared to meet death and danger at any time and in any form." Private Upton, who had recoiled at the sight of the wounded and dying, after a year of war wrote, "I am astonished at the calmness and almost indifference which I experience now walking over the battlefield. It is only when some shocking instance of mutilation meets my eye that I feel that sensation of horror which is natural for anyone to feel." In some instances, the dead even angered the living, as if the former somehow had betrayed their comrades by dying. When Indiana volunteers found the decayed bodies of two American soldiers along a road in central Mexico, the corpses were tossed unceremoniously over the edge of a nearby embankment. As Lieutenant Brackett explained, "I pitied them, but we could afford [them] no better burial." Captain Rogers later lamented engaging in a fist fight with his lieutenant, because "it occurred 10 feet from the corpse of poor [Lt. Josephus J.] Tatum who had died that day." Attitudes toward death changed as soldiers saw men die almost daily.[34]

Army regulations set down how funerals were to be conducted. As

with so many things in the army, one's rank was important, for it determined the size of the military escort that accompanied the body to the
grave site. The escort for the commanding general of the army consisted
of one regiment of infantry, two companies of cavalry, and six pieces of
artillery; for a major general, one regiment of infantry, two companies of
cavalry, and four pieces of artillery; for a brigadier general, one regiment
of infantry, one company of cavalry, and two pieces of artillery; for a colonel, one regiment; for a lieutenant colonel, six companies; for a major,
four companies; for a captain, one company; for a lieutenant, one platoon.
Funeral escorts for officers were commanded, whenever possible, by an
officer of the same rank; if none were present, then an officer of the
next highest rank took charge. The same principles applied to enlisted men.
Sergeants attached to the staff departments received an escort of sixteen men, commanded by a sergeant. A sergeant with a line regiment
received an escort of fourteen men, commanded by sergeant. A corporal received an escort of twelve men, commanded by a corporal. And a private
received an escort of eight men, commanded by a corporal. These standards obviously could not be followed on the battlefield or when the dead
numbered several a day. Coffins all but disappeared. Ballentine claimed
that the sick died so quickly at Puebla that they were buried without any
ceremony at all. Deceased officers always seemed to receive more consideration than men in the ranks, although the situation began to return to
normal in central Mexico after the fall of the capital, as the army took up
garrison duty throughout the country.[35]

For some American dead, however, Mexico was not their final resting
place. In a number of cases, friends and family collected funds to bring
dead loved ones home. "We have just received a request from the citizens
of New Albany to bring home four bodies of our fallen comrades," wrote
Scribner as his regiment prepared to leave Saltillo. More often than not,
those brought home had achieved some level of fame. Retrieved heroes
included Col. Samuel H. Watson; Capt. Randolph Ridgely; Capt. Robert
A. Gillespie; Lt. Col. Henry Clay, Jr.; and Capt. Samuel H. Walker. Lead-
lined caskets (thought best for preserving a body) were hard to come by,
and, in at least one case, a tin lining was substituted. Charcoal, placed
inside the casket with the corpse, helped to slow decomposition and ab-
sorb odor. Capt. Franklin Smith disapproved of shipping departed heroes
home, after he saw the rough pine coffins of several notables at Camargo
heaped in with all the other army stores and looking very much "like the
ordinary gun boxes of the ordnance department." He pondered, "How

vain and futile the attempt to impart the honors of the living to the dead . . . Better poor fellows that they had been left in the glory bed where they fell."[36]

The reflective Tennery penned a passage quite moving in its sentiment: "There they lay like warriors taking their rest, no more to be roused by the reveille or to suffer on the toilsome march of this life's journey." Earlier he effectively had summed up the uncertain lot of the soldier: "Such are the chances and fate and a soldier should always be prepared for death or life without a moments notice." Prepared or not, thousands of soldiers in Mr. Polk's army did not come home.[37]

NINE

The Land of the Montezumas

I venture to assert that there is not one of us to whom the service in Mexico is not a recollection surpassing in interest the most brilliant operation of the Rebellion.
—Gen. Lew Wallace, May 1876

What a beautiful and happy country this might be if there were good laws and the people virtuous.
—Lt. Ralph Kirkham,
6th U.S. Infantry

The memory of Mexico stayed with American soldiers who served there. Lew Wallace, the author of *Ben Hur,* was just one of many men who was mesmerized by the land and its people. Writing thirty years after the war, he summed up his feelings in an 1876 letter addressed to Indiana's Mexican War veterans: "I venture to assert that there is not one of us to whom the service in Mexico is not a recollection surpassing in interest the most brilliant operation of the Rebellion." He explained this fascination saying, "Mexico was a strange land to us all, and full of novelties." To judge from the words of other Americans who served in Mexico, Wallace was not alone in his impression.[1]

Although a foreign land, Mexico was not *terra incognita*. Americans had been reading about Mexico for at least forty years. Before it achieved independence, Mexico appeared as New Spain in the pages of geography books such as Jedidiah Morse's *Geography Made Easy* (in its eleventh edition in 1807). The writings and maps of Alexander von Humboldt further illuminated the region for the outside world. Americans had been neighbors to the Spanish for many years, and, piqued by Aaron Burr's failed filibustering expedition and Zebulon Pike's survey of the Southwest, curiosity about Mexico had been high. American volunteers fought against Spanish Royalists during Mexico's wars for independence, and word that a new republic had been born was greeted with enthusiasm in the United States. In his contemporary history of the Mexican Revolution, one American author praised the Mexicans, writing that, although "some individuals from the United States and the British Isles" joined in the fight against the Spanish, "the Mexican patriots have maintained the long and sanguinary struggle alone . . . and by their own valour [*sic*] and perseverance, have overcome both foreign and domestic tyranny." He also proudly noted that the U.S. recognized Mexico and other former Spanish colonies, while European nations waited. Throughout the war, American map makers provided a ready supply of maps of the region so that their countrymen could chart the movements of armies in the field.[2]

Visitors to Mexico already had produced a substantial body of literature on the country prior to the Mexican War. Three American diplomats, Joel R. Poinsett, Waddy Thompson, and Brantz Mayer, had published accounts upon their return to the U.S. The wife of a Spanish diplomat, Frances Calderón de la Barca, described her observations of the land and people in *Life in Mexico During a Residence of Two Years in That Country*. Mexico's northern provinces also received their share of attention in such books as Josiah Gregg's *Commerce of the Prairies; Or, The Journal of a Santa Fe Trader;* Lansford W. Hastings's *The Emigrant's Guide to Oregon and California;* and Richard Dana's *Two Years Before the Mast*. Unfortunately for Mexico, this publicity led to unwelcome American interest in these areas. Mexico's political instability spawned a series of revolutions—Texas' struggle for independence was just one—that also increased American awareness. After the Alamo and Goliad, public opinion in the U.S. began to turn against Mexico, as news of mass killings was heard. The ongoing war between Mexico and the new Republic of Texas during the 1830s and 1840s had its own chroniclers, who published stories of Mexican cruelty to prisoners captured at Santa Fe and Mier, reinforcing the notion that Mexicans were barbaric people. Some enterprising former travelers, like the celebrated

"Dr. Slater," who had lived in Mexico for two years before the war, capital-
ized upon interest in the region by giving lectures on "Mexican manners,
custom[s], &c." for a small fee. During the war, too, U.S. newspapers
frequently carried descriptions of the land of the Montezumas. Even with
accurate knowledge of Mexico available, however, most Americans probably had only an impressionistic view of the country and its people.[3]

Americans knew that they were entering an ancient world. The recent
appearance of William H. Prescott's *History of the Conquest of Mexico* vividly told the story of Cortés and Montezuma. Many soldiers turned to the
work as a guide to Mexico and its people. Visiting Aztec ruins became a
popular pastime in central Mexico for Americans retracing Cortés's own
invasion route. Even Winfield Scott climbed atop the famous pyramid at
Cholula, from which he reviewed the troops who would make it possible
to "sleep in the halls of the Montezumas." The Americans were mindful
that they were walking among Montezuma's descendants and expected to
find a people worthy of that noble's name. Once in the old Aztec capital,
soldiers shopped for idols, vases, and sacrificial knives to take home to show
that they had walked in the footsteps of history.[4]

The land offered a variety of landscapes and climates. The regions of
Mexico range from arid deserts to tropical forests and from high mountains to low coastal plains. Visitors who began their journey at Vera Cruz,
on the country's eastern Gulf Coast, would find themselves on a hot and
humid coastal plain. There lush vegetation covered the low ground, giving
the countryside the appearance of a tropical paradise. To avoid the deadly
diseases associated with coastal areas, however, most visitors moved inland
quickly. To the west, already visible from the coast, stood mountains. Some,
such as Orizaba at 18,000 feet, were high enough to maintain a covering of
snow all year round. Moving inland on the Spanish-built National Road,
the traveler began a long climb upward toward the eastern branch of the
Sierra Madres. A short distance past an opening through the mountain
pass at Cerro Gordo stood the city of Jalapa. By now the coast had been
left far behind, and the traveler had ascended to 4,300 feet in elevation.
Running westward again, the road continued to rise until it passed through
the village of Las Vegas, at an altitude of 8,000 feet. From this vantage
point, the traveler could see a vast plateau spread out below, bounded on
the western horizon by more mountains. Popocatepetl, the tallest mountain in the distant range, reached over 17,000 feet into the sky. After a brief
descent to reach the famed city of Perote, the National Road stretched on
across the plateau to Puebla. Snow-capped volcanoes and numerous Aztec
ruins provided breathtaking scenery. The highway began to rise again at

Puebla, climbing nearly 4,000 feet more to reach a summit where, to the west, a spectacular view of the Valley of Mexico greeted travelers. To reach Mexico City, the visitor continued on the National Road as it descended to the valley floor. At 7,400 feet, Mexico City looked much as it had three hundred years before, when it was conquered by Cortés. A traveler who continued on to the west encountered another mountain range, before descending to Mexico's western coastal plain and the Pacific Ocean.[5]

Northern Mexico, New Mexico, and California comprised a region very different from central Mexico. More arid, this vast area was not without its own diversity. The Rio Grande provided northern Mexico with water for crops and livestock, while the eastern branch of the Sierra Madres formed the basis of Mexico's mining industry. The plains adjacent to the mountains were dotted with villages and ranches. To reach Mexico City, one had to travel Rinconada Pass from Monterey to Saltillo and then strike southward over a long and frequently waterless road. Distance and terrain worked together to isolate New Mexico from both central Mexico and the U.S. The plains of West Texas and eastern New Mexico were home to migrating herds of buffalo and the nomadic tribesmen who followed them. The New Mexicans lived in scattered and isolated settlements such as Santa Fe, the capital of the province. Pueblo and Navaho Indians maintained

Cactus Gigantea, La Palma Bendita, Sword Palmetos, &. George C. Furber, The Twelve Month Volunteer, *Cincinnati: J. A. and U. P. James, 1848. Courtesy Daughters of the Republic of Texas Library*

their own villages. The mountains to the west had provided a rich hunting ground for fur trappers who used Taos as a base of operation. By the time of the war, a thriving trade had been established with Missouri to the east and Chihuahua to the south. Just west of Santa Fe and Taos ran the same Rio Grande that passed Matamoros. California, on the Pacific Coast, had been difficult to reach from the east, although explorers, adventurers, and settlers had trickled into the area. Californios lived chiefly along the coastal plain, although some had moved into the mountain valleys. Ports such as San Diego, Monterey, and Los Angeles provided an link to the world. (San Francisco's days as a great port lay ahead.) Although many of the local Indians still farmed the lands settled by missionaries, Californios raised cattle, selling hides and tallow to Yankee sea captains who visited the region. Like New Mexico, California was isolated from both Mexico City and the U.S. On the eve of war with the U.S., Mexico was a vast country that stretched from Guatemala on the south to Oregon on the north. Furthermore, it included the future American states of California, Nevada, Arizona, Utah, and New Mexico, as well as parts of Wyoming, Colorado, and Kansas.[6]

Mexico offered Americans who crossed her borders new and interesting sights. Many soldiers were startled by the prickly character of local plants and wildlife. Commenting on his journey through Texas, Lt. Adolphus Engelman observed, "All plants here have thorns, all the animals, stings or thorns, and all men carry weapons and all deceive each other and themselves." Pvt. Benjamin Franklin Scribner agreed with the description, writing, "The expression so common with us, 'All bushes have thorns, All insects have horns,' is almost true without exception. Even the frogs and grasshoppers are in possession of the last mentioned appendages." The soldiers of Kearny's command encountered thorny bushes near the Gila River, prompting one soldier to record the unexpected remark, "Considering the thorns it was as bad as a Florida hammock." One volunteer thought that Tampico must be Mexico's Eden, writing, "This seemed to be a garden spot, from which most of the thorns have been expelled."[7]

Reptiles thrived in the arid and topical climates of Mexico. Soldiers frequently encountered rattlesnakes, black snakes, and snakes of other colors and designs along the march and in their camps. Lt. Napoleon Tecumseh Jackson Dana, an officer with Taylor's Army of Occupation at Corpus Christi, forwarded several snake stories to his wife. One companion awoke to find a rattler coiled up at the foot of his bed. Another man was awaken when he felt a snake crawling over his bare legs. These incidents convinced Dana to elevate his bed above the ground to avoid such night visitors. Missouri volunteers marching to Santa Fe frequently encountered rattlesnakes, one of which crawled into bed with three officers. "It had slept between the first lieutenant and myself near the captain's face," wrote Lt. George R. Gibson. Marching near Camargo, Pvt. Thomas Tennery encountered a dead rattler in the road that measured "six feet long, four inches in diameter, with thirteen rattles and a button." Capt. Leander M. Cox saw a dead snake near Vera Cruz that measured nearly ten feet in length. For all the snake sightings, actual bites seem to have been rare. Although a "viper" bit one Illinois volunteer on the finger, prompt medical attention saved his life. The treatment he received was not described, although probably it consisted of large doses of whiskey, if the conventional treatment was applied. On Lobos Island, the predominant reptiles were not snakes but lizards. These animals frequently crawled into the men's knapsacks, but fortunately they were harmless. Another harmless creature, the horned toad, fascinated those who saw it and marveled at its fantastic appearance.[8]

Other creatures, smaller in stature, were much more bothersome, annoying privates and generals alike. As Captain Cox exclaimed at Vera Cruz, "This is truly an enemies [*sic*] country. The ground . . . is covered with

Grand Plaza, Camargo. John Frost, Pictorial History of the Mexican War, *Philadelphia: C. Desilver, 1848. Courtesy Mary Couts Burnett Library, Texas Christian University*

small red ants that crawl into every place and feed on every thing you have to eat." He continued to enumerate the pests: lizards as numerous as grasshoppers, tarantulas as big as a man's fist, mosquitoes and flies in swarms. Later, when his regiment marched inland, he added ticks to his list. Ants on Lobos Island had a fiery bite which left a painful welt. Soldiers in some areas of Mexico learned to check their shoes for scorpions and tarantulas before slipping them on in the morning. Fleas and lice made appearances as well. At Vera Cruz, Pvt. William S. Johnson reported that he "saw 2767 full-grown Fleas on one man." Lieutenant Gibson claimed that lice infested the entire town of Santa Fe. Another Missourian on his way to Santa Fe found, scribbled in his journal by a prankster, a parody of a Thomas Moore poem, dedicated to "a Spanish louse":

> *Oft in the stilly night,*
> *Ere slumber's chains had bound me,*
> *I feel the cursed creatures bite,*
> *As scores are crawling round me.*
> *O' not like one who treads alone,*
> *The banquet halls deserted,*
> *In crowds they crawl despite the groan*
> *Of him whose blood they started.*
>
> (Thomas Moore,
> "Oft in the Stilly Night")

Infrequent bathing and crowded camps provided ideal conditions for the spread of body lice, and few soldiers failed to encounter "gray backs" during their terms of service. One improbable story that appeared in Mexico City's *North American* ventured an explanation for the numerous lice around the Mexican capital. According to the story's author, the Aztec rulers, in an effort to rid their country of the pest, had offered a bounty for the creatures. The plan had the opposite result, however, as it encouraged Mexicans to "raise" lice in order to collect the reward. Roaches and moths bothered Lieutenant Dana; they invaded his trunk at Corpus Christi and ate so many holes in his clothing that some garments looked as if they had been riddled with buckshot.[9]

The strange noises made by some unfamiliar animals sometimes caused volunteers to think they were under attack. Private Scribner recounted how one night his regiment, camped on the Rio Grande, thought it heard Mexican bugle calls in the distance. Not wishing to be caught by surprise, the guard was increased and muskets ordered loaded. About 2 A.M., shots awoke the men, who quickly formed a line of battle while a party was sent out to locate the enemy. Upon its return, officers announced that all could go back to bed—the pickets had fired on baying wolves. Sentinels of an Illinois regiment near the Rio Grande one night called the sergeant of the guard. One guard said that an Indian was just outside the camp, while another claimed it was a bear. Upon further investigation, the sergeant determined that the unusual noises emanated not from an Indian or a bear, but from a large toad.[10]

The Mexican people seemed as strange as the land in which they lived. An 1842 census placed Mexico's population at 7,015,509. The rich ethnic heritage of the country reflected the mixture of Indian, European, and African groups. According to the census, Mexico's inhabitants fell into the following categories: 4,000,0000 Indians; 2,009,509 mixed-bloods; 1,000,000 whites; and 6,000 blacks. Thus, concluded the survey's author, Indians and blacks outnumbered mixed-bloods and whites by nearly one million. Interracial marriage had produced a variety of progeny. Different groups were called by specific names to denote their ethnic origins: *mulattos* were the children of one white parent and one black parent; *mestizos* were the children of one white parent and one Indian parent; and *zambos* were the children of one Indian parent and one black parent. Although Americans had seen mixed-bloods and Indians in the U.S., encountering so many diverse groups in Mexico served as a visual reminder that indeed the soldiers were in a foreign land. The Mexican government had issued a decree in 1829 expelling Spaniards from the country; although many left, some had managed to evade the order. Mexico's cities drew some European residents—mainly merchants and businessmen from Britain and France.[11]

Many Americans were unimpressed by their first encounters with Mexicans. Scribner, the young volunteer from Indiana, exclaimed upon seeing Mexican traders and their rickety oxcart near Point Isabel, "Are these the people we came to fight?" He continued, "You can form no idea of their wretched appearance, without thinking of their abject poverty and ignorance." Col. William B. Campbell of Tennessee expressed a similar opinion of the herdsmen along the Rio Grande, viewing them as members of a "miserable ignorant, filthy race." The Massachusetts farm boy, Barna Upton, thought the residents of Matamoros ignorant because none could read. "How strong the contrast with the people of New England," he mused. Others expressed surprise at the obvious differences in skin color between themselves and many Mexicans. One South Carolina volunteer who saw a group of Mexican prisoners in central Mexico remarked, "Not a white man among them, but some as black as Negroes as I ever saw." Captain Cox thought the Mexicans he was passing on the National Road in central Mexico

looked "very much like Indians" and were the most "ignorant and de-
graded" people he had ever seen. Lieutenant Engelman thought Mexican
men he encountered in San Antonio, Texas, looked like mulattos, the only
difference being that the Mexicans had straight hair. One Mississippi volunteer wrote home from his camp on the Rio Grande to say that some of
the Mexicans he saw looked like a mixture of "Choctaws and negro." He
quoted one of the black servants with his regiment, who supposedly asked
his master, "Misser Willis, why you no bring dem cow-hide 'stead of muskets, case dem folks got nigger in 'em [for] sure?" Many American soldiers
strongly believed that Mexicans as a whole were an inferior race of people.[12]

The opinions of the soldiers tended to differ according to whether the
Mexicans being described were male or female, however. Americans like
Lieutenant Engelman often used such terms as "dark," "cruel," and "lazy"
when referring to Mexican men but had different language for Mexican
women. He marveled that the Mexican women he saw in San Antonio
were as white as American women, explaining the phenomenon by saying,
"They might have been of Spanish decent." Wrote one Mississippi volunteer, "The Mexican women are very kind to our sick, and pity the wounded
much, embracing every opportunity of alleviating their distress, and promoting their comfort." One sick Missourian who passed through Saltillo
recalled seeing "the prettiest girl I saw in all Mexico," describing her marble-
white complexion, rosy cheeks, and "large dark swimming eyes, with their
accompanying heavy lashes." "Oh the beauty of the exquisite Spanish word
pobrecito (poor fellow!)," he exclaimed; "when heard from such lips" it was
"the sweetest of all sounds." Young Scribner, who had been appalled by
the rough appearance of the traders, was impressed by two women he saw
in Matamoros. They had "large, dark, eloquent eyes," "small beautiful feet,"
"beautiful delicate hand[s]," and, moreover, "intellect." Like many Americans, Scribner, when noting superior qualities of any Mexicans, added that
these women "appeared to belong to a higher station." It was natural that
soldiers, away from their sweethearts and wives, would be attracted by the
Mexican women. In Mexico City, the *North American* remarked that Mexican women had overcome their fear of Americans and that "their faces
grace" most places where soldiers find amusement. Observed Pvt. Frederick
Zeh: "Mexican women loved us; just their husbands, brothers, and fathers
hated us." More than a few romances blossomed between American soldiers and dark-eyed señoritas. Zo Cook, an Alabama volunteer stationed in
central Mexico, recalled an officer he knew who took a Mexican bride home
to Montgomery when the regiment returned home. He included the usual
racial disclaimer, "She was of pure Castillian blood." Cook contended that

many more war brides would have been taken to the U.S. if the army had made transportation available for the Mexican spouses of enlisted men. Forced to leave these women behind, "Some [soldiers] declared their intention to return to the[ir] loved one[s] after they were discharged, . . . but it is probable that not one fulfilled that promise." Reported another soldier when the army left Mexico City, "Only promises of a prompt return could dry the tears of our lovely girlfriends as we bade them farewell." The colorful Samuel Chamberlain contended that some Mexican women paid a high price for their fraternization when their American protectors left the country. If the fate of female collaborators in other wars is any indication, he was probably correct.[13]

Some Americans endeavored to learn Spanish, in order to converse with the Mexicans in their own language. One Missouri volunteer reported that several members of his company had made a list of Spanish vocabulary words. "They have become very erudite of late," he remarked. He and his

Mexican Belles. With and Without the Reboso. Brantz Mayer, Mexico As It Was and As It Is, *New York: J. Winchester, New World Press, 1846.*
Courtesy Richard Bruce Winders

friends later visited a local priest, from whom they received a Spanish lesson. Most soldiers, like Capt. William P. Rogers, satisfied themselves with merely learning terms that would enable them to complete simple transactions. Rogers's Spanish vocabulary, even after a year in Mexico, was extremely limited, consisting simply of the words for water, corn, corn bread, wheat bread, yourself, which, where, here, house, is, cow, cow's milk, goat, and goat's milk. Some soldiers seemed eager to find señoritas to help them master the language. Others relied on more formal methods; the wife of one officer of the 6th U.S. Infantry sent him a Spanish grammar book. Americans in Mexico City could purchase a book advertised in the *American Star* under the promising title, *An Easy Guide to the Spanish Language*. Its not clear how many Americans actually mastered the language, but most soldiers who kept journals or sent letters home included Spanish words or phases in their writings.[14]

Americans found some Mexican customs odd. Smoking was quite the rage among Mexicans. One Missouri volunteer in New Mexico claimed that every man and woman there was addicted to *cigaritos* and never went anywhere without tobacco and cornshucks. Even the children, he said, frequently asked their mothers, "Da me una cigarita, maman?" At Tampico, the favorite smoke was the *cigarro,* a little cigar of a quality that matched those from Cuba. Gambling appeared to Americans to be a vice widespread among Mexicans of all ages, with *monte* almost the national pastime. "One of the most distinguishing characteristics of this people," wrote one volunteer at Matamoros, "is their insatiable thirst for gaming." Blood sports also were popular, with bullrings and cock pits found throughout the country. Lieutenant Engelman claimed that every household in Saltillo kept "several fighting cocks." The skill displayed by Mexicans with the lasso amazed Americans. Engelman claimed that Mexican boys learned the art by practicing on chickens, becoming so adept that they could catch one "not only by the neck but also by either foot." Although Americans conceded that Mexicans were skilled horsemen, they did not approve of how men and women rode a horse together. In Mexico, the woman sat in front of the man, instead of the opposite order as in the U.S. The arrangement seemed indecent, as did the practice of some Mexican women who openly bathed in sight of the Americans. One young regular officer wrote his wife the startling news that Mexican women on the Rio Grande "bathe before us in the river and show themselves perfectly naked to the waist and sometimes lower." He gave her the improbable assurance that he had not watched them himself, saying that for her sake he would not look at them.[15]

Mexicans dressed differently from Americans, too. Pvt. George C.

Mexican serape. Brantz Mayer, Mexico As It Was and As It Is, *New York: J. Winchester, New World Press, 1846. Courtesy Richard Bruce Winders*

Furber described the typical costume of Mexican men: "short waisted pantaloons (called calzones), without suspenders; open on the outside seam of each leg nearly to the waistband, with a row of large gilt or silvered bell buttons down this outer seam, to close it as far as the taste of the [day] required." Made of cotton or buckskin, the pantaloons often were decorated with needlework and were held up by a "highly colored sash." Another pair of pantaloons, usually white or blue and called *calzoncillas,* were worn under the outer pair and showed through the opening on the outer seam. A shirt of linen or cotton, a silver-studded sombrero, and slippers or sandals for footwear completed the outfit in warm weather. Mexican women dressed simply, their costumes consisting of a cotton or linen chemise "cut much lower than in our country would be thought correct," "a short petticoat, and slippers without stocking." Their hair usually was worn "neatly braided," and their accessories almost always included "a pair of gold earrings." A shawl called a *rebozo* could be worn on the shoulder or used as a covering for the head. The dress of the women, claimed Furber, was "not only neat, but pretty." Another volunteer likened it to the dress of "German peasant women." The poorer classes wore simple cotton shirts and pants. One American officer reported that children (except the sons and daughters of the wealthy) went naked until age "seven or eight." Jackets were worn by men in some regions, but the universal garment used both for warmth and for protection from rain was the *serape*. Americans often admired the serape but thought that some Mexicans wore them mainly to conceal weapons. The clothing described by Americans such as Furber seems to have been worn by the average Mexican, with only the quality of material and design changing to match a person's social position.[16]

Americans found Mexican society much more rigid than that in the U.S. Ruth R. Olivera and Liliane Crété, two historians who have studied Mexican society during the period of the war, describe the various social classes. The upper class consisted of Creoles (whites of Spanish descent born in Mexico) and upper-class mestizos; these together controlled the country's church, army, and commerce. Below them were other mestizos who were small businessmen, landowners, shopkeepers, priests, craftsmen, professionals, and even some peasants. The one trait these diverse groups had in common was that all they had forsaken their Indian heritage and adopted the Spanish culture. According to Olivera and Crété, these people, who formed the core of the Mexican middle class, were passionately involved in politics. It was the upper class, however, who ruled the country. Blacks, mulattos, and zambos occupied the bottom rung of the social ladder. Most American soldiers had little interaction with Mexico's upper classes; as a result, they based most of their assumptions concerning Mexican society on the people they saw daily—members of the middle and the lower classes. Indians who clung to their traditional ways of life comprised the single largest class of Mexicans. Outside the accepted Creole world, Indians went about their lives, ignoring the other groups and in turn being ignored by them.[17]

Many Americans pitied Mexican peasants, whom they saw as trapped in debt peonage. Although slavery officially had been abolished in Mexico in 1824, landowners who controlled the large estates still relied on a system of forced labor. American soldiers who witnessed the system in action described how it worked. A landless peasant arranged with a landowner for the use of a house and a small plot to farm, in return for his labor. The peon received a wage, with about a third paid in cash and the remainder in credit at the landowner's store. Peons sometimes found it difficult to earn enough to pay both their rent and their bills at the store and sank heavily in debt to their employers. Unable to leave the owners' land until the debt had been cleared, peons stayed, with little hope of paying off their mounting debt. Some landowners reportedly took the system to the extreme, making children responsible for any debt that remained unpaid upon the death of their fathers. Lieutenant Engelman visited the hacienda of the influential Sánchez Navarro family near Saltillo and wrote, "Within the wall [enclosing the ranch compound] were several long buildings and a lot of little huts made of corn stalks in which some 200 lousy peons lived in misery while working off their debt." Debt peonage resembled the system of farm tenants and sharecroppers prevalent in the South after the Civil War. Americans familiar with their own system of forced labor thought debt peonage harsher than slavery. Furber exclaimed, "While thus in debt, even of but one dollar, he is as much a slave as the negro of the south, and is in far worse condition." He reasoned that slaves had more freedom of action and were treated better by their masters than were peons. Slaves, he contended, did not have to pay for food, clothing, or medicine, and were cared for in the old age by their owners. Peons, on the other hand, had to provide for all of life's needs out of their meager earnings and could be turned out to fend for themselves when they were no longer able to work. "These poor . . . unfortunate beings, the descendants of the lordly Montezumas," exclaimed one Pennsylvania volunteer, "are made beasts of burden, are sold and transferred from master to master and undergo a slavery far more abject than the negroes of the north." Appalled by the poverty of the peons, Americans chose to view their own form of slavery in a favorable light. The editors of the *American Star* exposed the evils of debt peonage to the army in a story they published at Puebla. Raphael Semmes, a young naval officer who accompanied Scott's column to Mexico City, provided an anecdote supposedly demonstrating that even black servants with the army understood the difference between the two systems. According to Semmes, Gen. William J. Worth asked two of his servants if they would like to trade places with the peons, and both said that they "preferred . . . to be the servants of gentlemen, rather than consort with 'poor white trash,' and especially poor Indian trash." Even so, regular officers camped along the Rio Grande in the spring of 1846 had problems with black servants' deserting their masters for freedom in Mexico.[18]

To many Americans who had seen fantastic technological innovations that heralded the coming of a great industrial age, Mexico appeared a backward country. Mexican farming especially seemed outdated. "The country in general is very badly cultivated," wrote Private Upton about the fields around Matamoros. The plow became a symbol of Mexico's agricultural and industrial inferiority. One regular officer stationed at Puebla told his father, "I saw some ploughing the other day by a pair of oxen, the plough made of rough wood not of the approved shape with a little iron point—it made a small furrow and a man followed, dropped the corn and covered it with his feet[,] keeping up with the slow pace of the oxen." He added, "The end of the pole is fastened to the yoke which is in turn fastened to the horns[. I]nstead [of] pulling from the shoulder they pull by their heads." One Kentucky volunteer described an even cruder variation, in which the ploughman used a simple forked tree limb shaped like a wishbone; one branch served as the plow blade, the second as the hitch, and the third as the handle. Private Furber discussed the crude farming tools he saw along the march from Monterey to Tampico. He began his description by saying, "The plows are similar to those of the ancients," and concluded with the observation that "every other implement is of the same style." Their two-wheeled carts, he said, typically were made of mesquite branches held together with rawhide. One Mississippi volunteer at Cedras contended that the Mexicans were at least two hundred years behind in all aspects of life. Another officer of the same regiment estimated that the gap was one thousand years! One Pennsylvanian claimed that the Mexicans still were using tools of "the same pattern as the Egyptians used five thousand years ago." A West Point–trained officer expressed the opinion held by most Americans when he wrote, "There are many circumstances . . . in which they are very far behind the civilized world."[19]

Americans laid much of the blame for Mexico's apparent backwardness on the Catholic Church. Asserted one Pennsylvania volunteer after seeing the great number of churches and monasteries in central Mexico: "Here the Church and the Church alone flourishes and the whole nation are taxed and oppressed to support and build up a system of religion which triumphs over all power and sympathizes not with the people in adversity." Lt. Ralph W. Kirkham, who attended the celebration of Corpus Christi Day in Puebla, wrote, "The more I see of the Romanish religion in this country, the more I am convinced that it is really idolatry." He contended that the common Mexican who did not know Latin had no idea what the priests said at mass or the meaning of the prayers they had been taught to recite. The results of such practices, he concluded, were "ignorance" and "superstition." A German immigrant serving in the regulars expressed a similar opinion when he wrote, "Unfortunately, in this land which is as

FIFTY DOLLARS REWARD.---The undersigned will give the above reward to whoever will produce sufficient evidence to convict the person who stripped his vessel (the Alert,) of her rigging and even went so far as to pull off sheets of copper from her bottom.
April 3---3t   GEO. SIMPTON.

AT AUCTION.--Brig PENSACOLA for sale.--Will be sold at public auction, on Monday, April 5th, at 2 o'clock, P. M., on the West beach, the brig PENSACOLA, Hallett, master, her tackle and apparal, to be sold in small lots.   a3-1tp

AT AUCTION.--Brig J. PETERSON for sale.---Will be sold at public auction, on Monday, April 5th, at 2 o'clock, P. M., on the West beach, the brig J. PETERSON, Baker, master, her tackle and apparal. Her hull and apparal will be sold separately. Also---a lot of Beef. Pork, and cabin stores. By order of survey.   a3-1tp

COLTS REPEATING ARMS--Rifles, Carbines, and Pistols.--The officers of the Army and Navy are informed that these arms can be obtained until the 10th inst., at the door on the left of the gate, going out to the Wharf,
    Private soldiers can be furnished when producing written permits from their immediate commanding officers.
    Citizens can also be supplied upon the written permission of the Governor of the city, Major General Worth.
Vera Cruz, April 3, 1847. 3t

Colt's Repeating Arms. American Eagle, *Vera Cruz, Apr. 3, 1847.*
Courtesy Daughters of the Republic of Texas Library

lovely as it is wretched, there is not the slightest trace [of Christian civilization], notwithstanding all the anxious devotion to ritual." Americans commonly criticized priests and monks, who as a group they believed to be corrupt. "The clergy," charged Kirkham, "are very immoral and ready to stoop to the very lowest acts of villainy and wickedness." Many Americans disliked the holiday atmosphere of the Mexican Sabbath, believing that the day should be spent in prayer and reflection. Instead, Sundays throughout Mexico were filled with cockfights, bullfights, gambling, and dancing. One volunteer who attended a mass in Santa Fe remarked, "They play the same tunes in serving god as they do in the phandango [*sic*]." Many diarists lamented that their countrymen often participated in these irreverent activities and neglected the true meaning of the day. Wrote Furber, "There is no Sabbath in camp; . . . not one man in twenty can tell whether it is Sunday or Thursday, Monday or Saturday; they know not, neither do they care." Susan Shelby Magoffin, a Santa Fe trader's wife who traveled to Saltillo with Doniphan's column, objected to the observance of the 4th of July when it fell on a Sunday, saying, "I wish they [the officers at Saltillo] had deferred the celebration til the 5th, they would have shown more stamina of character in observing the Sabbath religiously, and establishing the customs of the U.S. here, instead of following the example of this people in making it a feasting day." It is difficult to tell if these observers truly were outraged by the church as they saw it or if they merely were expressing the anti-Catholic sentiment that already existed in the U.S. during the 1840s. As one historian of the period wrote in explaining the reason for attacks on Catholics in Philadelphia in 1844, "Many American Protestants feared Catholicism because it seemed alien and anti-democratic." Mexican Catholicism seemed especially decadent and offensive to American sensibilities.[20]

The notion that Mexico had failed to live up to republican ideals angered Americans. The country frequently had undergone revolutions, and the landowners, church, and military seemed to have the people in a stranglehold from which they could not escape. Sgt. Thomas Barclay of Pennsylvania deplored the power of the church and the army: "Without their support no government can stand and with a tacit understanding they wink at the tyranny and excesses of each other." He concluded, "As in all countries of the west which throw off the Spanish yoke the experiment of a Republic has been unsuccessful." Mexico was not like the U.S., which had "a government which protects all and favors none, which will neither perpetrate or suffer a wrong and where the people themselves thro [sic] the ballot box select their rulers and thus are made responsible for the wisdom, justice, and economy of those they choose." According to Captain Rogers, Mexicans "profess to live in a republic and yet their laws are more oppressive than those of any civilized monarchy." Even Winfield Scott, after seizing Vera Cruz, proclaimed to the Mexican people that their true enemies were not his soldiers, but "those who misgoverned you."[21]

Many Americans believed that Mexico's failure to establish republican principles could be attributed directly to the backward condition of the Mexican people. "Although this is the finest soil and climate joined I have any knowledge of yet," claimed Col. William B. Campbell, "it will never be much of a country while occupied by the present race." Another volunteer, Thomas D. Tennery of Illinois, flatly stated that "the Spanish and Indian do not make a race of people with patriotism and candor enough to support a republic, much less to form and sustain one out of the present deranged fabric called the Republic of Mexico." Lt. Andrew Jackson Trussell of Mississippi also concluded that Mexicans were "a bad looking Race of people" who were unable to comprehend republican concepts. "Many, very many years must pass before the common people, the public of this miscalled Republic, will be sufficiently enlightened to enjoy the blessings of independence," wrote Capt. Robert Anderson.[22]

Americans entered Mexico with the zeal of crusading knights. Captain

Rogers admitted that the war would cause a great deal of bloodshed but reasoned that "it will improve the condition of the poor Mexican." Some Americans believed that their institutions and actions could serve as examples to teach the people proper republican ideals. The citizens of Tampico, for example, were given instructions in trial by jury, "a thing they had never heard of." If the Mexicans did not learn the lessons of democracy fast enough, however, they should expect to be pushed aside. "The Anglo Saxon race, that land loving people are on the move," proclaimed Sergeant Barclay with pride. Colonel Campbell exclaimed, "They [the Mexicans] are all semi Indians and must in a short time give place to the civilization of North America or North Europe." To a nation that had just undertaken the removal of the Cherokee, Choctaw, Chickasaw, Creek, and Seminole to a permanent Indian territory west of the Mississippi River, the conquest of Mexico seemed logical and even beneficial to both the conqueror and the conquered. Both acts were in keeping with the notion then popular that a "civilized" people had a right to the land, because they would make the land fruitful, thereby fulfilling God's command to be prosperous.[23]

Many American soldiers believed that the war was good for Mexico. Wrote one Illinois volunteer in Wool's column, "It's a great war, instead of the Americans coming being a detriment [and] hurting the Mexicans it is a blessing." The demand for goods and services created by the invading armies proved to be an economic bonanza for some farmers, ranchers, and merchants. Exclaimed Lieutenant Trussell, "It is not the intention of the Mexicans to make pease [sic] because they ar [sic] as a Majority of them is doing better now than they ever did." He continued, "They can sell what they have to sell for four times as mutch [sic] as they could before the Armey [sic] come among them and the Mexicans that wants Imployment [sic] can get it from the Americans and get four times as mutch [sic] for it as they could from their own peeple [sic]." After the fall of Mexico City, some Mexican businessmen and women hung out signs advertising "American Eating House" and "Mush & Milk," in order to attract American customers. Soldiers maintained that a number of peons profited from the occupation, a claim supported by the editors of the American Star. Trussell wrote his brother from northern Mexico, saying that "a grate [sic] number of Peones have bought their Freedom." He added, "At some placis [sic] on this line where the troops have been stationed for some time there is hardly a Peone to be found." General Taylor told Mexicans living along the Rio Grande that his "republican army of the Union" would restore freedoms lost Mexico's present "despots." According to Private Upton, the people of Matamoros were friendly and welcomed the Americans who would "get rid of their tyrannical rulers." John T. Hughes, a volunteer who heard Gen. Stephen W. Kearny's pledge of friendship to the citizens of Santa Fe, New Mexico, thought, "[The people] seemed to be well pleased with the change of government and the idea of being citizens of the American Republic." One Pennsylvania volunteer said that the citizens of Mexico City appreciated the law and order the Americans had brought. Several soldiers mentioned that U.S. troops in northern Mexico protected the people there from two feared enemies—Comanches and Mexican tax collectors.[24]

Like Lew Wallace, most Americans found Mexico a strange and novel land. The war gave them an opportunity to visit a world that they had only read or heard about. Americans viewed Mexico and Mexicans through the lens of their own culture, and they did not always like what they saw. While the land of the Montezumas itself had much promise, the people living there seemed to have little hope. American soldiers believed that they were bringing progress to a backwards region. They took pleasure in avenging old wrongs and punishing a wayward country that dared to called itself a republic. With these words, Lieutenant Kirkham voiced his fellow soldiers' opinion of Mexico: "What a beautiful and happy country this might be if there were good laws and the people virtuous."[25]

TEN

Mr. Polk's Army

There is no harmony in the Democratic Party. They are cut up into factions . . . [that are] looking more to the Presidential election of 1848 than to the principle or the good of the country.
—U.S. President James K. Polk

This just war . . . was waged by the Democracy.
—The Democratic Text Book,
1848 campaign pamphlet

"I believe we are bound to beat the Mexicans whenever and wherever we meet them, no matter how large their numbers." Lt. Ulysses S. Grant's words exemplified the attitude of both regulars and volunteers in the Mexican War: American soldiers were invincible in battle. Victories at Buena Vista, Cerro Gordo, El Brazito, Mexico City, Monterey, Palo Alto, Resaca de la Palma, Sacramento, Santa Cruz de Rosales, and Vera Cruz only confirmed the belief of many Americans that the sons of Washington, Harrison, and Jackson were natural-born warriors. Although flaws in this image exist, the U.S. military performed impressively during the war. The objectives laid out by President James K. Polk to his cabinet had been realized less than a year and a half after hostilities began. The army assembled by Polk was truly the "Army of Manifest Destiny," because it expanded the nation's boundaries all the way to the Pacific Ocean and gave the United States a leading role on the North American continent and eventually a place among the great powers of the world. The force also deserves to be called "Mr. Polk's Army," because its creation and operation clearly bore the president's stamp.[1]

President Polk took his duties as commander-in-chief seriously and personally directed army operations from the White House. The president's diary records meetings with his advisors in which the war's strategy developed. On May 30, 1846, for example, Polk spelled out his specific goals to his cabinet: "I declared my purpose to be to acquire for the United States, California, New Mexico, and perhaps some of the Northern Provinces of Mexico." These objectives, he said, had been included in "Mr. Slidell's secret instructions" and now, with the United States and Mexico at war, "the prospect of acquiring them was much better." Polk told his cabinet that the military should be used to take possession of "all these provinces" as quickly as possible. The meeting was the genesis of the campaigns led by Alexander Doniphan, Stephen W. Kearny, Sterling Price, and John E. Wool. On September 22, 1846, Polk and the cabinet discussed an expedition to Tampico to seize the city and its port. The topic arose again on October 10; this time the discussion included Vera Cruz. By November, Polk had decided that controlling Mexico's northern provinces was not enough to end the war and that, in order to force the Mexican government to come to terms, Vera Cruz and Mexico City must be taken. The capture of Vera Cruz in March 1847 was followed by a six-month campaign that ended with the capture of the Mexican capital. Through his diaries, the development and implementation of the war strategy can be traced directly to Polk. By September 1847, Polk had accomplished all the goals that he had enunciated sixteen months earlier.[2]

Polk personally involved himself in the operations of the army's staff departments. He and Secretary of War William L. Marcy regularly discussed the ongoing military operations, because, Polk explained, "I find it to be indispensable to give my personal attention to many of these details." His attention was required, he believed, because the old officers who controlled the staff departments were "entirely too slow" for wartime effectiveness, although they might have been adequate in peacetime. Displeased with the activity of the Quartermaster Department, the president called Thomas S. Jesup to the White House on several occasions to demand that he run his office more efficiently. During one such visit, Polk read Jesup and Commissary General George Gibson letters from officers in Mexico who claimed that the pair's mismanagement had caused needless suffering among American troops. When Jesup objected to hearing the anonymous accusations, Polk told him that the "President of the U.S." could handle this situation however he saw fit; Jesup, in short, should be quiet and listen. Adj. Gen. Roger Jones experienced Polk's ire when he was too slow in providing a list of vacancies in the officer corps that the president wanted, so he could fill them with privates who had distinguished themselves in battle. Throughout the war, Polk believed that the officers of the staff departments failed to support his administration's policies and even worked to thwart his efforts, so that he would fail.[3]

Polk employed a loose network of Democratic informants who kept him abreast of news at the front. Some were the men he had appointed as volunteer generals. Both Franklin Pierce and Caleb Cushing called on Polk only days after receiving their commissions. Generals Butler and Patterson, back from Mexico on leave during the spring and summer of 1847, frequently visited the White House. They confirmed what Polk suspected: Taylor and Scott did not support him. A steady stream of officers—some bearing tales, some seeking favors, some paying their respects—flowed through the president's office during the war. Polk gathered information during these visits to use against his opponents. Polk also received letters from Mexico that kept him current on events and the political climate of the army. Soon after the battle of Monterey, Polk received letters from Gen. Gideon J. Pillow and Capt. Robert B. Reynolds that were critical of Taylor for allowing the Mexican Army to withdraw from the city. The president read these pages to Marcy and noted in his diary, "These letters are confidential." It was after receiving letters from Pillow and Reynolds that Polk called Jesup and Gibson to his office and accused them of mishandling their departments. Polk also relied upon Col. Louis D. Wilson of the 12th U.S. Infantry for information. The president met with Wilson, an old friend from North Carolina, and discussed with him in detail the squabble between Scott and Nicholas Trist of the State Department. Colonel Wilson left Washington with dispatches for Scott but sickened and died soon after landing at Vera Cruz. When news of his death reached the president, Polk wrote in his diary, "He was a patriotic & highly intelligent man, and my personal friend. . . . I had a full and free confidential conversation with him on the subject of the War & the operations of the army in Mexico, & gave him my views fully."[4]

As commander-in-chief, Polk was called upon to settle disputes involving army personnel, and evidence indicates that party politics guided some decisions. In cases concerning Taylor or Scott, the president almost always sided against the two Whig generals. Polk's bias is evident in his diary and manifested itself in diatribes directed at the two soldiers. Shortly after the war began, the president used the case of Capt. George C. Hutter, an officer who had been dismissed from the service by John Tyler and now sought reinstatement, to criticize Scott. Wrote Polk, "It proved to me that Gen'l Scott was not only hostile, but recklessly vindictive in his feeling towards my administration." Opposed to Hutter's return to duty, Scott penned a letter accusing Polk of using the creation of the U.S. Mounted Rifles as a means of rewarding Democratic supporters by appointing them to the new regiment. Although Hutter was denied a commission at the time, in April 1847 Polk reappointed him to the 6th U.S. Infantry with the rank of captain. Scott again ran afoul of Polk when he removed Col. William S. Harney from command for insubordination. The president, who knew the colonel to be a "Democrat" as well as "one of General Jackson's personal friends," reprimanded Scott and returned Harney to duty. Capt. Philip Barbour, 3rd U.S. Infantry, previously had noted favoritism by the president toward Harney, writing in his journal: "He will not be touched being a protégé of General Jackson, whose ghost Mr. Polk is afraid of." Ghost or not, Polk consistently sided with Democratic officers in their disputes against Taylor and Scott. The most celebrated case arose after the fighting in Mexico City had ended. Three prominent Democratic officers—Maj. Gen. Gideon J. Pillow, Bvt. Brig. Gen. William J. Worth, and Capt. James Duncan—were involved in a conspiracy to discredit Scott by claiming that the Whig general had little role in the capture of Mexico City. Scott felt wronged and ordered the Democratic officers arrested. Countercharges by the accused followed. Polk, who always had disliked Scott and never had had confidence in his ability as a general, directed that the officers be restored to duty. Moreover, he removed "Old Fuss and Feathers" from command.[5]

Polk occasionally took sides in the internal disputes of volunteer regiments. One involved the appointment of a regular officer to command the 2nd Baltimore and D. C. Battalion. A District of Columbia resident, Charles Lee Jones, had approached the War Department in November 1846 for permission to raise a regiment for the war. Officials at first delayed giving Jones an answer, but later he felt encouraged enough to raise three companies at his own expense and hold them ready for the expected announcement of another call-up. Polk stunned Jones by accepting his companies but appointing George W. Hughes, a captain in the U.S. Topographic Engineers, to command them. Jones's father entered the fray, claiming that the president had promised to give his son the commission. The elder Jones, in a printed defense of his son, hinted that politics lay at the center of the affair: "I have a word to say to the suggestion in some of the newspapers devoted to the support of the Administration—that the Whig editors are preparing to make the President's conduct in this matter a ground of party attack on his Administration. I owe the Whig party so much good will at least, as to hope they may fall into no such mistake in party-tactics." Walter Jones was a person of no little importance, as he was a lawyer of national renown, the commander of the District of Columbia's militia with the rank of major general, and the son-in-law of the Revolutionary War figure, Charles Lee. The president and his agents, he claimed, had acted to preserve the "power and patronage" of the presidency and branded Polk a "thief" who had stolen the volunteers from his son. In a bipartisan spirit, Jones asserted that Americans should "sink for the present all political disagreements in the one great purpose of fighting their country's battles." General Jones asked for justice in the case of the Maryland volunteers, but Polk ignored his solicitation.[6]

The president did become personally involved, however, in a dispute involving the 1st North Carolina Infantry. Dissatisfaction over the governor's appointment of Col. Robert T. Paine had festered among the men of the 1st North Carolina Infantry since its formation. An able but unpopular officer, Paine attempted to instill discipline in the especially rowdy group of volunteers at Saltillo by ordering a punishment horse built as a warning. On the afternoon of August 14, 1847, a crowd of volunteers attacked and destroyed the offending device, which was located behind the colonel's tent. Not yet satisfied, the band returned the following night, shouting and throwing rocks at the colonel's tent. When Paine's guard refused to come to his aid, the colonel fired his pistols into the crowd, killing one volunteer and wounding another. A court of inquiry that looked into the affair found Paine's actions justified and upheld his decision to shoot. In August 1846, Scott had issued orders giving commanders in remote areas the authority to punish volunteers without first reporting to the War Department. Acting under these orders, Gen. John E. Wool summarily dismissed two officers and two enlisted men of the North Carolina regiment, who were the ring leaders of the mutiny. The matter, however, was not yet settled.[7]

The inquiry disclosed that politics had been a prime factor in causing the mutiny. North Carolinians had been angered when Gov. William A. Graham announced that he would appoint the regiment's field officers, instead of allowing the volunteers to elect them. Graham's selections drove his opponents into a frenzy, because, like the governor, both Col. Robert T. Paine and Lt. Col. John A. Fagg were prominent Whigs. Lt. Josiah S. Pender—one of the dismissed officers—explained the situation in a letter to Polk asking for the president's help: "State laws provided that the selection of field officers should be made by the regiment, but after the regiment had been completed our whig legislature took the selection from an entire democratic regiment, and gave the right of appointment to a whig governor, contrary to the wishes of nine-tenths of the regiment." Pender pointed out to the president that, when Paine had been a member of the state legislature, he voted for a resolution declaring that the "existing war with Mexico was brought about by the executive, [and] is unjust." Testimony at the inquiry disclosed an ongoing struggle between political factions within the North Carolina regiment. Several letters had been sent to the Democratic press in North Carolina "of a highly abusive character towards Colonel Paine." One letter called Paine "an old Whig rascal" and even suggested that he should be shot. Reports such as this, one witness surmised, were designed to keep the regiment in a constant state of turmoil by depicting Colonel Paine as a tyrant who cursed and beat his men: "The whig editors of newspapers condemn the war, and preach to the people the distress and suffering of the soldiers. The democrats, to balance accounts, accuse the colonel of a want of judgment, tyranny, and cruelty." Caught in the middle between the two rival parties, Paine found himself in the difficult position of commanding troops who refused to recognize his authority over them. The incident also demonstrated that, given the opportunity, Whig governors were not above using the power of patronage themselves.[8]

Although evidence presented at the inquiry revealed that the mutineers were motivated by their political hatred of Paine, Polk ordered the dismissed officers reinstated, because, he claimed, their "right to a trial by jury" had been violated. Pender had written the president, "We have never asked any indulgence, but only claimed the right that belongs to every American citizen; that of a trial." Pender and his friends received support for their claim of violated rights from fellow volunteers, when thirty officers of the 2nd Mississippi Rifles sent Secretary of Treasury Robert J. Walker a petition stating that Wool—a regular—had no right to dismiss any officer appointed to his position by a state governor. Polk's decision to send the officers back to their regiment not only struck a blow for the rights of volunteers, but also it struck down the original order issued by Scott.[9]

Despite his claim to the contrary, Polk used military service as a test of loyalty. Daniel Tyler, a veteran of the Mormon Battalion, claimed that the president issued the call for Mormon volunteers to determine if the sect could be counted on to support the U.S. He contended that Polk had secretly granted Sen. Thomas H. Benton permission to raise a band of Missourians to "fall upon" the Mormons "and use them up" if they failed to answer the call. Massachusetts became a target in November 1846, during the War Department's second call for volunteers, when Secretary of State James Buchanan suggested that the state be required to furnish one of the nine new regiments. The president disapproved of the idea at first but changed his mind the following day. As he and several members of his cabinet reasoned, "If [Massachusetts] obeyed the call all would be well. If she refused to obey it and acted as she did in the last war with Great Britain the country would know it." The state complied, depriving the president and his supporters an opportunity to chastise the Whig stronghold. In these cases, refusal to serve would have been viewed by Polk as proof of disloyalty—not only to him, but to the nation as well—and deserving of punishment.[10]

It is an oversimplification to conclude that James K. Polk exercised exclusive control over the army and the war. He did not. Although an active commander-in-chief, Polk faced a plethora of problems over which he had little or no control. Perhaps most important, factions within the Democratic Party were causing the party to split apart. Lamented the president, "Faction has made its way into the Democratic party in Congress, which parali[z]es all my efforts to prosecute the War vigorously." Democrats continually squabbled over slavery, territorial acquisition, and the coming presidential election. Writing about the schism, Polk complained, "There is no harmony in the Democratic Party. They are cut up into factions . . . [that are] looking more to the Presidential election of 1848 than to the principle or the good of the country." One supporter observed the president's plight, commenting, "Polk has many indifferent and many false friends in the House. The Democratic members confess (in confidence) that it is just as much as the administration can do to keep its head above water in Congress." In the midst of a war, Polk struggled to hold his party together so that it could harvest the fruits of victory once peace came. He came to view not only Whigs but some dissident Democrats as enemies who were all the more contemptible because of their disloyalty to him and the party. Reflecting the Democratic troubles, Whigs captured the House of Representatives in the midterm Congressional elections.[11]

Polk attempted to use his patronage power to bring Democrats into line and encourage party loyalty. The creation of the U.S. Mounted Rifles and the ten new regiments gave him more than 350 commissions to grant. New staff positions, as well as the numerous vacancies within the Old Establishment, were also his to fill. Although he may have set aside certain positions for associates, he could not possibly have awarded all these places to acquaintances. Instead, as Polk explained in his diary, he relied on "Members of Congress and others occupying high positions in Society" for suggestions. These individuals usually tried "to procure appointments for their friends." He admitted that their advice sometimes led him to make bad appointments, complaining, "When I act upon the information they give me, and make a mistake, they leave me to bear the responsibility, and never have the manliness to assume it themselves." Polk also blamed Democratic congressmen for the limited number of Whigs he appointed to the army, surmising that they wanted only their friends and supporters appointed to office. Soon after the passage of the Ten Regiment Bill, Polk noted that "the members of Congress called to recommend their constituents & friends for military appointments." They returned a few days later, prompting him to write, "Many Senators and Representatives called to urge the pretensions of their friends for these office[s]." Dispensing offices did not always have the desired effect of creating peace among factions. When a dispute erupted between New York politicians over an appointment from their state, Polk offered a compromise candidate, Brig. Gen. Enos D. Hopping, a man he knew was a political ally and personal friend of Marcy. Instead of being pleased, the secretary of war threatened to resign if another man he supported was not selected instead. Indignant at Marcy's outburst, Polk gave the general's commission to Hopping anyway, stating, "I had become perfectly indifferent whether . . . Mr. Marcy resigned or not." The secretary of war failed to carry out his threat, and the matter passed. Desire to curtail the president's power sometimes shaped Congressional action. According to one observer of the Congressional debates, Sen. John J. Crittenden, a Whig from Kentucky, personally disagreed with the Ten Regiment Bill, "but he threw his doubts against the Const. as he would thus be striking down the patronage of the Pres.!"[12]

Although patronage was necessary in order to maintain party cohesion, Polk found awarding military offices taxing. "I am ready to exclaim God deliver me from dispensing the patronage of the Government," the exasperated president wrote. Overwhelmed with office seekers, Polk exclaimed, "I have pushed them off and fought them with both hands like a man fighting a fire, and endeavored to drive them to the Secretary of War as the regular channel of approach to the President in matters relating to the military service." One of the most vexing aspects of the task was that many Congressmen, not satisfied with acquiring positions for their friends, clamored for military office for themselves. Rebuking them for this practice, Polk explained, "The passion for office among members of Congress is very great. . . . They create offices by their own votes and then seek to fill them themselves." He considered it a form of corruption and vowed not to give in to their demands.[13]

At any given time during the war, hundreds of office-seekers roamed the nation's capital, hoping to find benefactors who could exert influence on their behalf and win for them the coveted commissions. James L. Kemper was typical of the throng of aspirants. Kemper had hoped to go to Mexico as an officer of the 1st Virginia Infantry, but the young law-school graduate had been unable to secure a post. Undaunted, he set off for Washington, where he met with congressmen and other federal officials in an effort to gain their support. Kemper eventually enlisted the aid of a fellow Virginian, Secretary of the Navy John Y. Mason, who arranged an interview with the president. "Mr. Polk received us very graciously and promised to submit our claims in the cabinet meeting," wrote Kemper. The cabinet recommended Kemper for an appointment in the Quartermaster Department and sent the nomination to the Senate for action. There, however, action on more important matters—the debate on the Ten Regiment Bill was in full swing at the time—delayed Kemper's confirmation for weeks. In the meantime, Kemper passed his time in the company of other hopefuls, watching the political wrangling on the floor of Congress and taking in what entertainment he could find in the city. The number of office-seekers amazed Kemper, who found that "there are enough applicants here for commissions to make up an army at once. Members [of Congress] are regularly besieged." He noted that on one day alone five hundred applications were presented. He and his companions—only partly in jest—suggested forming themselves into a company and offering their services to the government *en masse*. In the end, though, Kemper's connections paid off, and the Senate bestowed upon him the rank of captain and the position of assistant quartermaster of volunteers. Unsure how to act in his new position, Kemper exclaimed, "I am mighty troubled about this time how to demean myself in my new authority; I am as so wedded to the habits and manners of a Civilian."[14]

Polk expressed ambivalence about his power of appointment. He predicted early in the war that the practice of patronage, although intended to bring the Democratic party together, would result in dissension among its members. Writing in April 1847 about the upcoming election in his home state, Polk identified patronage as a reason for his party's faltering popularity: "All the leading men in Tennessee know me personally, and many of them aspire to high commands in the army who could not be gratified." Some of these disappointed men now favored Taylor's candidacy as a possible means of advancement; thus they also could strike back at the president. Polk contended that, "throughout the Union," disappointed office-seekers were turning against the Democratic party over the issue of patronage. Sensitive to the charge of political abuse, the president denied that politics ever had affected his decisions, stating flatly at one cabinet meeting, "I had never suffered politics to mingle with the conduct of this war." In May 1846, he even asked several Whig senators to find him "a suitable person of the Whig party for Major" as well as "three or four Whigs for Lieutenancies" whom he could appoint to the new regiment of U.S. Mounted Rifles. When rebuked by Rep. Stephen A. Douglass for appointing a Whig to the new corps, Polk "told him that we were at war with a Foreign country" and that it was improper to use politics as a test; he therefore had resolved to appoint some Whigs to office in the army. While his course toward the matter of the Mounted Rifles may have seemed bipartisan, the president reserved the post of colonel and almost all other commissions in the regiment for Democrats. Polk may have tried to be impartial, but, throughout the war, his actions and his words reflected party politics.[15]

Throughout the war, Polk maintained his belief in the superiority of volunteers, despite the poor reputation the corps earned. In his second annual address, delivered on December 8, 1846, Polk praised the volunteers, exclaiming proudly, "Our volunteer citizen soldiers, who so promptly responded to their country's call, with an experience of the discipline of a camp of only a few weeks, have borne their part in the hard fought battle of Monterey with a constancy and courage equal to that of veteran troops." The president apparently discounted reports of criminal behavior, as little or no mention of rowdy acts committed by volunteers ever appeared in his diary. Writing in July 1848, while the military force raised for the war was being demobilized, Polk reaffirmed his stance, telling Congress: "Our standing army is to be found in the bosom of society. It is composed of free citizens, who are ever ready to take up arms in the service of their country when an emergency requires it." Polk continued his praise, stating, "Our experience in the war just closed fully confirms the opinion that such an army may be raised upon a few week's notice, and that our citizen soldiers are equal to any troops in the world." Although some of these words might be taken as political rhetoric, Polk demonstrated on numerous occasions that he held the regular army—at least its old officer corps—in disdain. In the president's mind, citizens made the best soldiers.[16]

The Ten Regiment Bill authorizing the expansion of the regular army did not imply that Polk had abandoned his preference for volunteers. Rather, as is indicated by his promises to become personally involved in the war's management, his advocacy of it reflected his desire to exert control over the army. The president was displeased with the slow pace at which state officials responded to calls for volunteers, and he wanted to extend his control over the raising of troops by federalizing the process. As he explained in a message to the House, in which he asked for a bill to authorize these new regiments, "The existing law, requiring that they [volunteers] should be organized by the independent action of the State governments, has in some instances occasioned considerable delay, and it is yet uncertain when the troops required can be ready for service in the field." Polk believed that these new regiments of "regulars" could be raised quickly and rushed to the front. An effort, led by Sam Houston, to convert the corps into volunteers narrowly failed. Learning of Houston's plan, the president remarked that he already had the power to call for volunteers, had he wanted them, but that he "deemed [an additional regular force] indispensable for the successful prosecution of the war." Unlike the situation with volunteers, Polk would have direct control over the mobilization, deployment, and even the appointment of all officers of these ten new regiments. The officer commissions for the new regiments were divided among various states, with each of the states responsible for filling its quota of troops. Polk ignored the "old officers of the army," who "Insisted that the 10 Regiments each be filled and organized & drilled for some time in the U. States before they [were] moved to the seat of war." The president won the battle to get his new regulars, but overall the regiments failed to live up to his expectations. Untrained, they were hurried to the front piecemeal, and some were not organized fully until after the fighting had already ended. They were disbanded once peace came, and their officers and men returned to their prewar occupations. In reality, the ten new regiments—which, to set them apart from the old regulars, were designated the New Establishment—actually were volunteers raised by the federal government.[17]

The regular army did not share Polk's enthusiasm for volunteers. Many regulars resented the intrusion of untrained men into their profession. Lt. George G. Meade called volunteers "amateurs" and was glad when some returned home following the Battle of Monterey. Lt. William S. Henry predicted that the public quickly would detect a difference between the two corps. He stated, "Before this war is terminated, the people will feel, by applying their hands to a very sensitive part of the person—the pocket—the difference between carrying on the war by volunteers and regulars." Meade also noted the expense of volunteers, stating, "They cannot take care of themselves; the hospitals are crowded with them, [and] they die like sheep." He further claimed, "They waste their provisions, requiring twice as much to supply them as regulars do." Lt. George B. McClellan said that volunteers lack the simplest knowledge of how to care for themselves as soldiers and that, as a consequence, they died "like dogs." According to him, the American public gladly would accept regulars and dispense with the volunteer system, if only it knew the true condition of the army in Mexico.[18]

The War Department and Polk were aware of the differences between regulars and volunteers. General Scott described the problem in a letter to the secretary of war dated January 16, 1847. Regulars, he stated, would have tents pitched, arms stacked, guards posted, and supper simmering, all within fifteen minutes of the evening halt. Volunteers, on the other hand, slept in the open, left their arms exposed to the elements, and ate their salt meat raw or fried. Scott informed Marcy that the volunteers cost the government a high price in wasted men and material. Volunteers, nevertheless, formed a larger proportion of the American military during the war than did regulars.[19]

The lack of discipline within volunteer ranks concerned the professional soldiers. According to Meade, while regulars "made war against the Army and Government of Mexico," the volunteers, by their many outrages, carried the war to the Mexican people. The effect, he claimed, was to incite hatred toward all Americans on the part of the Mexicans, who had their fences torn down, fields ravaged, and their bodies assaulted. Capt. Philip Barbour, writing to say that volunteers had killed a dragoon, referred to them as "Mohawks," a term that likened them to savages on the warpath. Other regular officers, including George B. McClellan, routinely ridiculed volunteers, referring to citizen-soldiers as "Mohawks," "Mustangs," and "Voluntarios." According to Capt. Robert Anderson, the authorities at Tampico stationed guards with fixed bayonets at all "places of amusement . . . even on the ballroom floor." He explained in words that ridiculed the volunteer system, "This is necessary to keep our free and independent citizens in order!" Lt. A. P. Hill, who entered a village after it had been sacked by angry volunteers, wrote, "'Twas then I saw and felt how perfectly unmanageable were volunteers and how much damage they did."[20]

The rivalry that developed between the two corps lasted throughout the war. One volunteer officer who served with Gen. John E. Wool's Army of the Centre, summed up the situation: "We have little contact with the Captains and Lieutenants of the Regular service, who seem to think themselves above us Volunteer officers, being cold and distant. Consequently we act the same way towards them." Napoleon Jackson Tecumseh Dana, a lieutenant in the 7th U.S. Infantry, was pleased that no volunteers had been with Taylor during the battles on the Rio Grande, because the country could see the worth of regulars. He explained, "We have got all the honor, credit, and renown for our gallant and much abused little army." The men and the officers of the two corps vied with one another for battlefield honors, sometimes engaging in rancorous arguments to prove that one unit or another had played the most critical role in a victory. Following the fighting at Monterey, for example, a three-way debate arose among the 1st Mississippi Rifles, the 1st Tennessee Infantry, and the 1st U.S. Infantry over which unit had captured an important Mexican position called the Tannery. In the end, it appeared that all three units had had a hand in the fort's fall, but none was willing to share the glory. In the Jacksonian spirit, those who felt themselves slighted often took their cases to the public through the press. Following the Siege of Puebla, one regular, Lt. Theodore Thadeus Sobieski Laidley, wrote that Pennsylvania volunteers "have established a paper and are heralding their daring exploits to the world, as well as some they did not perform, and anything complimentary to officers of the regular army cannot find admission."[21]

Volunteers believed that they suffered unfairly at the hands of regular officers. Col. William B. Campbell contended, "So strong a feeling of jealousy and op[p]osition [existed] to the volunteers, that while the command and controul [sic] and all its departments is in the hands of Regular officers, justice will never be done to the volunteers." Col. Samuel Ryan Curtis of the 1st Ohio Infantry agreed. Colonel Curtis, an 1827 graduate of West Point who had spent five years in uniform before resigning, was no stranger to the army. He found the friction between the two corps galling, stating that he felt "more mortified than indignant at the unnecessary desire manifested by the regular officers to put regulars forward and make them certain to be the authors of every acceptable movement." Writing from Matamoros as Taylor prepared his advance on Monterey, Curtis complained, "In fact the force here is that of the volunteers, their commanders ought to have a full share in the operations of the army and should be, if competent, placed in command suited to their ranks." Curtis could not hide his feelings when Scott failed to include his regiment in the force assembled for the attack on Vera Cruz: "To pass by us and select regulars from Saltillo and even from General Wool's column is saying plainly you are inferior and General Scott[']s letter does not avoid this plain and palpable preference for troops that have the stamp of regulars on them." Although bitter about the slight, Curtis asked his men to show their "superiors" that volunteers understood the duties of soldiers and could obey even disagreeable orders without grumbling.[22]

Curtis and others had a valid complaint, as the majority of volunteers were assigned garrison duty, thereby freeing the regulars for combat. In war, not all soldiers return home heroes, but many volunteers felt cheated out of the opportunity to prove themselves in battle. Taylor tried to soothe one disappointed regiment as it was about to leave Mexico unbloodied, saying:

> All must know who are in the slightest degree acquainted with military operations in carrying on a war in an enemy's country . . . that a considerable portion of the troops employed must be engaged in guarding depots, keeping open the lines of communications, escorting trains, etc., which are as important, arduous and dangerous as the duties of those engaged in battle.

According to Taylor, all assignments were equally important; volunteers, however, believed otherwise. Volunteers had expected a fight, and many became disenchanted with the war, once they realized that Taylor, Scott, and other leaders of the old army preferred regulars over them. One volunteer reportedly lamented as he stood guard duty one rainy night near the mouth of the Rio Grande, "I voted for old Polk G—d D—n him and here I am in the mud and rain and misery. I came out here to fight and instead of fighting I have to tread this mud for four hours[.] what a d—d fool I was—I ought to be in Hell for [being] a d—d fool." Although Polk and the American public may have favored volunteers, the generals of the Old Establishment relied upon regulars for most of the hard fighting that had to be done.[23]

Many writers have noted the fierce rivalry between regulars and volunteers, but few have attempted to explain why it existed. One clue to the difference in the two corps lies in Alexis de Tocqueville's celebrated *Democracy in America*, in which he identifies two different types of armies: aristocratic and democratic. In an aristocratic army, stated the Frenchman, "The officer is [a] noble and the soldier a serf, one rich, the other poor, the one educated and strong, and the other ignorant and weak." Strict discipline prevails, a discipline with which the soldier already is familiar before he enters the army, due to his initial low station in society. "In aristocratic armies," claims Tocqueville, "the soldier will soon become insensible to everything but the orders of his superior officers." The U.S. Army was based on this model; West Point–trained officers commanded soldiers who were expected to perform with mechanical precision. Additionally, soldiers in aristocratic armies lived apart from the citizens of the nation, a circumstance that led to alienation and animosity. The writings of many volunteers, and some by regular enlisted men as well, describe the regular army in similar terms. Conversely, Tocqueville posits that democratic armies—the armies of ancient Greece and Rome, for example—tended to be made up of "freemen and citizens," fostering "a fraternal familiarity among the officers and men." Sociable relationships, while rare among the officers and enlisted men of the regular army, were a hallmark of the volunteers. In democratic nations, Tocqueville contended, few men would choose the military as a career, a fact that makes it necessary to impose compulsory service. Although most Americans now associate compulsory service with the draft, the militia was a form of compulsion, as it subjected all free, able-bodied men between the ages of eighteen and forty-five to military service during times of emergency. In democratic armies composed of citizens, writes Tocqueville, "the love of freedom and the respect of rights" can be found throughout the ranks "if these principles have once been success-fully inculcated in the people at large." Unlike the situation in an aristo-cratic army, with its strict division between officers and enlisted men, war offers even the lowest soldier in a democratic army the opportunity for advancement.[24]

Tocqueville's concept of two different types of armies helps us under-stand the American military during the Mexican War. Although based upon European armies, the model accurately captures the American military during the nineteenth century. Americans even spoke and wrote of Polk's military in Tocquevillian terms. Regular officers were "aristocrats" and their men "musket-holding machines." The regulars existed on the fringe of civilian society and lived by a military code. Volunteers, on the other hand, were "free-born men" who expected to have the same rights as soldiers that they had as citizens: equality among peers, free elections, and trial by jury. The two systems were at odds and provided a constant source of friction in the American military during the Mexican War.[25]

The differences between volunteers and regulars manifested themselves in various ways. States that provided volunteers retained a strong attach-ment to, and pride in, their soldiers. The volunteers themselves tended to identify with their state, not with the federal government. Organized un-der state militia laws, volunteers usually elected their own officers; many wore state uniforms or even clothing of their own design. These factors helped the volunteers preserve their individual identities. Unused to the rigors of active military life, volunteers commonly chafed when expected to abide by strict army regulations. With time and training, however, they could do their "duty as volunteers and American Soldiers." But these citizen-soldiers remained "citizens" first and "soldiers" last.[26]

Service together allowed some regulars and volunteers to form objective opinions of one another. Capt. Robert Anderson confided to his journal that not only volunteers, but regulars, too, committed crimes against Mexicans. Campaigning together forced some regulars and volunteers to respect one another. Capt. Franklin Smith, a volunteer quartermaster stationed at Camargo, watched several companies of the 6th U.S. Infantry marching away in perfect step with drums beating and fifes playing and remarked, "I felt what it was like to be a warrior." Some volunteer officers even desired regular commissions when their own units mustered out. Colonel Campbell claimed that he wanted to continue in the service of his country as a regular, but he feared that "Mr. Polk would not appoint [him] to any thing" as he was a Whig. Another volunteer colonel, Samuel Ryan Curtis, also wanted a commission but waited in vain for one to come. Lt. Andrew Jackson Trussell unsuccessfully sought a regular commission through his brother in Mississippi.[27]

Writing shortly after the fall of Monterey, the 3rd U.S. Infantry's Lt. William S. Henry struck a conciliatory note that recognized volunteers as a part of the army: "The battle is over: the army both regulars and volunteers—or, more properly speaking, Americans—have proved themselves invincible." Although at times awkward and contentious, the American military fulfilled its mission in the Mexican War.

Polk and the Democrats hoped that Americans would reward their party for conducting a successful war against Mexico. One Democratic organ proudly proclaimed, "The Democracy have waged, to a successful termination, a glorious War." True, but many opponents viewed Polk and his Democratic supporters as aggressors who forced Mexico into fighting. They held the party responsible for the war. Polk, as the head of the Democratic party and commander-in-chief, had built a successful army that accomplished his goals of expanding his nation's boundaries. Party leaders could rightly claim that "this just war . . . was waged by the Democracy." Taylor's election to the presidency in 1848 was a bitter pill for Polk and the Democrats to swallow. Although Polk had built an army that conquered Mexico, in the end the Whigs emerged the true victors in the war.[28]

Epilogue

A Pyrrhic Victory

*[Lincoln] was a Whig, and took the position of the Whigs of
his day, many eminent Southern men included, which was
opposition to the declaration of war with Mexico, by the President, so long as that opposition would accomplish any purpose, . . . [he] objected to what he considered a false statement
as to the origins of the difficulties.*

—David W. Bartlett (Lincoln biographer)

Disintegration lay ahead for both of the great
Jacksonian parties. The issue of slavery had become inexorably linked to
the Mexican War. Northern Whigs, working with radical abolitionists, successfully had promoted the theory that slaveowners had conspired to bring
on the war, as a means of securing new slave territory. The issue wreaked
havoc among the Democrats, as Polk and his supporters scrambled to repair the damage inflicted by one of their own, Rep. David Wilmot of Pennsylvania. Wilmot broke ranks to sponsor an act to prohibit slavery in any
territory that might be acquired from Mexico as a result of the war. The
Wilmot Proviso, introduced in the House of Representatives on August 8,
1846, reopened the debate about slavery's future—a debate many Americans had hoped would end with the Missouri Compromise. Although the
bill passed the House on several occasions, it never made it through the
Senate. The Wilmot Proviso, with its promise of permanently free territory, provided a rallying cry for northerners who feared southern political
power and wanted to limit slavery's spread. The Mexican War doomed the
two great parties of Jackson's day by forcing their members to take sides on

the issue of slavery in the territories—indeed, on the very future of slavery itself.[1]

The decade following the war was a time of political realignment. Factions within both major parties sought new alliances. A common aversion to slavery allowed a loose coalition to be constructed of northern Whigs (called "Conscience Whigs," to set them apart from the "Cotton Whigs," who favored the institution) and northern Democrats who supported the former president, Martin Van Buren. The Van Buren faction of the Democratic party was called "Barnburners," because the actions of its members threatened to destroy the traditional Democratic alliance that had given the party a national constituency, much like the actions of a farmer who sets his own barn on fire to rid it of rats. The antislavery factions formed a definite sectional party hostile to the expansion of the peculiar institution into any newly acquired territory. As scholars have shown, not all northerners who embraced the Free Soil doctrine did so out of consideration for the slave. Many Free Soilers wanted to keep the territories open to white farmers and laborers and closed to slaves and free blacks.[2]

The Free Soil Party had a short but very important existence. In the election of 1848, dissatisfied New York Democrats deserted their party to cast ballots for Martin Van Buren, the Free Soil candidate, thereby denying the state's thirty-six electoral votes to Lewis Cass. Although they did not stand a chance of electing their own presidential candidate, the Free Soilers helped to spoil the election for the mainstream Democrats by splitting Taylor's political opponents. In the election of 1852, the Democratic candidate, Franklin Pierce, defeated Winfield Scott for the presidency. With only 156,149 cast for Free Soiler John P. Hale of New Hampshire, the party failed to win a single electoral vote. Like other third parties in the United States, the Free Soilers realized that strong principles by themselves do not win elections. By the election of 1856, the Free Soil movement had been co-opted by the new Republican party. Thus, after a brief stopover in the camp of the Free Soil Party, many disaffected Whigs and Democrats had become Republicans. Although the new party's candidate, John C. Frémont, failed to win the White House in 1856, the party was poised for a rise to national dominance.[3]

The Republicans in 1860 benefited from deep rifts in the Democratic party, once delegates meeting in Charleston, South Carolina, openly split into two faction along sectional lines over the issue of slavery. Consequently, northern Democrats reconvened at Baltimore, Maryland, to nominate Illinois Sen. Stephen A. Douglas for president; and southern Democrats reassembled at Charleston to nominate Vice President John C. Breckenridge.

Another group of politicians from the border states formed a compromise party named the Constitutional Union party. The Republican party, now in a four-way race involving the two factions of the Democratic party and the Constitutional Union party, gained enough votes amid the political confusion to place Abraham Lincoln in the White House.[4]

The Republicans, whose ranks included a large number of old Conscience Whigs and Free Soilers, gained dominance over political and intellectual thought and retained that influence throughout much of the last half of the nineteenth century. Republican policy and ideology reflected a history of opposition to the party of Jackson and Polk. The judgment on the Mexican War passed by Republicans after 1865 was the same as that of their political predecessors: the Mexican War had been a Democratic scheme to steal territory from Mexico so as to ensure slavery's growth and survival. The actions and opinions of party leaders bolstered that viewpoint. Republicans proudly pointed to President Lincoln's defiance of Polk, when he dared "Young Hickory" to show him the "spot" on a map where American blood was shed on American soil. Ulysses S. Grant, a man who, in the minds of many Republicans, had saved the Union, reinforced the concept that the war had been a dishonorable affair. He wrote in his memoirs: "The occupation, separation, and annexation were, from the inception of the movement to its final consummation, a conspiracy to acquire territory out of which slave states might be formed for the American Union." In another passage, Grant linked the war he fought to preserve the Union with the war against Mexico: "The Southern Rebellion was largely the outgrowth of the Mexican War. Nations, like individuals, are punished for their transgressions. We got our punishment in the most sanguinary and expensive war of modern times." An early Lincoln biography also took the South to task on behalf of the martyred president, declaring, "We have already stated the fact that [the slave power], desiring Texas for the extension of slavery, made war on Mexico, and seized and appropriated the coveted land. . . . But these aggressions had at last aroused the free states, and brought on at last the 'IRREPRESSIBLE CONFLICT.'" Thus, for Grant as well as for many other Republicans, the responsibility of the Civil War rested squarely on the shoulders of James K. Polk and the Southern Democrats.[5]

In a largely forgotten book that was published shortly after the turn of the century, Charles H. Owens examined the opinion, then current, that the Mexican War had been an unjustifiable war of aggression. Born of "Puritan" stock, Owens claimed that he had "worked for Frémont, voted for Lincoln and Grant—twice each, and for several more Republican presidents." Troubled by the prevailing view in recent histories that the United

States had forced an unjust war on an unoffending neighbor republic, Owens concluded that Americans had been taught to view the war through the "blue light of whig and abolitionist defeat." He contended that the prevailing negative American attitude toward the war was based on the old Whig opposition that had been carried over to the Free Soil and Republican parties and had gained national acceptance with the rise of the latter.[6]

The notion that the Mexican War was an unjust war still lingers, and the war is remembered with much bitterness in both Mexico and the United States. Otis A. Singletary's brief but important study of the conflict contains the following Whiggish passage:

> Still another reason for our apparent indifference to the Mexican War lies rooted in the guilt that we as a nation have come to feel about it. The undeniable fact it was an offensive war so completely stripped it of moral pretensions that no politician of that era ever succeeded in elevating it to the lofty level of a "crusade." The additional fact that we paid Mexico fifteen million dollars after it was over—"conscience money," some called it [a reference to Grant]—seemed to confirm the ugliest charges of those who had denounced the war as a cynical, calculating despoiling of the Mexican state, a greedy land-grab from a neighbor too weak to defend herself.

Without stating so in this passage, Singletary lays the blame for the war at the feet of Polk and his party. Another author, the noted military historian Robert Leckie, in a recent study of the republic's early military conflicts, also relied on young Grant to prove the war's injustice: "Young Sam Grant, already perceptive beyond his years, called it an unholy war . . . He spoke for many of his comrades when he castigated the war that resulted as 'one of the most unholy ever waged by a stronger against a weaker nation.'" To be sure, Grant described the Mexican War as "one of the most unjust wars ever waged by a stronger against a weaker," but these words were not written by "Young Sam." Instead they were penned nearly forty years after the war by a man who had saved his nation from disunion, who had been courted and claimed by the Republican party, who had served two terms as president of the United States, whose visit to Mexico City was received by a crowd of fifty thousand Mexican admirers, who was president of the Mexican Southern Railroad Company, who helped negotiate a free-trade agreement between Mexico and the United States, and who was struggling to finish his memoirs before dying of throat cancer so that he could provide for the financial needs of his family. William S. McFeely, Grant's biographer, correctly surmises that "by 1885, Grant had been both general and president, and the seasoned Republican dismissed his pre–Civil War allegiance to the Democratic party and accepted the Whigs as the forebears of the Republicans."[7]

As Grant indicated, many Americans had opposed the war, including some in the army. Wrote Col. Ethan Allan Hitchcock as he prepared to join Scott's column before the invasion of Vera Cruz, "I not only think this Mexican war unnecessary and unjust as regards Mexico, but I also think it hostile to the principles of our own government." Many historians, both in the United States and Mexico, are quick to point to a number of prominent Americans, including John Q. Adams, Henry Clay, Daniel Webster, Abraham Lincoln, and a host of army regular officers like Hitchcock who believed the war unjust. What is often overlooked, however, is that these men were Whigs, whose party stood in political opposition to Polk and the war. One Lincoln biographer summed up the slain hero's motives for his actions during the war: "He was a Whig, and took the position of the Whigs of his day." How could the attitudes of these Whigs who followed party principles be anything but hostile toward the war?[8]

As Republican victors in the great struggle for the Union, the "spoils" fell to them. Along with those spoils came the freedom to interpret the Mexican War as an evil scheme devised by Jackson's minions. According to William Graham Sumner, a Jackson biographer writing in the early 1880s, "The Texan intrigue and the Mexican War were full of Jacksonian acts and principles." Sumner declared that Jackson's invasion of Spanish Florida in 1818 had set the tone for the era; as a result, "the army and navy were corrupted by swagger and insubordination and by the anxiety of the officers to win popularity by the methods of which Jackson had set the example." Summing up the period, Sumner stated, "The filibustering spirit, one law for ourselves and another for every one else, gained a popularity for which Jackson was much to blame." Republicans placed the Democrats on trial and found them guilty of dividing the Union and robbing Mexico of its territory. Victorious on the battlefields of Mexico, Polk and his army fared poorly in the clash of political ideologies that followed in the war's wake.[9]

Notes

ABBREVIATIONS

ACAB   James Grant Wilson and John Fiske, eds., *Appleton's Cyclopedia of American Biography* (New York: D. Appleton and Company, 1888)

DAB   Dumas Malone, ed., *Dictionary of American Biography,* 20 vols. (New York: Charles Scribner's Sons, 1927)

DRTL   Daughters of the Republic of Texas Library

NA   National Archives, Washington, D.C.

SCUTA   Special Collections, University of Texas at Arlington

USMHRC   Manuscript Division, U.S. Military History Research Collection, Carlisle, Pennsylvania

CHAPTER 1. JACKSONIANS AT WAR

1. Samuel G. Goodrich, *The First Book of History for Children and Youth; by the Author of Peter Parley's Tales* (Boston: Carter, Hendee, and Co., 1834), 8.

2. John William Ward, *Andrew Jackson: Symbol for an Age* (New York: Oxford University Press, 1977), 13–16. None of the four presidential candidates running in 1824 received a majority of votes. The election passed to the House of Representatives, where Speaker Henry Clay (himself one of the candidates) threw his support to the incumbent, John Quincy Adams. Andrew Jackson and his supporters were irate. Adams's appointment of Clay to the post of secretary of state drew the cry "corrupt bargain," meaning that the election had been stolen.

3. The personal and political life of Andrew Jackson has been much studied. See esp. Robert V. Remini, *Andrew Jackson and the Course of American Empire, 1767–1821* (New York: Harper and Row, 1977); *Andrew Jackson and the Course of American Freedom, 1822–1832* (New York: Harper and Row, 1981); and *Andrew Jackson and the Course of American Democracy, 1833–1945* (New York: Harper and Row, 1984). Other important works include Lee Benson, *The Concept of Jacksonian Democracy: New York as a Test Case* (Princeton, N.J.: Princeton University Press, 1961); Marvin Myers, *The Jacksonian Persuasion: Politics and Belief* (Stanford, Calif.: Stanford University Press, 1957); Arthur M. Schlesinger, Jr., *The Age of Jackson* (New York: Little, Brown, 1945); Edward Pessen, *Jacksonian America: Society, Personality, and Politics* (Homewood, Ill.: Dorsey Press, 1969); Richard P. McCormick, *The Second American Party*

System: Party Formation in the Jacksonian Era (Chapel Hill: University of North Carolina Press, 1986). Although historians debate whether or not Jackson truly instigated the movement toward democracy, none doubts that great changes took place during his life or that these were continued by his supporters.

4. Charles Grier Sellers, *James K. Polk: Jacksonian, 1795–1843* (Princeton, N.J.: Princeton University Press, 1957), 23, 39, 43–55, 59–62. Born in 1777 in Virginia, Felix Grundy moved west to pursue a legal and political career that included service in the Kentucky Constitutional Convention, 1799; in the U.S. House of Representatives from Tennessee, 1811–14; in the Tennessee Legislature, 1815–19; in the U.S. Senate, 1820–48; and as U.S. attorney general under Van Buren, 1838–39. At the time of his death in 1840, Grundy again was Tennessee's U.S. senator.

5. Sellers, *Polk: Jacksonian,* 76–77, 94–98, 292–97, 352–75, 421, 469–71; Charles Grier Sellers, *James K. Polk: Continentalist, 1843–1846* (Princeton, N.J.: Princeton University Press, 1966), 85–107, 208–12.

6. Frederick Merk, *Manifest Destiny and Mission in American History* (Cambridge, Mass.: Harvard University Press, 1995), 27; Julius W. Pratt, "John L. O'Sullivan and Manifest Destiny," *New York History* 14 (1933): 213–34. Merk's 1963 classic remains one of clearest examinations of Manifest Destiny to date. Other important works include Thomas Heitala, *Manifest Destiny: Anxious Aggrandizement in Late Jacksonian America* (Ithaca, N.Y.: Cornell University Press, 1985); and Reginald Horsman, *Race and Manifest Destiny: The Origins of American Radical Anglo-Saxonism* (Cambridge, Mass.: Harvard University Press, 1981). The term Manifest Destiny is attributed to John Louis O'Sullivan, founder and editor of the *United States Magazine and Democratic Review.*

7. Bernardo DeVoto, *The Course of Empire* (Boston: Houghton Mifflin Co., 1952), 264–66, 344; John Francis Bannon, *The Spanish Borderlands Frontier, 1513–1821* (Albuquerque: University of New Mexico Press, 1974), 204, 209, 210; John R. Ficklin, "Was Texas Included in the Louisiana Purchase?" *Publications of the Southern Historical Association* 5 (Sept., 1901): 351–87; Bannon, *Spanish Borderlands Frontier,* 205, 208, 216, 217; Ward, *Andrew Jackson,* 8–10; Joseph Burkholder Smith, *James Madison's Phony War: The Plot to Steal Florida* (New York: Arbor House, 1983), 51–68; and Merk, *Manifest Destiny and Mission,* 19–20. For an insightful study of the Louisiana Purchase, see Alexander DeConde, *This Affair of Louisiana* (Baton Rouge: Louisiana State University Press, 1976).

8. Robert Ryal Miller, *Mexico: A History* (Norman: University of Oklahoma Press, 1985), 211–14. Two of the more recent studies of the Texas Revolution include Paul D. Lack, *The Texas Revolutionary Experience: A Political and Social History, 1835–1836* (College Station: Texas A&M University Press, 1992); and Stephen L. Hardin, *Texian Iliad: A Military History of the Texas Revolution, 1835–1836* (Austin: University of Texas Press, 1994). For the colonization of Texas by Americans, see Eugene C. Barker, *The Life of Stephen F. Austin, Founder of Texas, 1793–1836: A Chapter in the Westward Movement of the Anglo-American People* (Austin: University of Texas Press, 1990).

9. Barker, *Stephen F. Austin,* 257; Jewels Davis Scarbrough, "The Georgia Battalion in

the Texas Revolution: A Critical Study," *Southwestern Historical Quarterly* 63 (Apr., 1963): 511–32; Karle Wilson Barker, "Trailing the New Orleans Greys," *Southwestern Review* 22 (Apr., 1937): 213–40; Harbert Davenport, "The Men of Goliad," *Southwestern Historical Quarterly* 48 (July, 1939): 1–41; John B. Thomas, Jr., "Kentuckians in Texas: Captain Burr H. Duval's Company at Goliad," *Register of the Kentucky Historical Society* 81 (Summer 1983): 237–54; Alexander Dienst, "The New Orleans Newspaper Files of the Texas Revolution Period," *Southwest Historical Quarterly* 4 (Oct., 1900): 140–51. One author, James E. Winston, wrote extensively about American aid in the Texas Revolution in such articles as "Kentucky and the Independence of Texas," *Southwestern Historical Quarterly* 14 (July, 1912): 27–62; "Mississippi and the Independence of Texas," *Southwestern Historical Quarterly* 21 (July, 1917): 36–60; "New York and the Independence of Texas," *Southwestern Historical Quarterly* 18 (Apr., 1915): 368–85; "Pennsylvania and the Independence of Texas," *Southwestern Historical Quarterly* 17 (Jan., 1913): 262–82. For accounts mentioning U.S. soldiers at San Jacinto, see David Lee Child, *The Taking of Naboth's Vineyard; Or, History of the Texas Conspiracy, an Examination of the Reasons Given by the Hon. J. C. Calhoun, Hon. R. J. Walker, and Others, for the Dismemberment and Robbery of the Republic of Texas* (New York: S. W. Benedict and Co., 1845), 16; William Jay, *A Review of the Causes and Consequences of the Mexican War* (Boston: Benjamin B. Massey and Co.; Philadelphia: Uriah Hunt and Co.; and New York: M. W. Dodd, 1849), 28; Noah Smithwick, *Evolution of a State; Or, Recollection of Old Texas Days* (Austin: University of Texas Press, 1983), 93; Bill Walraven and Marjorie K. Walraven, *The Magnificent Barbarians: Little-Told Tales of the Texas Revolution* (Austin, Tex.: Eakin Press, 1993), 113–32.

10. For accounts of the ongoing conflict between Texas and Mexico, see George W. Kendall, *Narrative of the Texan Santa Fe Expedition* (New York: Harper and Brothers, 1844); Thomas Jefferson Green, *Journal of the Texian Expedition Against Mier* (New York: Harper and Brothers, 1845); Joseph M. Nance, *Attack and Counter Attack: The Texas-Mexican Frontier, 1842* (Austin: University of Texas Press, 1964); Sam W. Haynes, *Soldiers of Misfortune: The Somerville and Mier Expeditions* (Austin: University of Texas Press, 1990). During the Mexican War, American soldiers often referred to these incidents in their diaries and letters.

11. Robert V. Remini, "Texas Must Be Ours," *American Heritage* 37 (1986): 47; Justin Smith, *War with Mexico* (Gloucester, Mass.: Peter Smith, 1963), 1:116, 1:140. The definitive study of the international implications of the annexation of Texas is David M. Pletcher, *The Diplomacy of Annexation: Texas, Oregon, and the Mexican War* (Columbia: University of Missouri Press, 1975). Taylor's forces at Fort Jesup included the 3rd U.S. Infantry, 8 companies of the 4th U.S. Infantry, and 7 companies of the 2nd U.S. Dragoons.

12. Thomas Maitland Marshall, "The Southwestern Boundary of Texas, 1821–1840," *Southwestern Historical Quarterly* 14 (Apr., 1911): 273–93; Justin Smith, *War with Mexico*, 1:138, 1:139, 1:141, 1:142; U.S. Congress, House, *Message from the President of the United States to the Two Houses of Congress at the Commencement of the First Session of the Twenty-Ninth Congress: Report of the Secretary of War*, 29th Cong., 1st

sess., 1845, House Doc. No. 2, 194. Taylor's movement was explained in Secretary Marcy's report: "He was instructed to repel Mexican aggressions and protect the country from Indian invasion, to regard the Rio del Norte [Rio Grande] as its western boundary, and to select a position for his forces with reference to this frontier, but to leave unmolested Mexican settlements, and also military posts, should there be any such posts on the east bank of that river, which were in the occupation of Mexican forces previously to the period when Texas assented to the terms of annexation."

13. Justin Smith, *War with Mexico,* 1:88–101; Curtis R. Reynolds, "The Deterioration of Mexican-American Diplomatic Relations, 1833–1845," *Journal of the West* 11 (Apr., 1972): 213–24; Gene M. Brack, *Mexico Views Manifest Destiny, 1821–1846: An Essay on the Origins of the Mexican War* (Albuquerque: University of New Mexico Press, 1975), 140–49, 163–64.

14. James K. Polk, *The Diary of James K. Polk During His Presidency, 1845 to 1849* (Chicago: A. C. McClurg and Co., 1910), 1:354, 1:384–87; Justin Smith, *War with Mexico,* 1:145–50; U.S. Congress, House, *Military Forces Employed in the Mexican War: Letter from the Secretary of War Transmitting Information in Answer to a Resolution of the House, of July 31, 1848, Relative to the Military Forces Employed in the Late War with Mexico,* 31st Cong., 1st sess., 1850, Exec. Doc. No. 24, p. 9. The American losses included one lieutenant, two sergeants, and eight privates killed; and fifty-three men captured.

15. Polk, *Diary,* 1:384–98; James D. Richardson, ed., *A Compilation of the Messages and Papers of the Presidents, 1789–1902* (N.p.: Bureau of National Literature and Art, 1903), 4:442.

16. William Addleman Ganoe, *The History of the United States Army* (New York: D. Appleman and Co., 1924), 196; Justin Smith, *War with Mexico,* 1:139, 450; U.S. Congress, House, *Message from the President of the United States to the Two Houses of Congress, at the Commencement of the Second Session of the Twenty-Ninth Congress,* 29th Cong., 2d sess., 1846, House Doc. No. 4, pp. 68c and 68d; "Army Journal," *Niles' National Register,* May 23, 1846, p. 181, and July 11, 1846, pp. 292–93. Determining the actual strength of the army on the eve of the Mexican War is difficult, as the figures vary from source to source. "Army Journal," *Niles' National Register,* May 23, 1846, presents this estimate, by military division: Gen. John E. Wool's Eastern Division, 1,600 officers and men; Gen. Edmund P. Gaines's Western Division, 1,905 officers and men; Gen. Hugh Brady's 4th Military District, 286 officers and men; Gen. Zachary Taylor's Army of Occupation, 2,965 officers and men. These figures indicate a combined strength of 6,763 men and officers, almost 1,500 more than the figure cited by Ganoe. In any case, both numbers are below the strength authorized by Congress.

17. Charles K. Gardner, *A Dictionary of All Officers Who Have Been Commissioned, or Have Been Appointed and Served, in the Army of the United States* (New York: G. P. Putnam and Co., 1853), 28–30; U.S. Congress, House, *Message from U.S. President at Commencement of 2nd Session of 29th Congress,* House Doc. No. 4, pp. 3–4, 6.

18. U.S. Congress, House, *Military Forces in the Mexican War: Letter from the Secretary of War,* 31st Cong., 1st sess., 1850, Exec. Doc. No. 24, pp. 2–5.

19. John H. Schroeder, *Mr. Polk's War: American Opposition and Dissent, 1846–1848* (Madison: University of Wisconsin Press, 1973), 14–16, 19; Frederick Merk, *Dissent in Three American Wars* (Cambridge, Mass.: Harvard University Press, 1970), 39, 40; *Congressional Globe,* 29th Cong., 1st sess., 1846, pp. 785, 795.

20. Schroeder, *Mr. Polk's War,* 19; Andrew Jackson Trussell to John Trussell, Feb. 28, 1848, in Trussell Family Papers, Box GA 66–4, SCUTA; Walter T. Durham, ed., "Mexican War Letters to Wynnewood," *Tennessee Historical Quarterly* 33 (Winter 1974): 406–407; *Raleigh (N.C.) Star and North Carolina Gazette,* Oct. 27, 1847; *Raleigh (N.C.) Register,* Jan. 19, 1847.

21. Each regiment was authorized one colonel, one lieutenant colonel, ten captains, and twenty lieutenants. A full list of all officers who served in the regular and volunteer forces during the Mexican War can be found in Gardner, *Dictionary of Officers,* 28–32; William H. Robarts, *Mexican War Veterans: A Complete Roster of the Regular and Volunteer Troops in the War Between the United States and Mexico, from 1846 to 1848* (Washington, D.C.: A. S. Witherbee and Co., 1887); and Cadmus M. Wilcox, *History of the Mexican War* (Washington, D.C.: Church News Publishing Co., 1892), 609–95.

22. Gardner, *Dictionary of All Officers,* 30.

23. Thomas W. Cutrer, *Ben McCulloch and the Frontier Military Tradition* (Chapel Hill: University of North Carolina Press, 1993), 3–4.

24. Alexis de Tocqueville, *Democracy in America* (New York: Vintage Books, 1945), 2:287.

25. Wilfred E. Binkley, *American Political Parties: Their Natural History* (New York: Knopf, 1971), 239–40; James A. Rawley, *The Politics of Union: Northern Politics during the Civil War* (Lincoln: University of Nebraska Press, 1974), 29; Carl Sandburg, *Abraham Lincoln: The War Years* (Harcourt, Brace, and Co., 1939), 1:334–35; Emanuel Hertz, *The Hidden Lincoln: From the Letters and Papers of William H. Herndon* (New York: Viking Press, 1938), 299; Harry J. Carman and Reinhard H. Luthin, *Lincoln and the Patronage* (Gloucester, Mass.: Peter Smith, 1964), 150–65; J. C. A. Stagg, *Mr. Madison's War: Politics, Diplomacy, and Warfare in the Early American Republic, 1783–1830* (Princeton, N.J.: Princeton University Press, 1983), 164. For a study of the party politics and their effects on the army during its formative stages, see Theodore J. Crackel, *Mr. Jefferson's Army: Political and Social Reform of the Military Establishment, 1801–1809* (New York: New York University Press, 1987).

26. George G. Meade, *The Life and Letters of George Gordon Meade, Major General of the United States Army* (New York: Charles Scribner's Sons, 1913), 1:152.

CHAPTER 2. THE AMERICAN MILITARY ESTABLISHMENT

1. John F. Callan, *The Military Laws of the United States, Relating to the Army, Volunteers, Militia, and to Bounty Lands and Pensions, From the Foundation of the Gov-*

ernment to the Year 1863, (Philadelphia: George W. Childs, 1863), 87; Francis Heitman, *Historical Register and Dictionary of the United States Army* (Washington, D.C.: Government Printing Office, 1903; reprinted Gaithersburg, Md.: Olde Soldiers Book, Inc., 1988), 2:576–78. For information on the formation of the U.S. Army, see Russell F. Weigley, *History of the United States Army* (New York: Macmillan, 1967); and Russell F. Weigley, *Towards an American Army: Military Thought from Washington to Marshall* (New York: Columbia University Press, 1962).

2. Polk's diary best describes the personal interest he took in directing the war. Also see Paul H. Bergeron, *The Presidency of James K. Polk* (Lawrence: University Press of Kansas, 1987). For Polk as commander-in-chief, see Leonard D. White, *The Jacksonians: A Study in Administrative History, 1829–1861* (New York: Macmillan, 1954), 50–66.

3. Ivor D. Spencer, *The Victor and the Spoils: A Life of William L. Marcy* (Providence, R.I.: Brown University Press, 1959), 59–62, 137–74.

4. Callan, *Military Laws,* 85; Ganoe, *History of the U.S. Army,* 95; Henry L. Scott, *Military Dictionary: Comprising Technical Definitions; Information on Raising and Keeping Troops, Including Makeshift and Improved Matériél; and Law, Government, Regulation, and Administration Relating to Land Forces* (Yuma, Ariz.: Fort Yuma Press, 1984), 547; Heitman, *Historical Register,* 1:16; U.S. War Dept., *General Regulations for the Army of the United States, 1841* (Washington, D.C.: J. and G. E. Gideon, 1841); U.S. War Dept., *General Regulations for the Army of the United States, 1847* (Washington, D.C.: J. and G. E. Gideon, 1847); Robert R. Jones, ed., "The Mexican War Diary of James Lawson Kemper," *Virginia Magazine of History and Biography* 74 (Oct., 1966): 395; "The Sunday Question," *Journal of the Military Service Institution of the United States* 8 (1888): 356–57; William B. McGroarty, "William H. Richardson's Journal of Doniphan's Expedition," pt. 2, *Missouri Historical Review* 22 (1928): 212.

5. Fayette Robinson, *An Account of the Organization of the Army of the United States of America* (Philadelphia: E. B. Butler and Co., 1848), 1:32.

6. Henry L. Scott, *Military Dictionary,* 168, 283, 570–73.

7. Ibid., 110–11, 388–91; W. A. Cruffut, *Fifty Years in Camp and Field: Diary of Major General Ethan Allen Hitchcock, U.S.A.* (Freeport, N.Y.: Books for Libraries Press, 1971), 204–206, 220–21.

8. U.S. War Dept., *General Regulations, 1841,* 11, 12, 17, 22, 31, 32, 33.

9. Heitman, *Historical Register,* 1:38, 1:582. Col. Roger Jones served as adjutant general from 1825 until 1852. Jones began his military career in the Marine Corps in 1809. During the War of 1812, while a captain of artillery, he received a brevet to major for his services at the Battle of Chippewa. An additional brevet to lieutenant colonel was awarded for gallantry at Fort Erie. Jones advanced in grade by additional brevets for faithful conduct and died a brevet major general in 1852.

10. Robinson, *Organization of the Army,* 1:33, 39–40; U.S. War Dept., *General Regulations, 1841,* 135–54; Heitman, *Historical Register,* 1:39, 1:339. Col. George Croghan served as inspector general from 1825 until 1849. Entering the army as a captain in

1812, Croghan participated in the defense of Fort Stephenson, Ohio, in Aug. 1813. Croghan died in 1849.

11. Robinson, *An Account,* 1:40–42; U.S. War Dept., *General Regulations, 1841,* 287–339; Thomas Henderson, *Hints on the Medical Examination of Recruits for the Army; And on the Discharge of Soldiers from the Service on Surgeon's Certificate* (Philadelphia: Haswell, Barrington, and Haswell, 1840), 16. Heitman, *Historical Register,* 1:42, 1:619. Col. Thomas Lawson began his career in military medicine in 1809, when he entered the U.S. Navy. He served as a regimental surgeon during the War of 1812. Appointed surgeon general in 1836, Lawson held the post until his death in 1861. Surgeons held the rank of major, while assistant surgeons with five years of service were captains and those with less were lieutenants. For examples of matrons in the army, see John B. Porter, M.D., "Medical and Surgical Notes of the Campaigns in the War with Mexico," pt. 5, *American Journal of the Medical Services,* New Series, 35–36 (1858): 349, 351; Records of Matron Magdalene Rages [Reyes], in *Compiled Service Records of the Mississippi Volunteers in the War with Mexico* Washington, D.C., Roll No. 7, Microfilm Series M863, NA.

12. Robinson, *An Account,* 1:44, 45; U.S. War Dept., *General Regulations, 1841,* 35–37, 340–62; Heitman, *Historical Register,* 1:42, 1:968, 2:590; McGroarty, "Richardson's Journal," pt. 2, pp. 331, 341, 350. Col. Nathan Townson entered the service in 1812 as a captain of artillery. Recognized for his part in the action against the British at Fort Erie and Chippewa, Townson emerged from the war as a brevet lieutenant colonel. In 1822, he was appointed paymaster general, the post he held until his death in 1854.

13. Robinson, *An Account,* 1:54–55; U.S. War Dept., *General Regulations, 1841,* 179–256; Erna Risch, *Quartermaster Support of the Army: A History of the Corps, 1775–1939* (Washington, D.C.: Quartermaster Historian's Office, Office of the Quartermaster General, 1962), 231–99; Heitman, *Historical Register,* 1:40, 1:573. Col. Thomas Sidney Jesup entered the army in 1808 as a 2nd lieutenant but by 1813 had risen to the rank of major. He received two brevets for the battles at Chippewa and Niagara. In 1818, Jesup was appointed quartermaster general, the post he held until his death in 1860.

14. Robinson, *An Account,* 1:41, 56; U.S. War Dept., *General Regulations, 1841,* 257–86, 363; Heitman, *Historical Register,* 1:40, 1:453. Col. George Gibson entered the army as a captain of infantry in 1808. In 1818, Gibson was appointed commissary general of subsistence, the post he held until his death in 1861.

15. Robinson, *An Account,* 1:31, 81–83; U.S. War Dept., *General Regulations, 1841,* 160–78; Heitman, *Historical Register,* 1:33, 1:228–29, 1:943. Col. George Bomford entered the army as a 2nd lieutenant of engineers in 1804. He was appointed chief of ordnance in 1832. Bomford died in Mar. 1848, while American troops were still in Mexico. His successor, Col. George Talcott, began his military career in 1813. He held the post of chief of ordnance until his death in 1851.

16. Robinson, *An Account,* 1:60–61, 73, 75–79; U.S. War Dept., *General Regulations, 1841,* 154–60; Heitman, *Historical Register,* 1:43, 1:150, 1:966. Graduated 3rd in his class at West Point, James G. Totten entered the army in 1802 as a 2nd lieutenant of engi-

neers. Promoted to chief engineer in 1838, Totten retained the post until his death in 1864. Nineteenth in his class at West Point, John J. Abert declined an appointment upon graduation in 1811. Abert later accepted the appointment as chief topographic engineer in 1838, the post he held until his retirement from the army in 1861.

17. Ganoe, *History of the U.S. Army,* 196.

18. Heitman, *Historical Register,* 1:838; Robinson, *An Account,* 1:28, 41, 88; U.S. War Dept., *General Regulations, 1841,* 8, 9, 12, 13, 28, 29, 76–79; Henry L. Scott, *Military Dictionary,* 571. According to Scott, "The Regimental Staff embraces regimental officers and noncommissioned officers charged with the functions, within their respective regiments, assimilated to the duties of adjutant-general, quartermasters and commissaries. Each regiment has a regimental adjutant, and a quartermaster, appointed from the officers of the regiment."

19. U.S. War Dept., *General Regulations, 1841,* 13, 14, 76–79.

20. George Ballentine, *Autobiography of an English Soldier in the United States Army; Comprising Observations and Adventures in the States and Mexico* (New York: Stringer and Townsend, 1853), 122; Robert H. Ferrell, ed., *Monterrey Is Ours! The Mexican War Letters of Lieutenant Dana* (Lexington: University Press of Kentucky, 1990), 8; U.S. War Dept., *General Regulations, 1841,* 37; Stewart J. Miller, "Army Laundresses: Ladies of Soap Suds Row," *Nebraska History* 61 (Winter 1980): 421–36; William B. Skelton, *An American Profession of Arms: The Army Officer Corps, 1784–1861* (Lawrence: University Press of Kansas, 1992), 207–208; Cruffut, *Fifty Years in Camp and Field,* 207. The story of women's role in the early army has yet to be fully explored. Those interested in women and the war should see Peggy Cashion, "Women and the Mexican War" (M.A. thesis, University of Texas at Arlington, 1990).

21. Judge Zo Cook, "Mexican War Reminiscences," *Alabama Historical Quarterly* 20 (1957): 438–39; Thomas L. Karnes, *William Gilpin, Western Nationalist* (Austin: University of Texas Press, 1970), 196; William Y. Chalfant, *Dangerous Passage: The Santa Fe Trail and the Mexican War* (Norman: University of Oklahoma Press, 1994), 182–83; *Jackson (Miss.) Mississippian,* Nov. 11, 1847.

22. Robinson, *An Account,* 1:28, 29; Winfield Scott, *Infantry Tactics; Or, Rules for the Exercise and Manoeuvres of the United States Infantry* (New York: Harper and Brothers, 1840), 1:1, 1:4; Emory Upton, *The Military Policy of the United States During the Mexican War* (Washington, D.C.: Government Printing Office, 1914), 198–99; Rhoda Van Bibber Tanner Doubleday, *Journals of Major Philip N. Barbour and Martha H. Barbour* (New York: G. P. Putnam's Sons, 1936), 73, 75; Edward M. Coffman, *The Old Army: A Portrait of the American Army in Peacetime, 1784–1898* (New York: Oxford University Press, 1986), 162.

23. Winfield Scott, *Infantry Tactics,* 1:1; Henry L. Scott, *Military Dictionary,* 121, 395, 570; Robinson, *An Account,* 1:82, 85–88; U.S. War Dept., *General Regulations, 1841,* 2, 4, 6.

24. Winfield Scott, *Infantry Tactics,* 1:1, 1:2; Donald E. Graves, "Dry Books of Tactics: U.S. Infantry Manuals of the War of 1812 and After," pt. 2, *Military Collector and Historian* 38 (1986): 173–77.

25. Philip R. N. Katcher, *The Mexican-American War, 1846–1848* (London: Osprey Publishing, 1989), 14; Lester R. Dillon, Jr., *American Artillery in the Mexican War, 1846–47* (Austin, Tex.: Presidial Press, 1975), 19, 30, 63; Robinson, *An Account,* 2:174, 2:175, 2:181; U.S. War Dept., *General Regulations, 1841,* 19–20; Henry L. Scott, *Military Dictionary,* 61; Ganoe, *History of the U.S. Army,* 187, 554; William E. Birkhimer, *Historical Sketch of the Organization, Administration, Matériel and Tactics of the Artillery, United States Army* (N.p.: James J. Chapman, 1884; reprinted New York: Greenwood Press, 1968), 54–64, 305–307; U.S. War Dept., *Instruction for Field Artillery, Horse and Foot. Translated from the French, and Arranged for the Service of the United States, by Robert Anderson, Captain in the Staff of U.S. Army* (Philadelphia: Robert P. Desilver), 10. Anderson's artillery manual begins with this caution to officers: "Before commencing the service of their proper arm, the Artillery Soldiers should be instructed in the School of the Soldier and of the Company, as detailed in the *Infantry Tactics.*"

26. Henry L. Scott, *Military Dictionary,* 154–56, 426–27; Heitman, *Historical Register,* 1:66; Ganoe, *History of the U.S. Army,* 190. For a technical history of the dragoons, see Randy Steffen, *The Horse Soldiers: The Revolution, the War of 1812, the Early Frontier, 1776–1850* (Norman: University of Oklahoma Press, 1977).

27. Ganoe, *History of the U.S. Army,* 122, 179; U.S. War Dept., *Abstract of Infantry Tactics; Including Exercises and Manoeuvres of Light-Infantry and Riflemen; for the Use of Militia of the United States* (Boston: Hilliard, Gray, Little, and Wilkins, 1830), unnumbered page; Samuel Cooper, *A Concise System of Instruction and Regulations for the Militia and Volunteers of the United States* (Philadelphia: Robert P. Desilver, 1836), 3; *Army and Navy Chronicle,* 2:319–20, 329.

28. Marvin A. Kreidberg and Merton G. Henry, *History of Military Mobilization in the United States,* 63–64; "On the Militia, As a Means of Defense," *Army and Navy Chronicle,* 2:116–17, 8:195; Henry L. Scott, *Military Dictionary,* 643–44.

29. Russell F. Weigley, *The American Way of War: A History of United States Military Strategy and Policy* (New York: Macmillan, 1973), 4; Joseph R. Riling, *Baron Von Steuben and His Regulations, Including a Complete Facsimile of the Original Regulations for the Order and Discipline of the Troops of the United States* (Philadelphia: Ray Riling Arms Books Co., 1966), 7–13. Weigley concluded that Von Steuben was less than successful, but the Prussian's appearance does mark the moment at which American military began to emerge as a professional force.

30. Winfield Scott, *Memoirs of Lieut.-General Scott, LL.D., Written by Himself* (Freeport, N.Y.: Books for Libraries Press, 1970), 1:1, 1:11, 1:18, 1:29, 1:50, 1:57–63, 1:72, 1:86, 1:117, 1:119, 1:120, 1:121, 1:129, 1:137–46; John Frost, *The Mexican War and Its Warriors* (Philadelphia: H. Mansfield, 1848), 15–319; Heitman, *Historical Register,* 1:20, 870. For a critical study of the battles that elevated Scott to fame, see Donald E. Graves, *The Battle of Lundy's Lane: On the Niagara in 1814* (Baltimore, Md.: Nautical and Aviation Publishing Co. of America, 1993). Although several new biographies are now in production, the standard remains Charles W. Elliot, *Winfield Scott, the Soldier and the Man* (New York: Macmillan, 1937).

31. Winfield Scott, *Memoirs,* 1:119, 1:120, 1:205–208, 2:258, 2:259; Grady McWhiney and

Perry D. Jamieson, *Attack and Die: Civil War Military Tactics and the Southern Heritage* (Tuscaloosa: University of Alabama Press, 1982), 31; U.S. War Dept., *Abstract of Infantry Tactics;* Weigley, *American Way of War,* 67; Henry L. Scott, *Military Dictionary,* 51–53. By its Acts of Mar. 13, 1813, and Apr. 26, 1816, Congress had authorized the president to issue regulations governing the army.

32. Winfield Scott, *Memoirs,* 2:355–61; Kenneth R. Stevens, *Border Diplomacy: The Caroline and McLeod Affairs in Anglo-American Relations, 1837–1842* (Tuscaloosa: University of Alabama Press, 1989), 17–22.

33. "Popular Portraits with Pen and Pencil: Major General Gaines," *United States Magazine and Democratic Review* 22 (June, 1848): 549–57; Heitman, *Historical Register,* 1:442; Winfield Scott, *Memoirs,* 1:208–16; U.S. Congress, Senate, *Message of the President of the United States, in Answer to a Resolution of the Senate of the 5th Instant, Relative to the Calling of Volunteers or Militia into the Service of the United States, by an Officer of the Army, without Legal Authority; to the Measures Adopted for the Defense of the Southern Frontier, &c.,* 29th Cong., 1st sess., 1846, Senate Doc. No. 378, p. 30.

34. Heitman, *Historical Register,* 1:239, 1:307, 1:1060; Graves, *Battle of Lundy's Lane,* 221, 222. The brigade major bears the same relation to a brigadier as the adjutant does to a colonel of a regiment.

35. Heitman, *Historical Register,* 1:949. For an excellent biography of Taylor, see K. Jack Bauer, *Zachary Taylor: Soldier, Planter, Statesman of the Old South* (Baton Rouge: Louisiana State University Press, 1985).

36. Winfield Scott, *Memoirs,* 1:217–19, 1:225–33, 1:260–65, 1:270–74; Frost, *Mexican War and Its Warriors,* 11–21.

37. John Bemrose, *Reminiscences of the Second Seminole War,* ed. John K. Mahon (Gainesville: University Presses of Florida, 1966), 59, 78.

38. T. B. Thorp, *Our Army on the Rio Grande* (Philadelphia: Cary and Hart, 1846), 160–62; H. Montgomery, *The Life of Zachary Taylor, Twelfth President of the United States* (Buffalo, N.Y.: Derby, Orton, and Mulligan, 1854), 344; John James Peck, *The Sign of the Eagle: A View of Mexico, 1830–1855* (San Diego, Calif.: Copley Press, 1970), 155. Accounts of Taylor's dress and mannerisms abound in Mexican War literature. For examples, see Lew Wallace, *Lew Wallace: An Autobiography* (New York: Harper and Brothers, 1906), 1:155; George C. Furber, *The Twelve Month Volunteer; Or, Journal of a Private in the Tennessee Regiment of Cavalry, in the Campaign, in Mexico, 1846–47* (Cincinnati: J. A. and U. P. James, 1848), 329–30; James K. Holland, "Diary of a Texan Volunteer in the Mexican War," *Southwestern Historical Quarterly* 30 (July, 1926): 19. One author, T. B. Thorp, compared Taylor to his Mexican rival, Gen. Mariano Arista, and made the same comparison: Taylor was plain and unpretentious, while Arista was vain and aristocratic. Thorp's conclusion was simple—Taylor was a common man.

39. William Seaton Henry, *Campaign Sketches of the War with Mexico* (New York: Arno Press, 1973), 89; Weigley, *American Way of War,* 72.

40. William B. Campbell, "Mexican War Letters of Col. William Bowen Campbell, of

Tennessee, Written to Governor David Campbell, of Virginia, 1846–1847," *Tennessee Historical Magazine* 1 (June, 1915): 161.

CHAPTER 3. MR. POLK'S GENERALS

1. Polk, *Diary,* 2:139–40; Justin Smith, *War with Mexico,* 1:179; Zachary Taylor, *Letters of Zachary Taylor from the Battle-Fields of the Mexican War* (New York: Kraus Reprint Co., 1970), 22.

2. Polk, *Diary,* 2:181–85; Justin Smith, *War with Mexico,* 1: 258–61; Zachary Taylor, *Letters,* 90.

3. Henry L. Scott, *Military Dictionary,* 27, 166–67; Polk, *Diary,* 2:119, 2:411–13.

4. Polk, *Diary,* 1:418–21, 2:118, 2:119, 2:227–28, 2:328; 2:429–33; Ganoe, *History of the U.S. Army,* 143; Justin Smith, *War with Mexico,* 1:197–98.

5. Polk, *Diary,* 1:418.

6. Cruffut, *Fifty Years in Camp and Field,* 64–69. Numerous Whig officers chafed under the Democratic administrations of Jackson and Polk. Lt. Col. Ethan Allen Hitchcock, for example, wrote, "But an evil time was again at hand [at the U.S. Military Academy], for which General Jackson was responsible." Hitchcock faulted the president for allowing cadets to discuss party politics at West Point and later accused Jackson of blocking his promotion after he complained. For many army officers, anti-Democratic fights appear to have been sparked by personal reverses such as Hitchcock's.

7. Polk, *Diary,* 2:117–19, 2:439; Justin Smith, *War with Mexico,* 1:490–91; Zachary Taylor, *Letters,* 46, 185–86. Wagons were a sore point with Taylor, who came to believe that they had been withheld to impede his advance, so as to diminish his political chances. Both Polk and Justin Smith blamed Taylor's transportation problems on poor planning by the general.

8. Gardner, *Dictionary of All Officers,* 29, 31; Heitman, *Historical Register,* 1:20, 1:21.

9. Polk, *Diary,* 2:478–80, 2:481–82, 2:492–93, 3:30–32; Spencer, *Victor and Spoils,* 59–62, 137–74. For a discussion of the spoils system, see Pessen, *Jacksonian America,* 336–40.

10. Polk, *Diary,* 1:418, 2:235–38, 2:384–88.

11. Heitman, *Historical Register,* 1:20–21.

12. "Volunteer Officers," *Niles' National Register,* July 11, 1846, 294–95.

13. Robert C. Cotton, "Robert Patterson," *DAB,* 14:306–307; Michael Feldberg, *The Turbulent Era: Riot and Discord in Jacksonian America* (New York: Oxford University Press, 1980), 23, 32.

14. "Thomas Marshall," *ACAB,* 4:225; "Volunteers," *Niles' National Register,* July 25, 1846, p. 326.

15. Philip M. Hamer, "Gideon Johnson Pillow," *DAB,* 14:603–604; "Volunteers," *Niles' National Register,* July 25, 1846, p. 326; Ulysses S. Grant, *The Papers of Ulysses S. Grant,* ed. John Y. Simon (Carbondale: Southern Illinois University Press, 1967), 1:3. For a recent biography of Pillow, see Nathaniel C. Hughes, Jr., and Roy P.

Stonesifer, Jr., *The Life and Wars of Gideon J. Pillow* (Chapel Hill: University of North Carolina Press, 1993), 7. Hughes and Stonesifer determined that Polk and Pillow never were law partners, refuting the popular notion that they had worked together.

16. Homer Carey Hockett, "Thomas Lyon Hamer," *DAB*, 8:169–70.

17. Joseph Schaffer, "Joseph Lane," *DAB*, 10:579–80.

18. Robert E. May, *John A. Quitman: Old South Crusader* (Baton Rouge: Louisiana State University Press, 1985), 4, 7, 11, 15, 19, 21, 31, 32, 37–41, 64, 68–71, 98, 107, 108, 121, 122, 147–49.

19. "James Shields," *ACAB*, 5:509; James Gray, *The Illinois* (New York: Farrar and Rinehart, 1940), 144–45.

20. Roy Franklin Nichols, "Franklin Pierce," *DAB*, 14:576–80; Roy Franklin Nichols, *Franklin Pierce: Young Hickory of the Granite Hills* (Philadelphia: University of Pennsylvania Press, 1958).

21. "George Cadwalader," *ACAB*, 1:493–94; Feldberg, *Turbulent Era*, 32–32.

22. "Enos D. Hopping," *ACAB*, 3:262; Polk, *Diary*, 2:399–405.

23. Claude M. Fuess, *The Life of Caleb Cushing* (Harcourt, Brace, and Co., 1923), 2:3–81.

24. H. Edward Nettles, "Sterling Price," *DAB*, 8:216–17.

25. Polk, *Diary*, 2:406, 3:29.

26. "Volunteers," *Niles' National Register*, July 25, 1846, p. 326; Zachary Taylor, *Letters*, 45; Meade, *Life and Letters*, 1:152; Eba Anderson Lawton, ed., *An Artillery Officer in the Mexican War, 1846–47: Letters of Robert Anderson, Captain 3rd Artillery, U.S.A.* (Freeport, N.Y.: Books for Libraries, 1971), 19, 235; S. Compton Smith, *Chile Con Carne; Or, The Camp and Field* (New York: Miller and Curtis, 1857), 301; Cruffut, *Fifty Years in Camp and Field*, 266, 322.

27. Lawton, *Artillery Officer*, 19; Robert Ryal Miller, ed., *The Mexican War Journal and Letters of Ralph W. Kirkham* (College Station: Texas A&M Press, 1991), 82.

28. William Starr Myers, ed., *The Mexican War Diary of George B. McClellan* (Princeton, N.J.: University of Princeton Press, 1917), 43. McClellan referred to volunteers as "mustangs" because of the lanky Mexican horses they often rode.

29. Campbell, "Mexican War Letters of W. B. Campbell," 161, 166; Cruffut, *Fifty Years in Camp and Field*, 318; Lawton, *Artillery Officer*, 338; Allan Peskin, ed., *Volunteers: The Mexican War Journals of Private Richard Coulter and Sergeant Thomas Barclay, Company E, Second Pennsylvania Infantry* (Kent, Ohio: Kent State University Press, 1991), 200.

30. Peskin, *Volunteers*, 223, 226; J. Jacob Oswandel, *Notes on the Mexican War, 1846–47–48* (Philadelphia: n.p., 1885), 396, 456, 473; George Winston Smith and Charles Judah, *Chronicles of the Gringos: The U.S. Army in the Mexican War, Accounts of Eyewitnesses and Combatants* (Albuquerque: University of New Mexico Press, 1968), 451.

31. Lawton, *Artillery Officer*, 16; Campbell, "Mexican War Letters of W. B. Campbell," 152, 161; Peskin, *Volunteers*, 227; Joseph E. Chance, ed., *The Mexican War Journal of Captain Franklin Smith* (Jackson: University of Mississippi Press, 1991), 49, 56; Oswandel, *Notes on the Mexican War*, 133–34; Maria Clinton Collins, ed., "Journal

of Francis Collins, an Artillery Officer in the Mexican War," *Quarterly Publication of the Historical and Philosophical Society of Ohio* 10 (Apr. and July, 1915): 41, 102.

32. Meade, *Life and Letters*, 1:165; Adolphus Engelman, "The Second Illinois in the Mexican War: Mexican War Letters of Adolphus Engelman, 1846–1847," ed. and trans. Otto B. Engelman, *Journal of Illinois State Historical Journal* 26 (Jan., 1934): 426. Charles F. Hinds, ed., "Mexican War Journal of Leander M. Cox," pt. 2, *Register of the Kentucky Historical Society* 55 (1957): 221; and pt. 3, *Register of the Kentucky Historical Society* 56 (1958): 60. Josiah Gregg, *Diary and Letters of Josiah Gregg* (Norman: University of Oklahoma Press, 1941), 2:24; Campbell, "Mexican War Letters of W. B. Campbell," 142, 145; Isaac Bowen to his wife, Dec. 13, 1846, and Jan. 10, 1847, Isaac Bowen Papers, USMHRC; Maria Clinton Collins, "Journal of Francis Collins," 102.

33. Lawton, *Artillery Officer*, 338; S. Compton Smith, *Chile Con Carne*, 60; May, *Old South Crusader*, 194; Peskin, *Volunteers*, 207.

34. Engelman, "Second Illinois," 396, 400; Peskin, *Volunteers*, 207; Justin Smith, *War with Mexico*, 2:55, 352; Chance, *Mexican War Journal of Smith*, 30; John H. Moore, ed., "Private Johnson Fights the Mexicans, 1847–1848," *South Carolina Historical Magazine* 67 (1966): 224; Oswandel, *Notes on the Mexican War*, 246.

35. Albert G. Brackett, *General Lane's Brigade in Central Mexico* (Cincinnati, Ohio: H. W. Derby and Co., 1854), 73, 74.

36. Graham A. Barringer, ed., "The Mexican War Journal of Henry S. Lane," *Indiana Magazine of History* 53 (1957): 407; Peskin, *Volunteers*, 170; Nichols, *Franklin Pierce*, 161, 164.

37. Isaac Bowen to his wife, Dec. 4, 1846, Isaac Bowen Papers, USMHRC; Henry, *Campaign Sketches*, 252; Brackett, *General Lane's Brigade*, 24, 25; "Army of Occupation," *Niles' National Register*, July 24, 1847, 328–29. Hopping had been ordered to Mier to command a camp of instruction to train newly raised volunteer and regulars.

38. Polk, *Diary*, 2:175-76, 226–30, 240–42, 286, 292, 330–35, 349–52, 406, 408–409, 411–13; Thomas H. Benton, *Thirty Years' View; Or, A History of the Working of the American Government for Thirty Years, from 1820 to 1850* (New York: Appleton and Co., 1856), 2:678–79; Henry L. Scott, *Military Dictionary*, 167; "Speech of Mr. T. W. Newton Made on Feb. 26, 1847," *Appendix to the Congressional Globe* no. 16 (1847):430; Justin Smith, *War with Mexico*, 2:75, 2:365. The plan was premised on the "Articles of War," which state that, although the president cannot place a junior officer over one who is senior, Congress does have the power to create new military ranks. This loophole would have allowed Polk to appoint Benton to the higher rank, had Congress gone along. Benton blamed his defeat on three of Polk's own cabinet members: Secretary of War William L. Marcy, Secretary of the Treasury Robert J. Walker, and Secretary of State James Buchanan. In reality, John C. Calhoun was one of the most active opponents to Benton's appointment. Told by Congress that he could appoint Benton as commander of the army with the rank of major general, Polk saw that he still would have had to recall Scott, Taylor, Butler, and Patterson first. While willing to remove the first two, he bore no ill feeling toward

the two Democratic generals. Polk's close relationship with Benton soured from this point and finally ruptured completely over the court-martial of John C. Frémont, Benton's son-in-law.

39. Zachary Taylor, *Letters*, 150; Justin Smith, *War with Mexico*, 2:185–88; Polk, *Diary*, 3:269–80; Cruffut, *Fifty Years in Camp and Field*, 309, 318–19, 323. Two other Democratic officers, Bvt. Brig. Gen. William J. Worth and Capt. James Duncan, were Pillow's confederates in the letter-writing campaign against Scott. The *American Star* reprinted the *Leonidas* letter on Oct. 23, 1847, including these portions:

> Having achieved this brilliant and signal victory, Gen. Pillow immediately resolved to pursue the retreating forces of the enemy, and while his troops were flushed with victory, give battle to a larger force said still to be in San Angel, which he did, and drove them before him. He then sent an officer of his staff to Gen. Scott to say to him, if he would cause Gen. Worth to co-operate with him, he would sweep around the valley, and assault the strong works of San Antonio in the reverse, and carry that place, so as to open the direct route to the capital for the advance of his siege train upon the other battery on that road. Gen. Scott replied that Worth should co-operate with him. Gen. Pillow then moved rapidly around the valley at the head of his victorious forces. . . . During this great battle, which lasted two days, Gen. Pillow was in command of all the forces engaged, except Worth's division, and this was not engaged. Gen. Scott gave but one order, and that was to reinforce Cadwalader's brigade . . . [Pillow's] plan for the battle, and the disposition of his forces, were most judicious and successful. He evinced on this, as he had done on other occasions, that masterly military genius and profound knowledge of the science of war, which has astonished so much the mere martinets of the profession. His plan was very similar to that by which Napoleon effected the reduction of the Fortress of Ulm, and Gen. Scott was so perfectly well pleased with it that he could not interfere with any part of it, but left it to the gallant projector to carry it into its glorious and successful execution.

40. Polk, *Diary*, 3:255. The presidential election had turned into a three-way race: Democrats (Lewis Cass and William O. Butler) received 1,220,544 popular votes and 163 electoral votes; Whigs (Zachary Taylor and Millard Fillmore) 1,360,099 popular votes and 127 electoral votes; and Free Soilers (Martin Van Buren and Charles Francis Adams) 291,263 popular votes and no electoral votes.

41. Polk, *Diary*, 2:226–30.

CHAPTER 4. THE REGULARS

1. Isaac Bowen to his wife, Oct. 25, 1846, Isaac Bowen Papers, USMHRC; Marcus Cunliffe, *Soldiers and Civilians: The Martial Spirit in America, 1775–1865* (Boston: Little, Brown, 1968), 102; "Army Clothing," *Army and Navy Chronicle*, 2:109. The government routinely sold off stocks of condemned or out-of-date uniforms to the

public. Officers disapproved of the practice because they thought it showed disrespect for their profession. One officer complained to the *Army and Navy Chronicle:* "It is anything but grateful to the eye and feelings of the profession, to see its uniform disgraced by exposure to the public gaze upon the back of every negro and ragamuffin he meets with, and these are the only persons who will wear or purchase it." Thus, although unintentional, the government linked soldiers to the lowest elements of nineteenth-century American society.

2. Isaac Bowen to his wife, Oct. 25, 1846, Isaac Bowen Papers, USMHRC; Coffman, *Old Army,* 57; Cunliffe, *Soldiers and Civilians,* 121.

3. Justin Smith, *War with Mexico,* 1:143; Richardson, *Messages of the Presidents,* 4:411.

4. Coffman, *Old Army,* 162; U.S. Congress, House, *Message from the U.S. President at 1st Session, 29th Cong.: Report of the Secretary of War,* House Doc. No. 2, pp. 195–96; U.S. Congress, House, *Message from U.S. President at Commencement of 2nd Session of 29th Congress,* House Doc. No. 4, 53; "Volunteer Brigadier Generals," *Niles' National Register,* July 11, 1846, 292–93. This article in *Niles' National Register* reported that the five infantry regiments with Taylor on the Rio Grande needed six hundred to seven hundred men each in order to bring them to full strength.

5. U.S. Congress, *Message from the U.S. President at 1st Session, 29th Cong.: Report of the Secretary of War,* House Doc. No. 4, p. 54; U.S. Congress, Senate, *Petition of the Officers of the United States Army in Mexico, Praying [for] the Passage of a Law Providing for the Retirement of Old and Disabled Officers,* 30th Cong., 1st sess., Miscellaneous Doc. No. 11, 1–6; Ganoe, *History of the U.S. Army,* 262. During the Mexican War, more than 250 officers with Scott's army in central Mexico signed a petition circulated by Capt. Robert Anderson asking Congress to pass a retirement bill. The problem was not corrected until 1861, when Congress passed an act making it possible for ill or aged officers in good standing to retire and draw either their pay or their rations.

6. U.S. Congress, *Message from the U.S. President at 1st Session, 29th Cong.: Report of the Secretary of War,* House Doc. No. 4, 73–75; Grant, *Papers,* 1:51–52, 1:215; U.S. War Dept., General Order No. 43, Oct. 8, 1846; Cruffut, *Fifty Years in Camp and Field,* 198–99. Problems with the field officers of the two regiments of dragoons were not as great; therefore they were not mentioned in Jones's report.

7. Henry, *Campaign Sketches,* 129–30; Callan, *Military Laws,* 379.

8. Henry L. Scott, *Military Dictionary,* 11; John C. Waugh, *The Class of 1846, from West Point to Appomattox: Stonewall Jackson, George McClellan and Their Brothers* (New York: Warner Books, 1993), 68. Data on the number of West Point–trained officers was compiled from U.S. Adjutant General's Office, War Department, *Official Army Register, for 1841. Published by Order of the Secretary of War, in Compliance with the Resolution of the Senate, Dec. 13, 1815, and the Resolution of the House of Representatives, Feb. 1, 1830* (Washington, D.C., 1841).

9. R. E. Lee to Capt. John MacKay, June 21, 1846, Miscellaneous Mexican War File, Box GA 43, Folder 9, SCUTA.

10. Cunliffe, *Soldiers and Civilians,* 109, 158; Meade, *Life and Letters,* 1:162; Skelton, *American Profession of Arms.*

11. Cunliffe, *Soldiers and Civilians,* 111; Isaac Bowen to his wife, Oct. 25, 1846, Isaac Bowen Papers, USMHRC; *Army and Navy Chronicle,* 8:195. Cunliffe explores nineteenth-century attitudes toward the regular army, including the periodic furor over funding the U.S. Military Academy.

12. William Starr Myers, *Mexican War Diary of McClellan,* 17; Lawton, *Artillery Officer,* 192; Meade, *Life and Letters,* 1:149–50; Emma Jerome Blackwood, ed., *To Mexico with Scott: Letters of Captain E. Kirby Smith to His Wife* (Cambridge, Mass.: Harvard University Press, 1917), 155–56; Isaac Bowen to his wife, Nov. 13, 1846, Isaac Bowen Papers, USMHRC.

13. Coffman, *Old Army,* 87–88, 90, 91; George W. Ames, Jr., ed., "A Doctor Comes to California: The Diary of John S. Griffin, Assistant Surgeon with Kearny's Dragoons, 1846–47," pt. 3, *California Historical Quarterly* 22 (1943): 46; Grant, *Papers,* 1:57; Chance, *Mexican War Journal of Smith,* 82; Skelton, *American Profession of Arms,* 286–88, 295–97; "Politics and Officers," *Army and Navy Chronicle,* 2:108–109 and 2:315–16; Heitman, *Historical Register,* 1:798. Andrew Porter entered West Point in 1836 but left less than a year later, without graduating. He was commissioned a 1st lieutenant in the Mounted Rifles in May 1846 and promoted to captain in May 1847.

14. Peck, *Sign of the Eagle,* 79; Meade, *Life and Letters,* 1:128; Skelton, *American Profession of Arms,* 139. According to Skelton, even appointment to West Point (the first step toward a career in the officer corps) could depend on political connections; by the mid-1830s, it had been decided that each congressman could nominate a candidate from his congressional district; if no candidate was put forward, the choice then passed to that state's U.S. senators; if again no appointment was made, the selection went to the president.

15. R. E. Lee to Capt. John MacKay, June 21, 1846, Miscellaneous Mexican War File, Box GA-43, Folder 9, SCUTA; Peck, *Sign of the Eagle,* 79.

16. Polk, *Diary,* 1:412–16; Dana O. Jensen, "The Memoirs of Daniel M. Frost," pt. 3, *Missouri Historical Bulletin* 26 (1970): 200; Skelton, *American Profession of Arms,* 149.

17. Lawton, *Artillery Officer,* 83, 108.

18. Ibid., 84; Ferrell, *Monterrey Is Ours!,* 193; William Starr Myers, *Mexican War Diary of McClellan,* 16.

19. U.S. War Dept., *General Regulations, 1841,* 38; Isaac Bowen to his wife, Oct. 4 and Nov. 4, 1846, Isaac Bowen Papers, USMHRC.

20. John F. Meginness, "A Collection of Incidents Connected with the life of a Soldier (from his Enlistment) in Mexico, during a Part of the Campaign of 1847, from Vera Cruz to the Great [unclear word] City of Puebla Mex. Oct. 17th, 1847," in small notebook, John F. Meginness Papers, GA 119, SCUTA; Ballentine, *Autobiography of an English Soldier,* 9–14; Coffman, *Old Army,* 137, 139, 140, 144–45, 152; Cunliffe, *Citizens and Soldiers,* 113–14; Frederick Zeh, *An Immigrant Soldier in the Mexican War,* trans. William J. Orr; ed. William J. Orr and Robert Ryal Miller (College Station: Texas A&M University Press, 1995), 4; James Hildreth, *Dragoon Campaigns to the Rocky Mountains; Being a History of the Enlistment, Organization, and*

First Campaigns of the Regiment of United States Dragoons; Together with Incidents of a Soldier's Life, and Sketches of Scenery and Indian Character (New York: D. Fanshaw, 1836; reprinted New York: Arno Press, 1973), 79, 134–39. Although he served during the 1830s, Hildreth contended that most soldiers enlisted in the army because of some personal misfortune.

21. Coffman, *Old Army,* 137, 141; Cunliffe, *Citizens and Soldiers,* 115; George A. McCall, *Letters from the Frontiers,* ed. John K. Mahon. (Philadelphia: J. B. Lippincott and Co., 1868; reprinted Gainesville: University Presses of Florida, 1974), 334; Skelton, *American Profession of Arms,* 264; Zeh, *Immigrant Soldier,* 4, 7, 55. The most recent and comprehensive work on the San Patricio Battalion is Robert Ryal Miller, *Shamrock and Sword: The Saint Patrick's Battalion in the U.S.–Mexican War* (Norman: University of Oklahoma Press, 1989). Miller found that many of these soldiers deserted not for ideological reasons, but to escape harsh treatment in the U.S. Army. Others, out on drinking sprees, were captured by the Mexicans and coerced into the battalion. Besides Irishmen, Miller determined that other nationalities, including British, German, and even American, were well represented in the San Patricios.

22. Isaac Bowen to his wife, Oct. 25, 1846, Isaac Bowen Papers, USMHRC; Ballentine, *Autobiography of an English Soldier,* 31, 32, 115–20; William F. Goetzmann, "Our First Foreign War: Letters of Barna Upton, 3rd U.S. Infantry," *American Heritage* 17 (1966): 174–75.

23. Peck, *Sign of the Eagle,* 127; Peskin, *Volunteers,* 101, 236–37; John F. Meginness, Manuscript, John F. Meginness Papers, Box GA-119, 283, 287, SCUTA; Coffman, *Old Army,* 198; Zeh, *Immigrant Soldier,* 29; Cruffut, *Fifty Years in Camp and Field,* 183. According to Hitchcock, Lt. Don Carlos Buell caused a stir when he was tried and found innocent of unjustly striking a soldier with his sword. Scott disagreed with the court's decision, but Hitchcock and others resented the general's interference and successfully fought his efforts to have the matter reopened.

24. Henry L. Scott, *Military Dictionary,* 476; Samuel E. Chamberlain, *My Confession: The Recollections of a Rogue,* 194–95; Ballentine, *Autobiography of an English Soldier,* 246, 247, 282, 283; Skelton, *American Profession of Arms,* 265–73, Zeh, *Immigrant Soldier,* 40–42, 50. According to Private Zeh, one of his companions was "bucked and gagged" and then strung up by his thumbs, after he went on "strike" because the unit had not been paid on time. In a separate incident, Zeh relates that another soldier was sentenced to carry two cannon balls in his knapsack from dawn to dusk for sleeping while on guard duty.

25. Bemrose, *Reminiscences of the Second Seminole War,* 54; John F. Meginness Manuscript, John F. Meginness Papers, Box GA-119, 279, 283, SCUTA; Skelton, *American Profession of Arms,* 273–77. Skelton describes a number of cases of soldiers attacking officers in retaliation for ill treatment. Meginness plagiarized these remarks from Furber, *Twelve Month Volunteer,* 433. I put them in at this point because I believe that they express Meginness's true feelings toward the regulars.

26. John F. Meginness Manuscript, John F. Meginness Papers, Box GA-119, 280, 288, SCUTA; Peskin, *Volunteers,* 196; Hildreth, *Dragoon Campaigns,* 111–14. Hildreth echoed Meginness's argument that the army's infatuation with West Point denied

enlisted men the opportunity to advance beyond "corporal or sergeant." He suggested that a better system would be to allow half the army's officers to be furnished by the Military Academy, with the other half coming from the army's ranks.

27. Richardson, *Messages of the Presidents,* 4:405–13.

28. Ibid., 4:409.

29. Polk, *Diary,* 3:153, 154, 157, 158; William B. Cooke, *Speech of William M. Cooke, of Tennessee, in a Review of the War, Its Costs, and Executive Patronage; Delivered in the House of Representatives of the U.S., May 18, 1848,* 12; Skelton, *American Profession of Arms,* 141, 145–46. According to Skelton, Polk appointed two nephews to the U.S. Military Academy.

CHAPTER 5. THE VOLUNTEERS

1. Callan, *Military Laws,* 95–100, 108–10.

2. A comparison of state constitutions and articles establishing state militias was made using *The American's Guide: Comprising the Declaration of Independence; the Articles of Confederation; the Constitution of the United States; and the Constitutions of the Several States Composing the Union* (Philadelphia: Hogan and Thompson, 1841), 117, 118, 293.

3. Callan, *Military Laws,* 98, 235, 236, 336, 337.

4. Henry W. Barton, *Texas Volunteers in the Mexican War* (Waco, Tex.: Texian Press, 1970), 1–15; U.S. Congress, House, *Message from the U.S. President at 1st Session, 29th Cong.: Report of the Secretary of War,* House Doc. No. 2, p. 194; *General Zachary Taylor: The Louisiana President of the United States* (New Orleans: Louisiana State Museum, 1937), 31.

5. Richardson, *Messages of the Presidents, 1789–1902,* 4:413, 493; Polk, *Diary,* 1:403–404; Callan, *Military Laws,* 367.

6. U.S. Congress, Senate, *Message of the President, Relative to the Calling of Volunteers or Militia,* 29th Cong., 1st sess., Senate Doc. No. 378, pp. 19, 20, 27, 29, 30, 61; Callan, *Military Laws,* 367; U.S. Congress, House, *Mexican War Correspondence: Message of the President of the United States, and the Correspondence Therewith Communicated, between the Secretary of War and Other Officers of the Government upon the Subject of the Mexican War,* 30th Cong., 1st sess., Exec. Doc. No. 60, pp. 450–51, 495–96; U.S. Congress, House, *Military Forces in the Mexican War: Letter from the Secretary of War,* 31st Cong., 1st sess., 1850, Exec. Doc. No. 24, pp. 2, 4; "Popular Portraits: Gaines," 557; "General Gaines," *Niles' National Register,* Aug. 29, 1846, 406–408. Companies or regiments wishing to reorganize and enlist for twelve months Taylor allowed to remain with his army; he also informed the disbanded volunteers that the Quartermaster Department would hire individuals who did not want to return home.

7. Callan, *Military Laws,* 367.

8. *The Rough and Ready Songster: Embellished with Twenty-Five Splendid Engravings Illustrative of the American Victories in Mexico, by an American Officer* (New York: Nafis and Cornish, Publishers, 1848), 83, 84; *Southron,* Jackson, Miss., June 3, 1846;

"America's Guard," *United States Magazine and Democratic Review* 20 (Mar., 1847): 209–10; *Jackson (Miss.) Mississippian,* May 20, 1846; Lew Wallace, *Lew Wallace,* 1:114; R. C. Buley, "Indiana in the Mexican War: The Indiana Volunteers," *Indiana Magazine of History* 15 (Sept., 1919): 267.

9. Hinds, "Mexican War Journal of Cox," pt. 3, p. 56; *Rough and Ready Songster,* 20, 21; James W. Oberly, *Sixty Million Acres: American Veterans and the Public Lands before the Civil War* (Kent, Ohio: Kent State University Press, 1990), 10, 11; Andrew Jackson Trussell to John Trussell, Mar. 19, 1847, Trussell Family Papers, Box GA 66-3, SCUTA; Steven R. Butler, "Mexican War Bounty Land Warrants in the National Archives," *Mexican War Journal* 4 (Fall 1994–Winter 1995): 23.

10. U.S. Congress, House, *Military Forces in the Mexican War: Letter from the Secretary of War,* 31st Cong., 1st sess., 1850, Exec. Doc. No. 24, pp. 3–4.

11. For examples of calls for volunteers, see *New Orleans (La.) Daily Picayune,* May 31, 1846; *Southron,* Jackson, Miss., June 2, 1846; and U.S. Congress, House, *Mexican War Correspondence,* 30th Cong., 1st sess., Exec. Doc. No. 60, pp. 478–80. These letters set forth the organization of each volunteer regiment: (field and staff) one colonel, one lieutenant colonel, one major, one adjutant; (noncommissioned staff) one sergeant major, one quartermaster sergeant, two principal musicians; (and ten companies, each consisting of) one captain, one first lieutenant, two second lieutenants, four sergeants, four corporals, two musicians, and eighty privates.

12. "Volunteers," *Niles' National Register,* July 18, 1846, p. 312, and July 25, 1846, p. 326; Robert A. Brent, "Mississippi and the Mexican War," *Journal of Mississippi History* 31 (Aug., 1969), 205; *Southron,* Jackson, Miss., May 17, 1846; *Mississippi Democrat,* Carrollton, Miss., May 20 and 27, 1846; Buley, "Indiana in the Mexican War," 267; Daniel J. Ryan, "Ohio in the Mexican War," *Ohio Archeological and Historical Publications* 21 (1912): 280; Turner J. Fakes, Jr., "Memphis and the Mexican War," *West Tennessee Historical Society Papers* 2 (1948): 124, 125.

13. *American's Guide,* 51, 73, 88, 116, 145, 171, 188, 200, 253, 283, 284, 313, 325, 341, 360, 406. New York even allowed the men of each company to elect their own noncommissioned officers.

14. Franklin B. Cooling, ed., *The New American State Papers, 1789–1860: Military Affairs* (Wilmington, Del.: Scholarly Resources, Inc., 1979), 6:56; Winfield Scott, *Infantry Tactics;* Charles F. Hinds, ed., "Mexican War Journal of Leander M. Cox," pt. 1, *Register of the Kentucky Historical Society* 55 (1957): 35, 36; Campbell, "Mexican War Letters of W. B. Campbell," 139; Lew Wallace, *Lew Wallace,* 1:116; Luther Giddings, *Sketches of the Campaign in Northern Mexico in 1846–47* (New York: George P. Putnam and Co., 1853), 225–27. The first volume of Scott's *Infantry Tactics* includes "School of the Soldier" and "School of the Company" and was intended for use by company officers; the second volume includes "School of the Battalion" and "Instruction for Light Infantry or Rifle" and was intended for use by company and field officers; the third volume includes "Evolutions of the Line" and was intended for use by field and general officers.

15. Henry, *Campaign Sketches,* 127, 128. These statistics were generated while I was researching volunteer unit histories; the major source was Robarts, *Mexican War*

Veterans; Skelton, *American Profession of Arms,* 216–17, 220; and "West Point Vindicated," *Raleigh (N.C.) Register,* Apr. 13, 1847. According to Skelton, the highest number of officer resignations came in the 1830s, during the Second Seminole War. In 1836 alone, 117 officers (17 percent of the officer corps) left the army.

16. Isaac Bowen to his wife, Sept. 8, 1846, Isaac Bowen Papers, USMHRC. Figures compiled by author from Robarts, *Mexican War Veterans.*

17. Meade, *Life and Letters,* 1:276; William Starr Myers, *Mexican War Diary of McClellan,* 16.

18. Jensen, "Memoirs of Frost," pt. 2, *Missouri Historical Bulletin* 26 (1970): 95, 96; John R. Kenly, *Memoirs of a Maryland Volunteer* (Philadelphia: J. B. Lippincott and Co., 1873), 78, 79, 80, 482; Isaac Bowen to his wife, Sept. 8, 1846, Isaac Bowen Papers, USMHRC; Skelton, *American Profession of Arms,* 265; Heitman, *Historical Register,* 1:154. Mustered out of the volunteer service in May 1847, Aisquith received a captain's commission in the 1st U.S. Artillery the following November but was dropped from the army rolls again less than two months later. He then served in the U.S. Marines for five years. He died in 1856.

19. Kenly, *Memoirs of a Maryland Volunteer,* 78–80. Figures compiled from Robarts, *Mexican War Veterans.*

20. U.S. Congress, House, *Military Forces Employed in the Mexican War,* 22h; Durham, "Mexican War Letters," 404; D. E. Livingston-Little, ed., *The Mexican War Diary of Thomas D. Tennery* (Norman: University of Oklahoma Press, 1970), 75–76. Volunteers who enlisted for a second tour of duty included two brothers, James W. Wynne and Robert Bruce Wynne. Some of the remustered companies contained men from several states. Thomas D. Tennery, private in the 4th Illinois Infantry, wrote near Vera Cruz that several members of his company had joined Capt. R. C. Wheat's Company of Remustered Tennessee Mounted Volunteers.

21. Lew Wallace, *Lew Wallace,* 1:116; Campbell, "Mexican War Letters of W. B. Campbell," 134, 148. Statistics on political affiliation were compiled from unit histories.

22. Campbell, "Mexican War Letters of W. B. Campbell," 148; Peskin, *Volunteers,* 323, 324. From the "Soldier Editors," *American Star,* Mexico City, Nov. 26, 1847: "Soldier Editors. We have recently stated that Isaac Seymour, editor of the *Macon Messenger,* has been appointed Colonel of the Infantry battalion raised in Georgia, and A. P. Williams, of the *Detroit Advertiser,* Lieutenant-Colonel of the Michigan Regiment." The story identifies several other editors, saying that there are two or three in the Pennsylvania regiments, and four in the New England regiment, as well as a large number of printers serving with the army, too.

23. These statistics were compiled using state biographical directories while constructing unit histories of volunteer units.

24. Lawton, *Artillery Officer,* 36; Gregg, *Diary and Letters,* 1:218, 2:50; Engelman, "Second Illinois," 439, 440.

25. Meade, *Life and Letters,* 1:94; Kenly, *Memoirs of a Maryland Volunteer,* 165; Mary Ellen Rowe, ed., "The Mexican War Letters of Chesley Sheldon Coffey," *Journal of Mississippi History* 44 (Aug., 1982): 246.

26. Engelman, "Second Illinois," 426; Campbell, "Mexican War Letters of W. B. Campbell," 151; Chance, *Mexican War Journal of Smith,* 147; Giddings, *Sketches of the Campaign,* 280; Peskin, *Volunteers,* 94, 100, 101, 226.

27. Giddings, *Sketches of the Campaign,* 281; Lew Wallace, *Lew Wallace,* 1:117; Peskin, *Volunteers,* 101; Gregg, *Diary and Letters,* 2:219–20.

28. Kenly, *Memoirs of a Maryland Volunteer,* 25; Eleanor Pace, ed., "The Diary and Letters of William P. Rogers, 1846–1863," *Southwestern Historical Quarterly* 32 (Apr., 1929): 265; Campbell, "Mexican War Letters of W. B. Campbell," 150, 151; Reuben Davis, *Recollections of Mississippi and Mississippians* (Boston: Houghton Mifflin, 1890), 223.

29. *Southron,* Jackson, Miss., Sept. 23, 1846; John H. Moore, "Private Johnson Fights," 219; Reuben Davis, *Recollections,* 222, 232.

30. Peskin, *Volunteers,* 207–10; John Porter Bloom, "With the American Army into Mexico, 1846–1848" (Ph.D. diss., Emory University, 1956), 14; Andrew Jackson Trussell to John Trussell, Oct. 26, 1846, Trussell Family Papers, Box GA 66-3, SCUTA. As an indication of how important regimental politics were, Col. Reuben Davis said that, as his adjutant, he had to select a man he knew was incompetent, because he could not afford to offend the man's friends.

31. Giddings, *Sketches of the Campaign,* 280; Hinds, "Mexican War Journal of Leander M. Cox," pt. 1, 34, 35; Campbell, "Mexican War Letters of W. B. Campbell," 151.

32. "Volunteers," *Niles' National Register,* July 25, 1846, 325–26; Oswandel, *Notes on the Mexican War,* 16, 30–31, 33, 37, 38, 43; *New Orleans (La.) Daily Picayune,* Jan. 22, 30, 31, 1847; New Orleans *Courier,* Jan. 27, 28, and 29, and Feb. 1, 1847; Chance, *Mexican War Journal of Smith,* 66, 67; Reuben Davis, *Recollections,* 236; Pace, "Diary and Letters of Rogers," 265; Campbell, "Mexican War Letters of W. B. Campbell," 166.

33. Chance, *Mexican War Journal of Smith,* 90, 91; Peskin, *Volunteers,* 100, 258. Preston Brooks gained national notoriety in 1856, when, as a Democratic member of the U.S. House of Representatives, he viciously beat Charles Sumner in the Senate chamber. The reason for the assault: the Massachusetts senator, in his famous "The Crime Against Kansas" speech, made unflattering remarks about Brooks's uncle, Sen. Andrew P. Butler of South Carolina.

34. Peskin, *Volunteers,* 97, 250, 258; Oswandel, *Notes on the Mexican War,* 475, 483; Livingston-Little, *Mexican War Diary of Tennery,* 88.

35. Oswandel, *Notes on the Mexican War,* 390; Andrew Jackson Trussell to John Trussell, Oct. 26, 1846, Trussell Family Papers, Box GA 66-3, SCUTA; U.S. War Dept., "Court Martial Records of Lieutenant John Amyx, 2nd Mississippi Rifles," Record No. EE553, NA; Alfred J. Henderson, "A Morgan Country Volunteer in the Mexican War," *Journal of the Illinois State Historical Society* 41 (Dec., 1948): 394.

36. Andrew Jackson Trussell to James M. Trussell, Feb. 28, 1848, Trussell Family Papers, Box GA 66-3, SCUTA; Wilbur G. Kurtz, Jr., "The First Regiment of Georgia Volunteers in the Mexican War," *Georgia Historical Quarterly* 27 (Dec., 1943): 314–17; Livingston-Little, *Mexican War Diary of Tennery,* 18–20; Kenly, *Memoirs of a Maryland Volunteer,* 47–50; Report of Col. Alexander Mitchell, *Compiled Service*

Records of the Mississippi Volunteers in the War with Mexico, Washington, D.C., Microfilm Series M863, Roll No. 3, NA. Although it is impossible to determine the number of volunteers killed or injured by other volunteers, readers frequently encounter such tales in diaries and newspapers of the period. For a review of the mutiny involving the Georgia volunteers, see D. E. Livingston-Little, ed., "Mutiny During the Mexican War: An Incident on the Rio Grande," *Journal of the West* 9 (July, 1970): 340–45.

CHAPTER 6. TOOLS OF THE TRADE

1. U.S. War Dept., *Ordnance Manual of the Use of the Officers of the United States Army,* 1841 (Washington, D.C.: J. and G. S. Gideon, Printers, 1841), 1, 4; U.S. War Dept., *Ordnance Manual of the Use of the Officers of the United States Army,* 1861 (Washington, D.C.: J. B. Lippincott and Co., 1861), 13–14, 384–90. The bronze 6- and 12-pounders were designated "Model 1840" in the 1841 edition of the *Ordnance Manual.* Also see Lester R. Dillon, Jr., *American Artillery in the Mexican War, 1846–1847* (Austin, Tex.: Presidial Press, 1975).

2. U.S. War Dept., *Ordnance Manual, 1841,* 1, 4; U.S. War Dept., *Ordnance Manual, 1861,* 13–14, 19, 384–90.

3. U.S. War Dept., *Ordnance Manual, 1841,* 1, 5; U.S. War Dept., *Ordnance Manual, 1861,* 384–90.

4. U.S. War Dept., *Ordnance Manual, 1841,* 1, 6; U.S. War Dept., *Ordnance Manual, 1861,* 13–14, 19, 384–90.

5. U.S. War Dept., *Ordnance Manual, 1841,* 1, 5; U.S. War Dept., *Ordnance Manual, 1861,* 13–14, 19, 384–90. The Hale Rocket was too new to be listed in *Ordnance Manual, 1841.*

6. U.S. War Dept., *Instruction for Field Artillery, Horse and Foot,* 13–37; Dillon, *American Artillery,* 14; Jack Coggins, *Arms and Equipment of the Civil War* (Garden City, N.Y.: Doubleday and Co., 1963), 67; U.S. War Dept., *Ordnance Manual, 1841,* 77; Letter Addressed "Dear Major," Monterey, Mexico, July 12, 1847, in Smith-Kirby-Webster-Black Family Papers, USMHRC. A letter in the collection mentions "two percussion cannon locks attached to your Howitzers."

7. U.S. War Dept., *Instruction for Field Artillery, Horse and Foot,* 13–37, 46–47; Zeh, *Immigrant Soldier,* 17. Apparently not all artillery officers were familiar with the loading procedure, as one enlisted man reported seeing one officer instruct his crew in loading a mortar by reading aloud from a manual he pulled from his pocket.

8. U.S. War Dept., *Ordnance Manual, 1841,* 93–95, 181; Carl P. Russell, *Guns of the Early Frontiers: A History of Firearms from Colonial Times through the Years of the Western Fur Trade* (Lincoln: University of Nebraska Press, 1957), 161–64, 324; Ganoe, *History of the U.S. Army,* 169. Russell identifies four basic models for U.S. flintlock muskets: the Model 1795, produced 1795–1812; the Model 1813, produced 1813–17; Model 1816, produced 1817–44; and the Model 1840, produced 1840–48. The length of the bayonet varied with the model of musket.

9. U.S. War Dept., *Abstract of Infantry Tactics,* 1:31, 1:37–42, 1:102. According to the

manual, "Each command will be executed in one time (or pause), but this time will be divided into motions, the better to make known the mechanism." After troops learned to "Load in Twelve Times," they moved to "Loading in Four Times" and "Load at Will."

10. Ibid., 1:55–61.

11. Ibid., 1:158–60; Ballentine, *Autobiography of an English Soldier,* 108; Ganoe, *History of the U.S. Army,* 169; Head Quarters of the Army, Mexico [City], General Orders No. 375, Dec. 15, 1847.

12. U.S. War Dept., *Ordnance Manual, 1841,* 211; Frederick P. Todd, *American Military Equipage, 1851–1872* (Providence, R.I.: Company of Military Historians, 1974–78), 1:117–18; R. T. Huntington, *Accoutrements of the United States Infantry, Riflemen, and Dragoons, 1834–1839* (Alexandria Bay, N.Y.: Museum Restoration Service, 1987, 46–47. Headquarters of the Army, Adjutant General's Office, Washington, [D.C.], General Order No. 44, Oct. 30, 1844. According to U.S. War Dept., *Ordnance Manual, 1841,* the department originally purchased percussion caps on the open market.

13. Head Quarters of the Army, Mexico [City], General Orders No. 42, Feb. 3, 1848; Oswandel, *Notes on the Mexican War,* 488; Theodore F. Rodenbough and William L. Haskins, *The Army of the United States: Historical Sketches of Staff and Line with Portraits of Generals-in-Chief* (New York: Argonaut Press, 1966), 355; Todd, *American Military Equipage.* On Feb. 21, 1848, Oswandel wrote, "This morning we were ordered to get percussion cap muskets, our former ones being old Harper's Ferry flint muskets." Arsenals began converting flintlock muskets to percussion as early as 1843.

14. U.S. War Dept., *Ordnance Manual, 1841,* 96; Russell, *Guns of the Early Frontiers,* 176–88; Ralph E. Arnold, "The Model 1841 Rifle: The Famous 'Mississippi,'" *Gun Report* 21 (Sept., 1973): 14–21; Todd, *American Military Equipage,* 118. The right and left companies were light infantry companies and in theory functioned as skirmishers for their regiment.

15. Headquarters of the Army, Adjutant General's Office, Washington [D.C.], General Orders No. 38, Aug. 19, 1846; John T. Cairns, *The Recruit: A Compilation of Exercises and Movements of Infantry, Light Infantry, and Riflemen, According to the Latest Improvements. Respectfully Dedicated to the Recruits of the United States Army* (New York: Edward Walker, 1853), 104–108; Arnold, "Model 1841 Rifle," 15; George Winston Smith and Charles Judah, *Chronicles of the Gringos,* 384. Early in the war, the quartermaster at Brazos Santiago had difficulty supplying the 1st Mississippi Rifles with percussion caps, causing Col. Jefferson Davis to write him, "The caps are indispensable and we have none." That Davis's regiment was equipped with cartridge boxes instead of the rifleman's pouch and flask was determined from examining the *Combined Service Records of the Mississippi Volunteers in the Mexican War,* Washington, D.C., Microfilm Series M863, NA, Rolls 1–8.

16. U.S. War Dept., *Ordnance Manual, 1841,* 97–98; Russell, *Guns of the Early Frontiers,* 168; Ron G. Giron, *U.S. Military Edged Weapons of the Second Seminole War, 1835–1842* (New York: Edward Walker, 1853); Steffen, *Horse Soldiers,* 131–35; Cham-

berlain, *My Confession*, 58, 188; Todd, *American Military Equipage*, 154–55. Samuel Chamberlain claimed that he "often went to town day and night, armed with a Bowie Knife and the chamber of [his] Hall's Carbine."

17. U.S. War Dept., *Ordnance Manual, 1841*, 95; Russell, *Guns of the Early Frontiers*, 173; Todd, *American Military Equipage*, 154. The Model 1839 Musketoon appears as the Model 1840 in *Ordnance Manual, 1841*.

18. U.S. War Dept., *Ordnance Manual, 1841*, 95–96; Russell, *Guns of the Early Frontiers*, 200; Steffen, *Horse Soldiers*, 47, 49, 126–28; U.S. War Dept., *Ordnance Manual, 1841*, 136. Only two pistols are listed in *Ordnance Manual, 1841:* the Model 1819 and the Model 1836.

19. Russell, *Guns of the Early Frontiers*, 191–98, 214–18; Steffen, *Horse Soldiers*, 135–36; "Colts Repeating Arms—Rifles, Carbines, and Pistols," *American Eagle*, Vera Cruz, Mexico, Apr. 3 and 6, 1847; *American Flag*, Matamoros, Mexico, May 7, 1848; Bloom, "With the American Army into Mexico," 22. The *American Eagle* carried the following advertisement: "Colts Repeating Arms—Rifles, Carbines, and Pistols. The officers of the Army and Navy are informed that these arms can be obtained until the 10th inst., at the door on the left of the gate, going out to the Wharf. Private soldiers can be furnished when producing written permits from their immediate commanding officers. Citizens can also be supplied upon the written permission of the Governor of the city, Major General Worth." The *American Flag* in Matamoros later carried a similar advertisement.

20. U.S. War Dept., *Ordnance Manual, 1841*, 131–33; Todd, *American Military Equipage*, 177–78; Giron, *U.S. Military Edged Weapons*, 15–19, 20–28.

21. U.S. War Dept., *Ordnance Manual, 1841*, 132–33; Todd, *American Military Equipage*, 180–81; Giron, *U.S. Military Edged Weapons*, 29–30, 31–32, 33–45, 46–49, 50–53; Philip R. N. Katcher, *U.S. Infantry Equipments, 1775–1910* (London: Osprey Publishing, 1989), 39; Robert R. Jones, "Mexican War Diary of J. L. Kemper," 418. Eagle-head swords were silvered for infantry officers and gilded for artillery officers. An NCO sword (intended for use by both infantry and artillery) had been authorized in 1818 but was not manufactured in large numbers. The Model 1833 Foot Artillery Sword had been used as the infantry NCO sword until 1840, when that branch received its own pattern. Officers often became attached to their swords. Gen. Joseph Lane placed an ad in the *North American*, Mexico City, Mar. 11, 1848, after he lost his sword. Although originally he had paid only $16 for the sword, because of sentimental value he offered a $25 reward for its return. Of all the swords described in this paragraph, only the Model 1840 NCO sword appears in U.S. War Dept., *Ordnance Manual, 1841*.

22. U.S. War Dept., *Ordnance Manual, 1841*, 140; R. T. Huntington, *Accoutrements of U.S. Infantry, Riflemen, and Dragoons*, 13–14, 23, 26–27, 30–31, 46–47; Stephen Dorsey, *American Military Belts and Related Equipment* (London: Osprey Publishing, 1989), 4–5. A note in *Ordnance Manual, 1841*, warned, "The bayonet belt is about to be discontinued; the bayonet will be attached to a frog sliding on the waist belt." Many volunteers, however, continued to wear cross belts.

23. U.S. War Dept., *Ordnance Manual, 1841*, 135–36; R. T. Huntington, *Accoutrements*

of U.S. Infantry, Riflemen, and Dragoons, 33–37, 39–43, 44–45, 46–47, 48–51; Dorsey, *American Military Belts,* 19–20.

24. U.S. War Dept., *Ordnance Manual, 1841,* 141; Giron, *U.S. Military Edged Weapons,* 16; Dorsey, *American Military Belts,* 12–13.

25. U.S. War Dept., *Ordnance Manual, 1841,* 141; Dorsey, *American Military Belts,* 52–53; Arnold, "Model 1841 Rifle," 21; R. T. Huntington, *Accoutrements of U.S. Infantry, Riflemen, and Dragoons,* 41–42.

26. U.S. War Dept., *General Regulations, 1841,* 365–93; Francis Paul Prucha, ed., *Army Life on the Western Frontier: Selections from the Official Reports Made Between 1826 and 1845 by Colonel George Croghan* (Norman: University of Oklahoma Press, 1958), 61–62.

27. U.S. War Dept., *General Regulations, 1841,* 203–10, 364; Prucha, *Army Life on the Western Frontier,* 57; U.S. Adjutant General's Office, *Orders to Gen. Zachary Taylor of the Army of Occupation in the Mexican War, 1845–47,* Washington, D.C., 3 rolls in Microfilm Series M1034, NA; "Headquarters Army of Occupation, Corpus Christi, Texas, Aug. 31, 1845, Special Order No. 8," Washington, D.C., Microfilm Series M1034, NA, roll 2.

28. U.S. War Dept., *General Regulations, 1841,* 365–93; U.S. War Dept., *General Regulations, 1847,* 186–215. For an illustrated treatment of uniforms of the war, see Katcher, *Mexican-American War.* Chevrons for noncommissioned officers were first prescribed in *General Regulations, 1847.*

29. Katcher, *Mexican-American War,* 14; U.S. War Dept., *General Regulations, 1847,* 198, 203; U.S. War Dept., *General Regulations, 1841,* 192, 198, 203.

30. Simon B. Buckner to John Earle, Jr., and Co., Aug. 23, 1848, Miscellaneous Mexican War File, Box GA 42, Folder 12, SCUTA; Ferrell, *Monterrey Is Ours!,* 31; Robert R. Jones, "Mexican War Diary of J. L. Kemper," 416. Volunteer officers had to buy their own uniforms as well. Wrote Captain Kemper shortly after receiving his appointment, "This day a very busy one. Made preparations for setting out, ordered uniform, &c." According to "Army Uniform," *Army and Navy Chronicle* 10 (Jan. 30, 1840): 73–74, the dress uniform with all its trimmings was extremely unpopular among regular officers. One critic wrote to the paper, claiming that "an officer who now takes to the field finds himself encumbered with no less than *four band-boxes,* to carry his Regulation trappings and trimmings."

31. Ferrell, *Monterrey Is Ours!,* 7, 30, 46, 83, 87–88, 97; Robert N. Pruyn, "Campaigning Through Mexico With 'Old Rough and Ready,'" *Civil War Times Illustrated* 2 (Oct., 1963): 11; "Army Uniform," *Army and Navy Chronicle* 10 (Jan. 30, 1840): 73–74.

32. Ferrell, *Monterrey Is Ours!,* 171; Engelman, "Second Illinois," 409; Brackett, *General Lane's Brigade,* 31.

33. Smith and Judah, *Chronicles of the Gringos,* 381; General Orders No. 367, Head Quarters of the Army, Mexico, Dec. 7, 1847.

34. U.S. War Dept., *General Regulations, 1841,* 393; U.S. War Dept., *General Regulations, 1847,* 215; Goetzmann, "Our First Foreign War," 90; Ferrell, *Monterrey Is Ours!,* 7, 28, 171; Chance, *Mexican War Journal of Capt. Franklin Smith,* 65; Carl M. Becker,

"John William Lowe: Failure in Inner Direction," *Ohio History* 73 (1964): 80; Oswandel, *Notes on the Mexican War,* 254, 257; Smith and Judah, *Chronicles of the Gringos,* 346; McGroarty, "Richardson's Journal," pt. 2, 533; U.S. War Dept., Adjutant General's Office, Washington, [D.C.], General Order No. 35, July 6, 1848.

35. Risch, *Quartermaster Support,* 253; George Rutledge Gibson, *Journal of a Soldier Under Kearny and Doniphan* (Philadelphia: Porcupine Press, 1974), 120–24; *Southron,* Jackson, Miss., May 15, 1846.

36. Kenly, *Memoirs of a Maryland Volunteer,* 77; Katcher, *Mexican-American War,* 6–7; Lee A. Wallace, Jr., "The First Regiment of Virginia Volunteers, 1846–1848," *Virginia Magazine of History and Biography* 77 (1969): 53–54; Fuess, *Caleb Cushing,* 2:55; Randy W. Hackenberg, *Pennsylvania in the War with Mexico* (Shippensburg, Pa.: White Mane Publishing Co., 1992), 86; Bloom, "With the American Army into Mexico," 18; Chamberlain, *My Confession,* 32; *Woodville (Miss.) Republican,* June 27, 1846.

37. William Starr Myers, *Mexican War Diary of McClellan,* 38; John H. Moore, "Private Johnson Fights," 210, 217; Pace, "Diary and Letters of Rogers," 263; Kenly, *Memoirs of a Maryland Volunteer,* 154; Oswandel, *Notes on the Mexican War,* 114; McGroarty, "Richardson's Journal," pt. 1, 209; Daniel Tyler, *Concise History of the Mormon Battalion in the Mexican War* (Glorieta, N.M.: Rio Grande Press, 1969), 134. Information on volunteer uniforms is sketchy at best, as writers seldom described in detail what they actually wore. Private Richardson of Col. Sterling Price's Regiment of Missouri Mounted Volunteers remarked, "I immediately set about preparing [and] bought my regimentals." Such remarks are typical, with no clue given as to what the uniform looked like.

38. "Important Information for Volunteers," *Alexandria (Va.) Gazette,* Dec. 11, 1846; "Important Information for Volunteers," *Carolina Watchman,* Salisbury, N.C., Dec. 25, 1846; *Mississippi Democrat,* Carrollton, Miss., Apr. 14, 1847; Durham, "Mexican War Letters," 398; McGroarty, "Richardson's Journal," pt. 2, 339. Robert Bruce Wynne, a Tennessee volunteer, came home on leave and returned to Mexico with these items: a blanket, two checked shirts, and a coarse suit. Missourian William H. Richardson bought several items of clothing from his regiment's sutler: a small cotton handkerchief, $1; suspenders, $1; and a flannel shirt, $3.

39. Chance, *Mexican War Journal of Capt. Franklin Smith,* 38, 154; Pruyn, "Campaigning Through Mexico," 11; Chamberlain, *My Confession,* 123; Francis Parkman, *The Oregon Trail* (Boston: Ginn and Co., 1910), 10. Several regimental commanders sent agents, or even went themselves, to the U.S. to obtain replacement clothing.

40. Risch, *Quartermaster Support,* 225; Miscellaneous Mexican War File, Box GA-43, Folder 3, SCUTA; "Clothing for Soldiers," *American Star,* Puebla, Mexico, July 25, 1847; *American Star,* Mexico City, Sept. 30, 1847; "Sewing Women," *American Star,* Mexico City, Oct. 2, 1847; "The Clothing Bureau," *American Star,* Mexico City, Nov. 18, 1847; "Military Clothing," *North American,* Mexico City, Mar. 7, 1848. The *American Star* reported that the Quartermaster Department in Mexico City had put a number of local women to work in the Customhouse sewing uniforms for the army. The work was completed in November and the women em-

ployees dismissed. The department evidently also had employed Mexican seam-stresses during its earlier halt at Puebla.

41. Peskin, ed. *Volunteers,* 89, 189, 201, 294; Oswandel, *Notes on the Mexican War,* 384; Brackett, *General Lane's Brigade,* 35; Smith and Judah, *Chronicles of the Gringos,* 380. "Captures Clothing," *American Star,* Jalapa, Mexico, Apr. 29, 1847, published a list of captured Mexican uniforms: 816 uniform coats, 246 wool overalls, 125 linen overalls, 118 linen jackets, 12 linen shirts, 9 cotton shirts, 220 pairs of boots, 10 great coats, 170 cloth stocks, 201 unfinished uniform coats, and 1500 knapsacks containing additional clothing items. Shortly after the capture of Mexico City, one Pennsylva-nia volunteer, Pvt. Richard Coulter, wrote, "During the day managed to plunder, from the clothing here, a pair of red Mexican uniform pantaloons which happened to be opportune, as the ones I have are completely worn out." A Pennsylvanian in another regiment, J. Jacob Oswandel, noted on Nov. 10, 1847: "This morning, we received clothing from the Quartermaster and all old soldiers got a full suit from head to foot. This being the first regular clothing we drew since we have been in the United States service, and I assure you we all stood in much need thereof. It is now being nearly a year since we were in service, and if it had not been for the clothing we captured from the Mexicans one-half of our army would have to go naked."

CHAPTER 7. LIFE IN MR. POLK'S ARMY

1. "Steamers for the Rio Grande," *Weekly Union,* July 11, 1846. For logistical studies on the war, see Risch, *Quartermaster Support,* ch. 7; and Roger Gene Miller, "Winfield Scott and the Sinews of War: The Logistics of the Mexico City Cam-paign, Oct. 1846–Sept. 1847" (M.A. thesis, North Texas State University, 1976).

2. W. Williams, *Appleton's Southern and Western Traveler's Guide* (New York: D. Appleton and Co., 1849), 132–35; W. Williams, *The Traveler's and Tourist Guide through the United States of America, Canada, Etc., Containing the Routes of Travel by Railroad, Steamboat, Stage, and Canal* (Philadelphia: Lippincott, Grambo, and Co., 1851), 171–74, 204; W. S. Tyron, *My Native Land: Life in America, 1790–1870* (Chicago: University of Chicago Press, 1961), 155–204.

3. Thomas Bailey, "Diary of the Mexican War," *Indiana Magazine of History* 14 (1918): 134; Oswandel, *Notes on the Mexican War,* 14–27; Ann Brown Janes, ed., *Gathering Laurels in Mexico: The Diary of an American Soldier in the Mexican American War* (Lincoln, Mass.: Cottage Press, 1990), 3, 24; *Woodville (Miss.) Republican,* June 6, 1846; Giddings, *Sketches of the Campaign,* 28; Holland, "Diary of a Texan Volun-teer," 1–8. New York City, Newport, Wilmington, Baltimore, Charleston, and Mobile all hosted soldiers on their way to Mexico, but more passed through New Orleans than any other city.

4. Grant, *Papers,* 1:47–53; Benjamin Franklin Scribner, *Camp Life of a Volunteer: A Campaign in Mexico; Or, A Glimpse at Life in Camp by "One Who Has Seen the Elephant"* (Philadelphia: Grigg, Elliot, and Co., 1847), 13; Alfred J. Henderson, "A Morgan County Volunteer," 388; Janes, *Gathering Laurels in Mexico,* 4; *New Or-*

leans (La.) Daily Picayune, Jan. 24, 1847; *Southron,* Jackson, Miss., Feb. 5, 1847;
Thomas N. Love, "Remarks on Some of the Diseases Which Prevailed in the 2d
Regt. Mississippi Rifles, for the First Six Months of Its Service," *New Orleans Medical
and Surgical Journal* 5 (July, 1848): 3–13; Richard B. Winders, "The Role of the
Mississippi Volunteers in Northern Mexico, 1846–1848" (M.A. thesis, University of
Texas at Arlington, 1990), 122–25.

5. Most diaries of soldiers who experienced sea voyages recorded similar experiences.
For example, see Hinds, "Mexican War Journal of Leander M. Cox," pt. 1, 34–46;
Scribner, *Camp Life of a Volunteer,* 13–15; McGroarty, "Richardson's Journal," pt. 3,
530–32; Zeh, *Immigrant Soldier,* 7–9; Kenly, *Memoirs of a Maryland Volunteer,* 23–
35; William Starr Myers, *Mexican War Diary of McClellan,* 8; Goetzmann, "Our
First Foreign War," 85; Furber, *Twelve Month Volunteer,* 492–502; Holland, "Diary
of a Texan Volunteer," 31–32; Robert R. Jones, "Mexican War Diary of J. L. Kemper,"
423, 425; Blackwood, *To Mexico with Scott,* 103–11; Chance, *Mexican War Journal of
Capt. Franklin Smith,* 73; Janes, *Gathering Laurels in Mexico,* 4.

6. Winfield Scott, General Orders No. 21, Headquarters of the Army, Tampico, Mexico,
Feb. 19, 1847.

7. Scribner, *Camp Life of a Volunteer,* 14; Blackwood, *To Mexico with Scott,* 104–105;
Furber, *Twelve Month Volunteer,* 496; McGroarty, "Richardson's Journal," pt. 3,
531–32.

8. Hinds, "Mexican War Journal of Leander M. Cox," pt. 1, 35–36; Scribner, *Camp
Life of a Volunteer,* 14; Furber, *Twelve Month Volunteer,* 497–98.

9. Risch, *Quartermaster Support,* 245–46; Cruffut, *Fifty Years in Camp and Field,*
193–95.

10. U.S. War Dept., *General Regulations, 1841,* 261; Engelman, "Second Illinois," 377.

11. Goetzmann, "Our First Foreign War," 86; Engelman, "Second Illinois," 413–15;
Scribner, *Camp Life of a Volunteer,* 22, 50; Campbell, "Mexican War Letters of
W. B. Campbell," 135, 139; Alfred J. Henderson, "A Morgan Country Volunteer,"
388, 391, 392, 396.

12. S. Compton Smith, *Chile Con Carne,* 67; Engelman, "Second Illinois," 407–408.

13. Goetzmann, "Our First Foreign War," 87; Scribner, *Camp Life of a Volunteer,* 18;
Gibson, *Journal of a Soldier,* 135, 167, 193; McGroarty, "Richardson's Journal," pt. 1,
217, 221; Tyler, *Concise History of the Mormon Battalion,* 157; Brackett, *General Lane's
Brigade,* 28–29; Peck, *Sign of the Eagle,* 5, 29; Livingston-Little, *Mexican War Diary
of Tennery,* 24; S. Compton Smith, *Chile Con Carne,* 99–100; Furber, *Twelve Month
Volunteer,* 405, 406, 408; Alfred J. Henderson, "A Morgan County Volunteer," 400;
American Star, Mexico City, Oct. 17, 1847, p. 29, and Dec. 12, 1847; *North Ameri-
can,* Mexico City, Mar. 2, 1848; Lawton, *Artillery Officer,* 59–62; Janes, *Gathering
Laurels in Mexico,* 6; Robert Ryal Miller, *The Mexican War Journal and Letters of
Ralph W. Kirkham* (College Station: Texas A&M University Press, 1991), 73; Wil-
liam Starr Myers, *Mexican War Diary of McClellan,* 50; Kenly, *Memoirs of a Mary-
land Volunteer,* 52–53; Livingston-Little, *Mexican War Diary of Tennery,* 49, 66;
William Estes, "The Battle of Monterrey," *Fort Worth Gazette,* Jan. 5, 1885; Jefferson

Davis, "Autobiography of Jefferson Davis," *Bedford's Magazine* (Jan., 1890): 256–57; Zeh, *Immigrant Soldier,* 14–15.

14. Ferrell, *Monterrey Is Ours!,* 23; William Starr Myers, *Mexican War Diary of McClellan,* 20; McGroarty, "Richardson's Journal," pt. 2, 339; John H. Moore, "Private Johnson Fights," 215–16; Giddings, *Sketches of the Campaign,* 32–34.

15. *American Flag,* Matamoros, Mexico, May 7 and 19, 1847; Lawton, *Artillery Officer,* 16–17; Kenly, *Memoirs of a Maryland Volunteer,* 53; Estes, "Battle of Monterrey"; Jefferson Davis, "Autobiography," 256–57; McGroarty, "Richardson's Journal," pt. 2, 338; Zeh, *Immigrant Soldier,* 22–23, 49–50. The Tremont House in Matamoros was located near the steamboat landing; the Washington House, described as a grocery and restaurant, was located on the north side of the market square.

16. *American Star,* Mexico City, Sept. 25 and 28; Oct. 2, 7, 12, 17, 24, and 31; Nov. 30; Dec. 6 and 19, all 1847; and Jan. 9, 1848. *North American,* Mexico City, Feb. 3, 1848. The Old Kentucky Restaurant in Mexico City informed customers of its celebrated cook, "Old Caution." Mrs. Foyle later managed the American Company that performed at the National Theater. The owner of the Albion House promised that "his cooks are the very best in the city."

17. Cook, "Mexican War Reminiscences," 442–43; Justin Smith, *War with Mexico,* 2:72. At Puebla, Gen. William J. Worth issued a warning to his troops that the inhabitants of the city might try to poison them. His words angered the Mexicans, whom he had called cowards. Upon investigation, General Scott had the circular rescinded and rebuked Worth. The incident helped to sour relations between the two men and led to further disputes in Mexico City.

18. Livingston-Little, *Mexican War Diary of Tennery,* 25; Pace, "Diary and Letters of Rogers," 285; Engelman, "Second Illinois," 447; Lawton, *Artillery Officer,* 60; Brackett, *General Lane's Brigade,* 104; William Starr Myers, *Mexican War Diary of McClellan,* 92; S. Compton Smith, *Chile Con Carne,* 377–78; Robert Ryal Miller, *Mexican War Journal of Kirkham,* 98–99.

19. Scribner, *Camp Life of a Volunteer,* 18; Giddings, *Sketches of the Campaign,* 31; John H. Moore, "Private Johnson Fights," 211, 215; Peck, *Sign of the Eagle,* 94, 152; Robert Ryal Miller, *Mexican War Journal of Kirkham,* 10; Gibson, *Journal of a Soldier,* 359. Advertisement for an ice house located at Brazos Santiago, *Matamoros (Mexico) Reveille,* May 8, 1848.

20. U.S. War Dept., *General Regulations, 1841,* 264, 346–47; Engelman, "Second Illinois," 378; William Starr Myers, *Mexican War Diary of McClellan,* 35; Lawton, *Artillery Officer,* 75; Peck, *Sign of the Eagle,* 6. According to George R. Gibson, the government allowed officers in Santa Fe to draw rations because there was no money to pay their stipend. Gibson, *Journal of a Soldier,* 268.

21. U.S. War Dept., *General Regulations, 1841,* 17, 18, 209, 365; McGroarty, "Richardson's Journal," pt. 1, 211; Gibson, *Journal of a Soldier,* 214; Peskin, *Volunteers,* 125–26.

22. U.S. War Dept., *General Regulations, 1841,* 18, 209, 365; Brackett, *General Lane's Brigade,* 28–29; Lawton, *Artillery Officer,* 48; Engelman, "Second Illinois," 391; Robert R. Jones, "Mexican War Diary of J. L. Kemper," 419–23; Brackett, *General*

Lane's Brigade, 13–14, 96; Furber, *Twelve Month Volunteer,* 203, 204, 216; Maria Clinton Collins, "Journal of Francis Collins," 44; Hinds, "Mexican War Journal of Leander M. Cox," pt. 2, 225; Henry, *Campaign Sketches,* 32; William Starr Myers, *Mexican War Diary of McClellan,* 10, 30; Robert Ryal Miller, *Mexican War Journal of Kirkham,* 12–13, 21, 74, 83, 92–93, 96–97, 113; Gibson, *Journal of a Soldier,* 269–70, 272, 288, 312; McGroarty, "Richardson's Journal," pt. 1, 231; Tyler, *Concise History of the Mormon Battalion,* 125; S. Compton Smith, *Chile Con Carne,* 244; Robert E. May, "Invisible Men: Blacks and the U.S. Army in the Mexican War," *Historian* 49 (Aug., 1987): 464–67.

23. Scribner, *Camp Life of a Volunteer,* 23; Furber, *Twelve Month Volunteer,* 349; Lawton, *Artillery Officer,* 22; Peck, *Sign of the Eagle,* 71.

24. Scribner, *Camp Life of a Volunteer,* 17–18, 55; Gibson, *Journal of a Soldier,* 226; Andrew Jackson Trussell to John Trussell, Nov. 4, 1847, Trussell Family Papers, Box GA 66-3, SCUTA; Peck, *Sign of the Eagle,* 138–39, 151; Robert Ryal Miller, *Mexican War Journal of Kirkham,* 59.

25. Chamberlain, *My Confession,* 186–87; Brackett, *General Lane's Brigade,* 52; S. Compton Smith, *Chile Con Carne,* 31.

26. Alfred J. Henderson, "A Morgan County Volunteer," 389, 398; Livingston-Little, *Mexican War Diary of Tennery,* 8; Oswandel, *Notes on the Mexican War,* 258–59.

27. U.S. War Dept., *General Regulations, 1841,* 61–64; Goetzmann, "Our First Foreign War," 87; Rowe, "Mexican War Letters of Coffey," 250; Gibson, *Journal of a Soldier,* 235; Holland, "Diary of a Texan Volunteer," 18.

28. Scribner, *Camp Life of a Volunteer,* 23, 38–38; Furber, *Twelve Month Volunteer,* 120; Brackett, *General Lane's Brigade,* 30; Giddings, *Sketches of the Campaign,* 228; Robert Ryal Miller, *Mexican War Journal of Kirkham,* 3, 7, 20, 38; Chance, *Mexican War Journal of Capt. Franklin Smith,* 18; Gibson, *Journal of a Soldier,* 256, 344; McGroarty, "Richardson's Journal," pt. 2, 331; McGroarty, "Richardson's Journal," pt. 3, 515; *North American,* Mexico City, Oct. 26 and Nov. 12, 1847; "Opposition to the Ethiopians," *American Star,* Mexico City, Oct. 22, 1847; *Rough and Ready Songster.* From the "Yankee Doodle," *North American,* Mexico City, Oct. 5, 1847: "The fine orchestra attached to the National Theatre, on Thursday night treated the audience with Yankee Doodle. It was admirably executed, but one could hear little of the music, for the cheering made the huge walls fairly tremble."

29. Furber, *Twelve Month Volunteer,* 418–22; McGroarty, "Richardson's Journal," pt. 2, 341; Janes, *Gathering Laurels in Mexico,* 21. Mock trials were also a popular pastime. For an example, see Holland, "Diary of a Texan Volunteer," 2–3.

30. Rowe, "Mexican War Letters of Coffey," 244; Scribner, *Camp Life of a Volunteer,* 35–36, 37; Durham, "Mexican War Letters," 393; Engelman, "Second Illinois," 378, 387; McGroarty, "Richardson's Journal," pt. 1, 232; Lewis H. Wunder to Friend, Feb. 24, 1847, Wunder Papers, Mississippi State Archives, Jackson, Miss.; Hinds, "Mexican War Journal of Leander M. Cox," pt. 2, 227; Campbell, "Mexican War Letters of W. B. Campbell," 140; Andrew Jackson Trussell to John Trussell, Mar. 19, 1847, Trussell Family Papers, Box GA 66-3, SCUTA; Robert Ryal Miller, *Mexican War Journal of Kirkham,* 6; Pace, "Diary and Letters of Rogers," 271–72;

Peck, *Sign of the Eagle*, 97–99, 150; Robert Ryal Miller, *Mexican War Journal of Kirkham*, 17, 21, 24, 75, 82, 85, 89, 93, 102.

31. Engelman, "Second Illinois," 427; Pace, "Diary and Letters of Rogers," 280; Andrew Jackson Trussell to John Trussell, June 6, 1847, Trussell Family Papers, Box GA 66-3, SCUTA; Robert Ryal Miller, *Mexican War Journal of Kirkham*, 25, 28, 39–40, 69, 72, 90; Gibson, *Journal of a Soldier*, 266.

32. Dayton W. Canaday, "Voice of the Volunteer of 1847," *Journal of the Illinois State Historical Society* 44 (1951): 199–209; Robert L. Bodson, "A Description of the United States Occupation of Mexico, as Reported by American Newspapers Published in Vera Cruz, Puebla, and Mexico City, Sept. 14, 1847, to July 31, 1848" (Ph.D. diss., Ball State University, 1970), 1–27; Durham, "Mexican War Letters," 392; Gibson, *Journal of a Soldier*, 221, 360; McGroarty, "Richardson's Journal," pt. 3, 516; Andrew Jackson Trussell to John Trussell, June 6, 1847, Trussell Family Papers, Box GA 66-3, SCUTA. Also see Lota M. Spell, "The Anglo-Saxon Press in Mexico, 1846–1848," *American Historical Review* 38 (Oct., 1932): 20–31; Giddings, *Sketches of the Campaign*, 60; Janes, *Gathering Laurels in Mexico*, 8, 14, 17, 21; "The American Star," *American Star*, Mexico City, Sept. 20 and 23, 1847; "The North American," *Weekly Star for the United States,* Mexico City, Jan. 31, 1848. The office of the *American Star* in Mexico City was located at Calle de Medinas No. 6, half a block from the Customhouse. The price of the *American Star* was 12-½¢ per copy. The paper's name changed on Oct. 12, 1847, to *Daily American Star.* "The North American," *American Star,* Sept. 30, 1847, announced the arrival of its rival: "It is decidedly neat, and gotten up with all the taste of a Northern paper." On Nov. 3, 1847, the "Flag of Freedom," *American Star* announced that it had received several issues of the *Flag of Freedom,* but said that it was published in Puebla, not Jalapa.

33. Playbills from the American Theatre, Jan. 12 and 27, [1846], Miscellaneous Mexican War File, Box GA 43, SCUTA; Oswandel, *Notes on the Mexican War,* 226–27; Giddings, *Sketches of the Campaign,* 61–62; H. Judge Moore, *Scott's Campaigns in Central Mexico: From the Rendezvous at the Island of Lobos to the Taking of Mexico City, Including an Account of the Siege of Puebla* (Charleston, S.C.: J. B. Nixon, 1849), 123; "American Theatre" and "Theatre Del Progreso," *American Star,* Jalapa, Mexico, May 2 and June 12, 1847; *American Star,* Puebla, Mexico, June 12, 1847; "Theatre Del Progreso," *American Star,* Puebla, Mexico, June 20, 1847; "Theatre Del Progreso" and "Circus," *American Star,* Puebla, Mexico, June 24, 1847; "Theatre," *American Star,* Puebla, Mexico, July 11, 1847; "Circus," "Teatro Principal," and "Theatre," *American Star,* Puebla, Mexico, July 15, 1847; "American Theatre," *American Star,* Puebla, Mexico, July 18, 1847; "American Theatre and Circus," "Teatro Principal," "Circus," and "American Theatre," *American Star,* Puebla, Mexico, Aug. 1, 1847. *American Star,* Mexico City, Sept. 28; Oct. 5, 7, 13, 15, 16, 21, 30; Nov. 26 and 30, 1847. *North American,* Mexico City, Oct. 5, Nov. 23 and 26, 1847. Peskin, *Volunteers,* 217, 219; Brackett, *General Lane's Brigade,* 200; Peck, *Sign of the Eagle,* 99, 142, 147; Robert Ryal Miller, *Mexican War Journal of Kirkham,* 31, 35, 38; Gibson, *Journal of a Soldier,* 273–74. At Jalapa, the cost of the theater was $1 for a box seat, 50¢ for a seat in the pit, and 25¢ for a gallery seat. From the *American*

Flag, Matamoros, Mexico, Mar. 3, 1847, comes news of a theater of a different sort: Mr. Bensley's Circus. Acts included a rider, a vaulter, and a strong man. A story on May 19, 1847, reported that the Matamoros Theater had been leased by the "Matamoros Dramatic Association" and was being renovated to improve its facilities. According to the "Amusements," *American Star,* Mexico City, Sept. 23, 1847, Bensley's Circus later opened in the Mexican capital, shortly after the latter's capture.

34. Darwin Payne, "Camp Life in the Army of Occupation," *Southwestern Historical Quarterly* 73 (Jan., 1970): 337; James Longstreet, *From Manassas to Appomattox: Memoirs of the Civil War in America* (Bloomington: Indiana University Press, 1981), 20; Oswandel, *Notes on the Mexican War,* 229; Peskin, *Volunteers,* 216; Giddings, *Sketches of the Campaign,* 61.

35. Holland, "Diary of a Texas Volunteer," 5, 33; Rowe, "Mexican War Letters of Coffey," 249; Bloom, "With the American Army into Mexico," 229–30; "To the Editors of the American Star," *American Star,* Mexico City, Dec. 1, 1847; Furber, *Twelve Month Volunteer,* 178. Furber joked about finding several human skulls on the Wild Horse Prairie north of the Rio Grande, saying that one of them was "the head of Morgan, the anti-mason." The *Aztec Club* still exists today, maintained by descendants of the original members. The club's formation was announced in the "The Aztec Club," *American Star,* Mexico City, Oct. 26, 1847: "THE AZTEC CLUB. It may not generally be known that since the occupation of this capital by our troops, many of the most distinguished and gallant officers of our army, have formed themselves into a club, which has been styled by them, 'the Aztec Club.' The object of this club, so far as we can understand, is similar to those of the military clubs of England—that of coming together in friendly intercourse. Every general officer of the army, with the exception of one, is a member, and the club promises to be one of mutual and social benefit to all."

36. Chance, *Mexican War Journal of Capt. Franklin Smith,* 71; McGroarty, "Richardson's Journal," pt. 1, 227; Janes, *Gathering Laurels in Mexico,* 14; Engelman, "Second Illinois," 433; Furber, *Twelve Month Volunteer,* 76, 184, 509; William Starr Myers, *Mexican War Diary of McClellan,* 25–26; Jensen, "Memoirs of Frost," pt. 3, 204; Brackett, *General Lane's Brigade,* 166; S. Compton Smith, *Chile Con Carne,* 101–102; Giddings, *Sketches of the Campaign,* 231; Gibson, *Journal of a Soldier,* 213, 236; "The Coffee Houses," *American Star,* Mexico City, Oct. 20, 1847; "Liquor Shops, &c," *American Star,* Mexico City, Oct. 22, 1847.

37. Furber, *Twelve Month Volunteer,* 381, 403; Giddings, *Sketches of the Campaign,* 62; Oswandel, *Notes on the Mexican War,* 448–49; Janes, *Gathering Laurels in Mexico,* 18, 20.

38. Durham, "Mexican War Letters," 405; Pace, "Diary and Letters of Rogers," 271–72; Peskin, *Volunteers,* 103; Chance, *Mexican War Journal of Capt. Franklin Smith,* 86–87; Cruffut, *Fifty Years in Camp and Field,* 180. Lieutenant Colonel Hitchcock claimed in 1843 that "nearly 400 [members of the 3rd U.S. Infantry] have signed the pledge, including several officers."

39. Furber, *Twelve Month Volunteer,* 228–30; Chamberlain, *My Confession,* 65–66; Engelman, "Second Illinois," 383; S. Compton Smith, *Chile Con Carne,* 320–36;

Peck, *Sign of the Eagle,* 41–42; Giddings, *Sketches of the Campaign,* 230–31; Gibson, *Journal of a Soldier,* 268, 316; McGroarty, "Richardson's Journal," pt. 1, 230, 235, 350; and pt. 3, 519; Janes, *Gathering Laurels in Mexico,* 15, 21; *American Star,* Mexico City, Nov. 16, 1847; "James K. Polk," *North American,* Mexico City, Oct. 26, 1847. Horse racing provided a way for soldiers to gamble. According to *American Star,* Nov. 16, 1847, one popular pacer named "James K. Polk" reportedly could "pace 20 miles in one hour."

40. Brackett, *General Lane's Brigade,* 22; Scribner, *Camp Life of a Volunteer,* 44–45; Giddings, *Sketches of the Campaign,* 63; Furber, *Twelve Month Volunteer,* 233–34; Ferrell, *Monterrey Is Ours!,* 89, 91; Andrew Jackson Trussell to John Trussell, Jan. 9, 1848; Feb. 28, 1848; and May 5, 1848, all in Trussell Family Papers, Box GA 66-4, SCUTA; S. Compton Smith, *Chile Con Carne,* 100–104; Robert Ryal Miller, *Mexican War Journal of Kirkham,* 37–38; Gibson, *Journal of a Soldier,* 215–26, 224, 229, 233, 243, 265, 314; McGroarty, "Richardson's Journal," pt. 2, 332, 334–35; Oswandel, *Notes on the Mexican War,* 446; Chance, *Mexican War Journal of Capt. Franklin Smith,* 113–14; Holland, "Diary of a Texan Volunteer," 31.

41. Livingston-Little, *Mexican War Diary of Tennery,* 4; Andrew Jackson Trussell to John Trussell, May 5, 1848, Trussell Family Papers, Box GA 66-4, SCUTA; Oswandel, *Notes on the Mexican War,* 431.

CHAPTER 8. DOG CHEAP TO THE LIVING

1. Thomas R. Irey, "Soldiering, Suffering, and Dying in the Mexican War," *Journal of the West* 11 (Apr., 1972): 285; John H. Moore, "Private Johnson Fights," 209.

2. Heitman, *Historical Register,* 2:282; Henry L. Scott, *Military Dictionary,* 644, 649. Casualty figures for the war vary from source to source. One U.S. War Dept. document lists deaths due to battle at 1,429 and deaths due to illness at 10,885. The numbers of casualties used in this paragraph and in the table below come from information in Henry L. Scott's *Military Dictionary.*

	Deaths-Battle	Deaths-Illness	Discharges
Old Regulars	792	2,623	1,782
New Regulars	143	2,091	767
Volunteers	613	6,256	7,200
TOTAL	1,548	10,970	9,749

3. Heitman, *Historical Register,* 1:799; Louis C. Duncan, "A Medical History of General Zachary Taylor's Army of Occupation in Texas and Mexico, 1845–1847," *Military Surgeon* 65 (1929): 80; John Duffy, "Medical Practices in the Ante-Bellum South," *Journal of Southern History* 25 (Feb., 1959): 53–54. Appointed an assistant surgeon from civilian life (in Connecticut) in 1833, John B. Porter was promoted to surgeon with the rank of major in Oct. 1846. He retired in 1862 and died seven years later.

4. Risch, *Quartermaster Support,* 256; Duncan, "Medical History of Taylor's Army," 80, 82; Gibson, *Journal of a Soldier,* 141, 255, 260; Holland, "Diary of a Texan Volunteer," 11–12, 13; Zeh, *Immigrant Soldier,* 38; Peskin, *Volunteers,* 95.

5. Peck, *Sign of the Eagle*, 6, 7, 55; Scribner, *Camp Life of a Volunteer*, 21–22; William Starr Myers, *Mexican War Diary of McClellan*, 9, 27; Andrew Jackson Trussell to John Trussell, Mar. 19, 1847, Trussell Family Papers, Box GA 66-3, SCUTA; John H. Moore, "Private Johnson Fights," 204; Giddings, *Sketches of the Campaign*, 112–13; Gibson, *Journal of a Soldier*, 146, 175; McGroarty, "Richardson's Journal," pt. 1, 222–23, and pt. 2, 355; Tyler, *Concise History of the Mormon Battalion*, 159; Engelman, "Second Illinois," 371, 374; Ballentine, *Autobiography of an English Soldier*, 158; Brackett, *General Lane's Brigade*, 80; William Starr Myers, *Mexican War Diary of McClellan*, 33; Robert Ryal Miller, *Mexican War Journal of Kirkham*, 22; Zeh, *Immigrant Soldier*, 32, 34. According to McGroarty, "Richardson's Journal," pt. 1, William H. Richardson's unit used old salt-pork barrels to carry extra water on the march to Santa Fe—a practice that surely would have made water taste bad and may have promoted disease.

6. John H. Moore, "Private Johnson Fights," 212; Brackett, *General Lane's Brigade*, 53–55; 204; Gibson, *Journal of a Soldier*, 134, 146; Oswandel, *Notes on the Mexican War*, 110; Engelman, "Second Illinois," 372, 419; Scribner, *Camp Life of a Volunteer*, 47–49; Andrew Jackson Trussell to John Trussell, Mar. 19, 1847, and June 6, 1847, Trussell Family Papers, Box GA 66-3, SCUTA; Giddings, *Sketches of the Campaign*, 101. According to Giddings, Taylor's baggage train on the march from Camargo to Monterey consisted of "1 wagon to each division and brigade head-quarters, 4 pack mules to the field and staff of each regimental, 2 pack mules to the officers of each company, 1 pack mule to every 8 non-commissioned officers, musicians, and privates. Three wagons in addition were assigned to each regiment, one for the transportation of water, and two for such articles as could not be packed on mules" (101). George R. Gibson, whose company marched from Fort Leavenworth to Santa Fe, said that many men complained a painful ailment called "splints," which affected the shinbone and caused swelling of the lower leg (160–61).

7. Scribner's description of a march is fairly typical. Marchers on the Mexican highlands, however, often complained of the cold and the rain, rather than the sun and heat. Scribner, *Camp Life of a Volunteer*, 48; Janes, *Gathering Laurels in Mexico*, 8; Hinds, "Mexican War Journal of Leander M. Cox," pt. 2, 217; Peck, *Sign of the Eagle*, 38–39; Zeh, *Immigrant Soldier*, 25–26.

8. Gibson, *Journal of a Soldier*, 184; Peck, *Sign of the Eagle*, 38–39; Maria Clinton Collins, "Journal of Francis Collins," 101; Brackett, *General Lane's Brigade*, 54–55, 81, 99; William Starr Myers, *Mexican War Diary of McClellan*, 78–79; Giddings, *Sketches of the Campaign*, 114–15; Robert Ryal Miller, *Mexican War Journal of Kirkham*, 9; Oswandel, *Notes on the Mexican War*, 108.

9. McGroarty, "Richardson's Journal," pt. 1, 212, and pt. 3, 532; Kenly, *Memoirs of a Maryland Volunteer*, 211; S. Compton Smith, *Chile Con Carne*, 65; Smith and Judah, *Chronicles of the Gringos*, 223–325; Robert Ryal Miller, *Mexican War Journal of Kirkham*, 22; Gibson, *Journal of a Soldier*, 215, 249; Ames, "Doctor Comes to California," pt. 3, 63; William Starr Myers, *Mexican War Diary of McClellan*, 24; Hinds, "Mexican War Journal of Leander M. Cox," pt. 1, 46; Zeh, *Immigrant Soldier*, 26.

10. McGroarty, "Richardson's Journal," pt. 2, 337; Love, "Remarks on Some Diseases,"

3–13; Winders, "Role of the Mississippi Volunteers," 119–50; Lewis H. Wunder to Friend, Feb. 24, 1847, Wunder Papers, Mississippi State Archives, Jackson, Miss.; Brackett, *General Lane's Brigade,* 29; Andrew Jackson Trussell to John Trussell, Mar. 19 and July 10, 1847, Trussell Family Papers, Box GA 66-3, SCUTA; John H. Moore, "Private Johnson Fights," 216; "Mexican Hospitals," *North American,* Mexico City, Oct. 26, 1847; Giddings, *Sketches of the Campaign,* 30–31; Peck, *Sign of the Eagle,* 95. According to Gibson, *Journal of a Soldier,* 244, many Missourians at Santa Fe suffered from tonsillitis.

11. Meade, *Life and Letters,* 1:108, 1:139, 1:162; Love, "Remarks on Some Diseases," 13; Porter, "Medical and Surgical Notes," pt. 4, *American Journal of the Medical Sciences* 26 (Oct., 1853): 323; U.S. War Dept., *General Regulations, 1841,* 308; Smith and Judah, *Chronicles of the Gringos,* 346–47; Giddings, *Sketches of the Campaign,* 83.

12. Love, "Remarks on Some Diseases," 4; U.S. War Dept., *General Regulations, 1841,* 124–26; Thomas Henderson, *Hints on the Medical Examination,* 16–17; Gibson, *Journal of a Soldier,* 173; Henry Dwight Sedgwick, *Men of Letters: Francis Parkman* (Boston: Houghton, Mifflin, and Company, 1904), 333; Kendall, *Narrative of the Texan Santa Fe Expedition,* 1:13. The outdoors was thought to have curative powers, a notion illustrated by George R. Gibson when he wrote, "One of our greatest anxieties now is to reach the pure air and water of the mountains, where we expect a perfect restoration to health." Historian Francis Parkman explained the reason for his celebrated journey out west in 1846: "I hoped by exchanging books and documents for horse and rifle to gain three objects at once—health, use of sight, and personal knowledge of savage life." New Orleans newspaperman George W. Kendall, who joined the ill-fated Santa Fe Expedition, was "induced [in part] by the hope of correcting a derangement of health."

13. Duffy, "Medical Practices," 55–56, 60, 66; Love, "Remarks on Some Diseases," 10, 12; Porter, "Medical and Surgical Notes," pt. 1, *American Journal of the Medical Sciences* 23 (Jan., 1852): 23; pt. 3 *American Journal of the Medical Sciences* 25 (1853): 38–39; pt. 4, 313–14, 317, 329–30. Calomel was a mercury compound and caused mercury poisoning. In the procedure called bleeding, blood was allowed to pour from an open vein until the patient either vomited or fainted. Duffy details the procedure of cupping: "A glass cup was rinsed with alcohol, set on fire, and instantly applied to the skin [on the back of the neck]. After four or five minutes, when the vacuum had drawn blood to the surface of the skin, the cup was taken off and the scarificator, a triggered spring device which made several small cuts simultaneously, was then used. As soon as the incisions were made, the cup was again rinsed with alcohol, set ablaze, and quickly placed over the scarified area." The alcohol was intended as a fuel, not a disinfectant.

14. Porter, "Medical and Surgical Notes," pt. 4, 330–33. Also see Roger G. Miller, "Yellow Jack at Vera Cruz," *Prologue: Journal of the National Archives* 10 (Spring 1978): 43–53.

15. U.S. War Dept., *General Regulations, 1841,* 304–309; Giddings, *Sketches of the Campaign,* 82.

16. Robarts, *Mexican War Veterans,* 7; Louis C. Duncan, "A Medical History of Gen-

eral Scott's Campaign to the City of Mexico in 1847," *Military Surgeon* 46 (Oct.–Nov., 1920): 437–38, 607–609; U.S. Congress, *Report of the Secretary of War, Which Accompanied the Annual Message of the President of the United States, to Both Houses of the Thirtieth Congress, 1847* (Washington, D.C.: Wendell and Van Benthuyes, 1847), 680. An examination board meeting at New York City in Mar. 1847 interviewed 37 candidates for appointment to the Medical Department but determined that only 11 were qualified. Another board was to be assembled in Oct. 1847. For a detailed history of the Medical Department during the war, see Mary C. Gillet, *The Army Medical Department, 1818–1865* (Washington, D.C.: Center of Military History, 1987).

17. S. Compton Smith, *Chile Con Carne,* 59; Smith and Judah, *Chronicles of the Gringos,* 335; H. Grady Howell, Jr., ed., *A Southern Lacrimosa: The Mexican War Journal of Dr. Thomas Neely Love, Surgeon, Second Regiment Mississippi Infantry, U.S.A.* (Madison, Miss.: Chickasaw Bayou Press, 1996), 88; "Gen. Order No. 377," *American Star,* Mexico City, Dec. 17, 1847. General Order No. 377, issued by Scott on Dec. 16, 1847, ordered several assistant surgeons to report to Dr. Tripler. It also detailed the 2nd, 4th, and 8th Infantry, and a steward from the 2nd Artillery, to work in the various wards. Scott further ordered that every brigade would have one cook to every twenty men, and one nurse to every ten men.

18. Porter, "Medical and Surgical Notes," pt. 3, 29, 31; Smith and Judah, *Chronicles of the Gringos,* 345–46; Livingston-Little, *Mexican War Diary of Tennery,* 85; Lawton, *Artillery Officer,* 328.

19. Porter, "Medical and Surgical Notes," pt. 4, 332; Janes, *Gathering Laurels in Mexico,* 10–11, 15, 17, 19; Zeh, *Immigrant Soldier,* 76–84; Maria Clinton Collins, "Journal of Francis Collins," 66; Howell, *Southern Lacrimosa,* 88. During the Civil War, the U.S. War Dept. attempted to eliminate the problems caused by untrained hospital staffs by commissioning Asst. Surg. Joseph Janvier Woodward to write a handbook, *The Hospitals Steward's Manual, For the Instruction of Hospital Stewards, Ward-Masters, and Attendants, in Their Several Duties.* The manual details the roles and duties of the various attendants. Many of these roles and duties were the same as those performed by their Mexican War predecessors.

20. Smith and Judah, *Chronicles of the Gringos,* 336–37; Janes, *Gathering Laurels in Mexico,* 9–10, 17; Peskin, *Volunteers,* 85, 96, 293; Tyler, *Concise History of the Mormon Battalion,* 158, 160; McGroarty, "Richardson's Journal," pt. 2, 352–54; Robert R. Jones, "Mexican War Diary of J. L. Kemper," 420; Howell, *Southern Lacrimosa,* 91.

21. Lewis H. Wunder to Friend, Feb. 24, 1847, Wunder Papers, Mississippi State Archives, Jackson, Miss.; Scribner, *Camp Life of a Volunteer,* 26; Ballentine, *Autobiography of an English Soldier,* 206–207; Peskin, *Volunteers,* 96; Love, "Remarks on Some Diseases," 12.

22. Porter, "Medical and Surgical Notes," pt. 4, 332; Livingston-Little, *Mexican War Diary of Tennery,* 28; John H. Moore, "Private Johnson Fights," 215; Janes, *Gathering Laurels in Mexico,* 7, 18. Editors of the "The Media Staff," *North American,* Mexico City, Oct. 12, 1847, praised army doctors, saying, "No department of the army deserves more honorable mention than the staff of surgeons. . . . Night and

day they have had little rest, but toiled unceasingly to alleviate the sufferings of the sick and wounded. . . . All who have witnessed these battles will long remember the services of the medical staff."

23. Holland, "Diary of a Texan Volunteer," 14; Hinds, "Mexican War Journal of Leander M. Cox," pt. 1, 48, and pt. 2, 217; Engelman, "Second Illinois," 380–81, 427; Ballentine, *Autobiography of an English Soldier,* 233; Maria Clinton Collins, "Journal of Francis Collins," 66; Oswandel, *Notes on the Mexican War,* 401; Tyler, *Concise History of the Mormon Battalion,* 145–47; Durham, "Mexican War Letters," 407; McGroarty, "Richardson's Journal," pt. 3, 522; Gibson, *Journal of a Soldier,* 163–64, 262; "Infirmary," *North American,* Mexico City, Jan. 14, 1848; *American Star,* Mexico City, Dec. 12, 1847. The *American Flag,* Matamoros, Mexico, Mar. 3 and May 19, 1847, and May 7, 1848, advertised Dr. E. G. W. Schoenian's "Dispensatory." Examples of patent medicines to be had there are Gray's Patent Ointment, Martin's Fever Pills, and Dr. Billings' Carminative and Astringent Syrup. By May, the city boasted that a dentist, Dr. Pritchard, had arrived: "One tooth of gold plate, $4; two or more, $3 each; cleaning, whitening, or stopping with gold or silver, $1 each." The *American Star,* Sept. 25, 1847, advertised Dr. David William Seager, a dentist, and Dr. Graves, a doctor with "Vaccine virus" on hand for "all who may desire it." Dr. Claudon, "a member of the Faculty of Medicine of Paris," announced in the *American Star,* Oct. 14, 1847, that he had opened a hospital to treat "invalids." On Oct. 24, 1847, the paper announced the arrival of Mr. Stuart MacGoun, a specialist in diseases of the eye.

24. Porter, "Medical and Surgical Notes," pt. 3, 40–42; Smith and Judah, *Chronicles of the Gringos,* 328; Louis C. Duncan, "The Days Gone By: A Volunteer Regiment in 1846–7," *Military Surgeon* 65 (1929): 710.

25. Porter, "Medical and Surgical Notes," pt. 1, 20, 25; Henry, *Campaign Sketches,* 108; Hinds, "Mexican War Journal of Leander M. Cox," pt. 3, 54; Maria Clinton Collins, "Journal of Francis Collins," 349, 351; Robert Ryal Miller, *Mexican War Journal of Kirkham,* 58; Brackett, *General Lane's Brigade,* 99; Gibson, *Journal of a Soldier,* 149, 154, 174; Ames, "Doctor Comes to California," pt. 2, *California Historical Quarterly* 21 (1942): 351; Henry L. Scott, *Military Dictionary,* 649; Cruffut, *Fifty Years in Camp and Field,* 243. The number of accidental deaths within the army is as follows: Old Regulars, 139; New Regulars, 30; volunteers, 192; total, 361. The number of injuries from accidents was not reported.

26. Livingston-Little, *Mexican War Diary of Tennery,* 11, 80, 83; Engelman, "Second Illinois" 376, 393; McGroarty, "Richardson's Journal," pt. 1, 216, 219–20; Tyler, *Concise History of the Mormon Battalion,* 165; Brackett, *General Lane's Brigade,* 18; Bailey, "Diary of the Mexican War," 144; Peskin, *Volunteers,* 162; Chance, *Mexican War Journal of Capt. Franklin Smith,* 86–87; *Matamoros (Mexico) Reveille,* July 15, 1846; Holland, "Diary of a Texan Volunteer," 16. The *Matamoros Reveille,* July 15, 1846, reported a volunteer shot and killed; a volunteer drowned; and several volunteers lost when their small boat was swamped at sea and they unsuccessfully tried to swim to shore. The "Fatal Accident," *American Star,* Mexico City, Oct. 20, 1847, reported that Capt. James Wilson, a Kentucky volunteer, accidentally was shot and

killed by his lieutenant at Covington, Ky. The *North American,* Mexico City, Dec. 30, 1847, reported that a Kentucky volunteer had shot himself in the hand while handling a revolver in the Progreso Hotel.

27. Henry L. Scott, *Military Dictionary,* 252; Engelman, "Second Illinois," 384; Lee A. Wallace, "First Regiment," 61–62; Porter, "Medical and Surgical Notes," pt. 3, 33; Brackett, *General Lane's Brigade,* 162–63, 209; Chance, *Mexican War Journal of Capt. Franklin Smith,* 40–43; Ferol Egan, *Frémont: Explorer for a Restless Nation* (New York: Doubleday and Company, 1977), 423–25; John Bigelow, *Memoir of the Life and Public Service of John Charles Frémont* (New York: Derby and Jackson, 1856), 203–13; Ames, "Doctor Comes to California," pt. 3, 55; Robert R. Jones, "Mexican War Diary of J. L. Kemper," 400; Zeh, *Immigrant Soldier,* 43–44; Jay Monaghan, ed., *Private Journal of Louis McLane, U.S.N., 1844–1848* (Los Angeles: Dawson's Books Shop for the Santa Barbara Historical Society, 1971), 113.

28. Porter, "Medical and Surgical Notes," pt. 1, 25–30; pt. 3, 25, 26, 29. For an account of wounds and their treatment, see Smith and Judah, *Chronicles of the Gringos,* 343–45. Ames, "Doctor Comes to California," the diary of Asst. Surg. John S. Griffin, also contains first-hand accounts of wound treatment. The figures below for number of wounded come from Henry L. Scott, *Military Dictionary,* 649:

	Wounded in Battle	Died of Wounds
Old Regulars	1,803	329
New Regulars	272	76
Volunteers	1,318	100
TOTAL	3,393	505

29. Porter, "Medical and Surgical Notes," pt. 1, pp. 28–35, and pt. 2, *American Journal of the Medical Sciences* 24 (July, 1852): 29; Duncan, "Medical History of Taylor's Army," 100; Smith and Judah, *Chronicles of the Gringos,* 347–50; Robert R. Jones, "Mexican War Diary of J. L. Kemper," 414–15; Zeh, *Immigrant Soldier,* 31; Duffy, "Medical Practices," 66. While in Washington, D.C., Captain Kemper had a tooth extracted by a dentist who used ether. Wrote the Virginian, "Went to have my tooth drawn—dreadful operation. Took ether (Letheon) [which] doesn't seem to injured me at all." His comments seem to have been made in response to those who warned of the drug's ill-effects.

30. Smith and Judah, *Chronicles of the Gringos,* 344; Engelman, "Second Illinois," 444–49; Duncan, "Medical History of Taylor's Army," 602–603; A Mississippian, "Sketches of Our Volunteers Officers: Alexander Keith McClung," *Southern Literary Messenger* 21 (Jan., 1855): 10–11.

31. Grant, *Papers,* 1:85; George A. McCall, *Letters from the Frontier,* 453–54; Ferrell, *Monterrey Is Ours!,* 61; Duncan, "Medical History of Taylor's Army," 93; Maria Clinton Collins, "Journal of Francis Collins," 50–51; Robert Ryal Miller, *Mexican War Journal of Kirkham,* 47; Giddings, *Sketches of the Campaign,* 189–90.

32. Porter, "Medical and Surgical Notes," pt. 3, 29–30; Giddings, *Sketches of the Campaign,* 179–82; Ames, "Doctor Comes to California," pt. 2, 336–37; Goetzmann, "Our First Foreign War," 98; Robert Ryal Miller, *Mexican War Journal of Kirkham,* 44;

Peck, *Sign of the Eagle*, 50, 114; Nathan Covington Brooks, *A Complete History of the Mexican War: Its Causes, Conduct, and Consequences, Comprising an Account of the Various Military and Naval Operations, from Its Commencement to the Treaty of Peace* (Philadelphia: Grigg, Elliot, and Co., 1849; reprinted Chicago: Rio Grande Press, 1965), 145; Zeh, *Immigrant Soldier*, 43, 65. On lancers at Buena Vista, see James Henry Carleton, *The Battle of Buena Vista with the Operations of the Army of Occupation for One Month* (New York: Harper and Brothers, 1848), 93–94, 105, 111. Lieutenant Peck described the Americans' attack at Contreras: "Our troops managed to turn the enemy and at daylight assaulted from the rear with the bayonet, carrying the works in seventeen minutes."

33. Goetzmann, "Our First Foreign War," 90; Peck, *Sign of the Eagle*, 26, 115; Lawton, *Artillery Officer*, 140; Zeh, *Immigrant Soldier*, 17, 31–32; Robert Ryal Miller, *Mexican War Journal of Kirkham*, 46–49, 51, 60, 67; Gibson, *Journal of a Soldier*, 350–51; Oswandel, *Notes on the Mexican War*, 445; Scribner, *Camp Life of a Volunteer*, 20, 60; McGroarty, "Richardson's Journal," pt. 3, 351.

34. Livingston-Little, *Mexican War Diary of Tennery*, 22–23, 34, 36; Goetzmann, "Our First Foreign War," 98; Brackett, *General Lane's Brigade*, 59; Pace, "Diary and Letters of Rogers," 272.

35. U.S. War Dept., *General Regulations, 1841*, 90–91; Brackett, *General Lane's Brigade*, 96; Scribner, *Camp Life of a Volunteer*, 20; Holland, "Diary of a Texan Volunteer," 13; John H. Moore, "Private Johnson Fights," 226; Hinds, "Mexican War Journal of Leander M. Cox," pt. 2, 223; Livingston-Little, *Mexican War Diary of Tennery*, 7, 17; Furber, *Twelve Month Volunteer*, 87–88; Brackett, *General Lane's Brigade*, 29; Ballentine, *Autobiography of an English Soldier*, 223; Giddings, *Sketches of the Campaign*, 65, 83, 229; Peck, *Sign of the Eagle*, 138; Robert Ryal Miller, *Mexican War Journal of Kirkham*, 59–60; Janes, *Gathering Laurels in Mexico*, 12, 19; Gibson, *Journal of a Soldier*, 188, 201, 253, 276; McGroarty, "Richardson's Journal," pt. 1, 228, and pt. 2, 336, 356. After one funeral in New Mexico, Pvt. William H. Richardson remarked, "The muffled roll of the drum, and the firing of the farewell to the dead, did not have the tendency to cheer me." At Camargo, Luther Giddings recorded his oft-quoted line, "Scarcely a day elapsed that the muffled drums of some regiment in the wood, did not announce the departure of one or more poor fellows to the chaparral."

36. Scribner, *Camp Life of a Volunteer*, 72–73; Peskin, *Volunteers*, 292–94, 296, 297, 300; Janes, *Gathering Laurels in Mexico*, 22; Kenly, *Memoirs of a Maryland Volunteer*, 105–106; Chance, *Mexican War Journal of Capt. Franklin Smith*, 149–50; Brackett, *General Lane's Brigade*, 96; John C. Breckenridge, "An Address on the Occasion of the Burials of the Kentucky Volunteers, Who Fell at Buena Vista" (Lexington: Observer and Reporter Office, 1847), 158–59; *Wilmington (N.C.) Journal*, Dec. 18, 1846; "Remains of Officers Morris, Williams, and Fields," *American Eagle*, Vera Cruz, Apr. 6, 1847. From the "Next Door to the New Mexico Theatre," *American Star*, Mexico City, Oct. 14 and 15, 1847: "To those of our friends who have the sad duty to perform of sending the remains of some loved friend or brother-officer, to the land of his fathers, we call their attention to the advertisement of Mr. [Peter]

Wright, an American, in another column." Wright offered lead-lined coffins for sale.

37. Livingston-Little, *Mexican War Diary of Tennery,* 45, 65.

CHAPTER 9. THE LAND OF THE MONTEZUMAS

1. Lew Wallace, *Lew Wallace,* 2:895–96.
2. Jedidiah Morse, *Geography Made Easy: Being an Abridgement of the American Universal Geography* (Boston: J. T. Buckingham, Printer, 1807), 265–70; H. Huntington, Jr., *View of South America and Mexico* (N.p., 1825), 207–208; "Mitchell's Pocket Map of Texas, Oregon, and California," *Wilmington (N.C.) Journal,* June 26, 1846, and Feb. 12, 1847; "Maps," *Carolina Watchman,* Salisbury, N.C., Aug. 14, 1846.
3. Joel Robert Poinsett, *Notes on Mexico Made in the Autumn of 1822, Accompanied by an Historical Sketch of the Revolution, and Translations of Official Reports of the Present State of That Country* (Philadelphia: H. C. Carey and I. Lea, 1824); Waddy Thompson, *Recollections of Mexico* (New York: Wiley and Putnam, 1846); Brantz Mayer, *Mexico as It Was and as It Is* (New York: J. Winchester, New World Press, 1844); Frances Calderón de la Barca, *Life in Mexico during a Residence of Two Years in That Country,* 2 vols. (Boston: Charles C. Little and James Brown, 1843); William H. Prescott, *History of the Conquest of Mexico* (Philadelphia: J. B. Lippincott, 1843); Kendall, *Narrative of the Texan Santa Fe Expedition;* Green, *Journal of the Texian Expedition Against Mier;* Josiah Gregg, *Commerce of the Prairies: Or, The Journal of a Santa Fe Trader, During Eight Expeditions across the Great Western Prairies, and a Residence of Nearly Nine Years in Northern Mexico* (New York: Henry G. Langley, 1844); Lansford W. Hastings, *The Emigrant's Guide to Oregon and California, Containing Scenes and Incidents of a Party of Oregon Emigrants; A Description of Oregon; Scenes and Incidents of a Party of California Emigrants; And a Description of California; With a Description of the Different Routes to Those Countries; and All Necessary Information Relative to the Equipment, Supplies, and the Method of Traveling* (1845; facsimile ed., Bedford, Mass.: Applewood Books, 1994); Richard Henry Dana, *Two Years Before the Mast* (N.p., 1840); "Chapparal," *Wilmington (N.C.) Journal,* June 5, 1846; "Lectures on Mexico," *Wilmington (N.C.) Journal,* Oct. 30, 1846; "Chapparal," *Carolina Watchman,* Salisbury, N.C., May 22, 1846; "Population and Character of the Inhabitants of Mexico," *Carolina Watchman,* Salisbury, N.C., May 29, 1846; and "The Spaniards—Agriculture and Politics" and "Mexican Towns," *Carolina Watchman,* Salisbury, N.C., June 19, 1846.
4. Winfield Scott, *Memoirs,* 2:457–58; Campbell, "Mexican War Letters of W. B. Campbell," 165; "Mexican Antiquities," *American Star,* Mexico City, Oct. 23, 1847; "Aztec Club," *American Star,* Mexico City, Oct. 24, 1847; Robert Johannsen, *To the Halls of the Montezumas: The Mexican War in the American Imagination* (New York: Oxford University Press, 1985), 154–59.
5. For a brief but detailed description of Mexico on the eve of the Mexican War, see S. Augustus Mitchell, *Mitchell's Geographical Reader: A System of Modern Geography, Comprising a Description of the World, with Its Grand Divisions, America, Eu-*

rope, Asia, Africa, and Oceania. Designed for Instruction in Schools and Families (Philadelphia: Thomas, Cowperthwait, and Co., 1845), 177–89.

6. Ibid.

7. Engelman, "Second Illinois," 389; Scribner, *Camp Life of a Volunteer,* 22; Ames, "Doctor Comes to California," pt. 1, *California Historical Quarterly* 21 (1942): 214; Furber, *Twelve Month Volunteer,* 390.

8. Ferrell, *Monterrey Is Ours!,* 5; Frank S. Edwards, *A Campaign in New Mexico with Colonel Doniphan* (Philadelphia: Carey and Hart, 1847), 35; Gibson, *Journal of a Soldier,* 139–40, 155, 160, 175, 179, 185; McGroarty, "Richardson's Journal," pt. 1, 223; Livingston-Little, *Mexican War Diary of Tennery,* 30; Engelman, "Second Illinois," 385; Lewis H. Wunder to Friend, Feb. 24, 1847, Wunder Papers, Mississippi State Archives, Jackson, Miss.; Hinds, "Mexican War Journal of Leander M. Cox," pt. 1, 48; S. Compton Smith, *Chile Con Carne,* 270–73.

9. Zachary Taylor, *Letters,* 100; Hinds, "Mexican War Journal of Leander M. Cox," pt. 1, 48, and pt. 2, 214; Holland, "Diary of a Texan Volunteer," 21; Lewis H. Wunder to Friend, Feb. 24, 1847, Wunder Papers, Mississippi State Archives, Jackson, Miss.; Peck, *Sign of the Eagle,* 15; Brackett, *General Lane's Brigade,* 31; Engelman, "Second Illinois," 369, 429; John H. Moore, "Private Johnson Fights," 211; Gibson, *Journal of a Soldier,* 222; *North American,* Mexico City, Nov. 16, 1847; Ferrell, *Monterrey Is Ours!,* 17; Peskin, *Volunteers,* 103; Livingston-Little, *Mexican War Diary of Tennery,* 17, 24; S. Compton Smith, *Chile Con Carne,* 273–75; McGroarty, "Richardson's Journal," pt. 1, 234. Surgeon S. Compton Smith recounts that he treated tarantula bites by giving the patient, internally and externally, liberal doses of whiskey.

10. Scribner, *Camp Life of a Volunteer,* 40–41; Engelman, "Second Illinois," 390.

11. Mayer, *Mexico As It Was,* 300–301. For a recent study of Mexican society during the Mexican War period, see Ruth R. Olivera and Liliane Crété, *Life in Mexico Under Santa Anna, 1822–1855* (Norman: University of Oklahoma Press, 1991), 1991.

12. Scribner, *Camp Life of a Volunteer,* 21; Campbell, "Mexican War Letters of W. B. Campbell," 137; Goetzmann, "Our First Foreign War," 92; John H. Moore, "Private Johnson Fights," 223; Hinds, "Mexican War Journal of Leander M. Cox," pt. 1, 47; Engelman, "Second Illinois," 373, 385; Zeh, *Immigrant Soldier,* 42; *Southron,* Jackson, Miss., Sept. 23, 1846; *Raleigh Star and North Carolina Gazette,* Sept. 15, 1847; and *Raleigh Star and North Carolina Gazette,* Sept. 15, 1847. "The Anglo-Saxon and the Spaniard," an article published widely in U.S. papers, compared the characteristics of the two ethnic groups. See, e.g., *Raleigh Star and North Carolina Gazette,* Sept. 15, 1847.

13. *Mississippi Democrat,* Carrollton, Miss., Dec. 30, 1846; Engelman, "Second Illinois," 29; "Public Amusements," *North American,* Mexico City, Nov. 5, 1847; Edwards, *A Campaign in New Mexico,* 147; Zeh, *Immigrant Soldier,* 46, 84; Cook, "Mexican War Reminiscences," 457–58; Chamberlain, *My Confession,* 210–17; Colyer Meriwether, *Raphael Semmes* (Philadelphia: George W. Jacobs and Co., 1913), 65–66. Chamberlain claimed that he had several Mexican lovers, including "Carmeleita," whom he considered his wife. He found her "young and lovely . . . as fair as any

Anglo Saxon lady." According to his tale, she fell into the hands of her former master, a cruel husband from an arranged marriage, who carried her "to a lone ranch where she was outraged by Canales' whole gang of demons and then cut to pieces!"

14. McGroarty, "Richardson's Journal," pt. 2, 332; Furber, *Twelve Month Volunteer,* 207; Robert Ryal Miller, *Mexican War Journal of Kirkham,* 21, 37; "An Easy Guide to the Spanish Language," *American Star,* Mexico City, Nov. 3 and 30, 1847. American publishers produced pocket-size foreign-language dictionaries prior to the war, including *A Pocket Dictionary of the Spanish and English Languages. Compiled from the Last Edition of Neuman and Bartetti* (Philadelphia: Samuel Wakeling, 1840).

15. Edwards, *A Campaign in New Mexico,* 59–60; Furber, *Twelve Month Volunteer,* 403–404; Scribner, *Camp Life of a Volunteer,* 31, 223–25, 293; Engelman, "Second Illinois," 399, 437; Livingston-Little, *Mexican War Diary of Tennery,* 17; Meriwether, *Raphael Semmes,* 66; Ferrell, *Monterrey Is Ours!,* 89, 105.

16. Furber, *Twelve Month Volunteer,* 195–96; Engelman, "Second Illinois," 398, 437; "Soldiers," *North American,* Mexico City, Nov. 5, 1847; Peck, *Sign of the Eagle,* 29–30, 63; Zeh, *Immigrant Soldier,* 42. The *North American,* Nov. 5, 1847, ran the following notice warning to American soldiers in Mexico City: "Soldiers! When you request a blanket man to open and show whether he has arms, take the precaution to feel his wrists. His hands will be covered with his blanket when his breast is open and ten to one a knife is tied to one of them." According to Furber, the Mexican lower classes wore the *horongo,* a blanket similar to the serape.

17. Olivera and Crété, *Life in Mexico,* 20–21, 22–43.

18. Ibid., 146, 150; Engelman, "Second Illinois," 404, 420; Furber, *Twelve Month Volunteer,* 204, 207–12; Peskin, *Volunteers,* 181–82; "Mexican vs. American Slavery," *American Star,* Puebla, Mexico, July 25, 1847; Meriwether, *Raphael Semmes,* 67–68; May, "Invisible Men," 473–75. Although Olivera and Crété cite a modern study that discounts the existence of debt peonage, American soldiers claimed to have witnessed it.

19. Goetzmann, "Our First Foreign War," 92; Lt. Theodore Thadeus Sobieski Laidley to His Father, June 3, 1847, in A80.92s, Folder 1, DeGolyer Library, Southern Methodist University, Dallas, Tex.; Hinds, "Mexican War Journal of Leander M. Cox," pt. 2, 221; Furber, *Twelve Month Volunteer,* 219–20; Andrew Jackson Trussell to John Trussell, May 5, 1848, Trussell Family Papers, Box GA 66-4, SCUTA; Rowe, "Mexican War Letters of Coffey," 245; Oswandel, *Notes on the Mexican War,* 223.

20. Peskin, *Volunteers,* 196; Robert Ryal Miller, *Mexican War Journal of Kirkham,* 27, 78; Zeh, *Immigrant Soldier,* 48, 52, 84; Oswandel, *Notes on the Mexican War,* 209, 219; McGroarty, "Richardson's Journal," pt. 3, 517–18; Furber, *Twelve Month Volunteer,* 221, 349; S. Compton Smith, *Chile Con Carne,* 196–98; Pace, "Diary and Letters of Rogers," 264, 280; Stella M. Drumm, *Down the Santa Fe Trail and into Mexico: The Diary of Susan Shelby Magoffin, 1846–1847* (Lincoln: University of Nebraska Press, 1982), 209–10, 236; Feldberg, *Turbulent Era,* 10; William E. Connelley, *Doniphan's Expedition and the Conquest of New Mexico and California* (Topeka: William E. Connelley Publisher, 1907), 69.

21. Peskin, *Volunteers*, 181–82; Pace, "Diary and Letters of Rogers," 268; Winfield Scott, "A Proclamation to the Good People of Mexico," Head Quarters of the Army, Vera Cruz, Apr. 11, 1847.

22. Merk, *Manifest Destiny and Mission*, 157–64; Campbell, "Mexican War Letters of W. B. Campbell," 150; Livingston-Little, *Mexican War Diary of Tennery*, 37–38; Andrew Jackson Trussell to John Trussell, May 5, 1848, Trussell Family Papers, Box GA 66-4, SCUTA; Lawton, *Artillery Officer*, 237; Peskin, *Volunteers*, 182; Zeh, *Immigrant Soldier*, 52–54. For fuller discussion, see Heitala, *Manifest Destiny;* and Horsman, *Race and Manifest Destiny.*

23. Furber, *Twelve Month Volunteer*, 410, 427–28; Pace, "Diary and Letters of Rogers," 268; Peskin, *Volunteers*, 181; Campbell, "Mexican War Letters of W. B. Campbell," 150; Merk, *Manifest Destiny and Mission*, 31, 33–34. Anthony F. C. Wallace, *The Long Bitter Trail: Andrew Jackson and the Indians* (New York: Hill and Wang, 1993), 38. Wallace analyzed the philosophical foundations of the policy of Indian removal and linked it to Emmerich de Vattel, *The Laws of Nations* (1758). According to Wallace, "The right of the agriculturalist to acquire land for expansion was superior to the claim of the primitive hunter."

24. Engelman, "Second Illinois," 393, 403, 416; "Mexican vs. American Slavery," *American Star,* Puebla, Mexico, July 25, 1847; "The City," *American Star,* Mexico City, Oct. 7, 1847; Andrew Jackson Trussell to John Trussell, May 5, 1848, Trussell Family Papers, Box GA 66-4, SCUTA; Goetzmann, "Our First Foreign War," 93; "By the One Legged Sergeant," *A Sketch of the Life and Character of Gen. Taylor, The American Hero and People's Man; Together with a Concise History of the Mexican War* (Boston: John R. Hall, 1847), 13–15; Connelley, *Doniphan's Expedition*, 67, 201.

25. Robert Ryal Miller, *Mexican War Journal of Kirkham*, 78.

CHAPTER 10. MR. POLK'S ARMY

1. Grant, *Papers*, 1:105; James M. McCaffrey, *Army of Manifest Destiny: The American Soldier in the Mexican War, 1846–1848* (New York: New York University Press, 1992). In this book, McCaffrey coined the term "Army of Manifest Destiny."

2. Polk, *Diary*, 1:437–40, 1:149–51, 1:179–80, 1:231, 1:240–42.

3. Ibid., 2:117–19, 2:150, 2:429–33, 2:439, 3:22–23, 3:32, 3:80–81. It was believed that Adjutant Jones, who disagreed with the idea of appointing enlisted men as officers, tried to stall the president until a new class from West Point could graduate and make available more than enough candidates for the vacant positions.

4. Polk, *Diary,* 2:221, 2:441, 2:442, 2:443, 3:56, 3:57, 3:79–80, 3:85, 3:118, 3:152, 3:154; Heitman, *Historical Register,* 1:825, 1:1048. Both Robert B. Reynolds (Tennessee) and Louis D. Wilson (North Carolina) were appointed to the army by Polk.

5. Polk, *Diary,* 1:413–14; Heitman, *Historical Register,* 1:560; Doubleday, *Journals of the Barbours,* 102; Justin Smith, *War with Mexico,* 1:364–65, 2:185–86; Hinds, "Mexican War Journal of Leander M. Cox," pt. 3, 55. Capt. Leander Cox, a Kentucky volunteer in Mexico City at the time of the scandal, reported that "in all things pertaining to the war[, Worth] sides with the administration of Mr. Polk. I also

learn he has been hitherto a Whig in politics. . . . I conjecture that he has been induced to take such views by the hope of being the Democratic candidate for the next Presidency."

6. Walter Jones, *The Case of the Battalion Stated, with an Exposition of the Grounds Upon Which Chas. Lee Jones, Esq., Expected to Have Had Command of the Battalion (Consisting of Three Companies Raised by Himself in the District of Columbia, and Two To Be Raised in Maryland,) Conferred Upon Him, as of Right and Justice Due Both to Him and to the Officers and Men Who Had Volunteered to Serve Under His Command* (Washington, D.C.: J. and G. S. Gideon, 1847), 10, 11, 15, 22; Fanny Lee Jones, "Walter Jones and His Times," *Records of the Columbia Historical Society* 5 (1902): 139–50. Walter Jones claimed to have been driven to action "when I beheld the overwhelming power and influence of an *Administration* thrown against a private individual." In examining the party affiliations of the 8 captains of the battalion in question, Jones found that 5 were Democrats and 3 were Whigs. Jones claimed that, regardless of political affiliation, all had agreed to serve under his son, and all were upset at being placed under the command of a regular officer.

7. U.S. Congress, Senate, *Message from the President of the United States in Answer to a Resolution of the Senate, Calling for the Proceedings of the Court of Inquiry Convened at Saltillo, Mexico, Jan. 12, 1848, for the Purpose of Obtaining Full Information Relative to an Alleged Mutiny at Buena Vista, about the 15th August, 1847,* 30th Cong., 1st sess., Exec. Doc. No. 62, pp. 9, 101, 102, 103, 161, 162, 175, 181, 187, 204; *Mexican War Correspondence,* 30th Cong., 1st sess., Exec. Doc. No. 60, p. 448. Scott's order to Wool and Kearny read in part, "You may . . . grant discharges from the service of the United States, 'honorable' or otherwise, according to the conduct in [the volunteer] service, upon the presentation of such circumstances as may appear to you of grave interest to the officers themselves, or to the public service." Scott issued this order "considering [Wool's] remoteness from the general headquarters of the army."

8. U.S. Congress, House, *Message of the President Relative to the Dismissal from the Public Service of J. S. Pender, and G. E. B. Singletary,* 30th Cong., 1st sess., 1848, Exec. Doc. No. 78, p. 230; U.S. Congress, Senate, *Message from the President re Proceedings of Court of Inquiry at Saltillo, Mexico,* 30th Cong., 1st sess., Exec. Doc. No. 62, pp. 7, 80, 208. Josiah S. Pender entered the U.S. Military Academy in 1836 but failed to graduate.

9. U.S. Congress, House, *Message of the President Relative to the Dismissal from the Public Service of J. S. Pender, and G. E. B. Singletary,* 30th Cong., 1st sess., 1848, Exec. Doc. No. 78, pp. 7–10.

10. Tyler, *Concise History of the Mormon Battalion,* 117; Polk, *Diary,* 1:478; 2:237–39.

11. Polk, *Diary,* 2:307, 2:340, 2:341, 2:346, 2:347, 2:348, 2:368, 2:369; Robert R. Jones, "Mexican War Diary of J. L. Kemper," 398; Donald B. Cole, *Martin Van Buren and the American Political System* (Princeton, N.J.: Princeton University Press, 1984), 387–405; Andrew W. Young, *The American Statesman: A Political History Exhibiting the Origins, Nature, and Practical Operation of Constitutional Govern-*

ment in the United States and the Rise of Political Parties (New York: J. C. Derby, 1855), 808–909. Within the Democratic party, a faction was developing, led by ex-President Martin Van Buren, that was most troublesome for Polk and his supporters. Van Buren headed a rising group of party dissidents, later called Free Soilers. Going into the Democratic party convention in 1844, Van Buren had been the front-runner. When his own nomination was blocked by southern expansionists, Van Buren lent his support to Polk, an old political ally, after Gideon Pillow mounted a push for the Tennessean. Afterward, Van Buren believed that Polk had slighted his wing of the New York Democratic party in the makeup of the cabinet. He split with the president when Polk made William L. Marcy, a member of a rival New York faction, secretary of war. Henceforth, Van Buren was Polk's personal and political foe. The makeup of the 29th Congress (Mar. 4, 1845–Mar. 4, 1847) was as follows: 31 Democrats and 25 Whigs in the Senate; and 143 Democrats, 77 Whigs, and 6 others in the House. In the 30th Congress (Mar. 4, 1847–Mar. 4, 1849), there were: 36 Democrats, 21 Whigs, and 1 other in the Senate; and 115 Whigs, 108 Democrats, and 4 others in the House.

12. Polk, *Diary*, 1:478; 2:278–80, 2:375, 2:399–405; Robert R. Jones, "Mexican War Diary of J. L. Kemper," 408.

13. Polk, *Diary*, 1:466–67; 1:483, 2:323, 2:383.

14. Robert R. Jones, "Mexican War Diary of J. L. Kemper," 387–413, 418.

15. Polk, *Diary*, 1:413, 1:416, 1:478, 1:483, 2:236, 3:120.

16. Richardson, *Messages of the Presidents*, 4:483.

17. Polk, *Diary*, 2:294, 2:295, 2:346, 2:439, 2:457; Richardson, *Messages of the Presidents*, 4:508.

18. Meade, *Life and Letters*, 1:108, 1:139, 1:162; Henry, *Campaign Sketches*, 152; Skelton, *American Profession of Arms*, 210–12; William Starr Myers, *Mexican War Diary of McClellan*, 18.

19. Justin Smith, *War with Mexico*, 2:512–13.

20. Meade, *Life and Letters*, 1:108, 1:139, 1:162; Doubleday, *Journals of the Barbours*, 90; William Starr Myers, *Mexican War Diary of McClellan*, 16, 28, 79; Lawton, *Artillery Officer*, 46–47; James I. Robertson, *General A. P. Hill: The Story of a Confederate Warrior* (New York: Random House, 1987), 15–17.

21. Engelman, "Second Illinois," 395; Ferrell, *Monterrey Is Ours!*, 83; Jefferson Davis, *The Papers of Jefferson Davis*, ed. James T. McIntosh (Baton Rouge: Louisiana State University Press, 1981), 3:77–79, 84–88; Smith and Judah, *Chronicles of the Gringos*, 79–82; John Robert Blount, *Reminiscence of a Campaign in Mexico; by a Member of the "Bloody First"* (Nashville, Tenn.: John York and Co., 1849), 167–74; Lt. Theodore Thadeus Sobieski Laidley to His Father, Oct. 24, 1847, in A80.92s, Folder 1, DeGolyer Library, Southern Methodist University, Dallas, Tex.

22. Campbell, "Mexican War Letters of W. B. Campbell," 166; Heitman, *Historical Register*, 1:346; Joseph E. Chance, ed., *Mexico Under Fire: Being the Diary of Samuel Ryan Curtis, 3rd Ohio Volunteer Regiment, During the Military Occupation of Northern Mexico* (Fort Worth: Texas Christian University Press, 1994), 23, 108, 109.

23. R. C. Buley, "Indiana in the Mexican War: The Buena Vista Controversy," *Indiana Magazine of History* 15 (Mar., 1920): 309; Chance, *Mexican War Journal of Smith*, 48.

24. Tocqueville, *Democracy in America*, 2:286–87, 2:295–96; John A. Lynn, *Bayonets of the Republic* (Champaign: University of Illinois Press, 1984), 64, 100. Lynn notes that many of the characteristics ascribed by Tocqueville to a democratic army existed in the army of republican France. He concludes that French regulars and volunteers "did not always mix well." Lynn cites several leaders of the French Revolution whose words resemble those uttered in the 1840s by supporters of American volunteer system. General Dumouriez, for example, said, "The man who binds for a time his liberty in order to defend the public liberty, loses none of his rights as a citizens." One French republican viewed discipline "as an instrument of slavery created by aristocrats." A consistent philosophy appears to guide republican or democratic armies.

25. Tocqueville, *Democracy in America*, 2:287, 2:295–96.

26. Katcher, *Mexican-American War*, 6–8; Justin Smith, *War with Mexico*, 1:207; Kreidberg and Henry, *History of the Military Mobilization in the United States*, 71–72; Alfred J. Henderson, "A Morgan Country Volunteer," 398; McGroarty, "Richardson's Journal," pt. 2, 347. In "A Morgan Country Volunteer," the remark of Sgt. John B. Duncan following the Battle of Buena Vista typifies the state pride exhibited by volunteers: "Our men fought like tigers and Illinois has gained for herself and her sons immortal honor."

27. Lawton, *Artillery Officer*, 148; Chance, *Mexican War Journal of Smith*, 187; Campbell, "Mexican War Letters of W. B. Campbell," 150; Chance, *Mexico Under Fire*, 190; Andrew Jackson Trussell to John Trussell, Oct. 26, 1847, Trussell Family Papers, Box GA 66-3, SCUTA; William Seaton Henry, *Campaign Sketches*, 216.

28. George H. Hickman, *The Democratic Text Book, Being a Compendium of the Principles of the Democratic Party* (New York: Burgess, Stringer and Co.; Philadelphia: G. B. Zieber and Co., 1848), 7–8.

EPILOGUE: A PYRRHIC VICTORY

1. Schroeder, *Mr. Polk's War*, 46–48, 67–68, 71–72, 77, 79–80, 120, 124–27, 136–39, 146–47; Charles Buxton Going, *David Wilmot, Free Soiler* (New York: D. Appleton, 1924), chs. 7–14; Richard R. Stenberg, "The Motivation of the Wilmot Proviso." *Mississippi Historical Review* 18 (Mar., 1932): 535–40; Cole, *Martin Van Buren*, 409–11. An older work, Wilfred E. Binkley, *American Political Parties: Their Natural History*, chs. 4–9, presents a concise story of the evolution and devolution of the Whigs and Jacksonian Democrats. For an excellent analysis of the Wilmot Proviso and its affect on the Democratic party, see Chaplain W. Morrison, *Democratic Politics and Sectionalism: The Wilmot Proviso Controversy* (Chapel Hill: University of North Carolina, 1967).

2. Cole, *Martin Van Buren*, 409–11. For a discussion of Free Soilers and the struggle

for Kansas, see James A. Rawley, *Race and Politics: "Bleeding Kansas" and the Coming of the Civil War* (Lincoln: University of Nebraska Press, 1979).

3. Binkley, *American Political Parties,* chs. 7–9; Cole, *Martin Van Buren,* 409–19. Van Buren returned to the mainstream Democratic party after his defection in 1848. The Republican campaign slogan was a series of high ideals strung together to form a sonorous alliteration: Free soil, free speech, free labor, free men and Frémont. The first four phrases had been the rallying cry of the Free Soil Party. The Republican party also provided a home for a number of Nativists or Know Nothings.

4. Binkley, *American Political Parties,* ch. 9.

5. David W. Bartlett, *Life and Public Services of Hon. Abraham Lincoln* (1860; facsimile ed., Freeport, N.Y.: Books for Libraries, 1969), 29–32; William H. Herndon and Jesse William Weike, *Herndon's Lincoln: The True Story of a Great Life,* 3 vols. (Chicago: Belford, Clarke, and Co., 1889), 2:277–79; Isaac N. Arnold, *The Life of Abraham Lincoln* (Chicago: Jansen, McClurg, and Co., 1885), 101–102; Schroeder, *Mr. Polk's War,* 153; Ulysses S. Grant, *Personal Memoirs of U. S. Grant* (New York: Charles L. Webster and Co., 1894), 37–38, 45.

6. Charles H. Owen, *The Justice of the Mexican War* (New York: G. P. Putnam's Sons, 1908), 10, 18–19.

7. Otis A. Singletary, The Mexican War (Chicago: University of Chicago Press, 1960), 5; Grant, *Personal Memoirs,* 37; Robert Leckie, *From Sea to Shining Sea: From the War of 1812 to the Mexican War, the Saga of American Expansion* (New York: Harper Collins Publishers, 1993), 528; William S. McFeely, *Grant: A Biography* (New York: Norton, 1981), 35. On Grant's role in promoting good relations with Mexico, see David M. Pletcher, *Rails, Mines, and Progress: Seven American Promoters in Mexico, 1867–1911* (Ithaca, N.Y.: Cornell University Press, 1958), ch. 5.

8. Cruffut, *Fifty Years in Camp and Field,* 228–29; Richard Griswold del Castillo, *Treaty of Guadalupe Hidalgo: A Legacy of Conflict* (Norman: University of Oklahoma Press, 1990), 122; Bartlett, *Life and Public Services of Lincoln,* 29–32; Owen, *Justice of the Mexican War,* 47.

9. William Graham Sumner, *Andrew Jackson* (Boston: N.p., 1882), 358–59.

Bibliography

GOVERNMENT DOCUMENTS

Compiled Service Records of the Mississippi Volunteers in *the War with Mexico*. 9 rolls. Microfilm Series M863, National Archives, Washington, D.C.

U.S. Adjutant-General's Office, War Department. *Official Army Register, for 1841. Published by Order of the Secretary of War, in Compliance with the Resolution of the Senate, December 13, 1815, and the Resolution of the House of Representatives, February 1, 1830.* Washington, D.C.: J. and G. S. Gideon, Printers, 1841.

U.S. Adjutant-General's Office, War Department. *Official Army Register, for 1848. Published by Order of the Secretary of War, in Compliance with the Resolution of the Senate, December 13, 1815, and the Resolutions of the House of Representatives, February 1, 1830, and August 30, 1842.* Washington, D.C.: C. Alexander, 1848.

U.S. Adjutant-General's Office. *Orders to General Zachary Taylor of the Army of Occupation in the Mexican War, 1845–1847.* 3 rolls. Microfilm Series M1034, National Archives, Washington, D.C.

U.S. Congress, *Report of the Secretary of War, Which Accompanied the Annual Message of the President of the United States, To Both Houses of the Thirtieth Congress, 1847.* Washington, D.C. Wendell and Van Benthuysen, December, 1847.

U.S. Congress. House. *Message from the President of the United States to the Two Houses of Congress, at the Commencement of the Second Session of the Twenty-Ninth Congress.* 29th Cong., 2d sess., 1846, House Document No. 4.

U.S. Congress. House. *Message from the President of the United States to the Two Houses of Congress at the Commencement of the First Session of the Twenty-Ninth Congress: Report of the Secretary of War.* 29th Cong., 1st sess., 1845, House Document No. 2.

U.S. Congress. House. *Message of the President Relative to the Dismissal from the Public Service of J. S. Pender and G. E. B. Singletary.* 30th Cong., 1st sess., 1848, Executive Document No. 78.

U.S. Congress. House. *Mexican War Correspondence. Message of the President of the United States, and the Correspondence, Therewith, Communicated, between the Secretary of War and Other Officers of the Government upon the Subject of the Mexican War.* 30th Cong., 1st sess., 1848, Executive Document No. 60.

U.S. Congress. House. *Military Forces Employed in the Mexican War: Letter from the Secretary of War Transmitting Information in Answer to a Resolution of the House, of July 31, 1848, Relative to the Military Forces Employed in the Late War with Mexico.* 31st Cong., 1st sess., 1850, Executive Document No. 24.

U.S. Congress. House. *Report of the Secretary of War.* 29th Cong., 2d sess., 1846, House Document No. 4.

U.S. Congress. Senate. *Message from the President of the United States in Answer to a Resolution of the Senate, Calling for the Proceedings of the Court of Inquiry Convened at Saltillo, Mexico, January 12, 1848, for the Purpose of Obtaining Full Information Relative to an Alleged Mutiny at Buena Vista, about the 15th August, 1847.* 30th Cong., 1st sess., 1848, Executive Document No. 62.

U.S. Congress. Senate. *Message of the President of the United States, in Answer to a Resolution of the Senate of the 5th instant, Relative to the Calling of Volunteers or Militia into the Service of the United States, by an Officer of the Army, without Legal Authority; to the Measures Adopted for the Defense of the Southern Frontier, &c.* 29th Cong., 1st sess., 1846, Senate Document No. 378.

U.S. Congress. Senate. *Petition of the Officers of the United States Army in Mexico, Praying [for] the Passage of a Law Providing for the Retirement of Old and Disabled Officers.* 30th Cong., 1st sess., 1847, Miscellaneous Document No. 11.

U.S. War Department. *Abstract of Infantry Tactics; Including Exercises and Manoeuvres of Light-Infantry and Riflemen; For the Use of the Militia of the United States.* Boston: Hilliard, Gray, Little, and Wilkins, 1830.

U.S. War Department. *General Regulations for the Army of the United States, 1841.* Washington, D.C.: J. and G. E. Gideon, 1841.

U.S. War Department. *General Regulations for the Army of the United States, 1847.* Washington, D.C.: J. and G. E. Gideon, 1847.

U.S. War Department. *Instruction for Field Artillery, Horse and Foot. Translated from the French, and Arranged for the Service of the United States, by Robert Anderson, Captain in the Staff of U.S. Army.* Philadelphia: Robert P. Desilver, 1839.

U.S. War Department. *Ordnance Manual of the Use of the Officers of the United States Army, 1841.* Washington, D.C.: J. and G. S. Gideon, Printers, 1841.

U.S. War Department. *Ordnance Manual of the Use of the Officers of the United States Army, 1861.* Washington, D.C.: J. B. Lippincott and Company, 1861.

MANUSCRIPTS

Army of Mexico, First Division, Second Brigade. Papers. Manuscript Division, United States Military History Research Collection, Carlisle, Pennsylvania.

Bloom, John Porter. "With the American Army into Mexico, 1846–1848." Ph.D. dissertation, Emory University, 1956.

Bodson, Robert L. "A Description of the United States Occupation of Mexico as Reported by American Newspapers Published in Vera Cruz, Puebla, and Mexico City; September 14, 1847, to July 31, 1848." Ph.D. dissertatiuon, Ball State University, 1970.

Bowen Collection, Isaac. Manuscript Division, United States Military History Research Collection, Carlisle, Pennsylvania.

Cashion, Peggy. "Women and the Mexican War." M.A. thesis, University of Texas at Arlington, 1990.

Duncan Papers, James. Manuscript Division, United States Military History Research Collection, Carlisle, Pennsylvania.

Meginness Papers, John F. Special Collections, University of Texas at Arlington, Arlington, Texas.

Miller, Roger Gene. "Winfield Scott and the Sinews of War: The Logistics of the Mexico City Campaign, October 1846–September 1847." M.A. thesis, North Texas State University, 1976.

Miscellaneous Mexican War File. Special Collections, University of Texas at Arlington, Arlington, Texas.

Smith-Kirby-Webster-Black Family Papers. Manuscript Division, United States Military History Research Collection, Carlisle, Pennsylvania.

Trussell Family Papers. Special Collections, University of Texas at Arlington, Arlington, Texas.

Wettemann, Robert P. "The Enlisted Soldier in the United States Army: A Study of the Seventh Regiment, U.S. Infantry, 1815–1860." M.A. thesis, Texas A&M University, 1995.

Winders, Richard B. "Mr. Polk's Army: Politics, Patronage, and the American Military in the Mexican War." Ph.D. dissertation, Texas Christian University, 1994.

———. "The Role of the Mississippi Volunteers in Northern Mexico, 1846–1848." M.A. thesis, University of Texas at Arlington, 1990.

Wunder Papers, Lewis H. Mississippi State Archives, Jackson, Mississippi.

PUBLISHED SOURCES

The American's Guide: Comprising the Declaration of Independence, The Articles of Confederation, The Constitution of the United States, and The Constitutions of the Several States Composing the Union. Philadelphia: Hogan and Thompson, 1841.

Anthony, F. C. Wallace. The Long Bitter Trail: Andrew Jackson and the Indians. New York: Hill and Wang, 1993.

Appleton's Cyclopedia of American Biography. 6 vols. New York: D. Appleton and Company, 1888.

Arnold, Isaac N. The Life of Abraham Lincoln. Chicago: Jansen, McClurg, and Company, 1885.

Ballentine, George. Autobiography of an English Soldier in the United States Army; Comprising Observations and Adventures in the States and Mexico. New York: Stringer and Townsend, 1853.

Bannon, John Francis. The Spanish Borderlands Frontier, 1513–1821. Albuquerque: University of New Mexico Press, 1974.

Barker, Eugene C. The Life of Stephen F. Austin, Founder of Texas, 1793–1836: A Chapter in the Westward Movement of the Anglo–American People. Austin: University of Texas Press, 1990.

Bartlett, David W. Life and Public Services of Hon. Abraham Lincoln. 1860; facsimile ed., Freeport, N.Y.: Books for Libraries, 1969.

Barton, Henry W. *Texas Volunteers in the Mexican War.* Waco, Tex.: Texian Press, 1970.

Bauer, K. Jack. *Zachary Taylor: Soldier, Planter, Statesman of the Old South.* Baton Rouge: Louisiana State University Press, 1985.

Bemrose, John. *Reminiscences of the Second Seminole War.* Edited by John K. Mahon. Gainesville: University of Florida Press, 1966.

Benson, Lee. *The Concept of Jacksonian Democracy: New York as a Test Case.* Princeton, N.J.: Princeton University Press, 1961.

Benton, Thomas H. *Thirty Years' View; Or, A History of the Working of the American Government for Thirty Years, from 1820 to 1850.* 2 vols. New York: Appleton and Company, 1856.

Bergeron, Paul H. *The Presidency of James K. Polk.* Lawrence: University of Kansas Press, 1987.

Bigelow, John. *Memoir of the Life and Public Service of John Charles Frémont.* New York: Derby and Jackson, 1856.

Binkley, Wilfred E. *American Political Parties: Their Natural History.* New York: Knopf, 1971.

Birkhimer, William E. *Historical Sketch of the Organization, Administration, Materiél and Tactics of the Artillery, United States Army.* N.p.: James J. Chapman, 1884; reprinted New York: Greenwood Press, 1968.

Blackwood, Emma Jerome, ed. *To Mexico with Scott: Letters of Captain E. Kirby Smith to His Wife.* Cambridge, Mass.: Harvard University Press, 1917.

Blount, John Robert. *Reminiscence of a Campaign in Mexico; By a Member of the "Bloody First."* Nashville, Tenn.: John York and Company, 1849.

Brack, Gene M. *Mexico Views Manifest Destiny, 1821–1846: An Essay on the Origins of the Mexican War.* Albuquerque: University of New Mexico Press, 1975.

Brackett, Albert G. *General Lane's Brigade in Central Mexico.* Cincinnati, Ohio: H. W. Derby and Co., 1854.

Breckenridge, John C. "An Address on the Occasion of the Burial of the Kentucky Volunteers Who Fell at Buena Vista." Lexington: Observer and Reporter Office, 1847.

Brooks, Nathan Covington. *A Complete History of the Mexican War: Its Causes, Conduct, and Consequences, Comprising an Account of the Various Military and Naval Operations, from Its Commencement to the Treaty of Peace.* Philadelphia: Grigg, Elliot, and Company, 1849; reprinted Chicago: Rio Grande Press, 1965.

"By the One Legged Sergeant." *A Sketch of the Life and Character of Gen. Taylor, The American Hero and People's Man; Together with a Concise History of the Mexican War.* Boston: John R. Hall, 1847.

Cairns, John T. *The Recruit: A Compilation of Exercises and Movements of Infantry, Light Infantry, and Riflemen, According to the Latest Improvements. Respectfully Dedicated to the Recruits of the United States Army.* New York: Edward Walker, 1853.

Calderón de la Barca, Frances. *Life in Mexico During a Residence of Two Years in That Country.* 2 vols. Boston: Charles C. Little and James Brown, 1843.

Callan, John F. *The Military Laws of the United States, Relating to the Army, Volunteers, Militia, and to Bounty Lands and Pensions, From the Foundation of the Government to the Year 1863*. Philadelphia: George W. Childs, 1863.

Carleton, James Henry. *The Battle of Buena Vista with the Operations of the Army of Occupation for One Month*. New York: Harper and Brothers, 1848.

Carman, Harry J., and Reinhard H. Luthin. *Lincoln and the Patronage*. Gloucester, Mass.: Peter Smith, 1964.

Chalfant, William Y. *Dangerous Passage: The Santa Fe Trail and the Mexican War*. Norman: University of Oklahoma Press, 1994.

Chamberlain, Samuel E. *My Confession: The Recollections of a Rogue*. Lincoln: University of Nebraska Press, 1987.

Chance, Joseph E., ed. *The Mexican War Journal of Captain Franklin Smith*. Jackson: University Press of Mississippi, 1991.

———. *Mexico Under Fire: Being the Diary of Samuel Ryan Curtis, 3rd Ohio Volunteer Regiment, During the Military Occupation of Northern Mexico*. Fort Worth: Texas Christian University Press, 1994.

Child, David Lee. *The Taking of Naboth's Vineyard; Or, History of the Texas Conspiracy, an Examination of the Reasons Given by the Hon. J. C. Calhoun, Hon. R. J. Walker, and Others, for the Dismemberment and Robbery of the Republic of Texas*. New York: S. W. Benedict and Company, 1845.

Coffman, Edward M. *The Old Army: A Portrait of the American Army in Peacetime, 1784–1898*. New York: Oxford University Press, 1986.

Coggins, Jack. *Arms and Equipment of the Civil War*. Garden City, N.Y.: Doubleday and Company, 1963.

Connelley, William E. *Doniphan's Expedition and the Conquest of New Mexico and California*. Topeka: William E. Connelley, Publisher, 1907.

Cole, Donald B. *Martin Van Buren and the American Political System*. Princeton, N.J.: Princeton University Press, 1984.

Cooke, William B. *Speech of William M. Cooke, of Tennessee, in a Review of the War, Its Costs, and Executive Patronage; Delivered in the House of Representatives of the United States, May 18, 1848*. Washington: J. and G. S. Gideon, 1848.

Cooling, Franklin B., ed. *The New American State Papers, 1789–1860: Military Affairs*. 19 vols. Wilmington, Del.: Scholarly Resources, Inc., 1979.

Cooper, Samuel. *A Concise System of Instruction and Regulations for the Militia and Volunteers of the United States*. Philadelphia: Robert P. Desilver, 1836.

Crackel, Theodore J. *Mr. Jefferson's Army: Political and Social Reform of the Military Establishment, 1801–1809*. New York: New York University Press, 1987.

Cruffut, W. A. *Fifty Years in Camp and Field: Diary of Major General Ethan Allen Hitchcock, U.S.A.* Freeport, N.Y.: Books for Libraries Press, 1971.

Cunliffe, Marcus. *Soldiers and Civilians: The Martial Spirit in America, 1775–1865*. Boston: Little, Brown, and Company, 1968.

Cutrer, Thomas W. *Ben McCulloch and the Frontier Military Tradition*. Chapel Hill: University of North Carolina Press, 1993.

Dana, Richard Henry. *Two Years Before the Mast.* N.p., 1840.

Davis, Jefferson. *The Papers of Jefferson Davis.* Edited by James T. McIntosh. 5 vols. Baton Rouge: Louisiana State University Press, 1891.

Davis, Reuben. *Recollections of Mississippi and Mississippians.* Boston: Houghton Mifflin Company, 1890.

DeConde, Alexander. *This Affair of Louisiana.* Baton Rouge: Louisiana State University Press, 1976.

DeVoto, Bernardo. *The Course of Empire.* Boston: Houghton Mifflin Company, 1952.

Dillon, Lester R., Jr. *American Artillery in the Mexican War, 1846–1847.* Austin, Tex.: Presidial Press, 1975.

Dorsey, Stephen. *American Military Belts and Related Equipment.* London: Osprey Publishing, 1989.

Doubleday, Rhoda Van Bibber Tanner, ed. *Journals of the Late Brevet Major Philip Norbourne Barbour, Captain in the 3rd Regiment, United States Infantry, and His Wife, Martha Isabella Hopkins Barbour.* New York: G. P. Putnam's Sons, 1936.

Drumm, Stella M. *Down the Santa Fe Trail and into Mexico: The Diary of Susan Shelby Magoffin, 1846–1847.* Lincoln: University of Nebraska Press, 1982.

Edwards, Frank S. *A Campaign in New Mexico with Colonel Doniphan.* Philadelphia: Carey and Hart, 1847.

Egan, Ferol. *Frémont: Explorer for a Restless Nation.* New York: Doubleday and Company, 1977.

Elliot, Charles W. *Winfield Scott, the Soldier and the Man.* New York: Macmillan, 1937.

Feldberg, Michael. *The Turbulent Era: Riot and Discord in Jacksonian America.* New York: Oxford University Press, 1980.

Ferrell, Robert H., ed. *Monterrey Is Ours! The Mexican War Letters of Lieutenant Dana.* Lexington: University of Kentucky Press, 1990.

Frost, John. *The Mexican War and Its Warriors.* Philadelphia: H. Mansfield, 1848.

Fuess, Claude M. *The Life of Caleb Cushing.* 2 vols. Harcourt, Brace, and Company, 1923.

Furber, George C. *The Twelve Month Volunteer; Or, Journal of a Private in the Tennessee Regiment of Cavalry, in the Campaign in Mexico, 1846–47.* Cincinnati: J. A. and U. P. James, 1848.

Ganoe, William Addleman. *The History of the United States Army.* New York: D. Appleman and Company, 1924.

Gardner, Charles K. *A Dictionary of All Officers Who Have Been Commissioned, or Have Been Appointed and Served, in the Army of the United States.* New York: G. P. Putnam and Company, 1853.

General Zachary Taylor: The Louisiana President of the United States. New Orleans: Louisiana State Museum, 1937.

Gibson, George Rutledge. *Journal of a Soldier under Kearny and Doniphan.* Philadelphia: Porcupine Press, 1974.

Giddings, Luther. *Sketches of the Campaign in Northern Mexico in 1846–47.* New York: George P. Putman and Company, 1853.

Gillet, Mary C. *The Army Medical Department, 1818–1865.* Washington, D.C.: Center of Military History, 1987.

Giron, Ron G. *U.S. Military Edged Weapons of the Second Seminole War, 1835–1842.* New York: Edward Walker, 1853.

Going, Charles Buxton. *David Wilmot, Free Soiler.* New York: D. Appleton, 1924.

Goodrich, Samuel G. *First Book of History for Children and Youth. by the Author of Peter Parley's Tales.* Boston: Carter, Hendee, and Company, 1834.

Grant, Ulysses S. *The Papers of Ulysses S. Grant.* Edited by John Y. Simon. 15 vols. Carbondale: Southern Illinois University Press, 1967.

———. *Personal Memoirs of U. S. Grant.* 2 volumes in one. New York: Charles L. Webster and Company, 1894.

Graves, Donald E. *The Battle of Lundy's Lane: On the Niagara in 1814.* Baltimore: Nautical and Aviation Publishing Company of America, 1993.

Gray, James. *The Illinois.* New York: Farrar and Rinehart, 1940.

Green, Thomas Jefferson. *Journal of the Texian Expedition Against Mier; Subsequent Imprisonment of the Author; His Suffering, and the Final Escape from the Castle Perote.* New York: Harper and Brothers, 1845.

Gregg, Josiah. *Commerce of the Prairies: Or, The Journal of a Santa Fe Trader, During Eight Expeditions across the Great Western Prairies, and a Residence of Nearly Nine Years in Northern Mexico.* New York: Henry G. Langley, 1844.

———. *Diary and Letters of Josiah Gregg.* 2 vols. Norman: University of Oklahoma Press, 1941.

Griswold del Castillo, Richard. *The Treaty of Guadalupe Hidalgo: A Legacy of Conflict.* Norman: University of Oklahoma Press, 1990.

Hackenberg, Randy W. *Pennsylvania in the War with Mexico.* Shippensburg, Pa.: White Mane Publishing Company, 1992.

Hardin, Stephen L. *Texian Iliad: A Military History of the Texas Revolution, 1835–1836.* Austin: University of Texas Press, 1994.

Hastings, Lansford W. *The Emigrant's Guide to Oregon and California, Containing Scenes and Incidents of a Party of Oregon Emigrants; A Description of Oregon; Scenes and Incidents of a Party of California Emigrants; And a Description of California; With a Description of the Different Routes to Those Countries; and All Necessary Information Relative to the Equipment, Supplies, and the Method of Traveling.* 1845; facsimile edition, Bedford, Mass.: Applewood Books, 1994.

Haynes, Sam W. *Soldiers of Misfortune: The Somerville and Mier Expeditions.* Austin: University of Texas Press, 1990.

Heitala, Thomas. *Manifest Destiny: Anxious Aggrandizement in Late Jacksonian America.* Ithaca, N.Y.: Cornell University Press, 1985.

Heitman, Francis B. *Historical Register and Dictionary of the United States Army, from Its Organization, September 29, 1789, to March 2, 1903.* 2 vols. Washington, D.C.: Government Printing Office, 1903; reprinted Gaithersburg, Md.: Olde Soldiers Book, Inc., 1988.

Henderson, Thomas. *Hints on the Medical Examination of Recruits for the Army; And on the Discharge of Soldiers from the Service on Surgeon's Certificate.* Philadelphia: Haswell, Barrington, and Haswell, 1840.

Henry, William Seaton. *Campaign Sketches of the War with Mexico.* New York: Arno Press, 1973.

Herndon William H.; and Jesse William Weike. *Herndon's Lincoln: The True Story of a Great Life.* 3 vols. Chicago: Belford, Clarke, and Company, 1889.

Hertz, Emanuel. *The Hidden Lincoln: From the Letters and Papers of William H. Herndon.* New York: Viking Press, 1938.

Hickman, George H. *The Democratic Text Book, Being a Compendium of the Principles of the Democratic Party.* New York: Burgess, Stringer and Co.; Philadelphia: G. B. Zieber and Co., 1848.

Hildreth, James. *Dragoon Campaigns to the Rocky Mountains; Being a History of the Enlistment, Organization, and First Campaigns of the Regiment of United States Dragoons; Together with Incidents of a Soldier's Life, and Sketches of Scenery and Indian Character.* New York: D. Fanshaw, 1836; reprinted New York: Arno Press, 1973.

Horsman, Reginald. *Race and Manifest Destiny: The Origins of American Radical Anglo-Saxonism.* Cambridge, Mass.: Harvard University Press, 1981.

Howell, H. Grady, Jr., ed. *A Southern Lacrimosa: The Mexican War Journal of Dr. Thomas Neely Love, Surgeon, Second Regiment Mississippi Infantry, U.S.A.* Madison, Miss.: Chickasaw Bayou Press, 1996.

Hughes, Nathaniel C., Jr.; and Roy P. Stonesifer, Jr. *The Life and Wars of Gideon J. Pillow.* Chapel Hill: University of North Carolina Press, 1993.

Huntington, H., Jr. *View of South America and Mexico.* N.p., 1825.

Huntington, R. T. *Accoutrements of the United States Infantry, Riflemen, and Dragoons, 1834–1839.* Alexandria Bay, N.Y.: Museum Restoration Service, 1987.

Janes, Ann Brown, ed. *Gathering Laurels in Mexico: The Diary of an American Soldier in the Mexican American War.* Lincoln, Mass.: Cottage Press, 1990.

Jay, William. *A Review of the Causes and Consequences of the Mexican War.* Boston: Benjamin B. Massey and Company; Philadelphia: Uriah Hunt and Company; and New York: M. W. Dodd, 1849.

Johannsen, Robert. *To the Halls of the Montezumas: The Mexican War in the American Imagination.* New York: Oxford University Press, 1985.

Jones, Walter. *The Case of the Battalion Stated, with an Exposition of the Grounds Upon Which Chas. Lee Jones, Esq., Expected to Have Had Command of the Battalion (Consisting of Three Companies Raised by Himself in the District of Columbia, and Two To Be Raised in Maryland,) Conferred Upon Him, as of Right and Justice Due Both to Him and to the Officers and Men Who Had Volunteered to Serve Under His Command.* Washington, D.C.: J. and G. S. Gideon, 1847.

Karnes, Thomas L. *William Gilpin, Western Nationalist.* Austin: University of Texas Press, 1970.

Katcher, Philip R. N. *The Mexican-American War, 1846–1848.* London: Osprey Publishing, 1989.

———. *U.S. Infantry Equipments, 1775–1910.* London: Osprey Publishing, 1989.

Kendall, George W. *Narrative of the Texan Santa Fe Expedition*. New York: Harper and Brothers, 1844.

Kenly, John R. *Memoirs of a Maryland Volunteer*. Philadelphia: J. B. Lippincott and Co., 1873.

Kreidberg, Marvin A.; and Merton G. Henry. *History of the Military Mobilization in the United States, 1775–1945*. Department of the Army Pamphlet No. 20-212. Washington, D.C.: U.S. Department of the Army, June 1955.

Lack, Paul D. *The Texas Revolutionary Experience: A Political and Social History, 1835–1836*. College Station: Texas A&M University Press, 1992.

Lawton, Eba Anderson, ed. *An Artillery Officer in the Mexican War, 1846–47: Letters of Robert Anderson, Captain 3rd Artillery, U.S.A.* Freeport, N.Y.: Books for Libraries Press, 1971.

Leckie, Robert. *From Sea to Shining Sea: From the War of 1812 to the Mexican War, the Saga of American Expansion*. New York: Harper Collins Publishers, 1993.

Livingston-Little, D. E., ed. *The Mexican War Diary of Thomas D. Tennery*. Norman: University of Oklahoma Press, 1970.

Longstreet, James. *From Manassas to Appomattox: Memoirs of the Civil War in America*. Bloomington: Indiana University Press, 1981.

Lynn, John A. *Bayonets of the Republic*. Champaign: University of Illinois Press, 1984.

McCaffrey, James M. *Army of Manifest Destiny: The American Soldier in the Mexican War, 1846–1848*. New York: New York University Press, 1992.

McCall, George A. *Letters from the Frontiers*. Edited by John K. Mahon. Philadelphia: J. B. Lippincott and Company, 1868; reprinted Gainesville: University Presses of Florida, 1974.

McCormick, Richard P. *The Second American Party System: Party Formation in the Jacksonian Era*. Chapel Hill: University of North Carolina Press, 1986.

McFeely, William S. *Grant: A Biography*. New York: W. W. Norton and Company, 1981.

McWhiney, Grady; and Perry D. Jamieson. *Attack and Die: Civil War Military Tactics and the Southern Heritage*. Tuscaloosa: University of Alabama Press, 1982.

Malone, Dumas, ed. *Dictionary of American Biography*. 20 vols. New York: Charles Scribner's Sons, 1927.

May, Robert E. *John A. Quitman: Old South Crusader*. Baton Rouge: Louisiana State University Press, 1985.

Mayer, Brantz. *Mexico As It Was and As It Is*. New York: J. Winchester, New World Press, 1844.

Meade, George G. *The Life and Letters of George Gordon Meade, Major General of the United States Army*. 2 vols. New York: Charles Scribner's Sons, 1913.

Meriwether, Colyer. *Raphael Semmes*. Philadelphia: George W. Jacobs and Company, 1913.

Merk, Frederick. *Dissent in Three American Wars*. Cambridge, Mass.: Harvard University Press, 1970.

———. *Manifest Destiny and Mission in American History*. Cambridge, Mass.: Harvard University Press, 1995.

Miller, Robert Ryal. *Mexico: A History*. Norman: University of Oklahoma Press, 1985.

————. *Shamrock and Sword: The Saint Patrick's Battalion in the U.S.-Mexican War.* Norman: University of Oklahoma Press, 1989.

Miller, Robert Ryal, ed. *The Mexican War Journal and Letters of Ralph W. Kirkham.* College Station: Texas A&M Press, 1991.

Mitchell, S. Augustus. *Mitchell's Geographical Reader: A System of Modern Geography, Comprising a Description of the World, with Its Grand Divisions, America, Europe, Asia, Africa, and Oceania. Designed for Instruction in Schools and Families.* Philadelphia: Thomas, Cowperthwait, and Company, 1845.

Monaghan, Jay, ed. *The Private Journal of Louis McLane, U.S.N., 1844–1848.* Los Angeles: Dawson's Book Shop for the Santa Barbara Historical Society, 1971.

Montgomery, H. *The Life of Zachary Taylor, Twelfth President of the United States.* Buffalo, N.Y.: Derby, Orton, and Mulligan, 1854.

Moore, H. Judge. *Scott's Campaigns in Central Mexico: From the Rendezvous at the Island of Lobos to the Taking of Mexico City, Including an Account of the Siege of Puebla.* Charleston, S.C.: J. B. Nixon, 1849.

Morrision, Chaplain W. *Democratic Politics and Sectionalism: The Wilmot Proviso Controversy.* Chapel Hill: University of North Carolina, 1967.

Morse, Jedidiah. *Geography Made Easy: Being an Abridgment of the American Universal Geography.* Boston: J. T. Buckingham, Printer, 1807.

Myers, Marvin. *The Jacksonian Persuasion: Politics and Belief.* Stanford, Calif.: Stanford University Press, 1957.

Myers, William Starr, ed. *The Mexican War Diary of George B. McClellan.* Princeton, N.J.: University of Princeton Press, 1917.

Nance, Joseph M. *Attack and Counter Attack: The Texas-Mexican Frontier, 1842.* Austin: University of Texas Press, 1964.

Nichols, Roy Franklin. *Franklin Pierce: Young Hickory of the Granite Hills.* Philadelphia: University of Pennsylvania Press, 1958.

Oberly, James W. *Sixty Million Acres: American Veterans and the Public Lands Before the Civil War.* Kent, Ohio: Kent State University Press, 1990.

Olivera, Ruth R., and Liliane Crété. *Life in Mexico under Santa Anna, 1822–1855.* Norman: University of Oklahoma Press, 1991.

Oswandel, J. Jacob. *Notes of the Mexican War, 1846–47–48.* Philadelphia: N.p., 1885.

Owen, Charles H. *The Justice of the Mexican War.* New York: G. P. Putnam's Sons, 1908.

Parkman, Francis. *The Oregon Trail.* Boston: Ginn and Company, 1910.

Peck, John James. *The Sign of the Eagle: A View of Mexico, 1830–1855.* San Diego, Calif.: Copley Press, 1970.

Peskin, Allan, ed. *Volunteers: The Mexican War Journals of Private Richard Coulter and Sergeant Thomas Barclay, Company E, Second Pennsylvania Infantry.* Kent, Ohio: Kent State University Press, 1991.

Pessen, Edward. *Jacksonian America: Society, Personality, and Politics.* Homewood, Ill.: Dorsey Press, 1969.

Pletcher, David M. *The Diplomacy of Annexation: Texas, Oregon, and the Mexican War.* Columbia: University of Missouri Press, 1975.

————. *Rails, Mines, and Progress: Seven American Promoters in Mexico, 1867–1911*. Ithaca, N.Y.: Cornell University Press, 1958.

A Pocket Dictionary of the Spanish and English Languages. Compiled from the Last Edition of Neuman and Bartetti. Philadelphia: Samuel Wakeling, 1840.

Poinsett, Joel Robert. *Notes on Mexico Made in the Autumn of 1822, Accompanied by an Historical Sketch of the Revolution, and Translations of Official Reports of the Present State of That Country*. Philadelphia: H. C. Carey and I. Lea, 1824.

Polk, James K. *The Diary of James K. Polk During His Presidency, 1845 to 1849*. 4 vols. Chicago: A. C. McClurg and Company, 1910.

Prescott, William H. *History of the Conquest of Mexico*. Philadelphia: J. B. Lippincott, 1843.

Prucha, Francis Paul, ed. *Army Life on the Western Frontier: Selections from the Official Reports Made Between 1826 and 1845 by Colonel George Croghan*. Norman: University of Oklahoma Press, 1958.

Rawley, James A. *The Politics of Union: Northern Politics during the Civil War*. Lincoln: University of Nebraska Press, 1974.

————. *Race and Politics: "Bleeding Kansas" and the Coming of the Civil War*. Lincoln: University of Nebraska Press, 1979.

Remini, Robert V. *Andrew Jackson and the Course of American Democracy, 1833–1845*. New York: Harper and Row, 1984.

————. *Andrew Jackson and the Course of American Empire, 1767–1821*. New York: Harper and Row, 1977.

————. *Andrew Jackson and the Course of American Freedom, 1822–1832*. New York: Harper and Row, 1981.

Richardson, James D., ed. *A Compilation of the Messages and Papers of the Presidents, 1789–1902*. 10 vols. N.p.: Bureau of National Literature and Art, 1903.

Riling, Joseph R. *Baron Von Steuben and His Regulations, Including a Complete Facsimile of the Original Regulations for the Order and Discipline of the Troops of the United States*. Foreword by Frederick P. Todd. Philadelphia: Ray Riling Arms Books Company, 1966.

Risch, Erna. *Quartermaster Support of the Army: A History of the Corps, 1775–1939*. Washington, D.C.: Quartermaster Historian's Office, Office of the Quartermaster General, 1962.

Robarts, William H. *Mexican War Veterans: A Complete Roster of the Regular and Volunteer Troops in the War Between the United States and Mexico, from 1846 to 1848*. Washington, D.C.: A. S. Witherbee and Company, 1887.

Robertson, James I. *General A. P. Hill: The Story of a Confederate Warrior*. New York: Random House, 1987.

Robinson, Fayette. *An Account of the Organization of the Army of the United States of America*. 2 vols. Philadelphia: E. B. Butler and Company, 1848.

Rodenbough, Theodore F., and William L. Haskins. *The Army of the United States: Historical Sketches of Staff and Line with Portraits of Generals-in-Chief*. New York: Argonaut Press, 1966.

Rough and Ready Songster: Embellished with Twenty-Five Splendid Engravings Illustra-

tive of the American Victories in Mexico, by an American Officer. New York: Nafis and Cornish, Publishers, 1848.

Russell, Carl P. *Guns of the Early Frontiers: A History of Firearms from Colonial Times through the Years of the Western Fur Trade.* Lincoln: University of Nebraska Press, 1957.

Sandburg, Carl. *Abraham Lincoln: The War Years.* 4 vols. Harcourt, Brace, and Company, 1939.

Schlesinger, Arthur M., Jr. *The Age of Jackson.* New York: Little, Brown and Company, 1945.

Schroeder, John H. *Mr. Polk's War: American Opposition and Dissent, 1846–1848.* Madison: University of Wisconsin Press, 1973.

Scott, Henry L. *Military Dictionary: Comprising Technical Definitions; Information on Raising and Keeping Troops, Including Makeshift and Improved Materiél; and Law, Government, Regulation, and Administration Relating to Land Forces.* 1864. Reprint, Yuma, Ariz: Fort Yuma Press, 1984.

Scott, Winfield. *Infantry Tactics; Or, Rules for the Exercise and Maneuvers of the United States Infantry.* 3 vols. New York: Harper and Brothers, 1840.

———. *Memoirs of Lieut.-General Scott, LL.D., Written by Himself.* 2 vols. Freeport, N.Y.: Books for Libraries Press, 1970.

Scribner, Benjamin Franklin. *Camp Life of a Volunteer: A Campaign in Mexico; Or, A Glimpse at Life in Camp by "One Who Has Seen the Elephant."* Philadelphia: Grigg, Elliot, and Co., 1847.

Sedgwick, Henry Dwight. *Men of Letters: Francis Parkman.* Boston: Houghton, Mifflin, and Company, 1904.

Sellers, Charles Grier. *James K. Polk: Continentalist, 1843–1846.* Princeton, N.J.: Princeton University Press, 1966.

———. *James K. Polk: Jacksonian, 1795–1843.* Princeton, N.J.: Princeton University Press, 1957.

Singletary, Otis A. *The Mexican War.* Chicago: University of Chicago Press, 1960.

Skelton, William B. *An American Profession of Arms: The Army Officer Corps, 1784–1861.* Lawrence: University Press of Kansas, 1992.

Smith, George Winston and Charles Judah. *Chronicles of the Gringos: The U.S. Army in the Mexican War, Accounts of Eyewitnesses and Combatants.* Albuquerque: University of New Mexico Press, 1968.

Smith, Joseph Burkholder. *James Madison's Phony War: The Plot to Steal Florida.* New York: Arbor House, 1983.

Smith, Justin. *War with Mexico.* 2 vols. Gloucester, Mass.: Peter Smith, 1963.

Smith, S. Compton. *Chile Con Carne; Or, The Camp and Field.* New York: Miller and Curtis, 1857.

Smithwick, Noah. *Evolution of a State; Or, Recollection of Old Texas Days.* Austin: University of Texas Press, 1983.

Spencer, Ivor D. *The Victor and the Spoils: A Life of William L. Marcy.* Providence, R.I.: Brown University Press, 1959.

Stagg, J. C. A. *Mr. Madison's War: Politics, Diplomacy, and Warfare in the Early American Republic, 1783–1830.* Princeton, N.J.: Princeton University Press, 1983.

Steffen, Randy. *The Horse Soldiers: The Revolution, the War of 1812, the Early Frontier, 1776–1850.* Norman: University of Oklahoma Press, 1977.

Stevens, Kenneth R. *Border Diplomacy: The Caroline and McLeod Affairs in Anglo-American Relations, 1837–1842.* Tuscaloosa: University of Alabama Press, 1989.

Sumner, William Graham. *Andrew Jackson.* Boston: N.p., 1882.

Taylor, Zachary. *Letters of Zachary Taylor from the Battle-Fields of the Mexican War.* New York: Kraus Reprint Co., 1970.

Thompson, Waddy. *Recollections of Mexico.* New York: Wiley and Putnam, 1846.

Thorp, T. B. *Our Army on the Rio Grande.* Philadelphia: Cary and Hart, 1846.

Tocqueville, Alexis de. *Democracy in America.* 2 vols. New York: Vintage Books, 1945.

Todd, Frederick P. *American Military Equipage, 1851–1872.* 3 vols. Providence, R.I.: Company of Military Historians, 1974–78.

Tyler, Daniel. *Concise History of the Mormon Battalion in the Mexican War.* Glorieta, N.M.: Rio Grande Press, 1969.

Tyron, W. S. *My Native Land: Life in America, 1790–1870.* Chicago: University of Chicago Press, 1961.

Upton, Emory. *The Military Policy of the United States During the Mexican War.* Washington, D.C.: Government Printing Office, 1914.

Wallace, Lew. *Lew Wallace: An Autobiography.* 2 vols. New York: Harper and Brothers Publishers, 1906.

Walraven, Bill, and Marjorie K. Walraven. *The Magnificent Barbarians: Little-Told Tales of the Texas Revolution.* Austin, Tex.: Eakin Press, 1993.

Ward, John William. *Andrew Jackson: Symbol for an Age.* New York: Oxford University Press, 1977.

Waugh, John C. *The Class of 1846, from West Point to Appomattox: Stonewall Jackson, George McClellan and Their Brothers.* New York: Warner Books, 1993.

Weigley, Russell F. *The American Way of War: A History of United States Military Strategy and Policy.* New York: Macmillan Publishing Company, 1973.

———. *History of the United States Army.* New York: Macmillan Publishing Company, 1967.

———. *Towards an American Army: Military Thought from Washington to Marshall.* New York: Columbia University Press, 1962.

White, Leonard D. *The Jacksonians: A Study in Administrative History, 1829–1861.* New York: Macmillan Publishing Company, 1954.

Wilcox, Cadmus M. *History of the Mexican War.* Washington, D.C.: Church News Publishing Company, 1892.

Williams, W. *Appleton's Southern and Western Traveler's Guide.* New York: D. Appleton and Company, 1849.

———. *The Traveler's and Tourist Guide through the United States of America, Canada, Etc.; Containing the Routes of Travel by Railroad, Steamboat, Stage, and Canal.* Philadelphia: Lippincott, Grambo, and Company, 1851.

Woodward, Joseph Janvier. *The Hospital Steward's Manual, for the Instruction of Hospital Stewards, Ward-Masters, and Attendants, in Their Several Duties. Prepared in Strict Accordance with Existing Regulations and the Customs of Service in the Armies* of the United States of America, and Rendered Authoritative by Order of the Surgeon-General. Philadelphia: Lippincott and Company, 1862.

Young, Andrew W. *The American Statesman: A Political History Exhibiting the Origins, Nature, and Practical Operation of Constitutional Government in the United States and the Rise of Political Parties.* New York: J. C. Derby, 1855.

Zeh, Frederick. *An Immigrant Soldier in the Mexican War.* Translated by William J. Orr. Edited by William J. Orr and Robert Ryal Miller. College Station: Texas A&M University Press, 1995.

ARTICLES

"America's Guard." *United States Magazine and Democratic Review* 20 (March, 1847): 209–10.

Ames, George W., Jr., ed. "A Doctor Comes to California: The Diary of John S. Griffin, Assistant Surgeon with Kearny's Dragoons, 1846–47." 3 pts. *California Historical Quarterly* 21 (1942): 193–224, 333–57; and *California Historical Quarterly* 22 (1943): 41–66.

Arnold, Ralph E. "The Model 1841 Rifle: The Famous 'Mississippi.'" *Gun Report* 21 (September, 1973): 14–21.

Bailey, Thomas. "Diary of the Mexican War." *Indiana Magazine of History* 14 (1918): 134–47.

Barker, Karle Wilson. "Trailing the New Orleans Greys." *Southwestern Review* 22 (April, 1937): 213–40.

Barringer, Graham A., ed. "The Mexican War Journal of Henry S. Lane." *Indiana Magazine of History* 53 (1957): 383–434.

Becker, Carl M. "John William Lowe: Failure in Inner Direction." *Ohio History* 73 (1964): 75–89.

Buley, R. C. "Indiana in the Mexican War: The Indiana Volunteers." *Indiana Magazine of History* 15 (September, 1919): 260–92.

Butler, Steven R. "Mexican War Bounty Land Warrants in the National Archives." *Mexican War Journal* 4 (Fall 1994–Winter 1995): 23–30.

Campbell, William B. "Mexican War Letters of Col. William Bowen Campbell, of Tennessee, Written to Governor David Campbell, of Virginia, 1846–1847." *Tennessee Historical Magazine* 1 (June, 1915): 129–67.

Canaday, Dayton W. "Voice of the Volunteer of 1847." *Journal of the Illinois State Historical Society* 44 (1951): 199–209.

Collins, Maria Clinton, ed. "Journal of Francis Collins, an Artillery Officer in the Mexican War." *Quarterly Publication of the Historical and Philosophical Society of Ohio* 10 (April and July, 1915): 37–109.

Cook, Judge Zo. "Mexican War Reminiscences." *Alabama Historical Quarterly* 20 (1957): 435–60.

Davenport, Harbert. "The Men of Goliad." *Southwestern Historical Quarterly* 48 (July, 1939): 1–41.

Davis, Jefferson. "Autobiography of Jefferson Davis." *Bedford's Magazine* (January, 1890): 255–76.

Dienst, Alexander. "The New Orleans Newspaper Files of the Texas Revolution Period." *Southwest Historical Quarterly* 4 (October, 1900): 140–51.

Duffy, John. "Medical Practices in the Ante-Bellum South." *Journal of Southern History* 25 (February, 1959): 53–72.

Duncan, Louis C. "The Days Gone By: A Volunteer Regiment in 1846–47." *Military Surgeon* 65 (1929): 709–13.

———. "A Medical History of General Scott's Campaign to the City of Mexico in 1847." *Military Surgeon* 46 (October–November, 1920): 436–70, 596–609.

———. "A Medical History of General Zachary Taylor's Army of Occupation in Texas and Mexico, 1845–1847." *Military Surgeon* 48 (July, 1921): 76–104.

Durham, Walter T., ed. "Mexican War Letters to Wynnewood." *Tennessee Historical Quarterly* 33 (Winter 1974): 389–409.

Engelman, Adolphus. "The Second Illinois in the Mexican War: Mexican War Letters of Adolphus Engelman, 1846–1847." Edited and translated by Otto B. Engelman. *Journal of Illinois State Historical Society* 26 (January, 1934): 357–452.

Fakes, Turner J., Jr. "Memphis and the Mexican War." *West Tennessee Historical Society Papers* 2 (1948): 119–44.

Ficklin, John R. "Was Texas Included in the Louisiana Purchase?" *Publications of the Southern Historical Association* 5 (September, 1901): 351–87.

Goetzmann, William F., ed. "Our First Foreign War: Letters of Barna Upton, 3rd U.S. Infantry." 2 pts. *American Heritage* 17 (1966): 18–27, 85–99.

Graves, Donald E. "Dry Books of Tactics: U.S. Infantry Manuals of the War of 1812 and After." Pt. 2. *Military Collector and Historian* 38 (1986): 173–77.

Henderson, Alfred J. "A Morgan Country Volunteer in the Mexican War." *Journal of the Illinois State Historical Society* 41 (December, 1948): 383–401.

Hinds, Charles F., ed. "Mexican War Journal of Leander M. Cox." 3 pts. *Register of the Kentucky Historical Society* 55 (1957): 29–52; 55 (1957): 213–36; and 56 (1958): 47–69.

Holland, James K. "Diary of a Texan Volunteer in the Mexican War." *Southwestern Historical Quarterly* 30 (July, 1926): 1–33.

Irey, Thomas R. "Soldiering, Suffering, and Dying in the Mexican War." *Journal of the West* 11 (April, 1972): 285–98.

Jensen, Dana O., ed. "The Memoirs of Daniel M. Frost." pts. 1–3. *Missouri Historical Bulletin* 26 (1970): 3–23, 89–112, 200–26.

Jones, Fanny Lee. "Walter Jones and His Times." *Records of the Columbia Historical Society* 5 (1902): 139–50.

Jones, Robert R. "The Mexican War Diary of James Lawson Kemper." *Virginia Magazine of History and Biography* 74 (October, 1966): 387–427.

Kurtz, Wilbur G., Jr. "The First Regiment of Georgia Volunteers in the Mexican War." *Georgia Historical Quarterly* 27 (December, 1943): 301–23.

Livingston-Little, D. E., ed. "Mutiny During the Mexican War: An Incident on the Rio Grande." *Journal of the West* 9 (July, 1970): 340–45.

Love, Thomas N. "Remarks on Some of the Diseases Which Prevailed in the 2d Regt. Mississippi Rifles, for the First Six Months of Its Service." *New Orleans Medical and Surgical Journal* 5 (July, 1848): 3–13.

McGroarty, William B. "William H. Richardson's Journal of Doniphan's Expedition." 3 pts. *Missouri Historical Review* 22 (1928): 193–236, 331–60, 511–42.

Marshall, Thomas Maitland. "The Southwestern Boundary of Texas, 1821–1840." *Southwestern Historical Quarterly* 14 (April, 1911): 273–93.

May, Robert, E. "Invisible Men: Blacks and the U.S. Army in the Mexican War." *Historian* 49 (August, 1987): 463–77.

Miller, Roger G. "Yellow Jack at Vera Cruz." *Prologue: The Journal of the National Archives* 10 (Spring 1978): 43–53.

A Mississippian. "Sketches of Our Volunteers Officers: Alexander Keith McClung." *Southern Literary Messenger* 21 (January, 1855): 10–11.

Moore, John H., ed. "Private Johnson Fights the Mexicans, 1847–1848." *South Carolina Historical Magazine* 67 (1966): 203–28.

Pace, Eleanor Pace, ed. "The Diary and Letters of William P. Rogers, 1846–1863." *Southwestern Historical Quarterly* 32 (April, 1929): 259–99.

Payne, Darwin. "Camp Life in the Army of Occupation." *Southwestern Historical Quarterly* 73 (January, 1970): 326–42.

"Popular Portraits with Pen and Pencil: Major General Gaines." *United States Magazine and Democratic Review* 22 (June, 1848): 549–57.

Porter, John B., M.D. "Medical and Surgical Notes of Campaigns in the War with Mexico, During the years 1845, 1846, 1847, and 1848." 5 pts. *American Journal of the Medical Sciences* 23 (January, 1852): 13–37; 24 (July, 1852): 13–30; 25 (January, 1853): 25–42; 26 (October, 1853): 297–333; and New Series 35 (April, 1858): 347–52.

Pratt, Julius W. "John L. O'Sullivan and Manifest Destiny." *New York History* 14 (1933): 213–34.

Pruyn, Robert N. "Campaigning Through Mexico With 'Old Rough and Ready.'" *Civil War Times Illustrated* 2 (October, 1963): 10–15.

Remini, Robert V. "Texas Must Be Ours." *American Heritage* 37 (1986): 42–47.

Reynolds, Curtis R. "The Deterioration of Mexican–American Diplomatic Relations, 1833–1845." *Journal of the West* 11 (April, 1972): 213–24.

Rowe, Mary Ellen, ed. "The Mexican War Letters of Chesley Sheldon Coffey." *Journal of Mississippi History* 44 (August, 1982): 234–52.

Ryan, Daniel J. "Ohio in the Mexican War." *Ohio Archeological and Historical Publications* 21 (1912): 277–99.

Scarbrough, Jewels Davis. "The Georgia Battalion in the Texas Revolution: A Critical Study." *Southwestern Historical Quarterly* 63 (April, 1963): 511–32.

Spell, Lota M. "The Anglo-Saxon Press in Mexico, 1846–1848." *American Historical Review* 38 (October, 1932): 20–31.

Stenberg, Richard R. "The Motivation of the Wilmot Proviso." *Mississippi Historical Review* 18 (March, 1932): 535–40.

"The Sunday Question." *Journal of the Military Service Institution of the United States* 8 (1888): 356–57.

Thomas, John B., Jr. "Kentuckians in Texas: Captain Burr H. Duval's Company at Goliad." *Register of the Kentucky Historical Society* 81 (Summer 1983): 237–54.

Wallace, Lee A., Jr. "The First Regiment of Virginia Volunteers, 1846–1848." *Virginia Magazine of History and Biography* 77 (1969): 46–77.

Index

Benton, Thomas H. (*continued*) troops against the Mormons, 191–92
Bent's Fort, 119
Bissell, Col. William H., 79, 131
Black Hawk War, 28–29, 73
Blake, Lt. Jacob E., 157–58
Bomford, Col. George, 21, 213n 15
Borland, Maj. Solon, 79, 80
bounties, 71–72
Bowen, Isaac: on Butler, 45; on Hamer, 47; on letter writers, 59; on public's opinion of the army, 50; and reaction to winning brevet, 56; and war as opportunity, 51; on William E. Aisquith, 77
Bowles, Col. William A., 79
Brackett, Lt. Albert G.: on feelings about the dead, 164; on military dress, 88, 107; on music in camp, 129; and objections to wearing regular uniforms, 112; on types of soldiers, 128
Bradford, Maj. Alexander, 80
Brady, Col. Hugh, 27, 53
Bragg, Capt. Braxton, 126
Brazos Santiago, 124, 130, 141
Breckenridge, John C., 203
brevet rank, 56; definition of, 17; as means of advancement, 56; Scott-Gaines feud over, 27; Scott-Polk dispute over, 34; Worth's resignation over, 18
Brook, Col. George M., 53
Brooks, Capt. Preston, 85–86, 227n 33
Brown, Gov. Albert G., 73
Brown, Gen. Jacob, 26, 27
Brown, Maj. Jacob, 162
Buchanan, James, 192
Buckly, Capt. Benjamin C., 83
Buckner, Lt. Simon Bolivar, 105
Buena Vista, 161, 164
Burr, Aaron, 6, 168
Butler, Anthony, 7
Butler, William Orlando: and assessment

as general, 45–46; background and appointment of, 37–39; in election of 1848, 220n 40; as Scott's successor, 49; and visiting Polk, 188

Cadwalader, Gen. George: and assessment as general, 47; background and appointment of, 41
Calderón de la Barca, Frances, 168
Caldwell, Maj. George A., 64–65
camaraderie, 126–28
Camargo, 129, 141, 155, 157, 160, 165
Campbell, Col. William B.: 15; on advance of civilization, 184; on being a Whig, 78; on Butler, 45; on difference between regulars and volunteers, 81, 84; on hardship of commanding volunteers, 82, 85; mailing address of, 131; and opinion of Mexicans, 174, 183; on Pillow, 44; on politics in the army, 79; on Quitman, 46; on rations and the quartermaster's department, 118–19, 125; on rivalry between regulars and volunteers, 198; on Scott and Taylor, 30; in Seminole War, 77; and studying tactics, 74; and wanting a regular commission, 201
Cass, Lewis, 11, 49, 203, 220n 40
Cass, Major Lewis, Jr., 65
casualties: of regulars, 145; tables of, 239n 2, 244n 28; of volunteers, 147–51
Catholic Church, 13, 181–83
cavalry. *See* dragoons
Cerralvo, 119, 153
Cerro Gordo, 142, 163
Chamberlain, Samuel: on facial hair, 108; on gambling, 137; on Hall Carbine, 229–30n 16; on Mexican women, 176, 247–48n 13; paintings of, 111; on types of soldiers, 127–28; on uniforms, 109
chief musician, 22
Chihuahua, 132
Childs, Lt. Col. Thomas, 108
China, Mex., 160

Oswandel, Pvt. J. Jacob, 163; on captured uniforms to volunteers, 233n 41; and clothing situation, 111; on garrison duty, 138; in a play, 133; on slackers, 128; travels to the front, 114; on volunteers' response to haircut order, 108

Owens, Charles H., 204–205

Page, Capt. John, 162

Paine, Col. Robert T., 78, 190

Palo Alto, 9, 18, 30, 157, 158, 161, 162

Paredes y Arrillaga, Mariano, 8

Parkman, Francis, 110, 241n 12

Patos, 80

Patterson, Robert: and assessment as general, 44–45; background and appointment of, 39; as Democratic appointee, 43; and visiting Polk, 188

Pay Department, 17, 19–20, 101, 122

Peck, Lt. John J.: on bayonet use at Contreras, 244–45n 32; on death of friend, 127; on horrors of war, 163; on Mexican markets, 119; on political influence, 57; on Polk's treatment of army, 58; popularity of, 61

Pender, Lt. Josiah S., 190–91

Peyton, Col. Baile, 78, 160

Pierce, Franklin: and assessment as general, 47; background and appointment of, 41; presidential election of, 49, 203; and relationship with Polk, 43; and visiting Polk, 188

Pike, Capt. Albert, 82, 137

Pike, Zebulon, 168

Pillow, Gideon Johnson: and assessment as general, 43–44; background and appointment of, 39–40; and election for 1844, 250–51n 11; and feuding with Scott, 40, 48–49, 189; and writing to Polk criticizing Taylor, 188

Poinsett, Joel, 168

Point Isabel, 8, 174

Polk, James Knox: abusing patronage accusation of, 65, 190; as active commander-in-chief, 187; and annexation, 8; and appointing Taylor to command Army of Occupation, 28; and appointing two nephews to USMA, 224n 29; and appointing Westerners to the U.S. Mounted Rifles, 58; and appointment of Democratic officers, 64–66; and appointment of new generals, 35, 37; and appointments rejected, 42; and army disputes, 188–92; and association with Pillow, 39–40; and awarding patronage, 193; background of, 4–6; on brevet rank, 18; and calling volunteers, 10, 69; and claiming credit for victory over Mexico, 201; and criticism by a volunteer, 199; on factionalism in Democratic Party, 186, 192; and informants, 188; and lieutenant general plot, 48, 219–20n 38; and opinion of Whig department heads, 34; and opportunities to use patronage, 192; and problems as commander-in-chief, 13, 16; and problems with Whig generals, 32–36, 48; regular officers' criticism of, 59; and relations with army staff departments, 187–88; and reliance on volunteers, 63–64, 66, 69, 195; and relieving Gaines of command, 70; and requests for offices, 193; and seeing patronage a cause of party factionalism, 194; and siding with Democratic officers, 36; and supporting Democratic officers, 188–89; on Taylor and Scott, 32; and using service as loyalty test, 191–92; and Van Buren angered about appointment of Marcy, 251–52n 11; and war message, 9; Whig opposition to, 12

Polk, Maj. William H., 65

Porter, Surgeon John B., 161; career of, 239n 3; on causes of disease, 140; on diet for sick, 153; on hospitals, 153, 155;

on tents, 140; and treating dueling victim, 160; on treatment of disease, 151; and treatment for gunshots, 160; on untrained hospital staffs, 153, 154; 157; on vaccinating soldiers, 146; on yellow fever, 152

Porter, Lt. Andrew, 57, 222n 13

Prescott, William H., 169

Price, Sterling: background and appointment of, 42, 80; genesis of campaign by, 187

prostitutes, 157

Puebla, 125, 128, 132, 133, 154, 155, 181

punishment: as cause for revenge, 63; descriptions of, 62–63; and Lt. Don Carlos Buell's court-martial, 223n 23; as prescribed by the Articles of War, 62; and punishment horse, 62, 86, 190; as reason for desertion, 62; volunteers' dislike for, 85–87

Quartermaster's Department, 17; at company level, 23; and difficulty in supplying uniforms, 108, 233n 41; duties of, 20; and hiring Mexican seamstresses, 111, 232–33n 40; Polk's criticism of, 187; quartermaster sergeant in, 22; and rations, 118–19; regimental quartermaster in, 22; on sale of surplus clothing to the public, 220–21n 1; and sheltering army, 140–41; transportation of supplies, 20, 35, 114, 217n 7, 240n 6; and transporting troops, 114–18

Quitman, John A.: and assessment as general, 46, 47; background and appointment of, 40–41; and establishing a hospital, 153

Raith, Capt. Julius, 126

rations, 118–19. *See also* markets and restaurants

Republican Party, 203, 253n 3

Resaca de la Palma, 9, 18, 163

restaurants, 121, 123–25, 235n 16

retirement, 52, 221n 5

Reynolds, Capt. Robert B., 188

Richardson, Pvt. William H., 154, 232n 37, 240n 5, 245

Ridgely, Lt. Randolph, 158, 165

riflemen. *See* infantry

Ringgold, Maj. Samuel, 24, 105, 158, 161

Roane, Lt. Col. John S., 79, 80

Robinson, Fayette, 15, 21

Rogers, Capt. William P., 124; on difficulty of commanding volunteers, 82; on evils of drinking, 137; on lack of respect for the dead, 164; and learning Spanish, 177; and losing shoes, 109; and mail, 131; on Mexican tyranny, 184; on newspaper stories, 131; and volunteers unsuited for foreign duty, 85; on war as improvement for Mexico, 184

Roote, Col. Henry Jackson, 79

Rush, Thomas, 42

Saltillo, 119, 124, 132, 134, 136, 138, 157, 165, 175, 177, 180

San Antonio, 141, 159

San Pascual, 162

San Patricio Battalion, 60

Santa Anna, Antonio López de, 7

Santa Fe, 121, 129, 131, 133, 134, 138, 138, 141, 142, 173, 182, 185

Sargent, Pvt. Chancey Forward, 154, 156

Scott, Winfield, 14, 32; and appointment as general-in-chief, 27; on brevet rank, 18; and comparison to Taylor, 28–30; and climbing a pyramid, 169; on difference between regulars and volunteers, 197; as diplomat, 27; and dispute with Edmund P. Gaines, 27; early life and military career of, 25–27; and establishing hospital in Mexico City, 153, 242n 17; and feud with Pillow, 40, 48–49; and involvement with Whigs, 27; on Mexican

Scott, Winfield (*continued*) tyranny, 183; on military dress, 106–107; and military scholarship, 23–24, 26–27, 43; and plan to increase army's size, 52; and ordering manual supplied to volunteer officers, 73–74; and order to dismiss volunteer officers, 250*n* 7; and regulars, 198; and regulation for sea transports, 116–17; and relationship with Polk, 33–34, 188–89; on use of rifles, 97; as Whig candidate in 1852, 203; and Worth, 235*n* 17; and yellow fever fear, 151

Scott's Tactics, 23–24, 25, 225*n* 14

Scribner, Pvt. Benjamin Franklin: on army life, 113; and describing a march, 142–43; and first impression of Mexicans, 174; on friendship, 127; on ice, 124–25; on importance of mail, 130; on Mexican women, 175; and mistaking toad for the enemy, 173–74; and musicians in mess, 129; at New Orleans, 115; on obtaining water, 141; on plight of the sick, 155, 164; on rations, 118; on sending bodies home, 165; on thorns in Texas, 171

secretary of war, 16, 17

Semmes, Lt. Raphael, 180

Señora Cañete, 133

sergeant major, 22

servants, 125, 126, 129, 175

Shields, James: and assessment as general, 46–47; background and appointment of, 41; and being called a political general, 42

Shivors, Capt. William R., 111

Singletary, Otis A., 205

slavery, 114, 126, 175, 202

Smith, Capt. Charles Ferguson, 59

Smith, Capt. Ephraim Kirby, 56, 117

Smith, Franklin: on dress of dragoons, 110–11; on Patterson; 44–45; and seeing bodies shipped home, 165–66; on volunteer morality, 85

Smith, S. Compton: on character, 113, 128; on Cushing, 43; and dining on armadillo, 124; expressing pride in seeing regulars, 201; on gamblers disguised as teamsters, 137; on Mexican markets, 119; on poor diet as cause for disease, 143; on Quitman, 46, 153; on whiskey as cure for bites, 247*n* 9

Spanish, 6; Americans' effort to learn the language, 176–77; expulsion of, 174

spoils system, 36

Stephens, Lt. George, 158

Stevens, Lt. Isaac J., 161

Stockton, Commodore Robert F., 57

stragglers, 143

Subsistence Department, 17, 20

surgeons, 19, 22, 152, 154, 241–42*n* 16

sutlers, 19–20, 120–21, 232*n* 38

Tampico, 120, 121, 124, 126, 171, 184, 187

Taylor, Zachary, 8, 12, 32; baggage train of, 240*n* 6; and commanding Army of Occupation, 28, 52, 210*n* 16; as compared to Gen. Arista, 216*n* 38; as compared to Scott, 28–30; and Democratic officers, 79; and disappointed volunteers, 199, 224*n* 6; early life and military career of, 28; and Gaines's volunteers, 70; and mentioned as a candidate, 33; and military dress, 104, 106; on militia generals, 43; presidential election of, 49, 220*n* 40; proclaims war to free Mexico, 184; and promotion to major general, 53; and relationship with Polk, 33, 188; and using militia troops, 68; and victory at Lake Okeechobee, 28; as Whig, 30

teamsters, 20, 137

Temperance Movement, 13, 136–37, 238*n* 38

Tennery, Pvt. Thomas D.: and dead rattlesnake, 172; on death, 139, 164, 166; on lockjaw, 153; on Mexicans as a race, 183; on plight of the sick, 155;